Interviewing

Interviewing: The Oregon Method is an anthology of essays written by University of Oregon School of Journalism and Communication faculty and other experts in interviewing who are associated with the school. It is compiled and edited by the James Wallace Chair Professor in Journalism Peter Laufer and copy edited by Professor John Russial.

Interviewing

The Oregon Method

Edited by **Peter Laufer**
with **John Russial**

SECOND EDITION

The University of Oregon
School of Journalism and Communication

O | UNIVERSITY OF OREGON
School of Journalism and Communication

ETHICS. INNOVATION. ACTION.

Congress shall make no law respecting an establishment of religion, or prohibiting the free exercise thereof; or abridging the freedom of speech, or of the press; or the right of the people peaceably to assemble, and to petition the government for a redress of grievances.

—The First Amendment of the U.S. Constitution

For Ken Metzler

Contents

Foreword

JUAN-CARLOS MOLLEDA

Edwin L. Artzt Dean and Professor
University of Oregon School of Journalism
and Communication

Interviewing has long been one of the best tools in the journalist's tool-box. It is also one of the most important skills for all communicators, from advertising and public relations professionals to media researchers.

Today, organizations of all types—news outlets, businesses, nonprofits, government agencies and more—know that content is king and human-interest stories are what resonate best with all audiences. In New York, Mount Sinai Medical Center's marketing and communication depart-ment is structured as a newsroom with internal media specialists who act as enterprise reporters.[1] These corporate reporters are subject-matter experts (i.e., science and health) who cover a variety of beats and pro-duce quality written and multimedia content as information subsidies for a variety of national and international media outlets.

Moreover, research has confirmed that insider stories and authentic narratives can help establish an organization's identity with a unified, distinctive voice.[2] Intensive interviewing, through a variety of face-to-face and digital means, is one of the most direct and effective ways to uncover both individual and collective realities and multi-layered identities in ways that allow readers, listeners, users, consumers and clients to make sense of the complex world we live in.

Creative strategy and execution need to gather detailed insights to produce powerful impacts on consumer behaviors. Advertising professionals interview clients, peers, experts and targeted audiences to support their campaign planning and production. Dan explained that the importance of consumer insight has significantly grown over time.[3] The advertising industry is increasingly in need of taking the pulse of social and political moments that inform the strategic and creative choices, which solidify brand values and purpose in a complex marketplace. Interviewing techniques are critical to gathering useful data and distilling actionable insights.

The interviewing skills of listening and reflecting are essential to accurate and balanced reporting and compelling storytelling.[4] Asking questions and paying attention to answers and expressions lie at the core of communication best practices for all of us, no matter our professions. This is more important than ever for journalists, who are now challenged regularly on the quality, accuracy and impact of their work.[5] At a time when people around the world are increasingly divided along political, social and cultural lines, journalists and other storytellers have the responsibility to give voice to the voiceless, portraying their thoughts and actions in ways that are fair to their perspectives and clear to others who have not shared their experiences.

Although effective interviewing is most commonly associated with long-form journalism, it is a key ingredient for achieving sustained audience engagement with content of any length. In an era of soundbites, social media posts and video clips, every communicator must be able to capture the essence of a source, client or customer's story in as few words as possible. These brief comments can also motivate audiences to click through to longer stories and convince employees and shareholders to read strategic documents or browse additional inspiring testimonials.

For all its power, interviewing is surprisingly difficult to do well. Carperter, Cepak and Peng studied 10 journalistic interviewing competencies: articulation, empathy, interaction management, listening, news judgment, observation, open-mindedness, research, self-presentation and verification.[6] These competencies illustrate the complexity underlying the art of interviewing, which will always be a core skill set for professional and ethical communicators, no matter what directions technology takes us.

Interviewing knowledge and techniques are also essential to researchers and scholars. Graduate students and academic scholars in any field will benefit from the guidelines for in-depth qualitative interviewing they find in this book.

Interviewing: The Oregon Method represents some of the foundational skills we give our students to prepare them for their future—and, in turn, ensure the continued quality of content coming out of the professions we serve and influence.

NOTES

1. Moore, T. (2019, January–February). Turning employees into reporters. *PRWeek*, pp. 22–25.

2. Moore, T. (2019).

3. Dan, A. The heart of effective advertising is a powerful insight. *Forbes*, July 8. Retrieved Feb. 19, 2019, from https://www.forbes.com/sites/avidan/2013/07/08/the-heart-of-effective-advertising-is-a-powerful-insight/#79366c5d21d5.

4. Harro-Loit, H., & Ugur, K. (2018). Training methods of listening-based journalistic questioning. *Journalism Practice*, 12(7), 918–934.

5. Hautakangas, M., & Ahva, L. (2018). Introducing a new form of socially responsible journalism. *Journalism Practice*, 12(6), 730–746.

6. Carpenter, S., Cepak, A., & Peng, Z. (2018). An exploration of the complexity of journalistic interviewing competencies. *Journalism Studies*, 19(15), 2283–2303.

Introduction

PETER LAUFER

Interviewing was the first course I taught when I joined the School of Journalism and Communication faculty at the University of Oregon. That made sense. The interview is my stock in trade; it has been all my professional life. In fact, it's a crucial stock in trade for all of us. Every human interaction is some sort of interview.

Our earliest human records—paintings on cave walls, for example—are pictorial interviews.

"What did you do today?"

That's the question the cave wall artist asks his cave mate or himself.

The answer shows up marked on the wall.

"I took my spear and killed dinner for us."

Before I taught that first class I was lucky enough to go out for a leisurely coffee with Ken Metzler. It was a sunny and warm Oregon autumn day, and we sat together at a sidewalk café table a few blocks from campus talking interview—interviewing each other. By the time of our meeting, Professor Emeritus Metzler was already long retired from formal teaching, but he graciously shared with me some of his tricks from the classroom. When I showed him my tattered copy of his interview textbook— *Creative Interviewing*—he agreed to sign the flyleaf for me, but he did so with a schoolmaster's flourish.

"My book is dated," he announced, and then he proceeded to assign me the daunting and arduous task of writing a new interview textbook. Sad to report: not long after our meeting Ken Metzler died—mourned by colleagues lucky enough to work with him and by generations of students who profited from his teaching.

His assignment to me—that next textbook—lingered in the back of my mind as I used his fine book with my first cohort of Oregon students. He was correct. Although the creative concepts and philosophies he taught in the book are timeless, they were presented in a matrix of what was fast becoming a quaint pre-Facebook, pre-Twitter and pre-Google world of tape recorders and beepers, telephone answering machines and regular office hours.

I checked library and bookstore shelves for updated alternatives (not literally, of course, I trawled Amazon), and nothing I found seemed adequate to the task. Then one day, as I gazed at my colleagues gathered at a faculty meeting in Eric W. Allen Hall, I enjoyed a delightful eureka moment. Here was a think tank of interview experts poised to fulfill Metzler's appropriate assignment—a team of innovative journalism and communication educators and practitioners.

Interviewing: The Oregon Method is a product of that School of Journalism and Communication meeting. More than three dozen faculty and friends of the School collaborated to create this text—a wide-ranging guide to the practice of interviewing and a thought-provoking inquiry into the art of the interview. It was a pleasure to work on this project with my colleagues, and I am proud to introduce them and their work—chapter by chapter— here in this compilation.

PART I Interviewing Techniques

ONE **A Matter of Trust**

The more your source respects you,
the better the interview

BOB WELCH

The rigors of daily reporting demand ready access to interview
subjects. Bob Welch told Oregonians' stories for years in his
regular newspaper column, a job that required a seemingly
endless supply of subjects opening their hearts and homes
to him. Here he helps guide other journalists also facing
difficulties in getting sources to talk.

As journalists, we sometimes find that our best lessons are born out of
desperation.

For years, I had longed to write about the Mennonites of Oregon's
Willamette Valley, people not as severely cut off from the norm as the
Amish but cultural cousins, true nonconformists, the most conserva-
tive of whom live without television, smartphones, movies and insurance.
They're people—many farmers—who have never voted, served in the
military, attended a public school, seen a football game or worn a ring.
They're strangers and pilgrims—so-called by their Articles of Faith—who
purposely cloister themselves away from the American mainstream.

As I sat in the living room of two such people—an older couple—my
notebook was as barren as the fallow fields that lay beyond. The so-called
interview—my initial foray into the Mennonites—had begun nearly half

an hour before and the two were divulging information with the icy reserve of the Midwest giving way to spring. And, gradually, it dawned on me why.

It wasn't because they had something to hide; they didn't. It wasn't because they had other things to do; they were retired.

It was because of this: They didn't trust me.

For people who like their privacy, having a reporter from the city sitting in their living room was bad enough. And I hadn't scored any points when, in my initial phone call, I'd asked if we could meet for a cup of coffee. "We don't drink coffee," the man had said.

But now I realized there was more: When the "conversation" turned to farming—the two had been part of a grass-seed industry that purports itself to be the largest in the world—their already chilly dispositions froze completely.

Suddenly, the light went off for me, something I should have anticipated long before the meeting had taken place. For decades, farmers like these folks had been locked in a battle with environmentalists over the issue of yearly field burning. In late summer, after harvesting their grass seed, farmers would set fire to their fields to cleanse them and prepare for the next year's planting. It was cheap, fast and efficient. And, in the 1990s, legal.

But it also filled the valley skies with dark smoke that wreaked havoc with asthmatic people; that turned sunny afternoons into virtual darkness; and that led to a 23-car pileup on nearby Interstate 5 in which five people died and 37 were injured.

My newspaper, the *Register-Guard,* had long been a staunch opponent of field burning, arguing for years that the state legislature should ban it. And, to this couple, I *was* the *Register-Guard.* Never mind that I didn't write those editorials and that I'd actually spent two summers working with an Oregon State University project whose goal was to develop a tractor-drawn metal box that could burn fields without all the smoke. Clearly, I was The Enemy.

Then the idea hit. My father-in-law, an OSU agronomy professor, was a huge friend of local farmers, a grass-seed expert who'd literally been around the world sharing his knowledge.

"Say," I said, "I wonder if you might know my father-in-law, Harold Youngberg."

The man's forehead furrowed.

"You're Harold's son-in-law?" he asked.

I nodded.

"Well, sure I know him," he said while a hint of smile broke from his face like a glimpse of sunshine after one of Oregon's many cloudy days. "Harold's a great guy."

"Can I get you a piece of pie?" his wife asked.

A few months later, the 5,000-word, four-full-page, 14-photo spread was published. I had eaten dinner with the Mennonites, gone to church with them, milked cows with them and gone with them to deliver their farm products to the city. I spent months on the story. Interviewed dozens of people. And I'm convinced the only reason this journalistic crop-duster got off the ground was because the mention of my father-in-law suddenly stamped a seal of approval on my forehead in this couple's eyes. That approval was shared by this couple with other Mennonites. If Harold Youngberg had let me marry his daughter, they reasoned, then I could be trusted. *What can we help you with, Mr. Welch?*

Interviewing is a complex component of the storytelling process. In a sense, the journalist is something of a one-man band, challenged to simultaneously ask, listen, write, encourage, notice nuances of the subject and the environment—and anticipate his or her next question. But at its core, interviewing is a conversation whose success or failure is often dependent on one thing: trust.

Trust in a hurry, in many cases. Unlike with my Mennonite story, sometimes journalists must build that trust in mere seconds, making the experience a tad like journalistic speed dating. As such, the key to good interviewing is building a relationship in a hurry, almost like those time-lapse photo sequences you'll see of, say, a crowd filling a 100,000-seat football stadium.

It's too easy to think of interviewing in only mechanical terms: asking questions, getting answers, recording those answers. At the same time, a subterranean game is playing out between journalist and source, the latter of whom is, quite understandably, wondering: If I tell you something about myself or my job or organization, can I trust that you'll use that information wisely?

Each of us is a story that's uniquely our own. Naturally, we don't want that story misconstrued, misused or exploited. I have a friend whose 16-year-old daughter had been invited to her first school dance. The man scheduled a meeting with her date and politely but unequivocally helped the boy understand how highly the father valued his daughter and how deeply he did not want her hurt in any way—*if you know what I mean.* Likewise, people who share their lives with journalists are going to be concerned how we treat that information; they don't want to be hurt in any way either.

Certainly, public officials have responsibilities to be forthcoming with information—and the public's right to know outweighs any personal toll that the person might pay through the divulging of such information. But even in interviews involving public employees, journalists would be wise to understand the more human side of an interview upon which teeters this fragile thing called trust.

Granted, the concept of trust might strike some as too "touchy-feely" for the gritty business of journalism; Woodward and Bernstein, after all, weren't exactly Dr. Phil when they went after Nixon's henchmen. True. But the idea isn't to score style points; the idea is to gather the richest possible ingredients to serve readers, viewers and listeners with the richest possible story. To that end, understanding the subcurrents of the human relationship can only help us do that better.

So, how do you build trust with a source? Here are six ways:

1. KNOW AS MUCH ABOUT YOUR SOURCE AS POSSIBLE BEFORE YOU BEGIN THE INTERVIEW

Obviously, when you're racing to a rally or accident or hastily called press conference, you're not going to be able to download someone's résumé, hear their childhood exploits from a third-grade teacher or talk to work colleagues about what makes them tick.

But when possible, do so, if it's relevant to your story, whether it is written as a story or aired as a video or radio broadcast. Here's why: When you've done your homework on your source, he or she feels more *valued*—in the same way someone might feel more valued if a guest showed up at his or her house with a small gift. (Note: Do not show up at a source's house with a small gift.) Someone who feels valued is more likely to want to spend time with you and is more likely to share at a deeper level than someone who does not feel valued.

Alberto Salazar, once the fastest marathoner in the world, told a class of my students at the University of Oregon School of Journalism and Communication that he could tell within the first few minutes of an interview whether a reporter had done any homework or not. And he gauged his response accordingly. If someone clearly was prepared, he said, he'd offer the reporter a "deluxe burger" interview; if someone was asking how to spell his name and what sport he participated in, he'd give them a slab of meat on a bun. In other words, why go out of your way for someone who obviously hasn't gone out of his way for you?

The more you know about your sources, the less likely you are to offend them with your ignorance. My first professional interview was with an author/editor/scientist who specialized in astronomy. "So, Mr. Brogan," I said with a faux sophistication designed to belie my tender age of 22, "how did you get interested in *astrology*?"

I believe my Aquarius horoscope for that day must have said: *You will sabotage your interview before it even begins. You're basically a total loser, pal.*

Another time I arrived at the newspaper office and was told that I needed to fill in for our entertainment writer, who had a 9 a.m. phone interview with Mickey Hart, the Grateful Dead drummer. I made a complete fool out of myself, trying to break the ice with some lame comment about having played the snare drum in seventh grade.

If possible, come prepared.

2. MAKE A GOOD FIRST IMPRESSION

Dave Lieber, a columnist with the *Dallas Morning News*, made national TV for the job he did emceeing a high school talent show. When he was introduced, he came out from behind the curtain onto the darkened stage and promptly fell off the front edge. The good news? He wasn't hurt, and he made *America's Funniest Home Videos*. The bad? He totally distracted the audience from the purpose of the evening: to see a bunch of young people perform.

Try to avoid the metaphorical equivalent when it comes to an interview. Ease into things.

If that means throwing softball questions just so you can find a rhythm, so be it. If that means finding a few things in common just to establish some basic rapport, so be it. If you're in someone's office or home, look at the stuff on the walls—without disengaging from your source.

"Hey, I've stood at this same spot on the Grand Canyon. When were you there?" Or: "You graduated from Colorado in 2004? My sister was a year ahead of you in Boulder."

Bingo. You have something in common. And commonality is a component of trust. We tend to be wary of the unknown—not that we necessarily *should*—so it behooves us to find a few commonalities, particularly at the critical start of the interview.

Don't force it, of course. But just as realtors know a house's entryway can make or break a sale, so can the first few minutes of an interview make or break the experience. At the very least, practice the Hippocratic oath: *First, do no harm.*

ESPN's Jim Rome obviously wasn't concerned about such when, in 1994, he began a TV/radio interview with NFL quarterback Jim Everett by intentionally calling him "Chris Everett," the host's way of linking the football player to former pro tennis player Chris Evert. Never mind that Chris Evert won 18 grand slam singles championships—uh, and how many slams do you have, Jim?—Rome was implying that female tennis players are soft and so was Jim Everett. After a few warnings by Jim Everett, Rome continued to call him Chris, whereupon Jim Everett shoved aside the table and lunged at Rome. The stunned host fell off the elevated stage and, said Everett, "[curled] up like a little bunny . . . in the fetal position."

As I said, not probably the best way to start solidifying trust between you and your source.

3. LOOK AT THE INTERVIEW AS A CONVERSATION, NOT AN INQUISITION

That doesn't mean you can't get tough when necessary. But people put on the defensive are less likely to divulge information than people who are engaged in a spirited two-way conversation that they might actually be enjoying, even if it leans to the volatile side. A *"you-must-tell-me-this"* approach isn't apt to produce as much as an *"I'd-love-for-you-to-share-with-my-viewers/readers/listeners-your-thoughts-on-this"* approach. Like it or not, people are ego- and pride-driven. The adage is true: You catch more flies with honey than vinegar.

In most cases, it's counterproductive to make a source feel ramrodded. It doesn't work when telling a child to clean his or her room, and it rarely works with adults who you're hoping will spill their guts to you.

Treat a source as you'd want to be treated. Know when to push; know when to back off. And, above all, be sensitive to what might be blocking your source from sharing information.

I remember interviewing a World War II veteran, Capt. Fred Michalove of the Army Nurse Corps' 45th Field Hospital, for a book on the first nurse to die after the landings at Normandy, *American Nightingale*. He was 88 at the time of the interview.

I listened as he talked about the months before D-Day in June 1944, about coming across the English Channel on D+4 and about his landing craft hitting Utah Beach. Then, his mind would process images that he didn't want to share. "We were billeted in England with the Sirmons," he said.

Patiently, I would guide him back to that ship, to the landing craft and to the beach. Again, he would tell me about everything up until hitting the beach, then bounce me back to England.

Finally, I said, "Fred, what was it you saw on the beach?" He gulped. His eyes glistened.

"They were," he said, "hanging from the trees." "They" meaning paratroopers from the 82nd or 101st Airborne Divisions whose parachutes had gotten tangled in the trees upon the men's descent. The Germans had used the men for target practice.

You cannot force stories like that. You have to be patient, put yourself in the shoes of your sources and try to understand why they might clam up on some topics. Only then—on their terms, not your own—can you hope to hear the stories that need to be told.

4. BE AWARE OF "CONVERSATIONAL SIGNALS"

In a book by Georgetown University professor Deborah Tannen, *That's Not What I Meant!: How Conversational Style Makes or Breaks Relationships,* she writes about how communication is dependent on an array of styles: voice level, pitch and intonation, rhythm and timing, even the simple turns of phrase we choose are powerful factors in the success or failure of any relationship. And so it is with an interview, because what is conversation but a short-term relationship?

Regional speech characteristics, ethnic and class backgrounds, age, and individual personality all contribute to diverse conversational styles. If, as interviewers, we ignore such factors, our efforts to gain information can be impeded because trust depends, to some degree, on our willingness to respect the uniqueness of the people we're interviewing.

Some of this is common sense; you need to speak to a business leader differently than you would to a homeless street kid. The relaxed nature of an interview in the laid-back Northwest might not work as well in the more formal South. People are different for all sorts of reasons, and the more sensitive we are to that as interviewers, the more we can adjust our styles to compensate.

Weirdly, one of the proving grounds of this for me was Oregon's Blue Mountain, where I joined a group of elk hunters for a week to try to understand their passion to hunt. I'd written a lighthearted column saying, "I don't *get* hunting." Wasn't philosophically opposed to it, just didn't understand it. So, when invited to join this group using horses and pack mules, I said yes.

I wound up getting bucked off a horse with the dude-ranch name of Rusty and had a contact lens freeze in 2-degree weather but wrote a three-part series that readers seemed to enjoy. Why did it work? In part, I believe, because instead of trying to come across with city-slicker panache, I simply swallowed my pride and played the part of a guy who didn't have a clue what he was doing but would pull his weight nevertheless. I earned their respect with a combination of hard work, self-effacing humor and constant curiosity about all that was going on.

At the same time, I believe my willingness to try to "get it" added to the respect they developed for me; I was willing to enter their world, though outnumbered five to one, and assimilate, if even for a week, into the life of a hunter. (Though I had no interest in shooting a gun, nor would they have *wanted* me to.) By the end of the trip, I had been dubbed "Cowboy Bob" and been invited back for a second trip, which I did five years later, writing yet another three-part series.

While conforming to the culture at hand, you're sometimes going to experience times when you must take control of an interview. Say, when a source strays far from the focus of your story and you need to rein him or her in. The key to do that is to control the interview without the source feeling as if he or she is being controlled.

When I was a kid, Disneyland had a speedboat ride that allowed kids to actually think they were driving the boat. We weren't, of course; it was on rails beneath the water. And that's how sources need to feel: as if they're driving the boat, even though we know this boat is running on rails beneath the water.

The suggestion isn't to be duplicitous, just to nudge the interview this way or that with subtlety and respect that won't disturb the source. "Oh, that's interesting" you might nod as the person wanders from quantum physics to a family reunion in Des Moines, "but back to science: What was it that triggered your interest in all this?"

Look them in the eyes. Don't get too close. Don't stay too far away. And for heaven's sake, don't answer a call on your cell phone during the interview. Nothing says, "I'm unimportant" to a source more than you taking your attention off them and putting it onto something else.

5. PROVE YOUR TRUSTWORTHINESS OVER TIME

Occasionally, I've encountered people reluctant to let me interview them. "I've had a bad experience with the media," they'll often say. Your only option as a journalist? Point out that they haven't had a bad experience with *you*—assuming, of course, they haven't.

Point out previous articles you've written similar to the one you'd like to write about them. Refer them to sources you've interviewed whose circumstances might be similar to their own. In other words, show them your record. Your reputation. Your résumé. Better yet, hope that if they do their own research, the word on the street is that you're someone who can be trusted.

The end of a tennis match is reported in a few numbers: 6–2, 4–6, 6–1, for example. In fact, a victory is built game by game, point by point, shot by shot. And so it is with interviewing. Whether you're a veteran or rookie in the field of journalism, the key is understanding that the heart and soul of interviewing is earning trust, one shot at a time.

6. BE GENUINE

A huge part of trust is about being real. Being yourself. Not being the anchorman played by William Hurt in the 1987 film, *Broadcast News*, who musters artificial tears to intensify a story he's reporting on rape.

Early in my career, I found myself trying to pretend I was better than I was. If I wasn't quite sure I'd heard a quote right, for example, I wouldn't dare embarrass myself by asking a source to repeat it. That changed when I realized you could clarify an "I'm not sure" with one person in an interview but you couldn't in front of 60,000 readers at their breakfast tables or on buses, reading the glaring error in my story. Sources are less interested in *style* than *substance*. They're more willing to trust an interviewer who admits he or she didn't get something—"Could you repeat that?"— than someone who feigns perfection.

The old proverb is true: *Better to be a fool for five minutes than for 5,000 years.* You can fake that you got everything correct in the interview, but the proof comes when the story is aired or printed. There's nothing worse than making a mistake because your pride wouldn't let you stop and double-check something during an interview.

Don't be afraid to be human. Admit when you can't keep pace. "Wait, that was interesting; would you mind repeating what you just said?" It not only subtly feeds the person's ego but also earns you "trust points": *This interviewer cares about accuracy. I like that.*

Don't be afraid to reveal something about yourself. When I was thrust into interviewing a woman whose 4-year-old daughter had been kidnapped, I fretted as I drove to her house. How do I start? How do I build a semblance of rapport, given the emotional state the mother must be in? I still didn't have any idea when she opened the door, but what came out was simply what I was feeling: "I have a 4-year-old son at home," I said, "but I can't even begin to understand what this must be like for you."

We had a smidgeon of common ground: 4-year-old children. The interview went well. And she felt at least a smidgeon of empathy, which went a long way in her sharing her thoughts at this tumultuous moment in her life.

Finally, don't try to be someone you're not. Fueled by ego, I've tried feigning expertise in areas that I'm unfamiliar with. It doesn't work. Far better, I've found, to reveal your expertise in areas where it's real—and admit you're naive in certain other areas. Journalists get thrust into all sorts of situations where they're expected to become instant experts. We can't be. We can dig hard and learn fast. But, ultimately, we're better off reflecting the expertise of others than trying to cling to a facsimile of our own.

These are only six of many more ways you can build trust with a source. Never forget what the ultimate goal is: not just to get information, but to get people to share at deep levels so you can tell a compelling story. And the best way to tell a compelling story is to have people trust you so much that they will share their own stories.

In 2007, a World War II veteran featured in the Tom Hanks–Steven Spielberg HBO series *Band of Brothers* chose me to write his book. I interviewed Don Malarkey more than a dozen times in person at his home in Salem, Oregon. At one point, I asked him to tell me about life after the war. At first, he shrugged a bit, a common reaction for WWII vets.

"Couldn't have been easy," I said.

"No, no, it wasn't easy," he said.

That, of course, means nothing to the reader. Cleaning gutters isn't easy. Making good clam chowder isn't easy. But this was war: jumping into the darkness over Normandy on D-Day; seeing buddies die and have legs blown off in the cold and snow of Bastogne during the Battle of the Bulge; realizing a German soldier he shot was 16 years old. I needed more than "it wasn't easy."

But here's what I've come to realize: When asked a question, sources— to protect themselves from the pain—will conjure images in their minds but will translate those pictures into euphemistic summary statements that dilute the deeper experience. Later, after more gentle probing, Malarkey would tell me that not a day had passed when he hadn't seen the face of that young German boy. But, at first, he would only *tell* me, not *show* me, what the experience was like: *It wasn't easy.* Or: *People who weren't there don't understand.* Bones, but no flesh.

By building trust, the chances increase that we can mine the more vivid responses. By now, my doggedness to get Don's story had earned me points with him. I'd made more than 10 75-minute trips to meet with him, stayed as long as he wanted me to stay, left when he said he was too tired to go on. And I think being myself had helped. Over our many sessions, he had come to appreciate that I was tender with his memories, some of which moved him to tears, and tough with his propensity to not go deeply enough with his emotions.

I gently kept ratcheting down the questions, though allowing long pauses between answers to keep Don feeling relaxed and not make him feel pressured. He mentioned never forgetting about the boy. Told me a story of a truck backfiring as he walked down a street and how he instinctively took cover. Good stuff, but I sensed there was more. Finally, I said it: "Don, when the war was over, what's the worst moment of it coming back to haunt you?"

In a dark basement filled with war memorabilia, he took a swig of his Jack Daniels and stared off in space. "Every night after work," he said, "I'd go out for a drink. And when I drained my Scotch, every night I saw them at the bottom of my glass: the faces of all the buddies I left in Bastogne."

That's a story. That's showing. That's the gold we must find in our journalistic mining, which is more readily available when, at first, we build trust with a source.

TWO Interviewing Basics

10 steps to conducting good interviews

MARK BLAINE

In this chapter, Mark Blaine, who teaches and produces science writing, outlines the basic foundation needed for successful interviews.

In the first term that I taught at the University of Oregon School of Journalism and Communication, I was assigned to teach what was the most dreaded course of any offered in the J-school—Information Gathering, dubbed by students Info Hell, a course in which each student produced a 100-page annotated bibliography and essay in 10 weeks. I was eased into Info by Professor Kathy Campbell, who helped guide me through the weekly ups and downs of a course that demanded more words from most of the students than they had ever written.

We had a very structured approach, which involved library time equivalent to a part-time job, but the crux for most students came about the midpoint of the term—the moment when they had to go find interviews to go with the 30-plus annotations we were asking for. For me this was my favorite part, the time when the students left the conditioned air of the library and dipped their toes into real give-and-take journalism. That was the moment when projects began to become real. It also drove many students to tears.

It turns out that one of the most anxiety producing parts of Info Hell was the interview. Instead of a consistent flow of articles and book chapters, the students suddenly had to work with people who had lives and schedules and no requirement to help them finish their work. The outcome was uncertain and the stakes felt high. A month or more of work—and a feeling that they had a handle on their topics—could come apart in minutes when weak execution met a poor choice of living, breathing sources.

Enter the wisdom of Ken Metzler. Kathy prepared a top-10 list of interview basics, mostly at Ken's advising, but with contributions from other faculty, too. What we used—10 key points on a one-page handout—for the next few years in Info has lived on in several other courses as a kind of quick reference guide to journalistic interviewing. I've tweaked those 10 points and expanded a small amount on each of them for this chapter. The point isn't to make interviewing seem simplistic, but rather to offer a simple list to help students get started and stay on track.

Interviewing is about learning something you didn't know. It might be a personal detail that gives you insight into the character of your interview subject or an abstract concept that a researcher has studied for years. It's always someone's side of the story, a spoken impression of events or experience, heard by someone else—you—and retold. In that string of remembrance, retelling and interpretation, interviewers can learn much, but they must also be vigilant not to stray from the essence of what the source meant.

Consistent journalistic interviewing relies on a framework of basic techniques and habits. The 10 steps that follow are intended as a starting point for exploring deeper techniques and concepts presented later in this book.

1. WHAT ARE YOU ASKING ABOUT?

You'll need to have a clear sense of what you want to talk to your interview sources about before you go and talk to them. This might seem obvious, but knowing how your sources might contribute to the story means being able to briefly describe why you want to talk to them. Summarizing your intent for a story that's incomplete isn't as easy as it sounds.

As you do this, you have to leave room for how the story will inevitably change as you report it. That's one of the best parts of doing this work— surprise when a story unfolds in unexpected ways—and you want to leave room for it. So what do you say?

Try to distill the idea for the story. Practice saying, "I'm working on a story about . . . and I'd like to talk to you about . . ." This statement does two things: It forces you to get to the heart of what you're interested in and forces you to identify how that person might contribute to the story.

It really helps to say what you're working on and try to explain it to someone else. Do that multiple times and shape it as you learn more. This statement of intent is the thing that ultimately gets you out the door, but it also helps to guide the research and backgrounding that you need to do before you start the interview.

2. TALKING TO THE RIGHT PEOPLE

Talking to the right people means doing a thorough job of background-ing both the concept for the story and the people who are, or might be, involved. I tend to think about timelines and networks for stories as I'm backgrounding them.

Working backward and asking what came before the current situation helps to build the timeline and get a sense of when the story shifted and pivoted. Event-based (rather than date-focused) timelines help to iden-tify the key moments in the development of a story and start to build the framework of potential anecdotes that you might use. The idea of any interview is to get content that you can use to build the story, so by focus-ing on the key parts of the story at the background phase, you can isolate those moments in the interview and fill them out with richer detail and impressions from the interview subject.

Identifying the network of the story helps in two ways—by identifying connections between potential sources and understanding how the dif-ferent players in a story interact. Thinking in terms of networks and asking who might have been involved at various points in the story also helps diversify the sources for the story and fill any gaps in knowledge.

3. GETTING THE INTERVIEW

Asking for the interview involves combining parts one and two with simple courtesy and a little doggedness. First, you won't get an interview unless you ask the right way. The best approach is to diversify your efforts to make contact with someone by emailing and calling. Email alone is too easy to avoid, while just calling may result in your catching someone at the wrong time, particularly if you're aiming for a longer interview. You should have a clear sense of purpose and be able to say what you're after in a sentence or two after introducing yourself.

Be aware of the context in which you make contact. In some cases, reaching out to them while they're working may be problematic, especially if their employer has rules about speaking with the media while they're on the job or they work somewhere where it's difficult for them to step away for a moment. Try to make contact with them in the most appropriate way that you can identify—it's the beginning of setting the ground rules for the interview.

When you ask for the interview, remember to present yourself as a professional. Be well spoken and to the point on the phone. Write email that you've vetted for spelling and grammar errors.

You'll need to establish the parameters of the interview at this point as well—if you need 30 minutes, say so. If you'd like to spend half a day or more and follow the source through the day, you'll need to ask for that.

4. PLAN YOUR STRATEGY

What do you need your sources to tell you? How will you ask them about it?

If you're lucky, your source will be talkative and forthcoming, but some people struggle with the interview process. Sometimes the story you would like to talk to them about is very personal or sensitive. Sometimes it happened so long ago that it's difficult to remember. Other times they may be limited in what they can tell you by professional codes or laws. In each case, you should anticipate any reluctance and identify ways to get beyond those barriers to learn what you need to learn. Personal stories require you to build trust. Long-past events may require you to tap memory with photos or questions that ask about details that they haven't thought about in years. For sources constrained by legal or professional issues, such as an attorney or a police officer working on an investigation, you might ask questions that address more abstract concepts or nonspecific situations.

It's a good idea to identify key questions or concepts that you need to have confirmed or explained and remember to return to those key bits later in the interview if you haven't touched on them. It might also help to ask some sources the same question in multiple ways—with complex or difficult concepts it may take a try or two (or more) to get a clear, non-jargon-filled answer. With some sources, it might help to let them know that you'll be doing that so they know to explain things in the clearest language possible.

5. FIND A RHYTHM

Interviews have their internal rhythms—often there's a period of warm-up followed by the key questions that the interviewer needs answers to. Harder questions take more time, both to build to and to give room for reflection and follow-up. As you practice, you'll grow more patient and confident, and you'll learn to find those rhythms and use them to your advantage. Observe your subjects and try to fit with their question-and-answer rhythms—some people talk fast and interrupt, others respond to a slower approach. Politicians and others who speak for a living will have a set agenda for what they'll want to tell you—if you want more than that, you'll need to take more control of the question-and-answer exchange and find ways to break them out of their canned statements about a specific issue.

6. LISTEN

Most really effective interviewing happens in the follow-up questions, and you won't get to those if you're not listening. The point of interviewing your sources is for you to hear what they have to say, but too often, interviewers talk over their subjects or make long-winded statements that eat up precious interview time. It's critical to train yourself to ask a question and then wait for the source's answer and listen. Make note of anything that you should return to later to ask for clarification, but generally you want to let them go without interrupting. In short, learn to shut up.

Practice being comfortable with silence and pauses in conversation. Effectively using silence in an interview is probably more effective than any specific questions you ask. Most people want to fill silence—it makes most of us a little uncomfortable—and by letting the gaps in conversation unfold, you'll find that your sources tell you more, offer a little more insight, think a little harder. Try it.

7. HOW ARE THEY SAYING IT?

As you practice shutting up while conducting your interviews, learn to pay close attention to your sources' body language and other nonverbal cues. Your sources will say a lot in the way they carry themselves, how they hold their hands, whether they're relaxed or fidgety. Body language will tell you a lot about how the interview is going and, perhaps, how forthcoming the source is.

Also pay attention to your body language as you conduct the interview, because your source is taking the same nonverbal cues from you. You should appear interested and receptive. Sit up straight and be careful not to move too much. If you're interviewing people on camera, their eyes may follow your movements and be distracting. Realize also that some movements will move the conversation to a new place—I can't count the number of times that closing my notebook or putting my hand on the doorknob to the office unlocked some new insight from a source. In that case you just have to nod and commit the best parts to memory, and then write them down immediately after leaving. If it's a multimedia interview, those might be the starting points for a follow-up on-camera interview.

8. GET WHAT YOU NEED

While you're in the interview, be sure to assess the kind of information that you're getting and make sure that it's what you need to develop the story. This is where it's important to have a focus on several questions that you need clear answers to, and to remind yourself to ask those questions and follow up if the answers are incomplete.

Remember to ask about details—the stuff that's going to make your story real—and ask your source to tell you more about the specifics of a scene. Questions that connect to the five senses can be useful at this point and often provide insightful details about a scene.

Always ask if there's anything that you haven't asked that would be important to the story. Sources often have a very different perspective on events and they may share things that you never thought to ask.

9. WRAP UP

Thank your sources for taking the time to do the interview and ask what the best way to follow up will be. Give them some sense of your timeline— when do you expect to be finishing the story and where it will appear. Expect that during the wrap-up of the interview, sources may begin to open up in new ways, so be prepared for the interview to go a little longer than you expected and be ready to capture what they say.

10. DOWNLOAD

After your interview, immediately go and make sense of your notes. Ideally, you'd start transcribing at this point and connecting all of the information that you got from the source. Interview notes go bad quickly if they're not organized and clarified, so don't put that work off. Interview footage or recordings can also stack up quickly, and you should make a habit of staying ahead of the process by transcribing those parts of the interview, too.

Transcription also helps you think more deeply about the interview. What you get from a close reading and transcription of your notes will help you ask better questions the next time.

Finally, listen to your own voice if you've recorded the interview and try to critique your approach. It's awkward at best for most of us to listen to our own voice, but there's a valuable learning opportunity in those recordings. Pay attention to which questions worked well and which didn't. Think about your delivery and articulation of the questions.

10+. WRITE A THANK-YOU NOTE

Your sources are taking time out of their lives to help you and share something that's valuable to them, their stories. Respect their time and that contribution by acknowledging it with a short note thanking them.

THREE

Chameleon Interviewing

*How changing your approach can be the key
to a great interview*

LISA HEYAMOTO

Does effective interviewing require playing a role? Lisa
Heyamoto, who directs Oregon's broad-based journalism
introductory courses, believes that being flexible and
intuitive are the keys to building great rapport.

As a journalist, I've interviewed everyone from governors to farmers,
celebrities to soccer moms—sometimes within the space of a single week.
With each, my goal was always the same—to get them to open up and
share their story. But talking to a craggy oyster farmer while standing
knee-deep in the mud is a very different experience than sitting in a
plush hotel suite with an A-list actor, and each person requires a different approach.

Good interviews entail flexibility. The person, the place and the circumstances are going to change every time, and the journalist should
adapt to the shifting landscape. It's not enough to smile and nod in all the
right places, or to make sure to ask every question on your list. Instead,
you must always be aware of where the conversation is, where it's been and
where it needs to go. And then, of course, you need to get it there.

For some, this constant assessment is second nature. But for most, it takes practice. Great interviews are *guided* conversations with specific goals in mind, and sources respond differently to different guides. For that reason, it can be useful to subtly switch styles from interview to interview—and even mid-way through—depending on whom you're talking to and what you're asking.

You already do this sort of thing all the time. You present different sides of yourself according to what you want to project, or what others expect from you. Maybe you were the Supportive Boyfriend at your girlfriend's lacrosse championship. Perhaps you were the Angelic Grandchild at your Nana's 80th birthday party. It's possible that you are the Life of the Party on any given Saturday night. Playing up each of these personas doesn't make you any less *you*, and it doesn't make you some kind of phony. Changing your approach from situation to situation makes it easier to connect with people—the ultimate goal in both journalism and in life.

In interviewing, the approach you take depends not only on the person you're talking to, but also on the interview itself. For example, you would probably want to adopt a sympathetic style when interviewing someone about an emotional experience, but not when asking a reluctant official about sensitive documents. But if the latter interview somehow became about a relevant emotional experience, you'd likely want to switch gears.

Sometimes the appropriate style isn't immediately obvious. For example, people in positions of power often prefer a subordinate approach that both recognizes and respects their authority. But others might be more receptive if you meet them as an equal. Still others may expect you to take the lead. You never know until you're sitting across from someone, which is why a little intuition and agility go a long way. And, of course, some careful research beforehand is likely to yield valuable clues.

So what interviewing style might work for you? There are endless approaches you can try, and you'll doubtless develop your own arsenal of go-tos. But here are a few tried-and-trues that might help get you started.

THE STUDENT

Your first few interviews are hard—maybe even a little bit painful. You may have gleaned a million pearls of wisdom from your professors, painstakingly written a list of thoughtful questions and faithfully rehearsed what you plan to say, but there's no real way to know what an interview entails until you actually do it. It takes years to get really good at it.

So why pretend that you know what you're doing? You can acknowledge that you're still learning. While setting up your interview, tell your sources that you're new at this, and are going to try your best not to mess it up. Chances are, this will put them at ease. It might even inspire them to open up more than they otherwise would. If you get flustered or make a misstep, you can simply ask them to forgive your inexperience. In the right situations, they will not only forgive you, they'll end up rooting for you too.

Role Model   You.

Word to the Wise   Beware, however, of taking The Student too far. Revealing and even playing up your inexperience can never atone for wasting the source's time by either being disingenuous or unprepared.

THE "AW SHUCKS"

This is a variation on The Student and can be employed long after you leave college. The premise is basically this: "Aw shucks, I'm just a journalist trying to learn all about this fill-in-the-blank, and I need you to spell it out for me to make sure I understand."

Why would you essentially play dumb, you may ask? Well, because it gets the job done. People love explaining something they know to someone who doesn't. It's human nature. The Aw Shucks allows your sources to feel good about themselves while giving you the clear, comprehensive information you need. You already know that you're smart, and you can continue to prove it by putting pride aside in the name of a killer interview.

Role Model   Susan Orlean, a longtime writer for The New Yorker. "I don't play dumb or helpless, but I try not to come off as slick and sophisticated. It is useful, but the fact is that this is also the way I feel: far from home, nervous about the story, somewhat exposed. (One of my sources) had this kind of protective relationship with me: 'What's a little girl like you doing out here?' He was always acting exasperated at my goofiness, joking about how many times he had to tell me the name of a particular flower."

Word to the Wise   Similar to The Student, The Aw Shucks should never be used to mask the fact that you haven't done your research, and it is best employed when you're trying to distill complicated information down to its simplest explanation.

THE THERAPIST

One of the best profile writers is, in my opinion, a mild-mannered, mustachioed man named Gary Smith. A longtime writer at Sports Illustrated, Smith built his career on writing deep, insightful profiles that reveal more than the story of one person—they reveal something universal about the human condition. For example, a story about a college football coach who lied on his résumé instead becomes a meditation on why people lie. As one of his subjects told the *New York Times*: "People warned me he'd get deep inside my head, but I had no idea. That piece could have saved me 20 years of psychoanalysis." Smith is called the "Sports Whisperer" for a reason.

This kind of interviewing goes far beyond searching for the "what" and delves deep into the "why." It involves thinking deeply about who your source is and what story you're trying to tell, asking insightful questions and, most important, creating an environment where your source feels comfortable answering them.

But how do you do that, exactly? As with all interviewing, it takes both practice and patience. The Sports Whisperer himself told The Poynter Institute this:

A lot of times it's rephrasing a question three, four or five ways. A lot of us have the pat answer or the safe answer or the quick answer, [which] is the first answer we'll give. Sometimes it takes that many times of coming back at it in a slightly different way to unlock a little something more.

Role Model   TV mogul Oprah Winfrey. "If I'm in an interview with some-body and I think that they have said something that they really didn't want to reveal, I'll try to help them out. It's a dance we have here. Earning people's trust is letting them know that I'm not out to get them."

Word to the Wise   Without a respectful, honest approach and a keen sense of how your subject is responding to you, this interview style can quickly go from therapy to prying—and could even wind up offending rather than revealing. It all comes down to being sensitive and creating the right environment. After all, therapists put couches in their offices for a reason.

THE LAW AND ORDER

Have you ever noticed that every interview conducted on a police proce-dural TV show takes place on the go? The hard-boiled detectives ask the suspects a series of hard-boiled questions while inexplicably walking from some mysterious Point A to an equally mysterious Point B. Apparently, sta-tionary interviews make for boring TV.

I'm not advising you to conduct your interviews via the walk 'n' talk (unless, of course, you have to—and believe me, you might) but rather to pay attention to the way they're conducted. Detectives on police pro-cedurals like the *Law and Order* or *CSI* series are in the business of gath-ering information, and doing it quickly. So they get straight to the point and ask pointed questions, eschewing rapport building in favor of the fast answer. This accomplishes the twin goals of letting the interviewee know that they're serious—which could give reluctant sources a critical push—and possibly eliciting more straightforward answers.

Role Model   Radio personality Howard Stern. "The biggest criticism of my interviews is that I cut people off. I think my biggest asset is that I cut people off. It sounds like a contradiction, but the fact is you can't allow people to drone on. You are the orchestra leader. You are the one who is saying, 'My audience wants something new. I've got to get out of this. I gotta keep it fresh.'"

Word to the Wise Keep in mind that this is an extreme style of interviewing that is best used when speaking with a source who either really wants to talk or who really doesn't. The former is likely to give you what you need no matter what, and the latter might respond well to both your no-nonsense demeanor and the fact that the whole thing will be over soon.

THE EXPERT

When I was a reporter at the *Seattle Times,* I shared a cubicle wall with a journalist who covered the burgeoning biotech industry. I used to sit on the other side of that nubby, gray wall and listen to him interview scientist after scientist about the important details of their work. Most of the time, I wouldn't even understand what he was saying—and not just because I could hear only one side of the phone call. His knowledge of the subject was so deep that he could skip over the getting-a-basic-understanding portion of the program and go straight to the details. In other words, he spoke their language.

This style of interviewing is called The Expert, and is the opposite of The Aw Shucks. While best applied when dealing with technical subjects that involve specialized knowledge, it can be used anywhere where it's in your interest to have a particular expertise.

Role Model Financial journalist Michael Lewis. "The financial world has become way too complicated and very secretive. Since when did the stock market become a secret? And the journalists who report are at the mercy of their sources and easily manipulated. Stuff is hard to find out."

Word to the Wise Though you may be able to hold your own on a particular subject, never assume that you know everything when employing The Expert. Information may have changed, or you might have gotten it slightly wrong to begin with. If you're going to rely on a foundation of knowledge to support your interview, it's critical that you continually check in to make sure that it's accurate.

THE BEST FRIEND

We often don't think about how important active listening is during an interview. Sometimes we're ruminating on what the source has just said, or anticipating our next question, or wondering when they're going to stop talking about their golf game and just get back to the point already. But in the Japanese language, there is a specific term for the sounds and phrases listeners make to let the speaker know they're paying attention. It can be a bit startling to hear Aizuchi in practice for the first time, as the "yes's" and "Is that so's" and "Really's?" come in a steadier stream than most native English speakers are used to.

But take a moment to listen to two best friends talking and you'll realize that a truly fluid conversation is a two-player game in any language. Verbal prompts keep the speaker going, and are more likely to elicit well-told anecdotes from your source—which makes your job that much easier.

The Best Friend is an interview style that relies on building a strong rapport with your source and creating an environment where relaying information feels like a pleasure rather than a responsibility. It makes use of enthusiasm and encouragement relayed through facial expressions, body language and, of course, Aizuchi. When used well, it actually allows you to ask fewer questions, and the questions you do ask are less about gathering new information and more about urging the speaker to continue.

Consider this gem of a radio interview between Canadian Broadcasting Company's Markus Schwabe and a trucker named Penn Powell, who had been attacked not once, not twice, but three times by a tenacious beaver on a lonely bridge. It's one of those interviews journalists dream about, where just a few well-placed questions inspire the interviewee to deliver a ready-made story on a proverbial platter. In the nearly seven-minute interview, Schwabe speaks just a handful of times. This is what he says:

What happened?

(Laughs)

What happened?

Where were you going? What happened?

Now did you kill it?

Now did you have big boots on to protect your feet?

(Laughs)

Holy cow, Penn!

So how did you get him off?

Ouch!

So he was biting you?

Did you scream or yell at all?

Well, Penn, how did you get this beaver off of you eventually?

And so you took off I suppose . . .

How bad were you hurt, Penn?

It was pretty serious. . . .

Now, Penn, why do you think the beaver did this?

Now could this beaver have been rabid?

But he was stuck on the bridge. . . .

I guess, Penn, you've got a bit of a new respect for the beaver?

And the parts you didn't hear? Interview gold.

Role Model   TV journalist Katie Couric. "I think the more comfortable you make someone feel, the better interview you'll ultimately get. In terms of body language, I always try to be very warm and welcoming and I think it's really critical to put someone at ease."

Word to the Wise   The Best Friend is probably the most versatile interview style, and can be used on the widest variety of people. Take caution, however, because when it doesn't work, it really doesn't work. Some sources just won't be comfortable unless you set the structure for the interview, or their personality is such that they're not naturally inclined to just go with it. Keep trying to get them to open up in case their reticence is simply a case of shyness, but if you sense your approach is putting them off or making them nervous, it's best to try another tactic.

KEEPING THE "PERSON" IN "PERSONA"

Changing your style to complement your source is a great way to create a comfortable environment, and is most likely to yield the information you need. But shifting personas should be a subtle tool rather than a flashy act. People can tell when you're being disingenuous, and they won't respond well if they feel like the unwilling extra in some kind of performance. After all, changing your approach is intended to more effectively build rapport with your subject—not to make yourself the star of the show.

Remember that you're building a relationship, whether it's for an hour or the span of a career. By tailoring your approach to different sources and meeting them on their terms, you're showing respect for both them and their story. Journalism is ultimately about connecting people, and whether you're exposing injustice or the latest in celebrity gossip, every story starts the same: with the person on the other side of your notebook.

FOUR **The Art of the Interview**

*When it's done well, it's an exchange, a conversation,
an illumination*

JACK HART

Whether they are pit bulls or puppy dogs, newshounds who
conduct interviews can be hacks or artists. Jack Hart, former
Oregonian managing editor and former interim dean of the
School of Journalism and Communication, pushes students
toward art.

You can't write it if you don't have it.

Which is a fundamental truth that writing gurus too often over-
look. . . . None of us should ever forget that good reporting is the heart
of all good writing.

And because journalists gather the vast majority of their information
by talking to people, reporting is mostly interviewing. It follows, then,
that writing problems are often interviewing problems.

- Does the writing lack emotion? Maybe the writer's interviewing
  style put sources on the defensive, causing them to bottle up their
  feelings behind a facade of empty, officious pronouncements.

- Does the writing lack detail? Maybe the writer asked the kind of
  questions that produced abstractions instead of vivid specifics.

· Does the writing lack the great anecdotes that light up the work of fine feature writers? Maybe the writer needed to put more into the conversation so that the source would put more into hers.

Clearly, writing and interviewing go hand in hand. As John Brady, author of *The Craft of Interviewing*, notes, "Many editors consider the best interviewers to be, inescapably, the best writers."

So we'd be wise to heed the journalism professors, behavioral scientists, criminologists and others who study interviewing. They've examined how the best journalists, cops, social workers, psychologists, lawyers and other professionals dig out information with skillful questioning. What they've discovered is surprisingly consistent, and it suggests that there is indeed an art to the interview.

An art that, it seems, lies somewhere far removed from the stereotype most of us learned as cubs. . . .

THE MYTH OF THE JOURNALISTIC INTERVIEW

University of Oregon professor Ken Metzler, who pioneered journalism-school instruction in interviewing, says most of us grew up with a warped sense of what an interview should be. Our false ideal for the journalistic interview grew from the clamoring crowd of shouting reporters typical of old movies, the Mike Wallace ambush interview or the *Meet the Press* celebrity grilling, all confrontational interviews that may make great theater but produce little real information.

The *Meet the Press* model is illuminating. Metzler notes that the show's guest sits on one side of the set behind a counter that is, in effect, a little fort. Three or four reporters sit on the other side of the set behind their own fort. The moderator opens hostilities, and then guest and journalists lob bombs back and forth between their respective battlements until the moderator declares a ceasefire.

Most of us quickly learn that such show-biz interviews are practically useless for digging out truly revealing information. But not many of us realize how deeply the stereotype colors our perceptions or how different a successful interview should be.

The best interviews generate more information than either the source or the interviewer could produce separately. The interview sparks synergy, the burst of energy created when combining elements produces a whole greater than the sum of the parts.

That's the dimension Metzler was trying to tap when he titled his book "Creative Interviewing." And it's integral to his very definition of what makes an interview: "A two-person conversational exchange of information on behalf of an audience to produce a level of intelligence neither person could produce alone."

That suggests that successful journalistic interviewers put as much into their interviews as they take away from them. They reveal something of themselves. They let their sources know where they are going and how they hope to get there. They try to enlist sources in a common cause, even when those same sources are defensive or antagonistic.

What Metzler seems to be suggesting is that the difference between good interviewers and bad ones is largely a matter of attitude. The good ones have overcome the Mike Wallace stereotype. They see their interview subjects as partners in a joint effort. They are less concerned with expressing their own opinions than they are with truly seeing the world from the subject's point of view.

They are, in other words, absolutely nonjudgmental. Metzler notes that the psychologist Carl Rogers defined a successful communication as one in which Party B persuades Party A to say what he really thinks and feels, regardless of what Party B believes. A good interviewer, says Metzler, comes to the interview to listen and understand, not to accuse and judge.

That doesn't mean a good interviewer has to be a sucker. Savvy journalistic interviewers are politely skeptical, even though they don't communicate that skepticism to the subject. And neither are they the cynical scam artists that Janet Malcolm described when she said that every journalist is "a kind of confidence man, preying on people's vanity, ignorance or loneliness, gaining their trust and betraying them without remorse."

But an effective journalistic interviewer does have to put his own anger, righteousness and personal values aside, at least for a time.

I used to tell reporters to listen to the telephone interviews they heard taking place around them in the newsroom. The best writers sound calm, reassuring and genuinely interested. They never turn into shouters who berate sources, demand information or threaten consequences. It is only the hacks who push their weight around.

OPENING THE DOOR

Most professional journalists are remarkably effective at getting to the sources they need. In one sense, that's not surprising. As A.J. Liebling pointed out, "There is almost no circumstance under which an American doesn't like to be interviewed. We are an articulate people, pleased by attention, covetous of being singled out."

Still, some sources are reluctant. Maybe they've been burned by past interviewers. Maybe their colleagues look down on publicity hounds. Maybe they're just busy.

Whatever the objection to an interview, most of us know a few tricks for getting by it. John Brady asked several master interviewers to reveal theirs:

- Carl Bernstein, one half of the Woodstein Watergate duo, says he and Bob Woodward often approached reluctant sources by offering an opportunity to set the record straight. "You tell them that if you've been in error, they're in a position to show you where you went wrong. We didn't think we were in error very often, but it's an effective introduction."

- Book author Philip Marvin has his own version of the same technique. "Never ask to 'interview' a busy person," he says. "Rather, ask for an appointment to get his 'constructive criticism' of the background information you've already gathered."

· Alex Haley figured the best way to get an interview with a VIP was to charm the secretary. He sent flowers and ladled on the flattery. He said he'd even date a secretary to get good inside information or land a big interview.

But most of us aren't trying to land one of the big Alex Haley–style Playboy interviews that justify that kind of time and effort. We just want to get somebody to talk . . . in a hurry. And the toughest assignments involve getting a response from somebody's who's accused of something.

In that situation, Nat Hentoff recommends a tried-and-true technique familiar to most veteran newspaper interviewers. "My usual procedure," says Hentoff, "is to tell him that since he will be in the story anyway, for the sake of accuracy, I would much prefer to get his statement firsthand."

BUILDING RAPPORT

We trust those most who are most like us. And we talk most freely with those we trust. So successful interviewers usually work hard to find something in common with the interview subject. "The object," John Gunther once said, "is to get the subject relaxed, to make him really talk instead of just answer questions."

A little bit of common ground can bridge a chasm of personal differences. It's hard to imagine two more diametrically opposed personalities than those of Richard Nixon and Hunter Thompson. Yet Nixon once summoned—actually singled out and sent for—the doctor of gonzo for a private 90-minute conversation during a drive to the airport. The reason? Both men were fanatic NFL fans, and Nixon desperately wanted to talk football.

Savvy interviewers say they usually scout the interview subject's background to find points of commonality. When they walk into an office or home, they look for souvenirs or knickknacks that betray personal interests. Then they seize on those openings to establish some relationship. An over-the-mantel shotgun opens a conversation on bird hunting. A movie poster kicks things off with some talk about a favorite film.

Of course, some real research in advance of the interview can pay even richer dividends. We do lots of minor, hurry-up interviews that must, of necessity, be pretty much off-the-cuff. But no truly accomplished journeyman would risk a major interview without at least checking the clips. And most will do considerably more digging. John Brady says, "Experienced writers agree that for every minute spent in an interview, at least 10 minutes should be spent in preparation."

The risks of ignorance are great. Brady reports that when Vivien Leigh arrived in Atlanta to celebrate a re-release of *Gone With the Wind*, a reporter asked her what part she played in the movie. She told him that "she did not care to be interviewed by such an ignoramus."

And when a reporter asked Bernard DeVoto for an interview, the famed Harvard professor, historian and editor immediately agreed. Then the reporter said, "I'm sorry. I really didn't have time to look this up. Just exactly who are you, Mr. DeVoto?"

"Young man," DeVoto replied, "if you don't have time to look it up in *Who's Who* or your own library and find out, then I don't have time for you."

DeVoto gave good advice. *Who's Who* is a minimum bit of background. The regional and specialized biographical dictionaries, such as *Who's Who in the West* and *American Men and Women of Science* are even more detailed.

Research can go a lot deeper, of course. And it should for a really big interview. A review of the periodical indices such as the *Reader's Guide to Periodical Literature* or an online search will turn up most of what's been written about anyone. Public records can yield valuable background, especially for investigative interviews. The point is to use knowledge as a lever that will open up the source. Cornelius Ryan, the novelist who wrote *The Longest Day*, said one of the basic rules of reporting was that you should "never interview anyone without knowing 60 percent of the answers."

CONDUCTING THE CONVERSATION

All that preparation goes for naught if it doesn't translate into a candid, revealing interview. The experts agree on several factors that seem likely to help:

Have a plan for the overall shape of the interview   After warming up the subject with some small talk, ask "can-openers"—the softball questions that get the subject relaxed and talking. Educational and career history questions fit the bill. So do questions about family lore or hobbies or well-known accomplishments.

Do the real work during mid-interview. And save the real zinger, your Columbo question, for the very end. In fact, you may want to try the true Columbo technique—the signature move of the TV detective. You poke your head back in the door and ask the Columbo question as you are leaving. "Oh, I almost forgot. There's just one more thing. . . ."

Plan your interviews in logical order   Build to the big one so that you don't have to go back to a prime source for repeated questions as you uncover further information. Most sources will be happy to oblige if you call back once to iron out some details right before publication. That kind of a call will help convince them of your concern for accuracy—especially if you clear the way by asking permission for a call-back as you end the main interview.

But badgering a source with repeated calls is no way to build rapport or pry loose information, especially if the calls are accusatory. Not only will it create a hostile source, but it also exposes the reporter's own bad planning.

Rough out general topic areas you want to cover, but don't write out complete questions   A reporter who reads her questions creates a stilted, excessively formal environment that isn't likely to produce much information. Besides, specific questions rule out a flexible conversation that easily adapts to productive twists and turns.

Remember that specifics produce specifics   Abstract questions, conversely, produce abstract answers. Don't ask the new CEO how she felt about getting the job. Ask her what she was doing when she found out about it, whom she told first and what she said when she told that person.

Offer cues and memory jogs   Most of us have only a fuzzy recollection of most things. But we can remember a lot more if we have a specific event to hang things on. "You had just returned to Chicago when the war broke out. How did you hear about it? What was the first thing you did?"

Zero in on meaningful moments Metzler points out that some of the most productive conversation in a personality interview takes the source back to key points in the subject's life. Look for crossroads, he advises, by asking the source about a time when his life could have gone in different directions. "I understand you had two choices for grad school. What made you decide to choose Minnesota?" And, Metzler further advises, look for epiphanies. "Did you suddenly realize that you weren't cut out for the priesthood?"

Let the source know what you're up to Clearly explaining your purpose will help the source relax and will keep him on track. If you want somebody's interpretation of an event, tell her so. If you want descriptive detail to help you set scenes, explain that, too. Explain what you're NOT interested in, as well. That will help head off one of the chief interviewing problems—the discursive source who wants to talk about everything but the subject at hand.

Know the difference between interviewing for information and interviewing for story If you're out to write a narrative, you'll have to press your source for the kind of descriptive detail that brings it to life. "Think about walking down the ramp and onto the dock. What did the boat look like? Was the sun shining? What was the light like? Were there any gulls? What was behind the boat? Who else was standing on the dock?"

The better educated the source, the more you'll have to press. Education teaches us to abstract generalities from our experience. So well-educated sources leave out the vivid details that bring a scene to life. That's one reason Phil Stanford says that blue-collar sources make the best interviews. They often produce highly detailed descriptions of an event, rather than reporting their own conclusions or filtering out all the specifics that they think are unimportant.

Tell stories to get stories Good anecdotes almost always come out of a relaxed conversation in which the interviewer spins a yarn and the source replies in kind. The best anecdotes illustrate a major theme in the finished story. So a skillful interviewer will tell stories related to some key concept. "I hear Sally's an incredibly hard worker. Her mother says she used to study under the covers with a flashlight. Does she bring her work along when she spends time with you?"

Telling stories on yourself may open up the source even more. Not only does telling a story tend to produce a story, but revealing something private about yourself helps make a source feel safe enough to do likewise.

The famous yarn about Truman Capote and Marlon Brando illustrates both points. Capote interviewed Brando for a New Yorker profile, and Brando was uncharacteristically candid. He even talked about his mother's alcoholism.

A friend asked why he'd been so loose-lipped. "Well," said Brando, "the little bastard spent half the night telling me about his problems. I figured the least I could do is tell him one of mine."

Think about more than words   A high percentage of reporters' notebooks contain nothing but quotations. But the notebooks of the best newspaper writers are filled with much more. They scribble about details that catch their eye, movements and gestures by the interview source and their own thoughts about the meaning of what the source is saying.

Metzler advises his students to follow the SCAM formula. As the interview progresses, the interviewer will remind himself to think about (1) setting, (2) character, (3) action and (4) meaning. Cynthia Gorney, the *Washington Post* writer who won an ASNE writing award with, among other stories, a profile of Theodore Geisel, clearly follows something like the SCAM approach. Her profile of Geisel, better known as Dr. Seuss, created meaning by probing a key element of Geisel's character—his obsessive perfectionism—to explain his success. It revealed different aspects of that character with an action line that led readers on a tour of Geisel's La Jolla home. On one wall, Geisel had prominently displayed his father's 1902 rifle target, drilled in the bull, "to remind me of perfection."

Watch for nonverbal cues   Diamond wholesalers supposedly watch a client's eyes when he examines a stone. If they dilate, the client likes what he sees, and the price will be higher.

That may be apocryphal, but the fact remains that we constantly send an array of nonverbal signals. Sensitive interviewers will pay attention to body posture, gestures and muscle tension. And many good interviewers can recognize the distinctive change in voice quality that reveals when a source is lying.

Watch out for what the social scientists call "contagion bias"—the tendency to telegraph your own feelings unconsciously Interview experts like to recall the story of Clever Hans, the famed turn-of-the-twentieth-century German horse. The farmer who owned the animal would ask him the sum of two plus two. The horse would strike the ground four times with a hoof. Six divided by three? The horse would strike the ground twice.

The experts were baffled until they separated the horse from his owner by a screen, whereupon the horse suddenly lost his ability. It seems that the farmer visibly relaxed when the horse counted his way to the correct number. The horse saw the subtle cue and quit counting.

Human beings are even more suggestible. One experimenter showed a film of an auto crash and asked members of the audience to estimate its speed. Their average estimates varied from 31 mph to 41 mph depending on whether he asked if the cars "contacted," "hit" or "smashed."

Work at listening Average speech proceeds at 125 words a minute. Thought clips along at 500 words a minute. That means you can do a lot of mental drifting while your interview subject answers the last question. The best interviewers use that mental space as an opportunity to think about what the interviewee is saying, what it means and where the interview should turn next.

They also listen aggressively in ways that stimulate the source. They lean forward. They look into the source's eyes. They grunt and nod at appropriate times. They look so intensely interested that the source feels obligated to produce material that justifies all the attention.

What it all boils down to, in the end, is old-fashioned courtesy. Honest, interested, respectful interviewers score the biggest prizes almost every time. Hard-boiled, macho journalists who pride themselves on their cynical, tough-minded questions end up with more doors slammed in their face than good stories. And cagey manipulators sometimes out-smart themselves.

John Brady tells the story of Harry Romanoff, of the old *Chicago Herald-Examiner*, who, according to a colleague, could "play the phone like Heifetz playing the violin."

Romy, as he was known, was famous for impersonating VIPs to pry information out of reluctant sources. After a South Side shooting, he called the switchboard at St. Bernard's hospital, where some wounded cops had been taken. "This is the police commissioner," he said. "Connect me with one of my men there." He was patched through to the sixth floor, where a quiet voice said, "Yes?"

"This is the police commissioner," Romy repeated. "What's going on out there?"

The man at the other end gave him a detailed report. Romy was so impressed that he asked, "Who is this, anyway?"

"This is Police Commissioner Fitzmorris, Romy," said the quiet voice. "I knew you'd be calling."

FIVE

Changing Quotes

We never, ever alter them (except when we do)

TOM WHEELER

If you're, like, concerned, you know, about, um, what belongs between quote marks and what you can edit out of interviews, Tom Wheeler helps guide you through the seemingly endless variables on the Quotometer. Don't forget Cardinal Rule Number One.

As a young music journalist, I once interviewed a rock star on a hot afternoon at a festival called Cal Jam II. More than 300,000 sun-addled rock and rollers attended, and the scene was every bit as chaotic as you might imagine. The assignment was a big deal. I was new to Guitar Player magazine, and my interview with the co-headliner was to be next month's cover story.

I arrived on time at the prearranged spot, which turned out to be a stuffy backstage trailer in the parking lot of the Ontario Motor Speedway. There must've been a dozen people crammed in there, and the place reeked of hot asphalt, warm bodies, stale cigarettes, beer, and more beer. A couple of roadies, burly as Vikings, were barking on their walkie-talkies, swilling the free Coors and rooting through the sandwiches like truffle pigs. Just on the other side of a flimsy, accordion-style room divider, guitarist Ronnie Montrose was warming up for his set at earsplitting volumes. Flashbulbs popped when Mr. Guitar Hero strode into the room, accompanied by a miniskirted teenage companion; she sat on his lap for the duration of the interview, communing with her flip-top compact, adjusting her eyeliner and looking bored. (Oddly, when the photographers weren't taking flash pictures of my subject, they were taking flash pictures of each other. One of them was the girlfriend of another rock star, which apparently made her flashworthy in her own right.) My interviewee leaned toward me. With his arm around the girl, he grinned and hollered over the racket: "So what's your first question?"

This catastrophe produced enough coherent copy for the shortest cover story in the history of print. Fortunately, over the course of the weekend I interviewed my subject again as he held court at Benihana, and again over Chinese takeout during a break in the sound check, and again in the limo, and again on the telephone. From these five fragments I was able to cobble together a serviceable cover story. But should I drag my reader through the sequence of the original transcript, starting and stopping and circling about, returning repeatedly to the topic of, say, my interviewee's preference for Byrdland guitars over Les Pauls? Of course not. It would have been impossible to render a publishable interview without restructuring and without altering quotes, unless I was willing to inflict upon my readers interminable rambling and conversational detours and dead-ends—not to mention a heinous number of brackets and ellipses.

I recount this story not because it is unique but rather for the opposite reason. Interviewing musicians amid boisterous backstage hubbub is not uncommon, so for me, fixing a quotation was never much of an issue. But never having attended journalism school, and working for a staff whose entire ethical guideline was basically "What would Walter Cronkite do?" (which served us rather well, by the way), my question was, if I'm altering a quote, what are the rules?

The short answer: Convey the intent of the speaker, know your publication's policy, and embrace the fact that everything else is a matter of taste, style or judgment.

While taste, style and judgment are subject to continuing debates, the good news is, responsible journalists concur on the most fundamental principle. In my classes it's known as Cardinal Rule Number One: Preserve the speaker's meaning. This is an ethical matter, whereas knowing your publication's policy is a practical one. Policies vary, even among publications otherwise considered similar in mission and classification—specialty magazines, for example, or big-city newspapers. Editors' opinions vary widely as well, even among responsible professionals.

QUOTE THE QUOTABLE

Quotes present all sorts of challenges. One way to avoid some of them is to be judicious when deciding whether to use a quote in the first place. If it's irrelevant, scrap it, even if you went to a lot of trouble to get it. If you keep it, quote the quotable and paraphrase the rest. Is the comment quirky, colorful, revealing of the speaker's uniqueness or character? Is it otherwise memorable? As one journalist advised, there is no reason to quote Mrs. Jones if she says her husband snores "really loudly." But if she says he snores "like a walrus with a head cold," the writer might well consider a quote.

Paraphrasing is convenient. While the ideas belong to the speaker, the words belong to you, and your expression may be more succinct than your speaker's. So long as your paraphrase is accurate, you can in good conscience convey his or her opinions using the varied tools at your disposal—long sentences, short ones, precise terminology, metaphors, etc. But sometimes only a quote will do. In a profile or any lengthy coverage of an interviewee, readers want to hear your subject's voice. They want at least a sense of his or her humanity and personality.

Aside from when to use a quote, considerations include punctuation, where to place attributions and other technicalities. But here we will address the thornier issue of whether quotes must be verbatim, a question that vexes professionals, teachers and students alike.

What is verbatim anyway? Most professionals I know allow for the use of brackets to denote a word or phrase added for clarity, and ellipses to denote an omission. Such tweaks are sometimes included within a verbatim standard because the marks serve to inform readers of the alterations. Other, less transparent changes may also be acceptable, as we will see. (Speaking of transparency, a level of quote-massaging that could otherwise arch an eyebrow might be rendered acceptable with disclosure: "Our interviews with the mayor were conducted over a three-day period; her comments have been edited for brevity and clarity.")

Although the subtitle of this book is *The Oregon Method*, please consider this chapter to be *an* Oregon method. I dare not presume to speak for my colleagues, for if there is one topic upon which reasonable professionals disagree, it is the wrangling of quotes. With that preamble out of the way, I hope to convey my own approach and also to suggest tips for teaching it, should you find it reasonable.

IN THE CLASSROOM: SETTING THE STAGE

I begin by asking students if we can ever alter a quote. Typically, they respond with a chorus of no's accompanied by head shaking and tsk-tsking. Quotes are to be verbatim! And this is a fine place to start. I draw on the whiteboard a VU-type meter with a needle that swings across an arc from far left to far right. At left I place the name of a writer whose work I discovered years ago. I asked her once about her lengthy magazine piece on self-described dissident feminist Camille Paglia. Spread over two issues, it included far-ranging discussions of numerous topics. I asked her about altering quotes, and she said (I'm not going to say she admitted) that, why, yes, she might take words out of a speaker's mouth, put words into a speaker's mouth, or merge a comment from Wednesday evening's conversation with another from Friday morning. (Some students assume I am using the example to illustrate a sloppy or unethical practice. But, not so fast.)

On the far right side of my Quotometer, I print the name of a member of our school's Journalism Advancement Council, a distinguished veteran newsman who seemed to enjoy the role of the crusty curmudgeon. (I remember a meeting where he chastised the faculty for failing to flunk enough students.) One evening I ran into him in a bar. I reintroduced myself and broached the subject of altering quotes. With barely concealed disdain, he delivered the answer I was hoping for: You work for me and alter a quote, that's a firing offense. (At least, that's what I remember him saying; I'm sure of the point he made, and I'm sure he mentioned "firing offense," but I cannot with certainty recount his sentence verbatim. To play it safe, I'll paraphrase.)

Having labeled my VU meter's left-hand extreme with our sure-I-alter-quotes magazine writer, and the right-hand extreme with our clean-out-your-desk-and-get-lost newsman/curmudgeon, I place marks across the dial from left to right to denote incremental shades of gray. My point: As we sweep across the arc from left to right, toward an increasingly rigid verbatim standard, we are not necessarily moving from less ethical to more ethical.

But how can that be? In journalism, surely the altered quote is less ethical—or at least sloppier—than the one conforming to an unyielding verbatim standard. Before passing judgment on that poser, I ask students: Is it conceivable that we might quote an interviewee verbatim and yet do that person, and the publication, and our readers a disservice? Thus begins a rich conversation.

IN AND OUT OF CONTEXT

In thinking up examples, students invariably refer to quotations "taken out of context." But what does that mean, exactly? Unless for some reason we publish a full-length, unaltered, warts-and-all transcription (which few people would want to read), *every* quote, every published interview is "taken out of context," technically speaking. We eliminate redundancies, highlight the quotable and excise the relevant from the context of a larger conversation, much of which may be trivial.

I challenge students to be more specific: Let's hear examples of quotes that might be verbatim yet are misleading by virtue of their being removed from context.

The most egregious examples are simply those where words are snipped out or rearranged. Case in point: President Obama delivered a speech on Sept. 8, 2010, in Parma, Ohio, in which he said, "Under the tax plan passed by the last administration, taxes are scheduled to go up substantially next year, for everybody." Fox News cut the reference to the Bush administration. "Journalist" Sean Hannity cited "a rare moment of honesty" for the president and showed only this fragment of the quote: "Taxes are scheduled to go up substantially next year, for everybody." The onscreen text proclaimed—"Obama: TAXES ARE SCHEDULED TO INCREASE FOR EVERYBODY NEXT YR."

Many examples are less crass than the Fox News forehead-slapper, and students readily suggest more subtle scenarios. What if the speaker was kidding? What about body language? Might eye-rolling, a gesture, or a giggle alter the meaning of a spoken quotation vs. its printed version? A student predicts she's going to get a perfect 4.0 GPA this term. Her friend responds in an encouraging, good-for-you tone of voice: "Yeah, right!" But let's do it again with a smirk and a gimme-a-break attitude: "Yeah, right!" Identical on paper, the two versions are opposite in meaning. (Query: Should I have changed "gimme" to "give me"?)

ONE SIZE DOES NOT FIT ALL

Given good journalism's foundation in ethics and fairness, shouldn't we expect a single, all-purpose standard? Aside from our Cardinal Rule Number One, the short answer is no. (If you prefer, the short answer is "No.") For one thing, consider the speaker. Most people talk in a loose, conversational style that when committed to paper could use a touch-up here and there. By contrast, a political candidate's spoken announcement may be edited, vetted and focus-grouped to within an inch of its life before it ever hits a microphone. Diplomatic speech is even more precisely crafted and coded; the ambassador knows that her recap of the summit meeting will be parsed by nuance-obsessed analysts trying to sniff out any possible distinction between "optimistically cautious" and "cautiously optimistic." Such quotes are special cases. The safe bet: Every syllable is left intact, every addition or deletion duly indicated with brackets or ellipses.

The status of the speaker should be considered in tandem with the nature of the publication. Students are not shocked to learn that the senator's announcement appearing in the *Washington Post* might be held to a different standard than some celebutante's rehab memoir in a cheesy gossip magazine.

BIGGER THAN ELVIS?

Consider pull-quotes, extracted from their body copy and promoted to subheads or teasers. In 1991 Rolling Stone ran a piece on Joni Mitchell by the astute music journalist David Wild. The headline, in bold whopper type: "When I was the queen of rock, I sold more records than Elvis did when he was the king." Joni Mitchell always struck me as brilliant and arty. I wondered, how on earth could she say something so dumb? Reading the body copy, it turns out she wasn't boasting about her popularity or equating her significance with that of the revolutionary rock and roller. She was talking about the growth of the record industry, a commercial explosion no one foresaw. With pop music now a global phenomenon, she was saying, even a jazzy folksinger such as herself could outsell Elvis Presley in his heyday. I don't know how Mitchell or Wild responded to the out-of-context (and in my view shamefully misleading) pull-quote/headline, but I would have been miffed.

OOPS. I HIT "REPLY ALL."

Most students nod their heads when asked if they have a couple of Best Friends Forever who have shared so many experiences that they've developed a lingo of their own, with inside jokes, code words and arcane references that might well be misinterpreted if a once-private email were to go viral.

REMOVING IMPEDIMENTS CAN CLARIFY

With the students having concluded on their own that verbatim quotes might be misleading and therefore unethical, I ask: Might the flipside also be true, that altered quotes might be ethical? Can you think of tweaks that even the testy purist at the extreme right of our Q-meter might permit?

Students suggest that dropping out the "um"s and "er"s must be allow-able, and I know of no one who insists on keeping them. I quote a pas-sage from former colleague and Pulitzer Prize–winner Jon Franklin, who noted that one writer opined that removing "uh"s and "um"s from quotes "pushed the marker on the continuum a hair closer to fiction." Franklin disagreed: "Such utterances are commonly artifacts . . . like dust on the negative that the photographer removes to produce a more real (not less real) likeness. People grunt, moan, snort, and say repetitive things like, 'Okay?' The idea that filtering is legitimate, and maybe even the idea that journalism is legitimate, is based on the premise that removing impedi-ments to understanding can clarify. . . . The whole enchilada, taken with-out filters, is not nonfiction. It is white noise."

LOST IN TRANSLATION?

Any other exceptions that even our cranky old-timer might allow? Students wonder: What about correcting grammar? I had asked our col-league at the bar that very question. For the second time he looked at me as though I were an idiot and groused, *"Of course we correct the grammar!"* I thought (but didn't say), well, that particular door has been cracked open, no? Some professionals claim that the speech of elected officials or political candidates should never be corrected; others argue that all speakers should be treated equally. Either way, as a practical matter, con-sider that when different versions of a newsmaker's quotation are widely published, any discrepancies are likely to come to light.

The *AP Stylebook* is clear and uncompromising on the matter: "Never alter quotations even to correct minor grammatical errors or word usage." The AP's online statement of News Values and Principles elaborates: "If a quotation is flawed because of grammar or lack of clarity, the writer must be able to paraphrase in a way that is completely true to the original quote. If a quote's meaning is too murky to be paraphrased accurately, it should not be used."

Nevertheless, correcting grammar in quotes is an accepted practice among journalists, including many who consider themselves sticklers. I find the *Wall Street Journal*'s policy, for example, to be as responsible as AP's, yet more flexible and, frankly, more realistic, particularly when editing interviews intended to appear as Q&As or in feature formats other than so-called hard news. Its Style & Substance newsletter updates "The Wall Street Journal Essential Guide to Business Style and Usage." Volume 24, No. 6 (2011) specifies: "Spoken quotations . . . normally should be corrected to avoid the errors in grammar and word usage that can occur unnoticed when someone is speaking but are embarrassing in print."

What if the interviewee is a non-native English speaker? Theguardian .com is a publication of the *Guardian*, the UK-based newspaper founded more than a century and a half ago. In an April 2014 Mind Your Language blog, *Guardian* subeditor Saptarshi Ray suggests: "When it comes to people who are expressing themselves in a second tongue, an obsession with perceived accuracy can inadvertently make them sound confused, ignorant or, worst of all, dense." He gives an example of a line from an interview conducted in Spanish with the president of Venezuela. If translated precisely, it would have made him sound goofy. Comparing the unedited and edited versions, Ray asks: "So which is more 'accurate'— the exact words used by an educated man, a head of state no less, speaking in a second language, that make him seem doddery?" (His question also provides an example of another use of quote marks, in this case to point out that the word "accurate" is in his view subject to interpretation; a reference to "accuracy" in quotes is one step shy of saying "so-called accuracy." Another example is seen above, in my arguably heavy-handed use of quote marks around the word "journalist" in reference to Sean Hannity of Fox "News." Oops, I did it again.)

Sometimes it's an editor, not the interviewee, who speaks a different language. In one cover story, my interviewee referred to his primary guitar influence, "B.B." Knowing that my musician readers would get the reference, I decided against adding "[King]." When reprinted in Fachblatt, a German music magazine, "B.B." was converted to "Brigitte Bardot," now identified as an iconic Mississippi bluesman. Readers surely wondered, "Was die Hölle?"

YOU AREN'T ANYTHING BUT A HOUND DOG

What if the speaker is not formally educated? (If students don't ask these questions, I do.) As is often the case, there is no all-purpose answer. If we fix the grammar to avoid embarrassing the speaker, we may find ourselves on a slippery slope—adjusting here, tweaking there, smoothing away rough edges, polishing sentences into gems of prose. Before you know it, every interviewee sounds like a journalism major. A once colorful and unique personality now speaks with a voice that may be grammatically sanitized but is also homogenous, less soulful. (I'm reminded of the comedian who sang corrected-grammar versions of rock and roll songs: "You aren't anything but a hound dog," and, "I can't get any . . . satisfaction.")

On the other hand, if we leave in every inelegant turn of phrase, every shard of fractured syntax, the point of the quote is undermined by distractions. Some may accuse us of poking fun at the speaker, especially if we are perceived to be correcting the grammar of some interviewees but not others. On occasion, a writer may wonder about issues of culture. If she leaves in the speaker's street lingo and bad grammar, she may be accused of cultural bias. If she corrects it, she may be accused of a different sort of bias: Who are you to make him sound just like you? Who are you to disrespect his natural way of expressing himself?

What about accents and dialect? If we have our bayou songwriter talkin' 'bout drinkin' and missin' his momma and still lovin' his woman (even if she's a-cheatin' on him), readers may again find themselves distracted, a disadvantage that for me outweighs the benefit of capturing a sound. That's not to say we must never alter a spelling for effect. I remember a profile about John Fogerty, a singer whose pronunciation is a stylistic hallmark. The article referred to the early days of Creedence Clearwater Revival, when the band was burning up the charts—or, as the writer put it, "boinin' up the charts." I thought it was clever, but in any case these are matters of taste (your editor's, not just yours), rather than higher vs. lower standards. My own view on re-spelling for effect: A very little goes a long way.

Should we change "gonna" to "going to"? I don't wanna generalize, but for me such things are sorta distracting in print, so I encourage students to use correct spellings—most of the time. The *Wall Street Journal*'s Style & Substance newsletter offers a nuanced compromise: "In quoting oral conversation, don't routinely use abnormal spellings such as *gonna* and *nothin'* in attempts to convey regional dialects or mispronunciations. But such spellings may be appropriate when the usage is relevant or helps to convey a desired impression in a feature article."

Professionals often advise that if grammatical quirks are part of the speaker's personality and something he or she is known for, we should be more likely to leave them in. Indeed, fractured syntax can be charming. Changing "It don't make no never-mind" to "It doesn't matter" strikes me as a real shame. To fix such a thing is to wreck it, like correcting Yogi Berra's math or logic. (Who would argue with "Ninety percent of baseball is half mental"?) I once interviewed the great western swing guitarist Eldon Shamblin, a veteran of Bob Wills and the Texas Playboys. Describing the all-gold Stratocaster that Leo Fender had given him, he told me, "It's been banged and beat, and the frets is wore, but . . . it's been a good one." I circled "the frets is wore" and scribbled a note to the copyeditor: "Do not touch."

What do we do when someone obviously misspeaks? A guest once told one of my classes: "When I was a writer, I often said that if I ever became an editor, I would treat writers the way I wish I had been treated when I was an editor." As spoken, the comment makes no sense. Surely, she meant to say "when I was a writer" at the end of her sentence. Do we quote the statement verbatim, including the mistake, perhaps adding a [*sic*], which would only spotlight the error and further embarrass the speaker? Do we tell ourselves we are sure we know what she meant and then fix it? Ideally, I would get the speaker's permission to correct the quote; then again, how often are deadlines met under ideal circumstances? In any case, changing a quote to reflect what you're sure the speaker meant is risky business. Proceed with caution.

A BIG F*****G CHALLENGE

Inevitably, classroom discussion turns to how we handle swear words, obscenities and so on. I illustrate a common approach with examples on the board: sh*t, f— and the like. A comedian once told a writer that most of the time he was calm and normal but that when he gets in front of a camera he becomes "a desperate motherfucker," or as it appeared in the magazine: "motherf—ker." Students invariably think this "solution" is quaint and silly, but anyone who eavesdrops on college students can cite a generational shift. In one multimedia class, students were warned: no swear words in your videos. But an otherwise conscientious student turned in a project in which an interviewee uttered an obscenity. After being penalized, she confessed that for her such language is so common that the infraction hadn't even registered.

Regarding asterisks and hyphens, my view is that by mentally filling in the blanks I become a collaborator in reconstituting the word, which only magnifies its prominence. Of course, many editors would never allow such words onto their pages, knowing how readers would react. In any case, this is a good time to remind ourselves that spoken words often take on weight when committed to print. The casual, no-big-deal phrase uttered in passing now sticks out like a zit on prom night. My advice: Quote such language sparingly if at all; a little goes a long way. Your profile of a gangsta rapper appearing in a hip-hop blog will have different standards than a review of the same artist in, say, The New Yorker, so along with the speaker and the publication, bear in mind the sensibilities of your reader.

Also consider whether the speaker chose the word with some degree of care, to emphasize a point. I once asked Keith Richards how he thought the other members of the Rolling Stones would react to his recording a solo album and touring with a different band. He thought about it and rasped, "Well, this should wake the motherfuckers up." I have no interest in enhancing my street cred by quoting such language, but what was I supposed to do with that word? Change it to "blokes"?

DISTILLING THE ESSENCE

We spend a lot of time in the classroom addressing our responsibility to the speaker, and we should. But let us not forget our responsibility to the reader. Among William Zinsser's 18 books is the million-seller *On Writing Well*, a classic text that has instructed generations of journalists. Regarding the reader, he advises: "He or she deserves the smallest package. Most people meander . . . Your interview will be strong to the extent that you get the main points made without waste."

To that end, some writers stitch together chunks of quotes that were said at different times during an interview, or even on different occasions. During the multiple trials in the Janet Malcolm/Jeffrey Masson/New Yorker case, the technique was called "compression." Lee Gutkind (called by Vanity Fair "the Godfather behind creative nonfiction") authored the book *Keep It Real: Everything You Need to Know About Researching and Writing Creative Nonfiction*. He writes: "Janet Malcolm was finally cleared. But her experience shows that although compression may often be a sound choice artistically, it is also rife with danger. Other celebrated writers have come under fire for using this technique."

Then again, William Zinsser, hardly a firebrand regarding such matters, remarks in *On Writing Well*: "Therefore if you find on page 5 of your notes a comment that perfectly amplifies a point on page 2—a point made earlier in the interview—you will do everyone a favor if you link the two thoughts, letting the second sentence follow and illustrate the first . . . Play with the quotes by all means—selecting, rejecting, thinning, transposing their order, saving a good one for the end. Just make sure the play is fair." Elsewhere he advises: "Your job is to distill the essence." My former student Sean Smith, a veteran of Premiere, Newsweek and other publications, put it this way: "Just because I had to slog my way through a raw transcript doesn't mean my readers have to do it."

WRAPPING UP

While we accept that many of these decisions are judgment calls or matters of taste, we should not mistake that recognition for an anything-goes, loosey-goosey standard. Sloppiness is never good and often damaging. Zinsser reminds us: "You are dealing with a person's honor and reputation—and also with your own." The promise of a quotation is: This is what the speaker said, and if you had been there, this is what you would have heard. If we cannot make that promise, what is the point of a quotation? After all, we can always paraphrase.

But it's important to disabuse students of the notion that all problems are solved with inflexible rules. Removing taste and judgment from the equation dooms us not only to inevitable awkwardness but also, in all likelihood, to unfairness. The speaker's meaning and the journalist's wisdom should always trump unyielding adherence to technicalities. The benefits of what Prof. Franklin called "removing impediments to understanding" inform the ethos of any trustworthy nonfiction communicator, whatever the medium.

I think the best lesson we can impart is this: Sure, let us begin with the verbatim standard but depart from it if necessary to obey Cardinal Rule Number One. In determining such rationales, context is key. Who is our speaker? What might distinguish him or her from others? Which nuances of wording, tone or gesture might not transfer neatly to the page? What do readers bring to the table? What are their sensitivities?

Reporter Fawn Germer's article "Are Quotes Sacred?" appeared in the American Journalism Review's September 1995 issue. She explained that when being interviewed about changing quotations, nearly all of the journalists ended their discussions the same way the *Miami Herald*'s Gene Miller did: "'If I screwed up,' Miller said of his own quotes, 'fix it.'"

SIX **Getting Past No**

People are often reluctant to talk to journalists. Persuading people to open up is usually not a question of if, but when. Here's how to make the moment happen.

BRENT WALTH

Investigative journalist Brent Walth explains why potential sources might not want to be interviewed and offers suggestions for making people comofrtable enough to agree to answer a reporter's questions. Sometimes it's just a matter of time.

Why won't people talk to journalists?

There's a list: The people we seek to interview might be shy, unsure they will have anything important to say. Or they fear saying the wrong thing—embarrassing themselves, hurting someone's feelings, getting fired. Or they fear being misunderstood. Or misquoted. Because we journalists will print what we want and we don't care if we get our facts right and if we make others look bad. We journalists cannot be trusted.

OK, there's more—but that's enough to make us think twice when we ask someone for an interview.

And we should—not about whether you should seek that interview (you should) but about why people are reluctant to talk. Over three-plus decades as a journalist, I've interviewed thousands of people, and many agreed to talk right away. Many times I had to persuade people to talk to me, and when they did, they didn't truly open up. I regret that I didn't learn as much from them as I should have. A few got away entirely—and I may never know why.

I've thought a lot about *what* will get people to talk, *why* they won't talk and *how* I can persuade them to talk. All good questions—but perhaps not the best one: *When* will they talk?

The most important insight I ever got came from Julie Sullivan-Springhetti, a former colleague at the *Oregonian* and a Pulitzer Prize–winning journalist. (Every journalist I cite in this chapter, as it turns out, has won a Pulitzer.) Julie has a marvelous knack for getting people to open up. She's engaging, funny and has a big heart—that all helps. But people still turned her down for interviews. When that happened, one guiding principle made all the difference

"When people say they don't want to talk, they're not really saying '*No*,'" she told me. "What they are saying is, '*Not now*.'"

In other words, people will talk to us eventually. Here's why this is often true: People want to be understood. Our fellow humans want to be *known*—not in the same sense of fame or celebrity, but in hopes of having people understand their lives and their experiences and how they see themselves.

Our job as journalists is to help our sources see that the time to talk to us has arrived. How we do it matters.

The trouble with advice about interviewing is there are only a few truths that always apply. Approach people with sincerity and a true curiosity about what they might tell you. Prepare well and listen carefully. Take thorough notes that capture, as best you can, the person's exact words and meaning. Never make up quotes. Do not deceive about who you are and what you're doing. Keep your word. Don't lie.

Beyond that, it's complicated. The variables involving the interviewer and the source can shift moment by moment depending on the personalities, motives and intentions of each—not to mention how either is feeling in any given moment. For some sources, an interview is strictly transactional. Politicians, CEOs, professional athletes, corporate mouthpieces and other self-promotional animals all want more out of the interview than the journalist (or the public) stands to gain from the deal.

As a journalist, I've always been wary of people who are too eager to talk. The people whose stories need telling—and whose revelations may be the most compelling—are often the most reluctant.

We should address their reluctance in ways that are persuasive, honest and ethical. We talk about interviews as conversations, and as much as possible, they should be. Interviews don't position each participant on equal footing. They're an asymmetrical exchange in which you, the interviewer, hope to bring hidden information to the surface, while your subject decides moment by moment how much to reveal.

Author and former *New York Times* reporter Isabel Wilkerson recognizes this "power differential" between her and her sources, whose thoughts, ideas and life may soon be on display for all to see.

"We must have tremendous humility as we interview and understand the enormity of what our sources are doing when they talk to us. Sometimes they don't even realize it themselves," Wilkerson says. "Empathy is the balance to power."

With that in mind, here are some of the most common reasons people we seek to interview are reluctant to talk—and what we can do to help make the timing right.

People are reluctant to be interviewed when they don't feel important to your story.

Start by assuming everyone will be willing to talk with you.

I have watched many reporters, both young and experienced, convince themselves a source subject will never talk, or that the journalist won't learn anything new, or that the interview will make the subject uncomfortable, or that nothing will be gained by trying. "I have learned that no matter how hopeless the prospect might seem, it is always a mistake to assume that someone will not talk," James Stewart, an author and former *Wall Street Journal* writer and editor, says in his book *Follow the Story*. "In their anxiety that sources won't talk, reporters all but guarantee the failure they fear."

In other words, the reluctant one is not the source—it's the journalist.

Take a breath, get your courage up and make the call or introduce yourself face to face. Nothing beats the direct ask. Emails are good for opening the door but not for asking questions. You can't watch people respond or hear their voice. You can't even be sure they're the ones writing out the answers. (If it's a politician or CEO, you can bet the answer is absolutely not.)

How do you make your pitch? Be clear how the sources will make a difference. Do enough research about them to understand why they can contribute. Show them you've taken time to understand who they are and what they can mean to the story. Don't make it about helping you or *your* story—your sources can help your readers and the public better understand their world.

"Have a hook—an opening line that, like a good lead, makes the person want to know more," says Deborah Nelson, a former *Seattle Times* and *Washington Post* journalist, now an associate professor of investigative journalism at the University of Maryland. "Give them a headline that begs for explanation. Appeal to their curiosity and self-interest."

Nelson recommends having a backup if the first pitch doesn't work. "Delivery is *key*. Your voice should reflect your firm belief that the people you're calling should talk to you. If you express doubts, they'll have doubts. If you're feeling shaky, practice your opening lines out loud before you knock on the door."

Yes—knock on the door. Too many young journalists give up when their emails go unanswered. You can write more emails, or you can get creative. "Write them a letter explaining yourself. If that doesn't work, write them another letter to say you're still interested and still need their help," says Mike Rezendes of the *Boston Globe*'s Spotlight team. "If a source refuses to talk, you might try showing up on the front porch. Don't think of this as a hostile confrontation (although it can be). Sometimes sources will be impressed because you took the time and made the effort to pay them a visit."

Remember: It's not a question of if they will talk, but when.

People are reluctant to be interviewed when they don't understand what they can contribute.

Part of our desire to be understood is to be recognized for what we do and what we know about the world—that is, our expertise.

Let your prospective sources know you're interested in their knowledge—what they have learned, experienced and witnessed. A potential interview subject may think other people know more than they do—but you counter by pointing out no one else has his or her particular insights. You're asking for help—you want them to teach you so that you can help others understand.

People with expertise are everywhere, as I learned as a young reporter when I investigated bad landlords in Portland, Oregon. I figured the city housing inspectors knew everything, but they seemed unwilling to spill the names of the worst landlords in town. Instead they pointed to filing cabinets jammed with inspection files on several thousand properties and told me to dig out the story by myself.

The guardian of the files was a tall, elegantly dressed woman who had organized the records in a manner only she understood. When I asked her to explain her filing system, she instead launched into a running commentary about my hair (too long), my beard (scraggly) and my shirt (stained, torn and untucked). She enjoyed watching me struggle to find any meaningful pattern in the records.

"Mr. Short Hairy Man," she said after three days of this, "you are not very bright."

"Well," I told her, "I asked you for your help."

"You asked me how I organized the files," she said. "You did not ask me if I knew what is in them."

So I did, and she showed me the secret to her system and pointed me to the crummiest landlords in town. I told her she taught me a lesson: Everyone has expertise—they just need a reason to share it.

"Thank you," I said.

"You are welcome," she replied. "You still need a haircut."

People are reluctant to open up when the interviewer doesn't care about who they are as a person.

Even after you get people to talk with you, their sense of reluctance will still hover over the interview. How much should they say? Can they trust you? Did they make a mistake by agreeing to talk to you at all?

You can build trust by engaging people not only in what they know but in who they are. So show that you care—and you have to mean it.

It's a lesson I learned early on as a reporter but didn't always remember to follow. I once interviewed a former police detective who had investigated unsolved deaths of children—a difficult and wrenching topic. When we sat down to talk, the former detective told me she wanted to help but couldn't remember any details about the cases.

I left the interview emptyhanded and stumped. How could she not remember these cases? Maybe it was all too traumatic for her to discuss. But maybe I had gone about the interview the wrong way. I went back to my notes and saw that I'd jumped right in, asking about the unsolved cases without paying attention to the person with whom I was speaking.

When you interview someone for the first time, open with some form of this question: "Where do you come from?" I open the first day of my journalism courses by asking students to write out a quick response to this prompt, then read their answers out loud. They talk about their hometowns, yes, but they also speak of their families and faith experiences. They speak to their sense of identity. Many say that they've never been asked the question before and that they enjoyed finding ways to express who they are and what they value.

Well, I tell them, imagine how someone you interview will feel if you show the same interest in them.

And that police detective? I called her back and asked her out to lunch. When we sat down with our cheeseburgers and fries, she apologized again for not being helpful the first time we spoke.

"It's OK," I told her. "I forgot to ask you a question. Why did you want to become a police officer?"

"It goes all the way back to when I was little," she said. "It's a long story."

"I have time," I told her.

Our food cooled as she talked for an hour about her parents, her difficult childhood and her sense of wanting to protect her community. I spoke only to ask questions that encouraged her to keep going.

When she finished, I finally understood the courageous woman sitting across from me. And I didn't have to ask another question. "About those cases," she said. "I might remember a lot more about them than I realized. What is it you want to know?"

Then she told me everything.

People are reluctant to open up if you're not really listening to them.

As journalists, we often confuse our need to prepare for interviews with needing to show people how much we already know. We often introduce ourselves or open interviews with long recitations about what others have already told us and our conclusions so far.

I've done this myself and then winced when the interview subject says, "You seem to know it all. You don't need me."

We need to show our sources we've earned their time, but we are there to learn because we don't know enough, and they can help.

Reluctant sources—and almost everyone else you interview—will respond better to open-ended questions than to narrowly drawn yes-or-no queries. Sure, sometimes we need a thumbs up or thumbs down, but not when the purpose of our conversation is exploration and discovery.

Every yes or no question begins with a presumption, and our interview subjects are left to feel they have to agree with you, even when they don't, or disagree, which may not help build a connection. It's a difficult habit for us to break. We use yes-and-no questions all the time in daily conversation. So make an extra effort and listen for when your questions open with "Did you . . . ?" or "Do you . . . ?" or "Is it true that . . . ?"

Better to pause and begin again with a question that opens "What did you . . . ?" or "How did you . . . ?" or "Why did you . . . ?"

People will often pause in their answers, or just stop talking, when they feel as if they're done. Maybe they can't think of what to say next. Maybe they've just offered up the answer they've always given. But often our sources are gathering their thoughts or assessing how what they have just said has made them feel. We interrupt that process when we jump right in with the next question.

Instead, given them space to think. When your source pauses or seems to have finished answering, do this:

. . .

Nothing. Sit in silence. Smile, nod, whatever. No matter how much you want to fill the quiet, don't.

Instead, think of this blank space above as the place where your source will fill in with a more detailed, complex and revealing answer. (I'd like to have left two blank pages here to make this point, but the editor wouldn't let me get away with it.)

The silence nudges them to keep talking, think more about what they want to say and perhaps reveal something new. It can be awkward, that waiting silently. Do it anyway.

I once interviewed an evasive police chief whose agency had badly bungled a murder case. I asked him, "So what went wrong?" He shrugged—a dishonest gesture, because of course he knew what had gone awry. I could have challenged him with another question, but instead I stayed quiet. He stared back in silence. Eight minutes went by. Neither of us moved. I thought he was going to kick me out of his office. He didn't. Finally, the chief couldn't take the silence any longer. "We made a lot of mistakes," he said. He never looked me in the eyes again, but he talked, and for the first time told me the truth.

People are reluctant to open up when they're uncertain about what to say.

It's a scary thing seeking exactly the right words when whatever you say could go straight into a story and out on the web. It's even scarier when our sources are not sure exactly how to express themselves. This gets back to the power imbalance between the interviewer and the source.

One solution: Share the power.

Create a safe place for your sources to open up, explore ideas and talk through their fears about how their words might affect themselves and others. In interviews, we do that by setting the ground rules.

Don't assume that people know what "on the record" and "off the record" really mean. "Off the record" means that you can't use anything the source tells you. "On the record" means everything is fair game. It's the appropriate ground rule for politicians, corporate spokespeople and others who expect that they are talking through you to the wider world.

Many veteran reporters routinely use a middle path: *background.* Reporters define what "background" means in different ways, so be clear. I explain that background means I will not attach the source's name to anything I learn, but that I will be taking notes and that I can use the information to advance the story. Then I say this: I'll probably circle back to ask more questions and check what I've learned, and when I do, I will ask again if we can talk for the record.

Some reporters reject this idea out of some principled stand about having everything on the record. These journalists also miss a lot.

The protection of background allows your subject to relax, open up and provide fuller answers. You build trust and walk away with information, insight and leads that you didn't have before.

When you return with more questions, the ground rules are the same. Nothing goes in the record—from the past interview or the present one—unless the source gives permission.

I've rarely had anyone turn me down. Still, a source may be reluctant. Eric Nalder, a former *Seattle Times* investigative reporter, suggests going one easy step at a time.

"Pick out quotes that aren't too damning," Nalder says, "and say: 'Now what about this thing you said here. Why can't you say that on the record?' If they agree to put that comment on the record, go to another one in your notes and say: 'Well, if you can say that on the record, why can't you say this?' And so on. I have gotten an entire notebook on the record this way."

Nalder reminds us that, above all else, we have an obligation to keep our word.

"If they insist on anonymity, however," he says, "you must honor it."

Honor the reluctance, and keep the conversation going.

Regardless of the ground rules for the interview, that follow-up interview is invaluable.

How often do we leave conversations wishing we had said something we did not? Or remembered something we could have added? Your questions have now had time to sink in, and your sources may only now understand how they really feel about the subjects you discussed. To them, the interview is over, and they may regret not having a chance to say more.

So keep the conversation going. Wait a day or two, call back and convey how grateful you are for their willingness to talk with you. Before asking the questions on your list, ask your sources if they have been thinking about your earlier conversation. After all, they have traveled a great distance to come to this moment. Once again, listen carefully and take good notes as you reflect on reluctance that has turned into revelation.

SOURCES

Nalder, Eric. "Loosening Lips: The Art of the Interview." Investigative Reporters and Editors, 2007 National Conference, Tipsheet No. 2894.

Nelson, Deborah. "The Art of the Interview: The Reluctant Subject." Investigative Reporters and Editors, 2008 National Conference, Tipsheet No. 3243.

Rezendes, Mike. "Lucky 13 Tipsheet for Finding, Nurturing and Protecting Sources." Investigative Reporters and Editors, 2017 National Conference, Tipsheet No. 5201.

Stewart, James B. *Follow the Story: How to Write Successful Nonfiction.* Touchstone, 1998.

Wilkerson, Isabel. "Interviewing: Accelerated Intimacy," in Mark Kramer and Wendy Call, eds., *Telling True Stories: A Nonfiction Writer's Guide from the Nieman Foundation at Harvard University.* Plume, 2007

SEVEN

How to Interview Somebody Who's Lying

Tips include doing your homework, avoiding confrontation and paying attention to the medium

TODD MILBOURN

"You lying scum!" is probably not the right response when a reporter knows a newsmaker is not responding to questions with the truth. As a reporter, Todd Milbourn developed easy-to-use techniques for teasing honest answers out of interviewees.

If you want advice about how to interview somebody who's lying, there are few people better to ask than Stephanie McCrummen. McCrummen is a veteran reporter for the *Washington Post*. She's filed stories from Kenya, Egypt, Iraq and Mexico. But the most remarkable interview of her career took place in a little Greek restaurant in suburban Virginia on a Wednesday afternoon in November 2017.

Weeks earlier, McCrummen had published a front-page story documenting sexual assault allegations against Roy Moore, a U.S. Senate candidate in Alabama. Since then, McCrummen and her reporting team had been inundated with emails and phone calls about additional potential victims. One of the tipsters was a woman with an especially harrowing story. She gave her name as Jaime Phillips.

Phillips told the *Post* that Moore impregnated her when she was 15 and convinced her to have an abortion. She said she was interested in possibly taking her story public and wanted to meet with McCrummen in person during an upcoming visit to the Washington, D.C., area.

In the days leading up to the interview, *Post* researchers fact-checked the details of Phillips' account. But unlike the accounts from other women, several aspects of Phillips' story seemed strange. She'd been calling from New York, not Alabama, and used an encrypted text messaging service. The place where she claimed to work had no record of her employment. Most suspiciously, a *Post* researcher uncovered an Internet message on a GoFundMe page in which Phillips asked friends to help finance a move to New York, so she could take a job combating "the lies and deceit" of the mainstream media.

By the time McCrummen entered the restaurant and sat down across the table from Phillips, she was "99 percent sure" the woman's story wasn't just inconsistent—but a fabrication.

"I was walking into a situation where, barring some crazy coincidence or fluke, we were pretty sure that she was a fake, but we didn't know who she was working for," McCrummen told me in an interview.

Let's pause and think about this situation for a moment. *What would you do?* Let's say you're McCrummen. You have credible information that suggests a source is not telling the truth about an extremely serious matter, and you've just pulled out your notebook and recorder for an interview. What questions would you ask? What tone would you take? Would you confront the source directly or hang back and see what she says?

These are critical questions that many reporters face but aren't always prepared for. While the circumstances of McCrummen's interview are certainly extreme—Phillips turned out to be involved in a sting operation to trick the *Post* into reporting a false story—interviewing people who lie is a regular hazard of the job. It might even be more common in an era when political and business leaders seem to face few consequences for not telling the truth.

I've been there myself. As a newspaper reporter in California, I once interviewed a mattress store owner who used more than a dozen aliases as part of an elaborate fraud scheme, and I confronted a high-profile real estate CEO who lied about everything from where he attended college to his involvement in a multimillion-dollar housing swindle.

The cloak-and-dagger nature of lie-detection can be exciting, alluring and downright exhilarating. But it can also be confusing and full of pitfalls.

One common myth is that you can tell people are lying by their body language. While sources might sweat, wiggle in their chairs or fail to make eye contact, that's usually just a sign they're nervous or anxious, according to Robert Feldman, a psychology professor at University of Massachusetts-Amherst and the author of the book *The Liar in Your Life.* What's more, he told me that the physical "tells" people often give off are unique to them, so you have to spend years with somebody before you're able to reliably discern if that person is lying.

So how then can you tell if your sources are lying? And if you're confident they are, in fact, lying, how should you approach those interactions? Here are seven tips to make sure you enter your interview poised, prepared and well-positioned to pursue the truth.

STRATEGY #1: BEGIN WITH BACKGROUND

Uncovering lies begins long before the interview—with thorough and rigorous reporting. If you're suspicious of a source—and frankly, even if you're not—you should conduct a deep background check before your interview. That means going beyond a simple Google search. Run your source through LexisNexis. Check for lawsuits, criminal histories and bankruptcies. Examine property records and licenses. Talk to associates. Dig up that GoFundMe page.

Doing so won't just familiarize you with your source's personal history, it'll provide ammunition for questions. You can use this information to test a source's truthfulness. Envision yourself as the prosecutor who asks questions but already knows the answers.

When I walked into company headquarters for my interview with the crooked real estate CEO, I already knew his entire work and education history. So when he started saying things that contradicted the record, I was prepared to dig deeper. "You say you played baseball at Arizona State? That's interesting. I didn't know that. Tell me more?"

STRATEGY #2: DON'T PLAY YOUR CARDS RIGHT AWAY

If you catch sources in a lie, your impulse will be to call them out. Don't—at least not right away. Your goal should be to keep sources talking until they've shared all the relevant details. That's because the moment you confront them, they'll likely get defensive. They might even shut down entirely and leave the interview. At that point the source is no longer helpful for your reporting.

A much better strategy is to ask short, open-ended questions that politely challenge the source. Save any confrontation for the end.

McCrummen is a master at this. Her interview with Phillips, which later went viral, is filled with simple, probing questions, such as: "Can you explain this? … I just want to understand."

"If you just come in like gangbusters, that you're sure of everything, then it's going to be off-putting to the person," McCrummen said. "I wanted her to stay and answer my questions as much as possible."

Remember: as a reporter, your job isn't ultimately to expose people who lie—it's to get at the truth. That's a subtle, but important distinction. It means that liars can, at times, be valuable sources. Somebody who's lying still has a story to tell, and that story—if corroborated—can point you toward deeper understanding.

So be skeptical. But see where they go.

STRATEGY #3: BE CURIOUS, NOT CONFRONTATIONAL

Even in contentious situations, it's a good idea to lead with your curiosity. That can be hard to do, especially when you're confident somebody is B.S.-ing you. It's human nature to feel angry and under attack. Set aside those feelings. Don't take lying personally.

In McCrummen's case, she came to suspect that Phillips' end goal was to harm her professional reputation and that of the *Post*. The deception also sought to cast doubt on the verified stories of the women who were credibly accusing Moore.

Yet during the 20-minute interview, McCrummen stayed focused on the story and showed commitment to following all the threads.

"As the interview went on, I became increasingly curious, genuinely curious," McCrummen said. "I was interested to hear how she came to be sitting here. I really wanted her to tell me the real story. How do you come to have this job where you're trying to trick reporters? What's that about?"

STRATEGY #4: SILENCE IS YOUR FRIEND

If a moment of awkward silence falls upon your interview, resist the urge to jump in. Instead, give the floor to your source, who might come forth with something unexpected and revealing. Humans are social creatures, after all. You never know what your source might say to break an anxious pause.

"You want to know what the other person is going to fill the silence with. You want them to step into the breach, because you're trying to understand their thinking," McCrummen said.

STRATEGY #5: GET FACE-TO-FACE

The best venue for interviewing a potential liar is face-to-face. Feldman, the psychology professor, said people are less likely to lie when you're talking in person. There's a measure of accountability that comes with one-on-one interaction.

If you do conduct an over-the-phone interview, make sure to record the conversation. Recording interviews improves accuracy and offers you a layer of protection in the event your source later claims you got something wrong. Various apps exist to record conversations, but I'm old-school. I've found that plugging a $14 Olympus TP-8 ear microphone into a standard audio recorder works great. You just put your phone up to your ear, hit record and it captures both voices.

Different states have different rules for recording phone conversations, so be sure you understand the legal restrictions. Whenever I record a phone interview, I always begin with a short, non-threatening disclosure: "I'm going to record this just so I make sure I capture everything accurately. That okay?"

If the interview gets heated and the source hangs up on you, my advice is to call back immediately. As always, be polite, but persistent. "I'm sorry. I think we got disconnected."

STRATEGY #6: MIND YOUR MEDIUM

Television interviews, especially live television interviews, have unique characteristics. Yet in my experience as a local TV news producer, many of the same strategies apply. Ask punchy, precise questions. Avoid the lengthy, look-at-me-I-know-it-all preambles. Instead, be original. Be surprising.

In televised press conferences, reporters often ask questions that they think make them look good to colleagues in the briefing room. But it's much more revealing to ask a question that would be interesting to somebody who isn't already following the story.

That's what John Dickerson did during a press conference with President George W. Bush in 2006. While other veteran White House reporters peppered Bush with predictable Beltway-insider questions, Dickerson, now a CBS This Morning co-host, asked the kind of question a normal person would ask midway through a presidency: "What would you say is the biggest mistake you've made during your presidency, and what have you learned from it?"

The question seemed to catch Bush off-guard.

"I wish you would have given me this question ahead of time, so I could plan for it," said Bush, before launching into a vague, rambling non-answer that provided viewers valuable insight into the president's capacity for introspection.

For extended TV interviews, it's good practice to stay on topic. Sources who want to avoid the truth like to skip from one subject to the next. It's much better to probe deeply into one matter and come at that topic from different angles.

Finally, TV producers and executives must be extremely careful in deciding whether to book a person with a history of truth-bending for a live television interview. It's true that a correspondent will have an opportunity to challenge the source's answers, but the audience hears the misleading statement first, and that first statement often leaves a lasting impression.

A good way to protect the integrity of your news station's airwaves is to record the interview and use it as a foundation for a reported video package that includes the source's comments but also provides enough context to give viewers a full picture.

STRATEGY #7: BE HUMBLE

No matter how well-prepared you are for an interview, there are always things you don't know. You might be confident you've uncovered a deception and have public records to back you up. But there's still a chance you're not seeing the whole picture.

That's why McCrummen stresses the importance of humility.

"Even if it's a half-of-a-percent chance or whatever, you always have to leave room for the idea that you've gotten something wrong. I think that keeps you from taking that self-righteous tone, which is not good anyway," said McCrummen, who later shared a Pulitzer Prize for her reporting on Phillips and her connections to a covert journalistic sting operation called Project Veritas.

Make sure you're following your own ethical compass, as well. Always identify yourself as a reporter. Don't misrepresent what you're doing. Be mindful of the power you wield as a journalist, and treat sources—especially those who aren't familiar with the workings of the press—with respect. If you end up breaking a big story, the last thing you want is for your methods to come under scrutiny and distract from the larger issue.

Above all, you must keep in mind that even through the wildest of interview situations, journalism isn't about the journalist.

"It's not about you. It's not about judging people. It's not about embarrassing people or scoring points," McCrummen said. "It's about understanding. It's about eliciting information. It's about revealing something."

That something is truth.

EIGHT

Learning to Fly: A Student of the Journalistic Interview

It isn't just a matter of winging it;
there are lessons to be learned

SIERRA DAWN McCLAIN

Teachers, of course, learn from students. Oregon professional master's student Sierra McClain provides examples of how and why as she shares her early journalistic interviewing experiences.

As I write this, I am a young journalist in graduate school, brimming with eagerness and curiosity. When you read this, I will already have graduated and will be off on the next adventure. I have learned so much about interviewing already, and I look forward to learning more for the rest of my life. I'm excited to share with you some lessons I've learned so far.

COURAGE IS CAUGHT

"Courage, dear heart."—C.S. Lewis

Interviewing requires courage, but courage is hard to teach. You can read about it, write about it and aspire to have it. But I have found that the best way to get a courageous spirit is to catch it—by being around people who have it already. As a student of interviewing, I've been infected by the contagious courage of my professors, professional journalists I've met and the other students in my cohort. These people are not reckless, fearless or cocky. They are brave. They have showed me that courage is not the absence of fear, but the willingness to face fear and keep going. When you find courageous people, stick by them and learn from them.

DO IT AGAIN

> "Courage doesn't always roar. Sometimes courage is the quiet voice at the end of the day saying, (whispering), 'I'll try again tomorrow.'"
> —Mary Anne Radmacher[1]

Keep interviewing people. If you're scared and would rather stay at home, interview people. If you're not sure you'll ever be good at it, interview people. If you stutter and blush, interview people. Nearly everything worthwhile is challenging and demands practice.

When I was 16, public speaking terrified me. One day when I had to give a speech in front of my peers, I cried—at the podium. It was then I decided I didn't want to carry the weight of my fear any longer. So I bought a train ticket to Seattle and spent 10 days at a debate camp. I still wonder how I survived. After a debate round, one of the judges sardonically told me, "You need to get over your blushing problem." Oh, thanks. That's *great* advice. But I tried. I participated in competitive speech and debate in high school and college. I won national awards and was later invited to speak to thousands of people across the U.S.

But you know what? I'm still not over my blushing problem. When I'm nervous, my heart hammers in my chest and my skin turns red as spilled wine. And that's okay. I'm working on it. Maybe I'll never get over it. But I'm going to keep speaking and interviewing people. I am a brave journalist, and so are you. Keep interviewing. Do it again . . . and again . . . and again.

THE ANSWER IS ALWAYS NO IF YOU DON'T ASK

> William Wilberforce: "No one of our age has ever
> taken power."
>
> William Pitt the Younger: "Which is why
> we're too young to realize certain things are
> impossible. So, we will do them anyway."
> —from the 2006 film *Amazing Grace*

For three years, I worked with a man named Joe Polito who said to me at least once a week: "The answer is always no if you don't ask." I didn't like asking people for things, not even for their time. I didn't want to be a burden. And some things seemed unlikely or even impossible, so why bother? But Polito's words lodged in my brain. I started asking for impossible things, and I haven't ever stopped. Sometimes I get a no. Sometimes there isn't any reply, even when I follow up later. But many times, I get a yes when I least expect it.

As a young journalist, I'm still learning to ask for things even when I expect no for an answer—asking to work in places I've only dreamt of seeing, to interview people I don't expect will have the time, to learn from experts with incredible skills. I recently reached out to Declan Walsh, a *New York Times* correspondent based in Cairo whose front-page stories about Yemen's civil war shocked the world. I invited Walsh to Skype my interviewing class at the University of Oregon so that we could learn more about reporting in a crisis zone. He is a busy man and could have said no—but he said yes, and our Skype meeting with him was fascinating. I was reminded again that asking is always worth it. I've learned to be half-doer, half-dreamer. I've learned to have a solid Plan B, but to ask for Plan A, even if I don't think it'll happen. Journalism scoffs at the impossible. Remember that the answer is always no if you don't ask.

BE A REDWOOD TREE

> "In normal life we hardly realize how much
> more we receive than we give, and life cannot
> be rich without such gratitude. It is so easy
> to overestimate the importance of our own
> achievements compared with what we owe to the
> help of others."—Dietrich Bonhoeffer[2]

You may be familiar with the analogy of the redwood tree. The tallest tree in the world, named Hyperion, is a redwood that reaches 380 feet.[3] Towering redwoods have vast root systems, which often extend 100 feet and intertwine with the roots of other redwoods. Baby redwoods especially rely on older trees, latching onto their roots for stability and nutrients. In my time in the University of Oregon's journalism master's program, I have similarly found the need to spread out my roots and intertwine with others. You often hear that successful journalists are those who know how to network. That's true. But journalism is about more than just networking. It's about community.

I quickly learned the importance of relying on others while learning how to interview. For one news series I produced about underserved aging populations, I realized I would need to talk to experts on aging, politicians, educators, families and older adults in the local aging community. Although I found some people to interview through online research and community meetings, I wanted to dig deeper. I contacted Arline Link, a woman in her late 70s who has led events at the Lane County Fairgrounds for decades and is well-connected in the community. I explained my project to her, and she gave me the names and phone numbers of dozens of potential interviewees. Many of those people made it into my stories. You might say they became my stories.

My experience with Link taught me how much good can come from reaching out. I started asking my interview subjects, "Who else should I talk to?" Occasionally I got a shrug in reply, but usually my interview subjects had other ideas or contacts for me, and they were glad to help. Networking, crowdsourcing and asking for help are essential tools for the successful interviewer.

When you're building your network, don't underestimate the resources you already have. I often asked for ideas or interview contacts from friends, family, professors and strangers. Some of my best resources were the other students in my graduate cohort.

Finally, I am learning how important my little grove of redwoods will be in my future career. I had the opportunity to meet Tom Bowman, NPR's long-time Pentagon reporter, this summer. When I started applying for post-graduation fellowships, I asked Bowman if he could be a reference for me. He said he was happy to do so anytime. And I have an invitation to shadow him on the job the next time I'm in D.C.

I owe so much to the help of others, and I'm excited for the chances I get to help others now and in the future. To grow tall, we must build strong roots and intertwine our lives with others.

SAY YOU ARE A JOURNALIST—BECAUSE YOU ARE

> "You are braver than you believe, stronger
> than you seem and smarter than you think."
> —Christopher Robin to Winnie the Pooh[4]

It's hard to get started in journalism. It's easy to feel intimidated or inadequate, especially if you haven't held a reporting job or been published yet. When pitching my stories or asking people if I could interview them, I have often felt unqualified. One thing I've learned as a journalism student is that I have to be assertive and call myself a reporter. As my fellow graduate student Lloyd Lamoureux put it, "I am a writer. I write." You have to take yourself seriously, believe in your work and call yourself a professional.

I learned this for the first time not in journalism but in art. One wintry day when I was in fifth grade, I was meandering through the streets of Poulsbo, Washington, a town fashioned like an old Scandinavian village. At one shop, I met a window painter. She was perched atop a stool painting a picture on a window of a Swedish girl sledding. I told my mom, "I want to do that someday." Scroll forward to age 16. I remembered the artist and told my mom I still wanted to paint windows. "Then do it," she said. "Why wait?" So, I painted the windows of my house, took photographs and made a portfolio. Then I dressed professionally and carried my portfolio into businesses around my city. In each store, I asked for the manager, introduced myself as a professional artist and asked if they would like their windows painted for the holidays. The first store I walked into was a haircutting salon, and the manager hired me on the spot. I'm glad she did, or I might have given up, because the next several business managers said no. But I kept going, and soon I was painting the town—literally.

I've carried this lesson into my career as a new journalist. I am learning to assert myself and call myself a reporter. That doesn't mean I hide that I'm a student. In fact, it has often been useful to tell my interview subject that I'm new to this field and still in the process of learning. But I still call myself a journalist—and as a result, people have treated me like a professional and taken the interview seriously. We are all lifelong learners and we ought to give ourselves more credit. I can do this. You can do this. We are journalists.

BEAT A PATH TO WHERE THEY ARE

> "Isn't it splendid to think of all the things there
> are to find out about? It just makes me feel glad
> to be alive—it's such an interesting world. It
> wouldn't be half so interesting if we knew all
> about everything, would it?"—L. M. Montgomery[5]

Interviewing is about seeking. We seek out information, answers, stories. I love learning foreign languages, which often contain subtle shades of meaning. In ancient Hebrew, the word "seek," its root verb דָּרַשׁ *dârash*, literally means to tread or beat a path.[6] Seeking requires leaving the familiar road to beat a path through uncharted territory. This is the magic of good interviewing. It's natural, safe and easy to talk about your-self because that's a familiar road. It takes courage and intentionality to really get to know the person you are interviewing. It demands draw-ing someone out, asking thoughtful questions and listening, not merely with the intent to reply or to get what you came for, but with the desire to understand. An interview is an expedition. A journalist is an explorer trekking through an interesting world. You must venture deep into the undergrowth—pursuing a story, seeking a person, beating a path to where they are.

THE 50–10 RULE

> "It is the province of knowledge to speak
> and it is the privilege of wisdom to listen."
> —Oliver Wendell Holmes

A few years ago, I was sitting in a conference session about how to commu-nicate respectfully with people who have different perspectives. An audi-ence member asked the speaker, Alan Shlemon, how he builds rapport with people with whom he disagrees. Shlemon's answer has stuck with me. He said that if he has one hour with someone, he spends 50 minutes asking questions and listening, and only 10 minutes talking about him-self once he better understands where the person is coming from. This 50-10 rule, he said, helps him to find common ground—and allows him to openly disagree without building a wall.

People like to talk about themselves. Everyone wants to be listened to and noticed. Sharing a little about yourself and the story you're writing is crucial. Chiming in when you find commonalities is a great way to con-nect. But listening comes first. The better we listen and ask thoughtful questions, the more we build trust with our interviewees. The more we build trust, the more things they will share that we can learn from. The more we learn, the better we can write the story. And as Shlemon said, listening helps build bridges between divided people. That's exactly what journalists like you and I should be doing.

MEET IN THEIR SPACE

> "In the name of God, stop a moment, cease your
> work, look around you."—Leo Tolstoy

As an early career journalist, I felt it might be presumptuous to ask my interview subjects if I could meet them in their workspace or house. I was already intruding on their privacy by asking personal and probing questions. Wouldn't it be too much to invade their home? But I quickly learned how important it is to meet my interviewees in their space. An interview at a coffee shop or over the phone will work for some projects, but if you need to know and understand your interviewees for the story, then you need to see them in their element.

Sometimes, that meant silently watching my interviewee work in a studio or shop. Sometimes, it meant shadowing them on the job—sitting next to them on the bus on the way to work, watching their interactions throughout the day. Many times, it meant going to their house. I learned that it's important to ask permission up front: "I would like to interview you, and I want to meet you in your space."

I learned not to rush through my interviews, but to stop a moment, look around and drink in the scene. Then I wrote down what I saw, heard, felt, tasted and smelled from any place where I interviewed someone. I didn't include everything I wrote down in my stories, but I used the best details. When you interview, remember that the place is not only valuable in helping you understand the person; the place itself is a character in your story.

·

BRILLIANTLY DISGUISED

> "There is no such thing on earth as an
> uninteresting subject; the only thing
> that can exist is an uninterested person."
> —G.K. Chesterton[7]

We've all heard the cliché "Don't judge a book by its cover." I have had to relearn this again and again while interviewing. Sometimes, you will need to write a story about a subject that bores you, or even one you dislike. I have learned, both in journalism and in life, not to underestimate topics or people. In every subject, there is something that makes me think, "Wow." In every issue, there is a human story that matters.

There is *always* more to a person than what I can see. I have yet to meet a two-dimensional person. People are full of secrets and surprises. For one story I wrote, I interviewed an 80-year-old seamstress about her craft and the fabric store she has owned for 42 years. After the interview, I asked her, "What would surprise people about you?" I learned that she had adopted three daughters, two with handicaps. One of her daughters has severe cerebral palsy. Doctors said she would never walk and that she was mentally retarded. But she did walk, she has a doctorate in law and she has written 28 books. What a surprising story—and an opportunity to write a profile piece on her daughter. Don't assume you have someone figured out, even if you've done your background research and spent a lot of time with them. There are plenty of things in their life, both pleasant and unpleasant, that you don't know about.

Circumstances, too, are not always what they seem. What might look like a closed door or an insurmountable obstacle may be your best story yet. John W. Gardner, who served in President Lyndon B. Johnson's Cabinet, once described work as "a series of great opportunities disguised as insoluble problems."[8]

MADE FOR FLYING

> "May the wind under your wings bear you
> where the sun sails and the moon walks."
> —J.R.R. Tolkien[9]

I have no doubt you've heard the popular expression "Fake it 'til you make it." What you may not have heard is that you'll never make it. Now, hold on. I don't mean you'll never succeed. I only mean you will never get there, wherever there is—you will never have "arrived." Sure, you'll get better over time. Maybe you'll land that dream job, win a Pulitzer and change the world. But, as my professor Lori Shontz told me, no matter how far you go in your career, you'll always have to fake it a little. You'll always have to be flexible and ready for surprises. Journalism is a lifelong journey. If I'm a good journalist, I'll never stop learning. I'll always have to wing it a little. But that's okay. These wings were made for flying.

NOTES

1. Mary Anne Radmacher, "Courage Doesn't Always Roar," *MaryAnneRadmacher.net*, June 23, 2016, https://www.maryanneradmacher.net/apps/blog/show/44046084-courage-doesn-t-always-roar.

2. Dietrich Bonhoeffer and Eberhard Bethge, *Letters and Papers from Prison*, 1st American enlarged ed. (New York: Macmillan, 1972), 50.

3. Jessie Szalay, "Giant Sequoias and Redwoods: The Largest and Tallest Trees," *LiveScience*, May 4, 2017, https://www.livescience.com/39461-sequoias-redwood-trees.html.

4. Karl Geurs, "Pooh's Grand Adventure: The Search for Christopher Robin," accessed Dec. 22, 2018, https://www.scripts.com/script-pdf/16075.

5. L.M. Montgomery, *The Green Gables Collection* (Canada: Doubleday, 2008), 18.

6. Francis Brown, Samuel Driver, Charles Briggs, *The Brown-Driver-Briggs Hebrew and English Lexicon* (Peabody, Massachusetts: Hendrickson, 2010), 109.

7. G.K. Chesterton, *Heretics: Centennial Edition* (USA: CreateSpace Publishing, 2011), 13.

8. Robert McFadden, "John W. Gardner, 89, Founder of Common Cause and Advisor to Presidents, Dies," *New York Times*, Feb. 18, 2002, https://www.nytimes.com/2002/02/18/us/john-w-gardner-89-founder-of-common-cause-and-adviser-to-presidents-dies.html.

9. J.R.R. Tolkien, *The Hobbit, or There and Back Again* (Boston: Mariner Books, New York: Houghton Mifflin Harcourt, 2012), 106.

PART II Specialized Interviewing

NINE Profile Interviewing

Anecdotes, details, backstory, chronology—
all contribute to telling the story of a life

MIKE THOELE

Journalist Mike Thoele has been teaching interview tactics
and techniques for almost as long as interviewing has been
taught at American journalism schools. In this chapter he
guides students through the process of turning questions and
answers into life stories.

Each of us is the owner of a life. Each of us wonders how best to use it. Each
of us is fascinated with how others use theirs.

We need no better reason to pursue profiles. The interviewing and
crafting of profiles may be the highest and best form of journalism,
because nothing takes us closer to the core of the human condition, while
challenging our own humanity. To do profile interviews well requires
nearly every tool in the interviewer's kit. Over time, such work has the
effect of sharpening those tools, making them more effective, more relevant for other interviewing tasks. The interviewer's knowledge of what
works, and when, and where is enhanced.

In profile interviewing, we walk into another person's life. The time we
spend interviewing inside that life is only the most minuscule portion of
the time that our subject has spent actually living the life. And yet, from

our brief encounter, we expect to emerge with the capability of describing and explaining that life to the wider world. This is the fundamental audacity of being a nonfiction storyteller. Still, as daunting as the task may seem to the novice interviewer, it works. It can be done. And few things are as satisfying as pulling it off successfully.

The profile interview, of course, spans a wide spectrum. It ranges from encounters with all-too-polished respondents—celebrities, politicians, bureaucrats, entertainers, corporate bigwigs—to the so-called ordinary people, those whose stories have never been publicly told and perhaps never will be again. We face limitations in doing this work. If your outlet is some daily, weekly or monthly journalistic medium, whether web, video, audio or printed page, then the fences of budget, airtime or word count will work to confine you. Still, in one fashion or another, you will stand as biographer for your interviewee. But how different is our task from those who pen biography at book length.

Doris Kearns Goodwin, author of an epic biography of President Lyndon Johnson, once addressed the difficulty of her task: "The search after 'the whole man' is the biographer's dream. . . . If we are honest with ourselves the best we can offer is a partial rendering, a subjective portrait of the subject from a particular angle of vision, shaped as much by our own biography—our attitudes, perceptions, and feelings toward the subject— as they are by the raw materials themselves."

She thinks it's a tough job at book length. What about us, laboring to capture a life in a few minutes of screen or broadcast time, or in a few thousand words? The answer is that the profiler must interview broadly to be able to compress with confidence, clarity and readability. Ken Metzler, the inspiration for this book, was fond of saying, "Interviewing is sifting tons of ore to get a handful of nuggets." Never more true than with profile interviews.

THE ENTRÉE AND THE BACKSTORY

Profiles typically present the interviewer with two primary dimensions, one more apparent than the other. First and obvious is the entrée—the present or past or pending activity that draws us to the profile subject. On one end of the entrée scale might be somebody who does or did or is about to do something interesting. Say, the director of a play that's just opening, a war veteran with harrowing tales of combat, someone who's simply known as a quirky persona in her community, an activist who's fighting to preserve a river, or yesterday's semi-celebrity living quietly among us.

On the more brightly lit end of the entrée spectrum stand the newly prominent, those rising or attempting to rise to a new level of fame or accomplishment or celebrity. One of the conventions of profile writing is that we almost never do profiles on those who are fully arrived at their station. But we do profiles when already prominent people are in the process of ratcheting up to a new level of fame. It would be odd, for example, to do a full-blown profile piece on a sitting president in the middle of his second term. But quadrennially, when the presidential sweepstakes open once again, we do profile interviews with those hopefuls who, though already household words, are attempting the upward vault to the White House. In the same way, we do new profiles on former star athletes when they are named to the Hall of Fame or on prominent scientists or authors when they win the Nobel.

The entrée, in short, is whatever has drawn us to the story. But lying behind it is the backstory, and this is almost always the more interesting and important dimension of the tale—the dimension that we must find and understand to define our subject. What equation of interests and ability and experience and choice and chance combined to produce the person we are heading off to interview? Here our questions delve into life history, motivation, conflict and its resolution, and the evolution of character over a career or a lifetime. This is the heavy lifting of the profile interview. It's the part of the life that seldom is readily visible to us. In our interviewing, we must find it. This is where we come to understand our subject. And this, unfortunately, is the dimension most often neglected in shallow, amateurish profiles. It is what psychologists call "the work."

It's worth noting that all of us lead lives with multiple niches. Most profiles are niche profiles, focusing on one dimension of the life. The other niches are not ignored, but they become secondary. I once did a profile on a world-renowned surgeon who practiced in the unlikely venue of a medium-sized Oregon city, his accomplishments well known in New York and London and Moscow but largely unknown to those who lived in his community. The focus of my story in his city's newspaper was his lifetime of surgical trailblazing. But the doctor was also a world-class map collector. For another publication with a different focus and a different audience, I could have done the map story. His medical accomplishments would not have disappeared, but they would have taken a secondary position in the map story. If we do our interviewing well, we should likewise expect to find multiple niches in the lives of those we profile. Handled well, they provide interesting cross-lighting that adds depth of character to our subject. Over-emphasized, they become a distraction.

INTERVIEWING WITH STORY CONSCIOUSNESS

Reduced to their basics, the interviews we do on a profile project are essentially a shopping trip for the elements we will need to write or script our story. The corollary is that we can't do these interviews well without a sense of what it takes to build the story. Look closely at a successful profile piece and deconstruct it. What interviewing avenues did it explore? Consider this list:

- Basic biography, perhaps capsulizing those life dimensions that are not central to the story.
- Life chronology.
- Extensive, detailed exploration of the niches, biography and life aspects that are the focus of the story.
- Physical description of the central subject and perhaps of the setting.
- Characterization of the central subject.
- Solid and colorful quotes from the central subject.
- Formative influences. What shaped the person we see before us?

· Anecdotes that reveal character or personality or life challenges.

· Secondary interviews—acquaintances, fans, friends, knowledgeable observers, critics.

Interviewing with story consciousness means carrying that mental checklist with us, plus an awareness of any other elements that may be unique to the story at hand. To interview without story consciousness is to risk arriving at the writing or broadcast editing moment short of the ingredients needed to succeed.

The Narrow Window

Gary Smith, the only four-time winner of the National Magazine Award, is by my lights the best profile writer/interviewer in the country. His work, which for years appeared regularly in Sports Illustrated, is only tangentially related to the sticks and balls and scoreboards of sport. Instead, it is masterful stuff about the human condition. For one profile piece, Smith may work four months and do upwards of 50 interviews.

And the rest of us? In an era where we wrestle with the devilishly counterpoised pressures of a 24/7 news cycle and shrinking newsroom budgets, the interview window for viewing the life of the profile subject is small indeed. With our central subject, we will spend an hour or two, perhaps a full day, rarely as much as a week. The respondent's past is not truly within the frame of that tiny window. Much of what we will write about—the pivotal moments of a life—is action we can never witness. We were not at Omaha Beach with the World War II vet. We were nowhere close for the early death of the mother of that long-ago 12-year-old boy, now a man. Nor were we in the audience when today's Grammy winner stumbled off the stage after her disastrous solo in a high school musical. Instead, our interviewing must take us to those moments as narrated to us by our subject or by others who were present.

We must interview then, for moments not seen. In doing it, we need anecdotal depth and detail. Here is a truth: If you interview for a thousand years, no one will ever say to you, "I'm going to give you an anecdote now. Are you ready?" More often, anecdotes with great potential go glimmering past us in the flow of the interview, shadowy or captured only in the half-telling, barely recognized for what they might contribute to the story.

No, anecdotes are seldom delivered whole and entire. Only when we are on deadline, editing our tape or polishing our words, do we wish that we had asked more questions, sought more detail. Then it's too late. It's in the interview itself that we must recognize anecdotes for what they are or, more correctly, what they could be. It can be as simple as interrupting and saying, "Whoa, that sounds really interesting. I'd like to see that moment. How did that day begin?" In short, it's up to the interviewers to corral those half-told anecdotes before the conversation gallops away from them.

How well can it be done? What sort of anecdotal detail is possible? One of my favorite interview class reading assignments is a riveting 3,000-word account of an incident that spanned 16 seconds, with the interviews done a month after the event. Another, the second-by-second tale of a forest fire crew entrapped in a horrific "burnover," is 6,000 words covering 30 minutes; the interview work was done a full five years after the fire. In developing such moments-not-seen, remember to interview for physical detail. How did the setting look? What was the forest like? How many people were on the trail? What was the weather that day?

With people who have led variegated, well-traveled lives, anecdotal possibilities are abundant. So it's important to remember that choice is a writing and editing technique. To be sure, collect those anecdotes in your interview. But when assembling your final piece, judge them with a critical eye. Be able to recognize that some anecdotes are just good bar stories—interesting to listen to but adding little or nothing to our understanding of the character. The anecdotes that make our final cut should be those that illuminate a trait, a strength, a weakness or a defining experience of our central subject.

Just as with anecdotes, push for detail in all parts of the profile interview. In the telling of a life we may have years to cover. That means we must interview broadly—Ken Metzler's "tons of ore"—so we can write or edit tightly. A truly detailed understanding of a particular episode or stage in a life enables the writer or broadcaster, if necessary, to essay a succinct, specific, even colorful passage that summarizes that bit of life's passage. It's when we return from our interview with half-baked understandings that our stories turn to mush, as we attempt to make a crystalline presentation of material that we understand less than clearly.

Consider the Prime Responsibility in every interview. Put simply, it's this: Don't stop until you're certain that you've obtained from the respondent everything that person can contribute to the story you want to construct. The delight is in the details.

GOING FOR THE BACKSTORY

As we look through that narrow window afforded by our profile interview, we may gain insights into personality, core beliefs and current activities. But we must recognize that our respondent is not fixed in the moment, or in the personality, in which we find her. Our Grammy winner, for example, presents today as a confident, polished, outgoing performer a dozen years into a successful recording career. As a teenager she quaked in fear at the thought of singing before an audience. How do we interview our way to knowing that teenager? Perhaps the best way is point-in-time perspective. Don't just ask the interviewee what she thinks and feels now. Work to find out what she thought and felt *then*. Point-in-time questions will get you there. "If I had known you as a junior in high school, what would you have said you were going to do or be?" "If I had know you when you left Smallville for New York, what were you hoping for?" "If I had known you at 23, when that club owner said you should go for a recording contract, did it seem at all possible?"

The distant past is a route to comprehending the subtleties of the present. If we understand the events and circumstances that shaped our interviewee's early life, we deepen our understanding of the person now before us. We get there with some easy and obvious questions: "Where did you grow up?" "What did your parents do for a living?" "Did you have siblings?" "What kind of teenager were you?" And on and on, segueing to more complex questions about the influences and experiences that shaped a life.

For the typical-age undergraduates who largely compose the audience for this book, such explorations bring us to the Department of Life Is Not Fair. In profile interviewing you will step into the lives of people 20 years, 50 years, even 70 years older than yourself. To interview them well you must have at least a rudimentary understanding of decades and eras that you have never experienced. In that sense, your learning curve is far steeper than that of a veteran 30-year journalist. From your vantage point of the early 21st century, an understanding of at least the last seven or eight decades of the 20th is crucial if you want to write effective profiles. What do you know about the Great Depression, World War II, the Baby Boom generation, the civil rights era, second-wave feminism, the counter-culture movement, the birth of the computer age?

For the would-be profile interviewer, one of the several "timetables of history" reference books would be a good investment. If you can establish in advance the approximate age of your upcoming interviewee, you can then do preliminary "age-casting"—serious thinking about the macro-history and micro-history that might have shaped the life you are about to explore. Was he the right age to be subject to the draft in the Vietnam War era? Was she in that first wave of girls to have true high school athletic opportunities in the 1970s? Is he a second-career computer programmer who can remember doing data input with a typewriter? It's likewise valuable to gain an understanding of the interaction of generational personalities. Consider, for example, the great historical irony of the silent, strong "Greatest Generation" that won World War II and found itself destined to become parent to the generation that could not decide whether it was willing to fight in Vietnam.

In this sort of retrospective interviewing we want to look especially for the younger person's character traits or tendencies or influences, now reflected, and possibly a bit refracted, in the mature adult. Perhaps a teacher or coach played a key mentoring role. Perhaps a rambunctious boy grew to be an adventurous man. Perhaps the survivor of horrendous parenting came away determined to be a stellar parent. The old phrase is, "As the twig is bent, so grows the tree." In our profile interviewing, we must probe to see how the twigs were bent.

Serendipitous connections emerge from such interviewing. I once profiled a criminal defense attorney who took on the most controversial murder cases in his state and never failed to win an acquittal. Decades earlier, he had been a college football quarterback, remembered by his teammates for coming into the huddle, calling a play they hadn't used for two years and being able to tell every man his route or assignment on that play. Describing his success as a trial lawyer, he confessed to doing poorly at such lawyerly stuff as recalling important precedents or sections of the statutes. "But," he said, "when I get one of these murder cases, I make it a point to learn where everybody was on the night of the murder. I know what they were doing, where they were coming from and where they were going. I never forget those things, and they work for me in the trial." In the profile piece, that translated to a telling sentence that moved a youthful trait from the gridiron to the courtroom and defined the mature man.

DRAMA IN REAL LIVES

Erving Polster is a distinguished psychotherapist who started his college career decades ago as a journalism major. His writing predilections resurfaced in the mid-1980s, when he authored a book titled *Every Person's Life Is Worth a Novel*. It is built on his years of autobiographical therapy—getting his patients to write their own stories as a way of seeing significance, drama and essential value in their own lives. It's aimed, of course, at coaching people to write in the first person. "People don't grant the same importance to experiences in their own lives as they do to characters in romantic novels or television soap operas," Polster wrote. "Instead, they set high standards for interesting experience, sifting life's waters with a large-holed fishing net, letting a lot go through untouched."

For journalists, it's a simple matter to refocus Polster's message to writing in the third person, helping interviewers see drama and significance in the lives of others, even so-called ordinary people. As profile interviewers, we must tighten the holes in our own fishing nets and learn to probe for the details that reveal the significance of other lives. If we do, we will find that real lives have conflict and irony and dramatic tension. We must learn to recognize and understand those dimensions.

Real-life turning points are common, if only we will see them. A young man passes on college and joins the Marines. A couple decides to marry. A young mother is widowed. A job taken in desperation becomes a fulfilling career. A family business fails. An opportunity presents itself. A parent dies. An urban man bails out of the rat race and moves his family to the country. It takes only a little of this sort of interviewing work to learn that life's turning points often come as odd intersections of choice and chance. Sometimes we learn that the people we interview were propelled to success not by their own designs but by chance. In spite of choices they made, the path they resisted could not be avoided, and it worked well for them.

Sometimes, too, we do profile interviews on tragedies in the making, lives that have not gone well. In those lives we may come to recognize a different sort of turning point—loss of the last chance to change. In the interview we find a pattern of poor choices, sometimes with obvious foreshadowing of dire consequences. And then we arrive at the inevitable moment when a course change is no longer possible.

CHRONOLOGY

Interviewing our way to understanding the life of another is a task freighted with complexity. To understand the life we must first understand its sequence. Consider an adult who has been through one war, two marriages, four children, a half-dozen jobs, three marathon races, a midlife career change, a bankruptcy, a bout with cancer, and a successful run for the state legislature. To understand that life we must understand its sequence.

Fortunately, perhaps two-thirds of the profile subjects you interview will be more or less linear narrators. With a little help from you—"Let's see . . . you did those two years in the Army, so when you started college it was 1979?"—they will lead you past the mileposts of their life. But the other third will be verbal scatterguns. They'll give you interesting bits and pieces of their lives in no particular order. It all sounds good until the moment you're on deadline, trying to assemble the pieces into a coherent story. Then you realize you have no sense of the sequence in which the events of the life unfolded. And hence, you have no sense of cause and effect in the life. What actions produced which consequences and changes in the life? Did the bankruptcy lead to the career change, or was it an unwise career change that led to the bankruptcy? And was the divorce the result of the bankruptcy, or vice versa?

With the scattergun respondents, you must work harder to develop the life chronology in the interview. Chronology and sequence are key to understanding the life. That doesn't mean that your finished story must come off as a glorified logbook, peppered with years and dates. But it does mean that establishing an understanding of the life chronology is yet another example of ore-processing—interviewing broadly so that you can summarize succinctly. Sometimes, for longer pieces and certainly for books, you may find it helpful in the writing process to create and have at hand a brief listing of your subject's chronological milestones. Often, putting the chronology on paper causes relationships between life events to leap out at you, and you grasp foreshadowings or ironies or unintended consequences that will enhance the account you are writing. Even for short profiles or sketches, a grasp of chronology can facilitate a clearer telling of the life.

TYPECASTING AND DEMOGRAPHY

Creative storytellers, we are told, should avoid stereotypes and strive for originality. But let me offer a word in defense of stereotypes as the profile interviewer's friend. Consider a few: career woman, Philadelphia lawyer, absent-minded professor, business executive, sorority girl, lounge lizard, hayseed, redneck logger, small-town cop, movie star. Here's a simple truth about stereotypes. We all know what they mean. They comprise a cultural shorthand. *But stereotypes never fit perfectly, and it is the ways in which they don't fit that we write about—and interview about.*

Rust Hills, for many years the brilliant fiction editor of Esquire magazine, authored a wonderful little book called *Writing in General and the Short Story in Particular.* Yes, his venue was fiction. But what he wrote about was the quintessential business of telling lives. In short sections he details dozens and dozens of plot and storytelling devices, almost all of which are applicable to nonfiction accounts of real lives. And one of his prime lessons is that writers must differentiate their characters from type. In short, in our interviewing and in our storytelling our task is not to show how much the subject fits the type, but rather, how much he or she doesn't match it.

At the beginning of this chapter we introduced the concept of the profile entrée—the present or past or pending activity that draws us to the profile subject. So our subject might be a World War II veteran, a widget collector, an emerging local politician or a country pastor. In a sense, all of these are stereotypes. Lucky for us, because our potential readers will share those stereotypes. That will give us a common reference and a handy point of departure for our interviewing and our story in which we will focus on what's unique about this veteran, this collector, this politician, this pastor. This is where our story develops.

Just as a sense of modern history is important to the profile interviewer, so, too, is a sense of modern demographics. Understanding basic demographic trends, for example, will help us spot those interview subjects who are truly running against type. The small-city surgeon with the international reputation is a prime example, because such top medical talent almost always migrates to major urban centers.

Here's another: Demography tells us that high levels of parental income and educational achievement are strong statistical predictors of educational success for family offspring. To use just one example, the average SAT score for high school students from families earning over $100,000 a year is 100 points higher than the average for thousands of students whose families earn only $50,000 to $60,000. And only 3 percent of the students in the top 150 universities come from the bottom 25 percent of the earnings scale. Do dollars grow extra brain cells? Of course not. But the combination of parental wealth and education begets household advantages, high schools with better course offerings, SAT prep tutors and other benefits. At some level, we know these things intuitively. But when we take strong demographic awareness into our profile interviews we become attuned to people who are running against type. If we encounter the Ph.D. candidate whose parents have eighth-grade educations and work at menial jobs we will know that we're standing at the threshold of great story.

SECONDARY SOURCES

Every profile writer needs secondary sources to bring the central subject into sharper focus. Wisely chosen, they become a sort of Greek chorus, underscoring the story theme or providing unanticipated counterpoint. Even so-called ordinary people stories—the widget collector, for example—can benefit from at least one secondary source. Typically, some aspect of uniqueness or talent in the subject drives such stories. These uncontroversial tales almost always will benefit from a "validator," a secondary source who can attest to the originality or skill of the story subject. The validator adds credibility to both the story and the writer, taking the onus of braggart off the story subject.

More complex feature stories can benefit from a greater array of secondary sources. Consider the voices that might be found for a lengthy piece on a successful business figure:

- The person who witnessed an early turning point or key moment— *"I knew John when his father's business failed, and I could tell it had a really profound effect on John's own work ethic."*
- The friend or co-worker with insights outside the niche topic— *"Yes, John's a great business head and a civic leader, but not many people know that he's run five marathons and climbed Mount Kilimanjaro."*
- The colleague familiar with John's work—*"He was the person who made the difference in this project. Nobody else had as clear a vision of what we needed and how we were going to do it."*
- The distant expert who doesn't actually know John—*"I've seen at least 20 people in this country try the same thing, and I know of only one who's succeeded."*

- The knowledgeable critic—*"Everybody's falling all over themselves to praise John's golf course project, but nobody wants to talk about how he evicted all the elderly residents of a mobile home park so that he could build it."*

Despite their importance, secondary sources must be considered with the same caution as secondary niches in our subject's interests or skills. Handled well, those sources become a true Greek chorus, bringing a compelling play of light and shadow to the portrait we are building. But they can become a distracting sort of crutch—easy to find, easy to use and all too easy in the way they let us pad our stories and sidestep the heavy lifting of doing deep interviewing with the person who is the true focus of the profile.

Above all, the success of our profile pieces will hinge upon that empathetic ability to connect with the life of the subject, no matter how different the experiences and core beliefs of that life are from our own.

TEN Interviewing Scientists

*Success depends not only on understanding
the basic concepts and terms but also in
uncovering the scientist's driving passions*

JON PALFREMAN

When interviewing technical experts, journalists need to
come well prepared. Longtime PBS *Frontline* and *NOVA*
producer Jon Palfreman argues such preparation serves several
functions: gaining the confidence of media-shy scientists,
arming the interviewer with the knowledge to ask follow-up
questions in a colloquial manner and even discerning the
expert's excitement about the process of discovery.

Scientists are important sources for journalists. And not just because they
possess expert knowledge. Scientists matter because they are also people
driven by passions, and they have remarkable stories to tell. It's a mistake
to think of researchers as dull and unfeeling. Even Mr. Spock, *Star Trek's*
legendary Vulcan science officer, expressed emotions (usually accompanied by a raised eyebrow) when he talked about the laws of science. While
he coldly dismissed his shipmates' behavior as "illogical," he found many
of the phenomena the crew encountered as the Enterprise explored the
universe—from wormholes to temporal anomalies—totally "fascinating."

A major goal, therefore, in interviewing scientists is to understand
their quests and passions. It might be a purely curiosity-driven (Spock-
like) quest to understand the universe—pursued, for example, by theoretical physicists such as Richard Feynman[1] and Stephen Hawking.[2] It

might be the story of an unexpected empirical discovery of Nature, like Arno Penzias and Robert Wilson's fortuitous realization that they were listening to the hiss of microwave background radiation left over from the Big Bang.[3] It might be a crucial piece of evidence that humankind is irreversibly warming the planet; for example, Scripps scientist Charles Keeling's careful measurements over four decades that proved beyond doubt that anthropogenic (i.e., human-generated) carbon dioxide was accumulating in the atmosphere.[4] It might be the quest of a biomedical researcher to find a cure for a disease like cancer, Alzheimer's, or Parkinson's and, thereby, save a patient's life.

In each case, the task of the interviewer is to elicit the arc of the scientific quest, to mine the interviewee's driving emotions (from fascination to empathy) and to cut through the technical jargon.

Journalists who are successful at interviewing scientists generally possess three key attributes. One, they are actually interested in science. Two, they have the intellectual self-confidence to tackle hard subjects from nuclear physics to molecular biology. Three, they are ready to do the necessary preparation to fashion a list of smart questions that help rather than hinder a scientist's communication. Preparation is essential. Before interviewing a scientist, a journalist needs to know in broad terms the path of the researcher's life—where she lived, where she studied, the areas she has worked on, the conflicts and controversies she's endured. The journalist also needs to understand in broad terms the underlying scientific vocabulary of the researcher's field. A good reporter would not think of turning up to interview a musician without a knowledge of his musical creations; likewise, it makes little sense trying to interview a molecular biologist without some basic notions of what cells, proteins and genes are.

Let me illustrate the craft of scientific interviewing with two examples, one from the physical sciences, the other from medicine.

Some years ago, I did a big story about climate change and got the opportunity to interview some of the key scientific luminaries about their life and work. Going in, I needed to understand some basic scientific concepts and terms—for example, "fossil fuel," "the greenhouse effect,"

"anthropogenic," the difference between "weather" and "climate," etc.—
and to have a broad sketch of the biographies of the interviewees.

One of the scientists I interviewed was Charles David Keeling, a giant
of climate science. In 1956, as a young man, he moved to a research station located at 11,000 feet on a mountain called Mauna Loa in Hawaii,
and started monitoring the Earth's air. Over the next four decades, he
recorded the data for what became known as the Keeling Curve, the
foundational empirical evidence that established the reality of human-
induced global warming. My questions tracked his life's work. What was
his story? How did he come to go to Hawaii? His decision, it turned out,
resulted from a global scientific project called the International Geophysical Year, which provided the resources for him to take some state-of-the-
art gas analyzers and start monitoring the Earth's atmosphere.

CHARLES KEELING: This program afforded me an opportunity, even
   though I was just out of school and a very young man, to commandeer
   enough resources to see that these analyzers were put in several
   places, rather quickly at that. One analyzer was put in Little America,
   Antarctica. And shortly after, another one was placed on a mountain
   in Hawaii called Mauna Loa.

JON PALFREMAN: When you started making those measurements of
   CO_2 in the late '50s, did you notice anything right away?

CHARLES KEELING: At Mauna Loa Observatory we started the
   measurements in March 1957 and I expected the concentration of
   CO_2 would be perhaps almost dead constant. But that wasn't what
   happened. The concentration rose for several months and then it
   dropped. And it dropped all during the period from May until
   September, and then it started to rise again. As soon as we saw that
   much information, less than a year's worth of data, it was pretty
   obvious that we were looking at the breathing of the plants in the
   Northern Hemisphere, because they absorb carbon dioxide during
   their growing period in temperate and high latitudes, and then it's
   released again in a cyclic process in the wintertime.

JON PALFREMAN: But as the years went by, you noticed something else
   too, didn't you?

CHARLES KEELING: What we see, of course, is the seasonal cycle,
   which looks like a sort of a seesaw, up and down . . . But it's clear that

every single year the cycle is at a higher concentration level than it was the year before. Every year, the amount of carbon dioxide in the atmosphere has inched up a little bit. And the cumulative effect of this is that the concentration that was about 310 parts per million when I started [in 1956] has risen up to past 360 parts per million [in 1999].

Here's what that curve—a seesaw superimposed on an exponentially increasing trend—looks like. Current peak levels are around 400 parts per million.

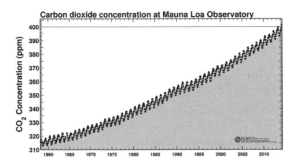

The upward curve of CO_2 concentration at Mauna Loa Observatory. Source: Scripps Institution of Oceanography.

JON PALFREMAN: How is this related to human activity?

CHARLES KEELING: It's hard for people to understand how much carbon dioxide is being put in the atmosphere, in absolute terms. But in relative terms, we can say as follows: that at the end of World War II, about a billion metric tons of carbon, in the form of CO_2, was being emitted to the atmosphere. When I started my measurements, it had risen to 2½ billion. At the present time, it's almost 7 billion.

Now for something completely different—a medical story. In November 1987, neuroscientists in Lund, Sweden, grafted fetal dopamine neurons (dissected from aborted fetuses) into the brain of a 47-year-old Parkinson's disease patient, launching a hopeful new era of neural grafting aimed at reversing the symptoms of that neurodegenerative disorder. Over the next two decades, some 300 cases were done worldwide. But after some promising initial results, two negative (and highly publicized) controlled trials (in 2001[5] and 2003[6]) brought the field to a virtual standstill. Now, proponents are pushing back, arguing that such studies were flawed. In researching this story, I interviewed Roger Barker of the John van Geest Centre for Brain Repair in Cambridge, England.

To undertake this interview, it was necessary to have a broad understanding of the principles of how clinical trials are organized for surgical procedures. While the FDA mandates controlled trials for new drugs and medical devices, the agency has no jurisdiction over new surgeries. Controlled trials are, therefore, very rare in surgery. And they're hard to do. The basic design is that investigators randomly assign patients to a treatment group and a "sham surgery" group. The treatment group gets the real operation, in this case fetal grafts. By contrast, patients in the control group are prepped for surgery and have a small hole drilled in their skulls; but no grafts are actually put in. Critically important, the study is blinded: patients and neurologists have no idea which group is which. This blinding controls for any placebo effect, which can be very large. Previous sham surgery trials for a very common arthroscopic procedure for osteoarthritis of the knee had found that the sham surgery group got the same benefit as the group getting the expertly performed operation.[7]

JON PALFREMAN: Placebo-controlled trials are viewed as the gold standard of clinical trials, but you think they can sometimes be counterproductive, don't you?

ROGER BARKER: It's not that you shouldn't ever do double blind placebo-controlled trials, but if you do them too early in the development of a therapy people think that you will get a definite answer. And if you haven't optimized the treatment, you're going to get a result that is hard to explain.

JON PALFREMAN: And your point is that if we haven't sorted out the dose, frequency, duration, etc., we might prematurely reject a therapy that could work.

ROGER BARKER: Absolutely. If I took 100 people with a chest infection, and I gave them 100 mg of ampicillin once a day for 3 days and then looked at the patients two days later, what would I find? Probably, the majority of them will still have a chest infection. So the conclusion would be that ampicillin, which is an antibiotic, is not useful for the treatment of infection—no more helpful than a placebo. And of course, the problem is that I've used the wrong dose, for the wrong amount of time, in a mixed group of patients, and the outcome led to a wrong conclusion.

JON PALFREMAN: So the fact that a trial fails doesn't mean the therapy is necessarily a hopeless failure?

ROGER BARKER: That's right. The history of experimental therapeutics shows that new therapies rarely work the first time. Recall what happened with heart transplants—people died only a few days after receiving the transplant. Based on our modern criteria for clinical testing, we would say that it's not working, let's just forget about it. But look what happened. Scientists studied the reason for failure—the rejection process—and once they mastered what was going on, heart transplants slowly became routine therapy. It was an iterative process. We learnt as we went along.

JON PALFREMAN: On the other hand, we can be fooled into thinking something is real when it isn't, can't we? Open label[8] studies of neural grafting appeared to work, but placebo-controlled trials couldn't demonstrate efficacy.

ROGER BARKER: I think the placebo effect is a vastly exaggerated phenomenon. I'm not saying that it's not real . . . but that randomized controlled trials to get round the placebo effect have made it difficult to prove new therapies actually work.

In both examples, success depends on the interviewer having a grasp of the story arc of the science, combined with a mastery of the basic concepts and terms.

Now, a few tips. If a scientist uses complex jargon that goes over your head, it's perfectly fine for you to say, "I don't understand." Most scientists sincerely want to become better communicators, and interactions with journalists are one of the ways they pick up those skills. Sometimes the jargon is simply a question of vocabulary. Biomedical researchers, for example, may use arcane terms when simpler ones would do just as well (e.g., *rostral* [near head], *caudal* [near tail], *anterograde* [moving forward], *retrograde* [moving backward], *proximal* [close], and *distal* [far]). Many technical terms involve concepts that a scientist can explain with a follow-up clause—for example, *enzymes* (regulatory proteins that speed up bio-chemical reactions), *autosomal dominant mutation* (one that produces a pattern of inheritance where 50 percent of the offspring, male and female, have the trait, e.g., Huntington's disease), *Large Hadron Collider* (a giant facility in Switzerland that smashes hadrons—subnuclear particles such as protons and neutrons—together to recreate the conditions of the Big Bang. Recently this machine detected a long-sought-after particle known as the Higgs boson) . . . and so on.

Finally, and most important, remember that science is not like politics. While there may be value in giving equal time to competing political viewpoints, this makes little sense in science. In science, some ideas (e.g., the flat Earth theory, the phlogiston theory of combustion, etc.) are plainly wrong. Science journalism, therefore, is committed to the balance of evidence rather than the balance of opinion. As physicist Richard Feynman famously argued in his analysis of the Challenger disaster (and NASA's attempt to cover it up), reality transcends politics. "Let us make recommendations to ensure that NASA officials deal in a world of reality in understanding technological weaknesses and imperfections well enough to be actively trying to eliminate them . . . *For [in] a successful technology reality must take precedence over public relations, for nature cannot be fooled.*"

NOTES

1. Richard Phillips Feynman, the Caltech-based Nobel Laureate, was perhaps the greatest science communicator that history has known. See *Surely You're Joking, Mr. Feynman!*, *What Do You Care What Other People Think?* and *There's Plenty of Room at the Bottom*. Feynman is highly quotable. One of my favorite Feynman aphorisms is "The first principle is that you must not fool yourself–and you are the easiest person to fool."

2. Stephen Hawking, a brilliant theoretical physicist and cosmologist stricken with advanced motor neuron disease, is unable to move without a wheelchair or speak without the aid of a speech synthesizer. His popular books such as *A Brief History of Time* have been astonishingly successful (that work stayed on the *Sunday Times* bestseller list for 237 weeks).

3. Penzias and Wilson shared the 1978 Nobel Prize for Physics for their serendipitous discovery of the microwave background residue of the Big Bang using Bell Labs' horn-shaped antenna in Holmdel, New Jersey. See Simon Singh, *Big Bang: The Origin of the Universe*.

4. In 1956, Charles David Keeling began monitoring the Earth's atmosphere from the Mauna Loa Observatory in Hawaii. He spent his whole professional life generating the Keeling Curve.

5. http://www.nejm.org/medical-research/parkinson-disease?subtopic=parkinson-disease&sort=cited&.

6. http://www.ncbi.nlm.nih.gov/pubmed/12953276.

7. J.B. Moseley et al., "A Controlled Trial of Arthroscopic Surgery for Osteo-arthritis of the Knee," NEJM 347(2) 81; (2002): A. Kirkley et al., "A Randomized Trial of Arthroscopic Surgery for Osteoarthritis of the Knee," NEJM 359 (11): (Sept. 11, 2008): 1097–107. Based on this data, the federal Medicare program stopped covering this procedure and it has more or less disappeared.

8. An open label study is an unblended uncontrolled study, one where patients and doctors have full knowledge that a treatment has been given and may "expect" to feel better.

ELEVEN

Interviewing Athletes

Going the distance with a source can result in a
winning story

CHARLES BUTLER

Securing good quotes from athletes requires patience and
persistence, teaches Charles Butler, who works hard to get
past the predictable "tough opponent" and "one game at
a time" answers. His lessons for reporting a thorough and
compelling sports story could be headlined with one more
sports cliché: "He knows what it takes."

For weeks—actually for months—I had been meeting with and interviewing Matt Long as he prepared to run a marathon. Now, in the scheme of
things what Long wanted to do, run 26.2 miles around the five boroughs
of New York City, seemed a bit pedestrian. Sure, if this had been the late
1960s or early '70s, when just a few soleful souls thought it was quixotic to
run 26.2 miles across the blacktop of Gotham, his goal might have seemed
exotic. But in the fall of 2008, thousands of men and women, moms and
dads, old people, middle-aged people and young people were running
this distance every weekend in races around the globe.

So what made it so essential for me to hang with Matt Long for so long,
interviewing him, among other things, about his daily mileage, his fuel
intake, his stride rate?

Matt Long had a special story: He was trying to run a marathon three years after getting crushed by a 20-ton bus.

I had first heard of Long when he *didn't* run the New York City Marathon two years earlier, in 2006. That year I was reporting on the race for Runner's World, the leading magazine covering the sport. Part of my coverage involved a race within the race: Each year a group of Big Apple firefighters face off against runners from the New York City police department. As I was reporting on that angle, one of the firefighters told me about Matty Long. In the previous year's race Long was a key member of the FDNY squad, clocking the team's fourth-fastest time and helping the firefighters beat the cops. But a few weeks after the marathon, Long was struck by a bus while biking to work—although struck just hints at the damage done. The bike impaled him, ripping a hole through his midsection. He lay under the bus, gushing blood, until being extricated and transported to a New York City hospital. There, a surgeon estimated that with his injuries and blood loss he had a 5 percent chance of surviving.

Long obviously lived, but according to his teammate he no longer was the athlete he once was.

When I heard this story, I knew I had to follow up. I worked for RW; we talked to athletes, both the illustrious and the less so, looking to tell their stories. When I first contacted Long a few days later, our conversation was brief, which was not that surprising. His firefighter friend had told me he "was dealing with things," both physically and mentally. We talked for a couple of minutes. I told him of my intent: interview him about his accident, his running, his life. Maybe there was a story. He listened, then politely yet firmly said, "Thanks but no thanks." End of phone call.

I didn't give up. About five months later, I decided to call Long again. This time he sounded more energized, and accommodating. We agreed to meet for coffee. When he arrived at a midtown Manhattan Starbucks, he looked nothing like a marathon runner, let alone a firefighter who had survived harrowing calls in the line of duty. He was gaunt, he relied on crutches to steady his gait, he wore a dark overcoat even though it was a warm spring New York City day. (Only later would I learn that the coat was hiding a colostomy bag.) We sat and talked for an hour or so. I got a bit about his backstory, about his life, about his running, about his near death. Finally I asked if he had plans to run again. I needed him to say yes in order for me to have a story. Runner's World likes stories about runners, not former runners. He waited a few beats before answering. Finally, he said he hoped to run one day. In fact, he wanted to run the six-mile loop in Central Park with his firefighting buddies and then go out for pizzas and beers. He would consider himself whole again if he could do that run. I asked when that might happen. He said, "I don't know."

I share this anecdote because if I had stopped there, if I had crossed Matt Long off my list of potential interview subjects, I never would have written what Runner's World would later headline "The Most Incredible Comeback Story You'll Ever Read." Nearly two years after our conversation, Long was back to running, and going a lot farther than six miles. He was training to run the New York City Marathon. I spent the better part of a year hanging with him and interviewing him as he went from barely finishing a mile to feeling confident he could do 26.2 of them. I interviewed him as he worked with his rehab doctors. I interviewed him with friends and co-workers. On the day of the marathon, I even accompanied him on the trip around New York. It took him 7 hours and 22 minutes, nearly twice as long as his previous marathon, and he did it with me running side by side, asking him questions as we moved slowly along. That marathon interview was the culmination of the incredible access I had, access that allowed me to get to know my source extremely well. I learned of the toll his accident had taken on Long as well as family members (especially his mom). I learned of Long's worries of never having a family of his own. I learned of the days when Long thought about ending his life. And I learned of how running and finishing a marathon—something so many people do—was so vital to his future well-being.

Through these intimate and extensive interviews I learned what I needed to tell a story.

Not every sports journalist can get such access. Today's sports writers and journalists are pulled by many demands and handcuffed by constraints that prevent them from connecting with their sources sufficiently enough to tell a satisfyingly complete story. If they're print or text reporters with a beat—say, the Yankees or the Patriots or Alabama football or UConn basketball—they are filing stories before, during and after a game. When not filing, they're tweeting about what they are seeing and hearing. For their parts, TV and radio reporters are busily crafting questions to elicit the pitch-perfect, quick-hit sound-bite that will fill a hole during a newscast. As soon as they get that bite they're off to find another one. It's content, and it's what the bosses want.

But is it deep and substantive and anything more than the obvious? Not often. You see, these days nuance too often takes a backseat to now.

That said, the best sports journalists are the ones who just don't want to repeat the score or the latest stat. And they sure as heck don't want to simply report the scripted clichés—"we worked as a team," "we gave 100 percent"—that any Nuke LaLoosh can deliver. They know that by being in sports they have the opportunity to bring drama and insight to their storytelling and to the sporting public. The *why* and the *how* and the *what if* a play had been called, a player had been benched, a shot had been made. How Serena Williams went from the streets of Compton to the highest echelons of her sport. Why Malcolm Butler knew where he needed to be to make a Super Bowl–winning interception. What made Matt Long run a marathon when his body was no longer built to do that. Those are the angles these reporters want because they make the assumption (a correct one) that those are the angles sports fans want. And sports fans are their readers, their listeners and their viewers. As such, these journalists need to get the athletes to share their thoughts. They need the time and access and openness from athletes that will allow them to transform these "heroes" into people the public can relate to.

The challenge? Getting the type of access I had with Matt Long so the interviews bear fruit—as well as quality quotes and insights. Athletes have their agents, their team PR managers, their sponsors who all can handcuff a reporter's desire to go deep with a subject. "Teams make it a priority to limit access and shield them from overuse, since their time is often in high demand," Jason Lloyd told Sports Illustrated a few years ago when he was a reporter for the *Akron Beacon Journal* covering the Cleveland Cavaliers during the LeBron James years. (He is now with The Athletic.) "In recent years, public relations staffs have worked hard to keep time with the most talented players down to a minimum. Quality work is often determined by access, and that's becoming a greater challenge each season."

One of today's most incisive sports journalists is Mina Kimes. She actually started her career as a business reporter but has transitioned to where her work appears in and on various ESPN platforms, including ESPN The Magazine. Her profile subjects have included such athletes as New Orleans Saints quarterback Drew Brees and Olympic gymnast Aly Raisman. One of her most discussed pieces was a 2017 profile of Aaron Rodgers, the Green Bay Packers quarterback. In the piece Kimes reveals more than Rodgers' take on football strategy. She gets him to discuss religion and politics and racial issues. But such revelations did not come without stipulations. Before her interview with Rodgers got rolling, the QB actually pulled out his own recording device. "It was not an experience I had had before," Kimes later would say. "He is really cautious, very private. He is also anxious about being misinterpreted, which comes with some of the territory of being famous. He doesn't want to be misheard."

Pros aren't the only ones seeking protection. Just consider the cocoon insulating student-athletes at major universities from the media. For instance, some weeks sports reporters for the student-run *Daily Emerald* at the University of Oregon are lucky to get five minutes with the starting quarterback or the leading scorer on the basketball team. That's hardly enough time to probe for material that might be useful in a preview story or to tease out anecdotes helpful in a feature story or to do any reporting of an investigative nature.

And such limitations can put student-journalists at loggerheads with the teams they cover.

In 2016, reporters for the *Emerald* were pursuing a story about a football player who apparently had had a number of off-field transgressions. In order to confirm some of their reporting, one of the student-journalists contacted a member of the football team—not a wise move, at least in the eyes of some university officials. According to the university sports information office, making contact with an athlete without first getting clearance from that office was verboten. When the sports information department chief learned about the infraction, he called the reporters into his office and threatened to take away credentials for an upcoming football game.

"[The sports information officer] made it pretty clear that he didn't like what we were doing and that we went against their protocol," recalled Jarrid Denney, the *Emerald*'s sports editor at the time. Denney doesn't contest the fact that he and his fellow staffers had violated a rule. In this case, though, they felt the rule needed to be broken. "Their protocol was not allowing us to do our jobs," Denney says. "We made the decision to burn that bridge and do what we needed to do to get what we felt was a meaningful story that we needed to tell."

They got the story, and more. The incident led the university's general counsel to review how the sports information office handled this situation and to consider whether any First Amendment violations had been committed. The counsel eventually found that the sports information officer had been heavy-handed in threatening to revoke a credential but that no press freedoms had been compromised. "From our interviews," the general counsel later wrote in a report to the university president, "we conclude that most student athletes appreciate the media access rules and perceive them as being enforced with the media in order to protect student-athletes. We find no evidence to support the allegation that the Athletic Department restricts student athletes' ability to address the media."

Perhaps, but by restricting the media's access to these athletes, university officials are potentially doing more of a disservice than service. They are preventing the athletes from growing personally and professionally; they're preventing them from learning how the media works in "the real world." Many sports information departments will say that they put rules in place regarding access in order to safeguard a student-athlete's free time. If a member of the media could call an athlete at any moment, the argument goes, such calls would cut into an athlete's study hours or free time away from the sport. The reality is the athlete's commitments to his or her team—from summer training sessions to traveling to games—steal more time from the athlete's schedule than a few interviews with the media.

Reluctantly, the student journalists have learned to live with the restriction. "I think the way colleges do it make things harder than they have to be," says Denney, who has gone on to report for MLB.com since graduating from Oregon. "I understand that you are dealing with 18- and 19-year-old kids and they might have to run to class and they are not a pro. . . .

I understand that there has to be guidelines in place or you would have some bulldog reporter calling athletes every day. But I think it turns into a big contest of them trying to lord their coverage and restrict anything that may be written about the teams and keeping their 18-year-old athletes from talking to a reporter when they are not supervised. It doesn't seem anyone is winning. Reporters don't get to write stories they want to write, and the athletic department is getting upset with these cases. It isn't working."

Considering such roadblocks, you might think covering sports would be on the bottom rung of beats for an aspiring journalist. But among my more ardent students (such as Denney) sports reporting remains a primary lure. I'll often poll my students before each term to see which journalist they most want to emulate. Rarely will they say a Bob Woodward or a Joan Didion. The most frequent names mentioned are those of sports journalists, with ESPN's Scott Van Pelt and Fox Sports' Erin Andrews often leading the way. The two are successful in their respective lines of sports journalism, and each is immensely popular (just check out the number of followers on their Twitter accounts). On screen they appear knowledgeable, confident and relaxed. But what the students usually are not aware of is the work these two journalists did on the way to their current positions. They don't see how Van Pelt and Andrews cultivated and built relationships with sources, thus allowing them to feel comfortable in their roles as interviewers.

Take Van Pelt, for instance. He is perhaps ESPN's biggest name, following the path of Keith Olbermann and Dan Patrick as a marquee draw on SportsCenter. On his late-night show Van Pelt will interview a compelling athlete from one of that evening's contests. The interviews are, at most, four minutes long, and usually include some light-hearted banter, a trademark of the Van Pelt repertoire. But he also works in tougher questions, intended to draw out the athlete and give viewers something they're not likely going to get from the typical postgame locker room scrum between an athlete and deadline-driven reporters. Whether it's by virtue of his talent or his place on the ESPN billboard, Van Pelt seems to get more from athletes than rival interviewers do.

Van Pelt would also say he's practiced in the art of interviewing thanks to honing his skills when the lights were not so bright. Twenty years ago, before he had made his name at the Worldwide Leader, Van Pelt was working at the Golf Channel, a network with a considerably smaller audience than ESPN's. He was there learning the sport and getting to know golf's stars. But he also made a point of looking out for the rising stars, developing relationships with them before the rest of the media pack did. The investment paid off when one of those up-and-comers—a golfer by the name of Tiger Woods—sprinted up the ranks. "I had met [Woods] very early on when he was a freshman at Stanford," Van Pelt told the *Times-Picayune* newspaper in 2013. "I was young enough that we were able to establish some common ground and rapport. He figured out early on that I was not out to get him. People always tell me, 'You're good friends with Tiger.' I tell them 'No, I'm not, we're professionally friendly.' He knows he can trust me."

Eventually, when Woods started winning professional tournaments, Van Pelt's past connections came in handy. For instance, after Woods won his first Masters in 1997, Van Pelt nabbed Woods for what turned out to be a surprisingly long interview. Initially, the sit-down was slated to go five minutes or so. Instead, Van Pelt got 45 minutes. "He was into it, and we just kept going," Van Pelt recalled to the *Times-Picayune.* "When I went back to the Golf Channel, I said this isn't like a piece; this is a show. They freaked out because Tiger was so open." In fact, Woods was so voluble with Van Pelt that he had little left when an ESPN crew came calling for an interview. "I'm sorry; that's just how the business goes sometimes. But that goes back to the fact that we had a relationship, and to this day [Woods] jokes with me that my career is directly attributable to him, which I suppose is true, because if he wasn't great and I didn't have this access, then ESPN wouldn't have wanted me in the first place."

As Van Pelt points out, access to athletes gives a sports reporter credibility. It's also the conduit for turning a mundane Q&A into something potentially memorable. Access comes from developing relationships, which is not easy. It takes, as the best sports reporters will tell you, a lot of "hanging around" time. Being in the locker rooms long before a game begins (and before other reporters show up). Waiting around after a press conference to get the smallest nugget of news that no one else is hearing. Talking (as Van Pelt showed) to the up-and-coming athletes who are often willing to share insights because so few reporters are talking to them.

Ronald Blum has been covering Major League Baseball and World Cup soccer for the Associated Press for more than 30 years. He got the job at the AP shortly after graduating from Columbia University, where we were classmates. I'm not sure how Ronald ever found time to study when he was in school. He seemed always to be at a game; if he wasn't covering something for the school paper he was stringing or freelancing for an off-campus pub. He has the stamina required of a baseball beat reporter: report, interview, write; report, interview, write (sleep, a little); report, interview, write; repeat. Over the years he has come to intimately know the sport's biggest stars as well as the executives running the games. And he's built relationships that give him better access than any drive-by reporter.

"Baseball is a little easier [to develop relationships] than the other major sports because it is every day," Blum told me recently, "and everyone knows each other and lives with each other. You are seeing people for six weeks of spring training and then a decent part of 162 games over 186 days and maybe a postseason for a week to a month." Being around the athletes that much allows a reporter like Blum to get familiar with interview subjects, and that helps when it comes to knowing the right time to ask a particular question. "You talk to a Buck Showalter (the former Baltimore Orioles manager), who gives long, thought-out answers, a lot differently than you talk to a Kevin Cash (manager of the Tampa Bay Rays), who tries to end interviews after three to four minutes," Blum explained. "And you can't ask Joe Torre a lot of open-ended questions; each answer will turn into seven minutes of storytelling. If you ask him what he thinks of a guy, you get a 10-minute story about what Bob Gibson did in the 1970s. His clock runs out after three questions. You spent 25 minutes with him and gotten just three questions answered."

But Blum, who has interviewed everyone in baseball from A (A-Rod) to Z (Don Zimmer), has learned that to get the best interviews—the ones that provide him with insights other beat writers don't get—he often has to outthink the competition. Working for the AP, which thrives on getting stories fast and first, Blum knows that he can't always wait to get a couple of hours with an athlete in order to go deep into the player's background. He's learned that he has to strike when the moment presents itself. An example he shared with me involved a story he wrote in spring 2018 just after the St. Louis Cardinals beat the New York Mets, thanks to two home runs by Paul DeJong. The obvious postgame questions would have involved asking DeJong, "What pitch were you expecting?" and "How do you feel after such a big day?" But weeks prior to DeJong's big game, Blum had been researching the shortstop and discovered that he was from a family of classical music enthusiasts. Blum, who sometimes covers opera for the AP, spotted an angle, especially because few ballplayers know their Brahms from their Babe Ruths. Now he just needed the right moment to bring it up to DeJong. The two-homer game did just that.

"Normally that's a pregame-type question. Postgame everyone is trying to rush away," Blum said. So, then, how did Blum approach DeJong with such an untypical topic? While most of the other reporters were talking to the St. Louis manager after the game, Blum rushed over to DeJong to get a few solo minutes with him. "Reporters get really annoyed if you try to ask a question like that after someone hits two home runs and when they're all on deadline." Blum got DeJong to answer his questions about classical music, and then used the insight to craft a lead with references to trumpets, pianos and homeruns, a litany you don't often see in a typical baseball recap.

Blum had done his homework and used it to effect. He also combined access with craftiness, and sometimes being crafty—being able to pose the incisive question at the appropriate time—is enough of a prompt to get an athlete to share a little bit more than a reporter normally might expect. Dan Patrick is among today's top sports interviewers. His 30-plus-year career includes long stints at CNN and ESPN. For the past decade he has hosted one of the premier weekday sports-talk shows on radio. Unlike a lot of sports radio that relies on phone calls from listeners to fill time, Patrick schedules extended interviews with athletes, coaches and executives. While the interviews are often entertaining (in fact, hilarious), Patrick is also known for breaking news. He's learned what works—and what doesn't—to get a subject to open up, even when time is tight.

One approach he rails against is the "Tell me about . . . " prompt. In Patrick's opinion, too many reporters fall back on that tack when interviewing athletes. It fails to ask a question—and often just elicits the expected and the drab.

The better route? Patrick says stick with asking fundamental questions that invariably produce high-quality results. "*Why* is a great question." Patrick told Esquire magazine a few years ago. "Always ask a question that is going to get someone to talk."

Patrick gave the example of an interview he did with Patrick Ewing, the former college and NBA star. During the course of an eight-minute-or-so telephone interview, he asked Ewing why he had decided to go to Georgetown University and not the University of North Carolina when he was an intensely recruited high school athlete. (Had he gone to North Carolina, Ewing would have teamed with another future star, Michael Jordan.) On the surface the question seemed a bit mundane; it had been 30 years since the pursuit of Patrick Ewing by college coaches was a national story. But Dan was curious, and his curiosity produced an answer from Ewing that still has currency in today's tumultuous times.

"North Carolina was a very good school," Ewing said, "but, you know, when I went down there they put me in that Carolina Inn, and there was a big Ku Klux Klan rally when I was there. And I'm like, 'You know what? I'm not coming down here.'"

The beauty of sports reporting is that many athletes do have stories and opinions beyond the expected, the clichéd. But too frequently sports reporters—especially less experienced ones—use their limited time with an athlete to either confirm information they already know or get quotes they can already anticipate. The result? Boring answers, which lead to boring storytelling.

"With interviewing athletes a lot of the challenge is getting them to think outside of the script of the usual sports clichés," Austin Meek, the sports columnist for the (Eugene) *Register-Guard*, told me. "I think most athletes that you interview have dealt with some degree of media training and also have just grown up with seeing athletes interviewed. And there are certain clichés you hear a million times in sports interviews, and if you are not careful and if you are not intentional about the questions you ask, it is really easy for athletes to follow that script and not really think about the question or the answer. The first thing I try to do is not use any of those clichés in the question. Avoiding that language in the question is important if you want to avoid that language in the answer."

Case in point: Meek recalls the time when he was covering the Kansas State University basketball team and interviewing one of its players. In the course of the interview, Meek got him to look back at his high school playing days during which the player had been homeless at different points. "I don't remember if there was a magic question or magic word that I said to get him to feel comfortable to open up about it, but we just gradually worked up to it," Meek said. "When he got to the point when he was willing to tell the whole story, he just kind of put it out there. That is the goal, I think, of interviewing: to work up to the point where it's not like you have to poke and prod and pull everything out of the subject. If they are comfortable and there is a trust level built up, then a lot of times they want to share the story. They are comfortable doing it, and you don't have to work that hard."

Austin Meek has a wonderful job. He's the lead sports columnist in a market with big-time college sports—namely, University of Oregon sports. But he also has the opportunity to search for and find the "off-the-radar" story that keeps readers coming back to their local paper. He's a must-read because you never know what you might discover in an Austin Meek piece. One day you might find he's interviewed Phil Knight of Nike. Another day you'll see he's uncovered the hidden story of a community college basketball coach. I tell my students: If you want to be a sports journalist, read Austin Meek. He should be as much of a role model as anyone who is on the national stage. His work showcases the hallmarks of good sports journalism: excellent writing married to exceptional reporting.

You can't have one without the other, and you (often) can't have the reporting without a good interview. To get the good interviews, to work your way around barriers like a stiff-arming sports information department or athletes and coaches who just want to provide the obvious, you have to work a bit smarter, a bit harder than the average reporter. You have to do what Austin Meek and Ron Blum and others do: "hang around" a little longer than everybody else. It's a proven formula. Frank Deford became legendary thanks to the profiles he wrote for Sports Illustrated, profiles on such athletes and sports figures as Jimmy Connors and Bobby Knight and Howard Cosell. One all-time classic was his piece on a retired Bill Russell. The reader meets Russell through a road trip the basketball great and the writing great take together from Oregon to Oakland. With all that "hang time," Deford crystalized the essence of Russell in 3-D.

Before he died in 2017, Deford noted how getting such access to sports figures is considerably harder for writers these days—and what is lost because of that. "It's unfortunate, because I think we were better able to present these guys as human beings, simply because we got to know them better," Deford told Smithsonian. "It wasn't because we were better writers, or anything like that, but when you have that access, and that intimacy, you can write about a person with more authority."

I know what Deford speaks of when he talks of access and its importance. But I also know you can still get it, if you work at. In the piece I wrote about Matt Long I was able to reveal why he needed to run a marathon for reasons that in many ways had nothing to do with running. I shared how, as a New York City firefighter, he had dealt with the losses that came on September 11, 2001. At first he was reluctant to discuss this part of his life. But the more I hung around, the more comfortable he became discussing 9-11, a day that would trigger his running life. And not until Long and I were actually running the marathon did he open up about a younger brother who had been dealing with his own personal struggles—and how his brother was seeking inspiration from the marathon as much as Matt was. The details helped to round out his story.

And I was also able to share the darkest thoughts Long had when he was recovering from his accident. I learned of them about three weeks before his comeback marathon. One afternoon I accompanied him to a rehab appointment. I watched as therapists worked on his thighs and knees and shoulders, and I talked to his doctor about his chances of getting to the finish line. It was another day of reporting, of hanging around. Then Long and I went to Central Park for a short run, about three miles. We talked about a lot of little things—about living in New York City, about his favorite bars, about basketball, about stuff. But then, for some reason,

I decided to ask Long something that I had wondered about for a long time, but had never felt OK asking. Considering all the pain he had been through, physical and emotional, and the way his life had changed since the accident, and the fact that his body could no longer do what it used to do, and that the dreams he once held—to find someone special, to have a family of his own—now seemed out of reach, did he think ever of, well, ending his life? He waited a few seconds before answering. Then he said yes, he had thought about it—but never went through with it for the following reason: It seemed that one night during his recovery he kept complaining to a visitor about all the things he would never have the chance to do because of his injuries. The complaining went for several minutes. But then, for some reason—a reason he couldn't quite determine—he just stopped whining. "And I remember saying, 'You know, a lot of people want stuff. People want this, people want that. People want to win the lottery. But just because you want something doesn't mean you're going to get it. You got to, you know, work for it.' So right there I just said, 'I will run. And I will run a marathon.' "

He gave me an emotional, genuine response. It filled another hole in his story. The only problem? We were running as he told me this anecdote, and I wasn't running with a recorder or pencil and paper.

When we got out of the park and back to where our bags were, I asked him if he wouldn't mind telling me his answer one more time. As we stood on a New York City corner, Matt Long talking, me scribbling, a story of an athlete took shape.

TWELVE

Interviewing for Television News

Different story formats call for different approaches

REBECCA FORCE

Successful TV interviewing requires dealing with complications unknown to the scribe laboring with only a pencil and pad. Veteran TV assignment editor Rebecca Force helps students use the right tools and ask the right questions for different types of stories.

Some techniques for conducting interviews are reporting basics, no matter what the publishing platform. There's a dog-eared checklist most successful journalists follow, whether they work in print, broadcast, magazine or multimedia. They prepare by:

- researching their story
- figuring out who knows the most about the topic and who is affected by it
- persuading some of those people to be interviewed
- writing out a list of questions (hopefully intelligent ones based on the research)

- asking open-ended questions
- maintaining eye contact to avoid distracting the interviewee
- asking only one question at a time
- listening to answers without interrupting
- asking follow-up questions as needed
- asking for details and anecdotes
- keeping their opinions to themselves
- remembering that they are seeking information on behalf of the public.

And, reporters sometimes try to put interviewees at ease before they begin—but not always.

That's what reporters do. But how they do it varies greatly depending on the medium for which they report. And the different media are accompanied by different baggage.

To say that broadcast news has baggage is an understatement. In fact, it also has cameras, video cards, audio recorders, lights and tripods in addition to the bags containing cables, power adapters, batteries, microphones and perhaps a sandwich for lunch.

For many interviews conducted for inclusion in broadcast news stories, that gear will be needed. So, it will be loaded into the back of the news mobile most days. Whether some or all of it gets used depends on the story being pursued and the form that story is going to take.

If the story has significant community impact, the checklist and most of the gear in the back of the car will be utilized as will the ingenuity, persistence, organization and skill of the journalists who use all those tools. But not all broadcast stories get the full treatment.

There are four basic forms of news pieces that appear on television:

The Read: a short (20 to 30 seconds) news brief that has no video and is read by an anchor in the studio.

Interviews for this form are frequently fast and to the point. In this hypothetical example* it's early morning as the reporter makes a call:

> "Hi, Detective Smith. We received a tip that the mayor was seen running down the middle of the street naked last night. Did you roll on any such reports?"

Smith says the police were called out on a complaint about indecent exposure, but the incident report has not yet been filed. The reporter writes a read saying only that police were called out after an as-yet unidentified person was reported running down the street naked and that there will be more information as it becomes available.

The Voice Over (VO):   a short (20 to 40 seconds) story read by the anchor while video relating to the content of the story is aired.

The reporter now has some video and a little more information provided by a credible source who has contacted her:

> "What's that you say? You have cell phone video of the mayor running down the street naked? Can we use it? We'll credit you. Great! Send me a link to the video. Spell your name for me. Now, tell me when you shot this footage. Why were you downtown at that time? Are you the one who called the cops? Were you there when they arrived? Oh, right . . . you shot the whole thing. Would you come by the station later for an interview? Great. How about 10 this morning?"

The reporter gets the video, edits it to blur some sensitive areas of the image and writes a VO script updating the story and noting that the person whose face is visible appears to be the mayor. The story makes it into the second morning report.

---

* This hypothetical situation is focused on interviewing—not on writing, ethical considerations, legal considerations, newsroom politics, equipment failures, crabby colleagues or abbreviated lunch breaks. These realities receive only passing attention here. In addition, the timeline herein is entirely fantastic; nothing happens this fast, or this smoothly.

The Voice Over-Sound on Tape (VO-SOT):   a slightly longer story that starts as a read, becomes a voice over, and then adds a brief portion of a recorded interview related to the story topic.

By now, the entire newsroom staff knows what the reporter is working on. The assignment editor had planned on having the reporter work on a story about neighborhood flooding because of storm runoff overloading the city's drainage system. Now the assignments are being reshuffled, and the reporter who has been working the mayor's story is told to continue with it, to have a VO-SOT ready for the noon show and to work on a package for the evening newscast. The reporter works with a photographer to set up the interview with the eyewitness: Two chairs facing each other, four lights to illuminate both the interviewee and the reporter, two microphones, and one camera behind the reporter aimed at the source. The reporter has now done a little research into the source and has prepared questions. The interview lasts 22 minutes and covers most of the questions the reporter has already asked on the phone as well as observations and reactions to the prior night's scene. The reporter now has the cell phone video as well as an interview detailing the event. The reporter calls Detective Smith again and learns that the incident report is still unfinished. She then writes a story showing part of the video, identifying the eyewitness, paraphrasing much of the interview to help shorten the time it takes to tell the story and using one quote from the eyewitness:

> "I told him to put some clothes on, and he yelled back at me that he had nothing to hide."

Out of the 22-minute interview, the reporter has used eight seconds of video to visually introduce the eyewitness, and a 5-second quote.

Now, the reporter turns her attention to preparing the package for the evening newscast.

The Package: a self-contained story narrated by a reporter that usually contains information gleaned from research and interviews as well as short clips (actualities) from a couple of recorded interviews. A package is typically about 90 seconds in length.

It's now 11 a.m., and the reporter calls the mayor's office at city hall. She is told that the mayor has called in sick. She then calls the mayor's home (she has great contacts) but the call goes to a recording. She leaves a message telling the mayor why she's calling and asks for an interview. The reporter and the photographer then drive the news car (already loaded by the photographer while the reporter was making calls and writing) to the mayor's home. The mayor's lawyer answers the door, says that the mayor will not be giving interviews and that there will be no further comment. The photographer shoots the entire exchange. As they are leaving, reporters from the local paper, two other television stations and one radio station are pulling up to the house.

When they get back to the station, the producer rushes the reporter to the studio for the noon newscast where she updates the story and introduces the VO-SOT. Afterward she walks back into the newsroom where she sees the station manager, the news director and the mayor's lawyer arguing loudly. The lawyer is yelling about libel. The news director snaps that reporting the truth is not libelous. The station manager is calling for calm and trying to call the station's lawyer.

The reporter urges the lawyer to talk to his client about doing an interview to explain last night's events. The lawyer says the station can't prove the naked person was the mayor. The reporter then plays the cell phone clip in which the mayor rejects his need for clothing. The lawyer leaves.

The reporter calls Detective Smith again. He tells her the incident report has been submitted, and no, he won't read it over the phone. She and her photographer head for the police station. The report reveals the responding officer insisted on a Breathalyzer test. Smith says the police chief is going to hold a news conference in a half hour. The chief is bombarded with questions but declines to answer most of them, confirming only that the mayor was escorted to his home and that the district attorney would be reviewing all information to determine if any charges should be filed.

The reporter writes the story, using pithy quotes from the eyewitness interview, the mayor's quip from the cell phone video, a clip of the lawyer's statement at the mayor's house and quotes from the police chief. She draws no conclusions about what was behind the event and focuses her story on what is known, and what's next. She has been allotted 90 seconds for the story; she asks for more time. The producer gives her 10 more seconds.

She and the photographer drive to city hall where they record the reporter's closing standup for her story. They rush back to the station where the photographer starts editing the story.

The tired and hungry reporter is about to leave for home when the mayor shows up in the newsroom and offers to do a live interview with her, saying there is more to this than meets the eye. The newscast producer and news director agree to allot 3 minutes for the interview. The reporter tells the mayor they can do the live interview, but she wants to prepare for it by recording an in-depth interview with him first. He agrees. The night photographer sets up lights and mics, and the reporter conducts a 40-minute interview in which the mayor discusses his problems with drinking, gambling and finding just the right tailor.

During the live interview a half hour later, the reporter asks four questions. The mayor confirms the cell phone video is of him, acknowledges he has a substance problem, asks for understanding and pledges to get help. By the time she asked, the reporter knew the answers to her questions; she asked them so her viewers would also know the answers.

The reporter had to interrupt the mayor once to refocus the interview when he started to wander off topic. The live interview comes in six seconds over budget.

The reporter has a start on her day tomorrow. Her taped interview with the mayor has been wide-ranging. She's a good journalist, and she listened carefully when he mentioned he'd noticed his problems getting worse a few months ago. She asked him what he thought triggered the change, and he talked about sadness, depression and feelings of being trapped by others' expectations. She followed up, and now she knew she would need to interview a lot of experts in the mental health and addiction fields who might help others who saw themselves in the mayor's story.

Time is the limiting factor for broadcast news. If our hypothetical journalist was reporting for a normal 30-minute newscast, her finished pieces would be short, but she would still need to collect all the information she could garner in order to effectively trim it to only the essentials for a

90-second story. If she reports for a broadcast magazine show, her budget will be three to four times longer; for documentaries, she'll have even more time. The actualities may be a bit longer, but they will still be pithy.

The 17th-century French theologian/philosopher/mathematician Blaise Pascal wrote at the end of a lengthy letter: "I have only made this letter longer because I have not had the time to make it shorter," thus capturing the dilemma faced by generations of broadcasters who shorten, tighten and craft carefully—and grieve for the details and quotes left on the cutting room floor.

THIRTEEN

Interviewing for Radio, Podcasting and Audio

In both planning and execution, remember that the medium matters

DAMIAN RADCLIFFE

Especially in this era of the ubiquitous podcast, interviewing for audio storytelling requires a focus on our aural environments. Former BBC journalist Damian Radcliffe calls attention to techniques, such as collecting natural sound and embracing the power of emotion, that make interviews come alive.

Audio is enjoying a creative and critical renaissance right now.[1] Radio continues to have the largest reach of any entertainment medium in the U.S.;[2] and podcasting—driven by the rise of listening to audio on smartphones and smart speakers, coupled with low barriers to entry, and the creative possibilities of this unregulated broadcast arena—is experiencing its own golden age.[3]

BACKGROUND: WHY AUDIO IS SO HOT RIGHT NOW

As a result, we've seen a wide range of news outlets move into the audio space, including traditional print publications such as The New Yorker,[4]

New York Times,[5] *Washington Post*[6] and the *Guardian*.[7] For some, such as Slate, audio is now responsible for nearly a quarter of their revenue[8] and is an area of continued investment and experimentation.[9]

Meanwhile traditional radio providers, such as NPR, the BBC and ABC in Australia, continue to make available their broadcast output for on-demand (and often offline) consumption, meaning that—as with TV—you can listen to programs when you want, not when they are broadcast. The ability to time-shift the media you consume represents a major change in media habits.

Broadcasters are also producing digital-only content—from the podcast extras on the BBC's flagship film show *Kermode and Mayo*,[10] through to more artistic forms of expression and experimentation.[11]

Alongside this, we're also seeing brands moving into the audio space, often driven by similar desire to capitalise on the podcasting phenomenon.[12] Everyone from universities,[13] through to banks,[14] apps[15] and soft drink[16] companies, seem to have a podcast. (Disclaimer: So do I.[17])

Arguably, the primary drivers for this growth of investment and interest in audio are threefold:

1. The opportunity to tell unique stories (or the stories behind the stories) in a manner not possible with other media

2. Using audio to deepen relationships with existing audiences (for newspapers, that also involves doing so via a different medium) and

3. Finding new audiences and revenue streams.

The growth of the medium is a boon for journalists. Audio skills are more desirable than ever, and the range of places where you can ply your trade grows by the day.

With audio too big to ignore,[18] opportunities abound for journalists who can make use of the medium—either in a dedicated audio role, or as part of their wider journalistic toolkit.[19]

What follows in this chapter is some key advice on how to interview for radio, or podcasts, and how interviewing for the medium differs from other platforms. At the end, I offer a series of links to recommended sources for those keen to know more.

CONTEXT: HOW RADIO IS DIFFERENT FROM OTHER MEDIA

Audio can be a highly powerful outlet for storytelling. With origins in campfire storytelling, it's a medium that's as old as language itself.

Why is that? Well, first, it encourages audiences to use their imagination. Unlike when watching TV, you cannot see the person being interviewed, or where that person is. Instead, audiences pick up on audio cues, such as natural sounds and background noise (as well as assumed knowledge, e.g., of what a place looks like), as well as description used in the audio narration to "paint pictures" of the scene—and people—they are listening to.[20]

Edward R. Murrow's broadcasts from London during World War II are a great example of this. We cannot see what is happening, but through Murrow's evocative descriptions, and the natural sound captured in his recordings, we can immediately picture the scene in front of him.[21]

Second, and perhaps more important, audio is also a deeply personal medium. As the librarian, writer and podcast lover Jill Fuller explains:

> "Whether told by the hearth or through earbuds, when the story starts, I am no longer alone. I am surrounded by other people, other ideas, stories unfamiliar but strangely recognizable. I am in the room with the dying man, I am walking through the migrant camp, I am holding the child's hand, I am watching the television episode, I am witnessing the artist's careful brushstrokes. The space between myself and the world beyond shrinks, and shrinks again, until it is no thicker than a sound wave."[22]

Audio interviews allow you to hear directly from sources. Hearing them speak can bring a story, or a person, to life, in a manner that words alone cannot.

Take, for example, a 2010 NPR interview with the legendary Rolling Stones guitarist Keith Richards.[23] The transcript alone is insufficient to convey the full depth of the interview.

If you just read that, you miss out on the tone of the interview, as well as some of the other colourful details. You would miss Richards' playfulness (I find him to be quite flirty with the host), the sound of him flicking his cigarette lighter during various parts of the interview or the fact that he sounds a lot more "posh" than perhaps you might expect if you've never heard him speak before.

Or consider an interview with former white nationalist Derek Black, featured in the *New York Times'* podcast The Daily.[24] Does listening to Black talk about his experiences directly change your perception about him? Do you view him differently?

Audio can be at its most powerful and deeply personal when communicating stories which carry an emotional punch. Hearing people talk about the loss of a loved one, their voices cracking with raw emotion, is so much more gut-wrenching and wrought when you hear it. I would argue that words alone are unable to have the same impact.

StoryCorps, a New York based nonprofit which aims "to record, preserve, and share the stories of Americans from all backgrounds and beliefs," has an archive full of hard-hitting material. Listen to the pieces featuring a "guardian angel," Thomas Weller,[25] or the discussion between Iraq war veteran Tracy Johnson and her mother-in-law—after Tracy's longtime partner, Staff Sgt. Donna Johnson, was killed in Afghanistan—and I defy you not to be moved.[26]

Great audio interviewing does more than just convey information. Done well, it can convey personality, emotion and a sense of place. Interestingly, in all of these StoryCorps examples, the interviewer is removed from the recording. "Getting out of the way," just one technique audio producers can deploy, enables us to just hear from those telling the story, and the pieces are all the more potent because of it.

Below are five recommended areas for those keen to improve their audio interviewing, and interviewing for audio, skills:

1. Decide on your storytelling and interviewing format
You can tell stories with audio in myriad ways.[27] This ranges from roundtable discussions to documentaries, features or more traditional interviews.

Determining which format you want to use will shape the way you approach your interviews.

An interview conducted for an edited podcast, is, inevitably, different from a live, time-restricted, show. The most obvious difference is that you have the beauty of time.

That can lead to long detailed discussions, such as Marc Maron's hour-long interview[28] with then-President Obama in 2015. (Can you recall another environment in which you've heard an interview with the former president which lasts this long?) It can also help create an environment where your interviewee has time to settle in and feel comfortable.

Similarly, the types of stories you are telling may also require you to interview differently.

Interviewing elected officials for a news story, for example, may require a more traditional, probing (and perhaps confrontational) approach than a human interest story.

Lastly, you also need to decide how you want to record your audio. Is your show, or segment, live? Or perhaps recorded and broadcast "as live"?

If so, it means there's no scope for editing and you're on the clock. In this scenario, your interviewees need to be focused and pithy (but not too pithy; you want them to talk more than the interviewer!). You also need to have the confidence to interrupt them, either to move the story on, ask for clarification or to keep the focus of the discussion on track.

Alternatively, if you're producing a podcast or an interview which will be hosted online (and thus free of restrictions in terms of running time), how much time do you want to spend editing? If at all?

In contrast to broadcast radio, where you're always up against the clock, online-only shows and interviews can be as long as you like. But, that doesn't mean that they don't need to be produced and (quite possibly) edited. In fact, I would argue that a lot of podcasts[29]—freed from traditional time constraints—are too long.

2. Preparation is key

Doing your homework is fundamental for any successful interview. You need to have researched the person you are interviewing and the subject that person will be talking to you about.

Not only is this professional, but it's a sure-fire way to garner the respect of your interviewee. In my experience, good prep leads to better interviews, as interviewees tend to be more responsive when they know you've done your homework.

And although all interviewers should be good active listeners— responding to answers and cues, in a manner which means that you are willing to deviate from previously prepared questions—no matter how good an active listener you are, good prep helps to ensure that the interview goes smoothly.

In a live audio environment, other types of interview preparation are also essential:

- *Ascertain if this is the right person to interview.* Your interviewee may know the subject matter, but that doesn't necessarily mean that person is a great fit for a live interview. Audio producers need to consider a number of other factors:
  - *Voice:* Most people's speaking voice is fine, but occasionally you'll find an interviewee whose voice is grating (whiny, nasal, etc.).
  - *Accent:* Can they be understood, especially when you cannot see them? Visual cues—such as body language and lip reading— can help us to navigate any issues we might have understanding accents. When you only have the audio to listen to, however, these additional cues are absent. You therefore need to ensure that your interviewees can be understood.
  - *Clarity of answers:* Is the person you're talking to engaging? Can the interviewee explain ideas and concepts (from scientific findings through to a "this happened" narrative) in a manner which anyone can understand?
- *Conduct a pre-interview.* You want to find out about any issues with these three areas (voice, accent or clarity of answers) before you go on air. As a result, most live shows will conduct a pre-interview as part of their production process.

  Typically, a pre-interview involves a producer, or researcher, talking to a potential interviewee ahead of the show. This is useful to not only address any potential concerns but also as a means to identify the areas that person is likely to touch on in an interview.

Thus, the pre-interview should be seen as an integral part of your research process. It can garner new ideas and questions as well as provide a forum (if required) to give your interviewee some tips and feedback *before* airtime. In many cases, the pre-interview lasts longer than the actual interview.

If the pre-interview throws up any issues, the best way to deal with it is to be polite.

Letting an interviewee down gently and respectfully is important. You don't necessarily need to mention the real reason for not putting someone on air.

Instead, I'd recommend thanking them for their time, pointing out how helpful the conversation has been in shaping your plans for the story, and perhaps suggesting that time restrictions mean you cannot feature everyone you've been talking to about this subject.

Such an approach not only saves face, but it's frequently true too.

- *Getting the technical quality you need.* Ideally, you'll conduct your interview face-to-face (of which more later). But, that's not always possible.

  Interviews conducted down the phone ("phoners") have always been a staple for audio shows. Increasingly common are interviews conducted via Skype, Zoom or other online platforms. If you are having to go down this route, I'd recommend the following:
  - *If the interview will be live, always do a test run:* Mimic the circumstances of the upcoming live interview as much as possible. This enables you to ensure that the technology works. Can you get through and hear each other? Is the interviewee's environmental setting quiet enough?
  - *If the tech doesn't work, what are your alternatives?* Does the interviewee need to use a different microphone (e.g., through one built into a headset or a laptop)? Does the interviewee need to be closer to/farther away from the mic?

- *Can you contact that person via a different route?* For example, if you're talking to someone on a mobile and reception is fuzzy, is it possible to phone a landline instead?
- *Ensure you—and your interviewee—are using headphones to avoid "bleeding":* When you're talking to someone—and you'll know this from conversations you've had on speaker phone—it can be very distracting to hear yourself looping back through someone else's speaker. Using headphones ensures that both parties avoid this scenario.

3. Location, location, location
Where you record your interview matters.

- *Interviewing in the field.* There are times when getting out of the studio makes a huge difference to your interview. A few quick examples:
  - Want to discuss the impact of the California drought with a farmer? Do the interview out in the fields. Sounds—from animals to machinery, even the wind—will help to give a sense of space and place.
  - Telling a story about the Toyosu fish market in Tokyo, or Pike Place in Seattle? Be sure to talk to your interviewees in their native environment. Again, the setting of the interview can be a key ingredient in the storytelling.
  You don't have to do this for your entire piece, or indeed your entire interview, but interviewing on location, especially if it's in the right location—namely one that is intrinsically linked to your story—can add real colour and flavour to your content.
- *Wear headphones.* Recording on location can sometimes bring with it major technical challenges. These are different from recording in a studio, or at home. This is especially true in noisy or echoey environments.

  Subsequently, it's smart to do a test run first. Of course, the ambient and background sounds from your test run may be different on the day of the interview itself. Nonetheless, I would recommend:

- Wear decent headphones for your recording. Plug it into the recording device and listen through your headphones to the recording, *as you capture it.*
- If you can't hear the sound that's being recorded properly, then the odds are you audience will struggle to hear it too. Better to find this out at the time, instead of in the edit, resulting in an unusable interview, or one you have to go and re-record.

- ***If in doubt, move.*** Your job is, in part, to make an interviewee sound good. Certainly from a technical perspective. Nobody wants to give an interview in which they cannot be heard![30]
  - If the recording quality is compromised (coffee shops are a good example of this. They're a good place to meet but often a bad place to record), try to move to a different location. If this isn't possible, reschedule the interview.
  - You're the expert. Your interviewee will respect your professional judgement. Just explain why you need to move or reschedule.
  - As a fallback, you may be able to move to another part of the room/space you're in; you can change location altogether.

    Try to make it a neutral location if it doesn't tie in with the story. (If you're interviewing a California farmer in a Starbucks, it will seem a bit odd to the listener, unless you can make a link—which you explain in the piece—to the location, e.g., the farmer might supply milk to the coffee shop.)
  - Recording in a car can sometimes be a good back-up. Unless it's raining heavily. Or you're in a noisy location with lots of passing trucks and cars, in which case—again—you may need to include some explanatory context.

    Nonetheless, cars have good soundproofing. Just be sure that you're comfortable getting in a car with an interviewee. You should never put yourself unnecessarily in harm's way for the sake of an interview.

4. Let's get physical

Audio brings its own set of tips and recommendations for success. Because you're not on camera, and it's just your voice that gets heard, there are a

few additional things you can do to ensure that your voice and delivery—
and that of your interviewee—sounds its best:

- **Smile.** Worried about sounding monotone or bored? A simple
  trick is to smile while you are talking. I don't mean a full-on
  Cheshire Cat, but a smile—even if slightly forced (remember this
  is radio, no one can see you)—will make you sound more
  engaging.

- **Stand if you can.** Standing up—as opposed to sitting or lying
  down—changes your diaphragm and how you sound. You
  automatically sound brighter and more interested.

- **Consider your body language.** If you're naturally expressive,
  someone who talks with your hands, don't tone this down just
  because you cannot be seen. Again, this helps with projection,
  injecting vigour and energy into the timber of your voice. Just try
  to avoid bashing the microphone with your flailing limbs.

- **Silent affirmation.** In real life, we constantly provide signals of
  understanding and encouragement to the people we're talking to.
  Often that's small noises such as "uh-huh," "ah-ha," "yes," etc.
  - That's fine in day-to-day conversation but tends to be a real
    no-no in audioland. It's distracting and off-putting and sounds
    intrusive. Instead, you want the words of your interviewee to be
    as clean as possible.
  - Michael Barbaro, host of the the *New York Times'* excellent
    podcast The Daily is an honourable exception to this rule. His
    audible reactions ("hmmm") to the revelations of his
    interviewees often mimic our own as listeners.
  - Audio interviewers need to use silent affirmation—lots of
    nodding and eye contact—instead as a means to provide mid-
    interview feedback. Ideally, you want to get out of the way and
    only be heard when you're asking a question.

5. Getting the most out of your interviewee

Some of the best audio interviews are conversational. In fact, they don't
sound like an interview at all. They sound like natural, free-flowing dis-

cussions, which we have the opportunity—and privilege—of being able to eavesdrop on.

Here are a few quick recommendations in that area:

- **Ask great questions!** The best interviewers ask the questions you want answered and you would have asked. Or they ask a question which you'd never thought of but wish you had.

  Much of this comes from preparation, but it also stems from the ability to pivot away from a pre-prepared script, based on the responses provided by an interviewee.

- **Vary your style of questions, depending on your needs.** For news stories, direct—sometimes closed—questions are sometimes appropriate.

  - For example, you might be interviewing public officials who do not want to answer your questions but instead push their own pre-prepared lines. In this scenario, closed questions can be your friend, as they help to reduce opportunities for wriggle room, rambling and an unfocused response.

  With human interest stories, the best questions tend to be open-ended. Encourage the interviewee to do most of the talking and to provide the colour and detail. Terry Gross at NPR is a master of this. If you read the transcripts from her show, Fresh Air, then you can see skill in action.

  - Gross' 2017 interview on school segregation with the journalist Nikole Hannah-Jones, for example, is a good case study.[31] It's clear that she knows the answers to many of the questions she's asking Hannah-Jones, but they're phrased in such a way that her interviewee tells the story. Gross is merely the (expert) facilitator of it.

  Questions which ask: "So, how did . . . " or "Tell us about," or "Can you explain . . . " help to tee up these types of responses.

- **Coach your interviewee if you need to.** Nikole Hannah-Jones is a journalist, and most journalists are great storytellers. They're often wonderful to interview for that very reason. Not everyone you want to talk to will be as comfortable in front of a mic or as great at telling the story.

In my view, it's fine to coach your interviewees, not telling them what to say, but perhaps in offering encouragement in terms of *how* they say it.

One way to do this is to briefly outline beforehand what you're looking for from the interview. Another option is to do this during the interview by asking questions which steer what you're looking for, e.g., "Can you tell us more x."

You can also ask an interviewee to retell a story, or to tell it more punchily ("That was really interesting, but we're pushed for time, so I wondered if there's a quicker way to say that"). However, I often find the first take is the most genuine, so try to get what you need live, or through your follow-ups.

- *Decide when you're going to hit record.* If your interview isn't live, there's often a merit to ensuring your tape recorder is running from the moment you arrive at the place of the interview.

  This enables you to capture natural sound, which helps to set the scene, right off the bat. That could be you getting out of the car, walking along a gravel footpath, ringing the doorbell, meeting the source for the first time, etc.

  That said, I *wouldn't* record your full interview without notifying your interviewee that you're rolling. You can, of course, have your tape rolling anyway. But, you must behave ethically! Be sure to tell your interviewees when they're "on the record" and ensure that you don't broadcast any of the recording prior to that.

  Some people "freeze" or clam up when they know they're being recorded, even if they're a great talker the rest of the time. Every audio producer will have encountered a scenario when a great conversationalist turns monosyllabic the moment that a tape recorder starts running.

  Making your interviewee comfortable is a skill. For a pre-recorded interview, my suggestion would be to start rolling from the beginning but to keep the initial conversation light so that the equipment becomes part of the furniture. Soon the interviewee forgets the tape is rolling (or at least stops freaking out about it), and all you need to do is edit out the background stuff at the start.

· *Edit sparingly.* The best producers—like the best copy editors— edit in such a fashion that you cannot see (or hear) where the edits are. It's fine to move around the order of a story.

It's also fine to only use key extracts. In fact, if you've recorded a 30-minute interview for a 3-minute segment, I'd recommend not trying to edit down the entire conversation. Pick the choicest bits. You can always précis some of the other parts of the discussion in your intro/conclusion.

I often get asked about editing out silences, um's, argh's, etc. My general recommendation would be not to do this. Why not? Well, first, it's very time-consuming.

Second, if an interviewee has paused (within reason) before answering your question, the listener needs to hear that. The silence tells us something.

Perhaps that the interviewee is considering your question before answering it. Cutting the silence to speed things up means you're essentially manipulating the interview and misrepresenting how your interviewee behaved and responded.

That can potentially be problematic if your interview is about a polemic topic, when a rapid response could create the impression of arrogance or make the interviewee appear glib. Your reaction to a response might be different with the pause kept in.

It's fine to edit. Of course. Just do so in a manner which is honest and true to the tone of the interview and your interviewee. Authenticity, in all journalism and especially in audio, is the bedrock of our profession.

FURTHER RESOURCES

NPR Training website:https://training.npr.org/

Online Learning

Writing for the Ear: https://courses.poynter.org/courses/course-v1:newsu+
    reportingwritingfortheear+sdc17/about
Telling Stories with Sound: https://courses.poynter.org/courses/course-v1:
    newsu+storytellingtellingstorieswithsound+sdc17/about

Technical Skills—Transom Articles on Podcasting Basics:

Voice Recording Gear: http://transom.org/2015/
    podcasting-basics-part-1-voice-recording-gear/
Software: http://transom.org/2015/podcast-basics-part-2-software/
Levels and Processing: http://transom.org/2015/
    podcasting-basics-part-3-audio-levels-and-processing/

Inspiration and Ideas

http://earbud.fm/—listener-recommended episodes (with great synopsis)
    hosted by NPR.
Ten years in your ears, Slate: http://www.slate.com/articles/arts/ten_years_in
    _your_ears/2014/12/best_podcast_episodes_ever_the_25_best_from_serial
    _to_the_ricky_gervais.html
100 outstanding pieces of audio for 2017, Bello Collective: https://bello
    collective.com/100-outstanding-pieces-of-audio-for-2017-c328b3cae530

NOTES

1. https://www.adweek.com/tv-video/npr-iheartmedia-ceos-explain-why
-were-in-the-golden-age-of-audio/ although previous decades have also deployed
this moniker. https://www.nytimes.com/1982/05/01/business/radio-networks
-new-golden-age.html and more commonly the period immediately pre- and
post-World War II. http://history.sandiego.edu/gen/recording/radio2.html
2. https://www.nielsen.com/us/en/insights/reports/2018/state-of-the-
media--audio-today-2018.html
3. https://digitalcontentnext.org/blog/2018/05/10/7-reasons-you-should-pay
-attention-to-podcasting/

4. https://www.newyorker.com/podcast

5. https://www.nytimes.com/spotlight/podcasts

6. https://www.washingtonpost.com/podcasts/

7. https://www.theguardian.com/podcasts

8. https://digiday.com/media/slate-pivot-to-words/

9. https://podnews.net/press-release/slate-what-next and https://slate
.com/culture/2018/05/introducing-lend-me-your-ears-slates-new-podcast-on
-shakespeare-and-politics.html

10. https://www.denofgeek.com/movies/wittertainment/36847/
wittertainment-the-worlds-flagship-film-review-programme and https://www
.bbc.co.uk/programmes/boolvdrj/episodes/downloads

11. http://australianaudioguide.com/podcast/soundproof/

12. https://www.fastcompany.com/40533210/branded-podcasts-are-the-ads
-people-actually-want-to-listen-to

13. https://www.polis.cam.ac.uk/about-us/talking-politics

14. https://www.umpquabank.com/blog/open-account-podcast-baratunde
-thurston/

15. https://slackhq.com/work-in-progress

16. https://redbullracing.redbull.com/article/cheers-dan-podcast

17. Demystifying Media podcast https://apple.co/2zx7zqZ

18. http://mediashift.org/2015/02/why-journalism-schools-should-join-the
-new-golden-age-of-radio/

19. https://www.inc.com/sarah-peck/why-you-should-still-start-a-podcast
-even-though-there-are-thousands-already-out-there.html

20. http://jayallison.com/new-york-city-24-hours-in-public-places/

21. https://www.youtube.com/watch?v=W8oTLlQc_LI

22. https://bellocollective.com/folklore-fragments-storytelling-in-a-podcast
-world-b4c45dcb9c2

23. https://www.npr.org/templates/transcript/transcript.php?storyId
=130722581

24. https://www.nytimes.com/2017/08/22/podcasts/the-daily/former-white
-nationalist-derek-black.html

25. https://soundcloud.com/storycorps/storycorps-337-just-pass-it-on

26. https://storycorps.org/listen/tracy-and-sandra-johnson/

27. https://medium.com/damian-radcliffe/a-history-of-audio-storytelling-10
-seminal-moments-and-timeless-formats-d6od0134b9fa

28. https://www.youtube.com/watch?v=gAnMYuQhocE

29. For example, the Tim Ferris podcast https://tim.blog/podcast/ —
although with more than 300 million downloads, what do I know!

30. For an example of where this happened to me, listen to https://www

.byuradio.org/episode/d5987fa0-f471-414a-ac9e-c897a13eb77e?playhead=1137&
autoplay=true

31. https://www.npr.org/sections/ed/2017/01/16/509325266/how-
the-systemic-segregation-of-schools-is-maintained-by-individual-choices
> transcript https://www.npr.org/templates/transcript/transcript
.php?storyId=509325266

FOURTEEN **Audio-Visual Interviewing**

*The gear is fundamental, and audio equipment
is most important*

DAN MORRISON

If that priceless interview you've secured is designed
to perform as audio—for radio or a podcast, as the
soundtrack for a film or a video report, to augment
an in-person presentation before a live audience or a
webcast, to voice a website slideshow or as a piece of
performance art—it's worthless if the technical quality
fails the "What did he say?" test. Globetrotting
multimedia journalist Dan Morrison offers a step-by-
step guide for securing sound as sharp as a perfectly
focused photograph.

Everything has changed. We're all journalists now.

You hear that a lot these days, but it's not true. Only those trained in
the profession of journalism are journalists. What is true, however, is that
professional journalists are required to use skills they could not have
imagined as part of their job description before the digital revolution.
When I graduated with a degree in photojournalism in 1984, if you could
take a photograph that was in focus, well exposed, and well composed
with a coherent caption, you could make a comfortable living as a professional photojournalist. No more. Now when I go out on assignment I take
a pack full of gear to collect video and audio as well as still images, and I
have to know how to use that gear at a professional level.

I don't even call myself a photojournalist or call my students photo-
journalists anymore. We are visual journalists. And we probably should

call ourselves audio-visual journalists. We go out and not only shoot still images, but interview our subjects using video digital single-lens reflex cameras (video DSLRs) and sync-up the audio with tracks we collect with audio recording devices. It was called backpack journalism and the One Man Band approach when it first became the norm, but now it is so ubiquitous it is simply journalism.

Here's an example: I have an assignment to interview a subject. There are three components to my completing this task: gear, information gathering techniques and production.

The gear is the most important, and of that component, audio gear is by far the most critical.

Audio rules. Period.

If you don't have usable audio when you return to your office, you have nothing.

The newer video DSLRs have onboard microphones that collect usable-quality audio, but only in ideal situations. Most journalists seldom work in ideal situations. Conducting an interview in the local coffee shop may seem like a good idea, but it won't work. You'll end up with audio that is really nothing more than noise. People talking in the background. People paying for their coffee. People dropping dishes into the sink. Noise.

With a professional shotgun microphone or lavalier microphone, you can sometimes get away with conducting an interview in a less than ideal setting. It's better to collect clean audio with no distracting background noise. A library, for obvious reasons, is a good setting. Any room with drapes and books on bookshelves also works well. In a pinch you can always conduct the interview in a car.

There are several options for collecting audio for your interview depending on your budget. The onboard mic works in ideal conditions. A mini-shotgun mic is slightly better. We use Azden mics in the School of Journalism and Communication, which cost less than 100 bucks, and they are acceptable. One thing to be aware of when using the less expensive mini-shotgun mics is they can sometimes pick up microwave telephone signals, which will leave you with an audio track ruined by a buzzing sound.

A full-size professional shotgun mic, such as a Rode, with XLR cables, will cost a few hundred dollars, but the audio is clean and clear. And your audio must be clean and clear. The mics can be set to uni-directional or omni-directional, depending on your needs. The XLR cables prevent the audio recording device from picking up static buzz.

Lavalier mics, generally just called lavs, work especially well in interview situations. The mic should be placed about six inches from the subject's mouth, and you need to be careful to keep clothing such as jacket lapels or hair from hitting the lav mic during the interview. Hair hitting a lav mic sounds like thunder. Lav mics are standard equipment, but they can be distracting. It looks like your subjects have an insect on their shirt or blouse. If you do choose to use a lav mic, have your subjects drop the mic cord down inside their clothing so that it is hidden. A good lav mic, such as the Audio-Technica brand, with XLR cables, will cost about $150.

No matter which mic you use, wind is your enemy. Wind will utterly destroy your audio. Wind that you barely feel on your skin will ruin your audio. Any wind that moves a leaf on a tree—even slightly—will kill your audio.

There are numerous devices to protect your mic from wind. The foam rubber windscreen fits over the mic head and is the least expensive. The furry windsock (lovingly called a "dead cat") works better and works with stronger wind. The blimp works even better yet. All these devices sell for less than $100. You can even buy tiny "dead cats" to go on a lav mic, but it makes your subject look like her throat is about to be attacked by a miniature porcupine.

If you have the luxury of working with a sound person, boom poles are often used, but most of us seldom have that luxury. All shotgun microphones come with a mount that will connect to the hot shoe on top of your camera, and that is the easiest setup if you are using a shotgun.

Once you have determined which mic you will use, you need to decide which digital audio recording device you plan to use. There are numerous brands of professional recording devices out there, but my students normally use the Zoom brand. They are professional quality, not terribly expensive and reliable. The Zoom H2n is a good recorder, small and easy to toss in your kit bag. It works well and costs about $150. But the better choice for just a bit more money is the Zoom H4n. True professional audio for just over 200 bucks.

The important advantage of using a lav mic attached to a Zoom H4n is it allows you to videotape your subject during the interview from any distance you choose. Nice to have the close headshot that shows the emotion in the eyes of your subject during the interview, but sometimes you might want your subject walking through a field during the interview. A lav mic with a Zoom H4n is perfect for that scene.

Audio has to be clear and clean. And the magic numbers are −12 and −6. A professional audio recorder shows the db levels while you are recording. Your db levels should always bounce between −12 and −6. This means doing a sound check before you begin your interview. Different audio recording devices use different procedures for the sound check. The Zoom H2n does a sound check as soon as it is turned on, but the Zoom H4n does a sound check only when you push the recording button one time. Many people have come back with no audio because they forgot to push the record button the second time to begin actually recording the audio.

When collecting professional-quality audio, just looking at the db levels on your recording device is not good enough. Again, it is possible to record electrostatic buzz that the human ear is unable to detect. And the human brain is trained to filter out distracting noise, something the recording device cannot do. You probably will not hear the hum of the air conditioner or the refrigerator or the bubbling sound of the subject's tropical fish tank filter, but the recording device will pick it up, ruining your interview.

You must listen to your audio input into your recording device with professional-quality headphones. All professional audio recorders have headphone jacks for this purpose. When doing the sound check with your headphones on, if your db levels are dancing between −12 and −6 and your sound is clean and clear, you can then hide the recording device out of the frame; tuck it into your subject's back pocket or clip it on his or her belt.

Remember to collect natural sound, commonly just called nat sound. Nat sound is just the ambient sound of wherever you are. If you are going to conduct the interview in a quiet room, collect five minutes of the ambient sound of that room. If you are conducting an interview on location in the field, collect five minutes of the ambient sound of that location. There is a good chance you will use some B-Roll in your final package (B-Roll is any video other than the interview with your subject) and you may need to lay nat sound under that B-Roll. Or nat sound may just be the right thing to have, even under the interview audio. If you are conducting an interview with a water-quality engineer on location at the water plant, it makes sense to have the sound of moving water at least in some part of your final package.

Okay, that takes care of sound. Now you have to collect usable video.

Because I am a journalist who works alone most of the time and must be able to pack all my gear in one bag that will fit in the overhead bin on a domestic airline, I use video DSLRs. I use the Nikon D800, but that is merely a personal choice. Canon also manufactures a fine line of professional video DSLRs.

To record an interview with a video DSLR, you must have a tripod, or at least some device that will stabilize your camera. The only time you can record an interview with a hand-held camera is if you are being chased through the woods by the Blair Witch. Hand-held, shaky video will not work. At all.

Once you have mic'd your subject and done a sound check, set your camera up on a tripod at eye level with your subject. This is true at all times. If you are interviewing a small child, your camera must be at eye level with that child. If you are interviewing a 7-foot-tall basketball player, well . . . good luck.

You frame your subject using the Rule of Thirds. This means your subject will either be on the left side of the frame or the right. If on the left, your subject should look across the frame to the right at about a 45-degree angle. If on the right, your subject should look to the left. You should leave just a bit of room in the frame from the top of your subject to the top of the frame. Do NOT have the subject look directly into the camera lens. This is called breaking the fourth plane and startles the viewer. Stand just to the side of your camera and remind them to look at you, not the camera.

If you are conducting multiple interviews, remember to alternate your framing, one subject on the left looking to the right, the next subject on the right looking to the left. Never have two subjects in the same frame. It is always distracting and the viewer will spend as much time watching the person who is not talking as watching the person who is.

Remember to be well prepared for the interview. Nothing is more embarrassing than to ask a subject a question that he or she has answered hundreds of times before. Or worse, to ask a question that will offend your subject and end the interview.

If you are lucky enough to interview subjects who have been interviewed numerous times, they know to speak in soundbites. If not, you will have to coach them a bit. Tell them to remember to include your question in their answer; this doesn't mean they should repeat verbatim your question, rather they should somehow include it in their answer. Your voice will be edited out when you produce the multimedia package, so if the answer is a yes or no or a sentence fragment, it will be worthless.

Example:

Q: How long have you lived in this cabin in this tree?
A: Five years.

Which leaves you with audio in your final product that says simply, "Five years." Which makes no sense at to your viewer. What you actually want:

Q: How long have you lived in this cabin in this tree?
A: I have lived in this cabin in this tree for five years.

Do not talk over your subject. It is normal to try to encourage your subject during an interview, but if you must do it, do it with a head nod. If you are constantly mumbling, "Yes. Uh huh. Yep. Yeah, me too," you will have audio that you cannot use. Keep quiet.

Inform your subjects you are going to leave just a bit of a pause between when they finish their answer and your next question. This will make your editing much easier.

Be polite during your interview, but make sure you get material you can use. If your subject begins to slip into giving yes or no answers or sentence fragment answers, remind them—politely—to include your question in their answer.

If a jetliner flies over during your interview, or a police car drives by with its siren on, stop the interview and wait until it is quiet again, apologize to your subject, then re-ask the question. It is your interview. You get usable material. If distracting noise occurs during your interview, politely stop the interview, make small talk with your subject and resume when it gets quiet again.

Remember to keep your subject on track. And also remember you are probably going to use only a few minutes of the interview in your package. There is no sense recording more than about 20 minutes of audio for a three-minute package. And it will make your editing process a nightmare if you have to wade through an hour of audio just to find three minutes of usable soundbites.

It is a good idea to bring a notepad with you to note the timecode on your recorder when your subject says something you know you will use in the final product. This also helps in the editing process.

The most important thing you as the interviewer can do during the interview is to listen. Listen carefully to what your subject says. You may have done all the background research in the world prior to the interview, and you may have prepared a dozen well-thought-out questions based on that research. But if your subjects go off on a much more interesting direction, go with them. Be prepared to wing it. The best interviews sound like a conversation, not a set of rote questions and answers.

Example:

You've been given the assignment to go out to farmer Smith's farm to interview him about the two-headed calf he reported born the day before.

Q: Mr. Smith, what do you think is responsible for your milk cow giving birth to a two-headed calf?

A: Well sonny, I believe it all began when the aliens from Planet Xenon began coming down here a few months ago and started doing experiments on not only my cows, but also on my wife, LuAnn.

Wrong Next Question:

Q: Okay, well, is this the first time your cow has ever given birth to a two-headed calf?

Right Next Question:

Q: Wait, what? Excuse me? Did you just say aliens from Planet Xenon have been doing experiments on your wife? Can you please go into more detail about that?

Always remember to ask your subjects at the end of an interview if there is anything they would like to talk about that you failed to ask. (Except for farmer Smith, not sure I'd go there . . .)

You have collected your stills, your video and your audio. Save your material on an external memory device. Our students use LaCie external storage devices; they are reliable and relatively affordable. These days you can get 500 gigabytes of memory for about $150 and a terabyte for about $200.

We use Final Cut Pro X in our school, but others use Avid or Premier. This is not a chapter on non-linear editing software, but it is easy to sync an audio track with the video track using these software packages. Remember when you are editing your work that the sound level coming out of your computer speakers or headphones is meaningless. The only level that matters is the audio db level meter. You can have your sound speakers turned up to maximum volume and think you have good audio when in fact the audio levels are only at about –20. And your viewers are going to hear that level, the –20, which is unacceptable.

So there it is. Let's sum it up. I get an assignment to do an interview with a subject. I'm on my own, as usual. I grab my backpack (I personally like the Mountainsmith Camera Spectrum Recycled Backpack, about 80 bucks), toss in two Zoom H4n audio recorders (a backup is always a good idea), my Rode shotgun mic with XLR cables and camera hotshoe mount, my two Audio-Technica brand lav mics with XLR cables (again a backup), my Sony earphones, my two Nikon D800s with a 24mm f/2.8 lens and an 85mm f/1.8 lens, a couple of dead cats (I have them in red, blue, black and green), extra batteries for everything, then strap my tripod onto the outside of the pack and I'm ready to go to work.

And now I need to get farmer Smith to explain to me more about those aliens from Planet Xenon.

FIFTEEN

Interviewing by the Numbers

Query the data as well as your source

SCOTT R. MAIER

Journalism does not live by words alone. As Scott Maier
makes clear, understanding numbers and explaining
them to the audience are crucial skills in many interview
scenarios.

The mayor is about to announce his new city budget, but as an enterprising reporter you've scored in advance a summary of the budgetary high-
lights. Scanning the numbers, you quickly see that the mayor seeks a
$4 million spending increase—a headline story for sure. With the mayor's
news conference still an hour away, you enter the budget totals for each
city department into an electronic spreadsheet. Not trusting your math,
you plug the percentage-change formula into the Excel spreadsheet. With
a few clicks, you find that the mayor's so-called Safe Streets, Clean Streets
budget provides only a 3 percent raise for police and 10 percent raise for
sanitation—while spending by the mayor's office nearly doubles! But wait.
The story gets even better. Closer examination of the numbers reveals a
$1.8 million budget gap—unaccounted spending hidden in the mayor's
budget. Armed with the data, you are ready to confront the mayor with

probing questions about his budget priorities and invisible spending of public tax dollars.

Far-fetched? The scenario is indeed fictitious. I use this underhanded budget as a class exercise to introduce journalism students to computer-assisted reporting. But the storyline keeps repeating itself in real life. Just days after completing this in-class exercise, a journalism student could hardly contain his bemusement when he learned that a $450,000 accounting error was largely responsible for a budget deficit crippling the city government he was covering. Another journalism student did the math and discovered that the numbers touted by a local tourism board were totally off. The budget exercise, pioneered by the *Miami Herald*, has led to fiscal exposés by journalists elsewhere.

The moral of this tale is that numbers can lead to better questions, to revealing interviews—and to better stories.

I can practically hear readers respond, I'm a storyteller, not a numbers person. But numbers have become as essential as words for journalists to understand and to explain what is happening in our world. As the late Victor Cohn noted in his authoritative guide, *News & Numbers*, "We journalists like to think we deal mainly in facts and ideas, but much of what we report is based on numbers. Politics comes down to votes. Budgets and dollars dominate government. The economy, business, employment, sports—all demand numbers . . . Like it or not, we must wade in."[1]

Cohn was right: there is no escape. In a study of 500 local news articles, I found that nearly half of the stories involved some sort of mathematical calculation or numerical point of comparison.[2] Moreover, numbers-based stories got the best play, dominating the front page of news, metro and business sections. So let's wade in.

A good reporter will conduct background research before conducting an interview. This often involves collecting biographical and contextual information. In addition, I suggest digging out key numbers to guide your interview. This will help put you, not your source, in control of the interview. Chances are your source already has a favorite figure or two that illustrates the story he or she intends to tell. But you can enliven the discussion by offering numbers that give a fresh, perhaps even contradictory, perspective.

Your first task then is to "interview the data." By that I mean you need to work through the morass of figures in a spreadsheet or annual report to understand how the numbers are used, and then to probe deeper for revealing patterns or puzzling results. A good starting point is to pose a series of "I wonder . . ." questions. For example, if I obtained the latest crime statistics for my college or university, I might ask, "I wonder if campus crime is on the rise? . . . I wonder, do the crime statistics include offenses that occur at off-campus student housing . . . I wonder why so few sexual assaults are reported?" Most revealing may not be what you found but what doesn't seem to add up or to make sense. "Querying data is just like asking someone a question," says MaryJo Webster, a veteran data journalist. "You must decide how to phrase the right question to get the right answer. And each question usually leads to more questions. Just like an interview."[3]

Reporters too often shy away from discussing numbers in an actual interview because they are insecure about their quantitative abilities or they fear numbers are boring. Either way, they are missing out on story-telling opportunities.

Not sure what the numbers mean? Use your ignorance to your advantage. Ask the expert to explain in simple terms (for your readers, of course) what the figures represent. Call for images, similes and real-life examples that give the numbers perspective and context. Still confused? Try the "Columbo approach," made famous by the television detective who played befuddled but got the goods by asking, "Aw shucks, help me understand." As the source patiently goes through the statistics, you get a step-by-step explanation that transforms complexity into bite-sized information easy to digest. This may seem as awkward as asking Lady Gaga to square dance, but consider how commonly reporters are called on to inquire about issues and events outside their expertise. It's part of a reporter's job description.

In fact, the Columbo technique works so well it's a good story-telling device even when you think you know what the numbers mean. By having the source clearly explain a statistical concept, you get the authority to discuss the numbers in illustrative terms showing why, for example, a rare event really isn't unusual. (The answer: the chances of winning the lottery are less than getting struck by lightning, yet someone gets the jackpot. It's just not likely it will be you.) Inviting your source to describe the data also is a good way to double-check your own understanding of the numbers. Better to learn that you are mistaken in an interview than to later have to publish a correction of a misreported number.

With a solid understanding of the numbers, the reporter is in a good position to anchor a story with credible data. But using the numbers correctly is not sufficient. As the adage in computer-assisted reporting goes, "People, not numbers, tell stories." The expert you are interviewing is likely to also be a promising source for finding people that the data represent. A good reporter doesn't end the interview without contacts leading to the real-life stories behind the numbers.

Sometimes reporters go astray because they don't know what to do with the data that the expert provided in the interview. Even if they quote a source correctly, a number may be misconstrued because the context is off the mark. For example, when the press reported my research on news accuracy, some reporters mistakenly said my study involved 400 news stories—when in fact it involved 400 news stories for *each* of 20 newspaper markets. Once the mistake was made, it was repeated time and time again because no one bothered to check the math.

As problematic as misuse of numbers is the unquestioning use of figures. Often numerical errors made by the media—and unquestioningly repeated—are self-evident if reporters and editors simply asked if the figures make sense. For example, no one questioned a newspaper report trumpeting a 200 percent drop in the price of an expensive vaccine, a decline that would have pharmacists *paying customers* to haul away the bargain medicine. Research indicates that such readily apparent math errors are routinely published in the news.[4] The problem isn't so much that reporters can't do the arithmetic (we're talking fifth grade math here) but that they lack the confidence to apply common-sense judgment when working with numbers in the news.[5]

One reason that journalists find numbers so vexing is that the data are open to interpretation. Even a mathematically correct figure can be dramatically misleading. For example, you might consider a career shift if told that the average starting salary for geography students at the University of North Carolina exceeds $100,000—until you learn that the figure is wildly inflated by the mega earnings made by basketball star Michael Jordan (UNC class of '86). So in this case the arithmetic mean (total salaries divided by number of students) is not very representative of what a typical geography major earns; better to use the median (middle value) as a descriptive value.

Just because numbers can be twisted doesn't make them meaningless. In fact, just the opposite: Readers rely on the media to sort through the conflicting, confusing morass of data. In this respect, figuring out how numbers best tell a story is already part of a journalist's repertoire. As Pulitzer-winner Sarah Cohen explains in *Numbers in the Newsroom*, "[S]electing the right number for just the right place in a story depends on the same news judgment you use in selecting just the right quote, anecdote or image. It's our job to put *everything* in a story, not just the words or pictures."[6]

The lesson here is that journalists need to use numbers to expose—not parrot—hyperbole or unsupported claims voiced by sources seeking to spin news coverage. So next time you are assigned a complex story, scope out the numbers before heading out for your interviews. Wielding the data, you will ask better questions, probe what's truly new and important, write with greater authority and precision—and get more stories on the front page.

A journalistic bromide proclaims, "If your mother says she loves you, check it out." Good advice. And be sure to ask, how much and what data supports her claim?

NOTES

1. Victor Cohn, *News & Numbers: A Guide to Reporting Statistical Claims and Controversies in Health and Other Fields* (Ames: Iowa State University Press, 1989), 3–4.

2. Scott R. Maier, "Numbers in the News: A Mathematics Audit of a Daily Newspaper." Journalism Studies 3, no. 4 (2002): 507–519.

3. MaryJo Webster, "Data State of Mind." IRE Journal (Winter 2014), 11.

4. Scott R. Maier, "Accuracy Matters: A Cross-Market Assessment of

Newspaper Error and Credibility." Journalism and Mass Communication Quarterly 82, no. 3 (Autumn 2005): 533–551; Scott R. Maier, "Numbers in the News: A Mathematics Audit of a Daily Newspaper." Journalism Studies 3, no. 4 (2002): 507–519.

5. Patricia Curtin and Scott R. Maier, "Numbers in the Newsroom: A Qualitative Examination of a Quantitative Challenge." Journalism and Mass Communication Quarterly 78, no. 4 (2001): 720–738.

6. Sarah Cohen, *Numbers in the Newsroom: Using Math and Statistics in the News* (Columbia, Mo.: Investigative Reporters and Editors, 2001), ix.

SIXTEEN **Interviewing for Solutions**

With a different set of questions, journalists can produce stories that show what's working

KATHRYN THIER

No news may be good news at times, but news need not be all bad. Kathryn Thier teaches how reporting about problems can—and at times should—focus on solutions.

Telling stories about people trying to solve problems in their communities, nonprofits working to make a difference and government programs aimed at alleviating social ills is nothing new for journalists. What is different is the emergence of solutions journalism, a systematic practice for finding and creating "rigorous reporting on responses to social problems."[1]

Not to be confused with advocacy or "feel-good" features, solutions journalism employs the same standards of traditional "objective" journalism, even as its framing of stories differs. Solutions journalists do not promote solutions or include their opinions; they report on existing responses to social problems with the same detachment as if reporting on the problems alone. Unlike features, which focus on individuals and are often uncritical, solutions journalism stories' main character is the response itself and that response must be structural, rather than ephemeral.

Solutions journalism's proponents argue that journalism's reliance on conflict as a dominant news value should shift toward a more holistic representation of society. We know from research that audiences are depressed by the news and that trust in media has suffered in recent years. That audience disengagement is troubling for democracy on several levels. When audiences tune out, they lose not only the information critical for civic functioning, but also the will to engage in civic action. If the media portray problems as insurmountable, why should people pay attention or attempt to solve them? Solutions journalism's advocates say that providing examples of what's working—as well as what isn't—can counteract those trends.

When journalists highlight only the negative, audiences can be unsure how to respond. If the purpose of journalism is to "provide citizens with the information they need to make the best possible decisions about their lives, their communities, their societies, and their governments," then reporting on what works offers people knowledge about choices.[2] If new law enforcement statistics reveal—and journalists report—that crime is rising in a community, what should residents do with that information? And how should they suggest their elected officials respond? Hire more police officers? Increase funding for after-school programs aimed at at-risk youth? Without knowing what similar communities facing similar problems found (or did not find) effective, your news audience may lack the information it needs to engage as civic actors.

Creating the type of journalism that provides citizens knowledge of what is possible starts with a reporter asking different questions: first, of herself and then, of others.

INTERVIEWING TO FRAME AND FIND SOLUTIONS STORIES

The first step in reporting a solutions journalism story is to flip the frame 180 degrees. Pulitzer Prize–winner Tina Rosenberg, who co-founded the nonprofit Solutions Journalism Network, often shares the story behind her first solutions-oriented piece. She was working at the New York Times

Magazine in 2000 and proposed a story about how pharmaceutical companies (and U.S. officials) pressured governments in developing countries not to make or distribute generic drugs. As a result, many people died from lack of access to life-saving medication available in wealthier nations. Her editor said the topic was "familiar" and "too depressing."[3] So she wrote instead a cover story about how Brazil was making generic drugs and supplying them for free to its citizens, putting pressure on other countries to do the same and pharmaceutical companies to drop their opposition. What it took to create, in Rosenberg's words, this "stronger and more effective and impactful story"[4] (besides a "no go" from an editor) was reframing her initial question about what was newsworthy. In this case, selecting uniqueness as the dominant news value was the key.

To find solutions stories journalists need to ask themselves: *Is a solutions-oriented angle the story?* When a national crime report is released, instead of devoting ink to the "Top 5 Most Dangerous Cities in America" journalists should write about the five on the bottom of the list or the five where crimes rates fell the most compared to last year—and explain how they got that way. At its heart, the best solutions journalism is explanatory reporting.

We'll come back to data in a minute, but first, a bit about how journalists can find these solutions stories when no news peg is immediately apparent. As beat journalists work their beats, SJN suggests asking sources, *Who's doing it better?* when it comes to issues of community concern. Local officials, nonprofit leaders or people engaged in reform usually know how to fix a problem even if they lack the resources to do so. Sometimes the solution will exist in a journalist's own coverage area; other times journalists may need to report on similar communities tackling the same issues. Sometimes they can do both. For example, the *Minneapolis Star-Tribune* partnered with the Solutions Journalism Network on a series called Muslims and De-Radicalization: What Works? Stories included efforts by Minnesotan Somalis and police to keep local youth from radicalizing, as well as other attempts by communities with Muslim immigrants in Maryland and Europe.

Another question journalists should ask themselves before beginning a solutions story, according to SJN: *Which slice of an issue does my community really care about?* Solutions are almost always incomplete but instead make progress against the social ill for some groups and not others. For instance, homelessness comes in different forms—chronic and short-term—and affects many subgroups, including veterans, families, youth, the mentally ill and people experiencing drug and alcohol addiction. Responses to homelessness will vary by community and demographics. Utah reduced chronic homelessness about 90 percent using the Housing First model, which provides housing for the chronically homeless and then help with underlying issues, rather than requiring homeless people to prove sobriety or enter counseling before receiving shelter. As part of its coverage about chronic homelessness in the Bay Area, the *San Francisco Chronicle* wrote about Utah's success as a possible response. By contrast, reporters in a community with more short-term homelessness should seek to cover approaches that help people who experience homelessness for shorter periods.

Looking at a "slice" can also overlap with searching for positive outliers in data. As mentioned above, reporters should ask different questions of data, such as *Who are the best performers—and why?* Below are questions SJN suggests reporters ask to frame and find a solutions story by examining data from a different lens.

Data Slice	Example
Comparison to peers	Which city has the lowest rates of homicide?
Change over time	Who has improved voting records the most in the last decade?
By method/ best practice	Which VA hospital has the shortest wait time?
By subgroup	Who's done best to reduce obesity among Hispanics?
By cost	Who has reduced dental costs the most?
By coverage	Who's doing well at getting low-income patients into preventive care?
By disparity	Who has most reduced the gap between African-American and Caucasian high school graduation rates?
By policy	Which state/city policies are most successful in preventing teen smoking?

Compiled by the Solutions Journalism Network.

Journalists can easily see how the examples above are a 180-degree turn on their typical take on data reporting.

An interview technique I suggest journalists use to suss out solutions stories is appreciative inquiry. Appreciative inquiry flips the interview frame from a transaction to a relationship by asking interviewees, broadly speaking, *What is possible now?* (For a fuller explanation of appreciative inquiry, its relationship to journalistic interviewing and its connection to solutions journalism, see the chapter on appreciative inquiry interviewing by Mike Fancher in this book.) In my solutions journalism classes at the University of Oregon's School of Journalism and Communication, I invite community members engaged in addressing social problems in our city, county and state to an "appreciative inquiry summit." Students ask our guests to tell a story about coming to believe in the power of their community and to describe how they won an imaginary award for work with that community. (These questions were adapted from thinking about appreciative inquiry by Peggy Holman of the nonprofit Journalism That Matters.) By asking community members themselves to define the story from an asset-based approach, the student journalists uncover story ideas they and their subjects had not considered. Community members often say that they appreciate the different interview approach and that it causes them to think differently about their own work. Student journalists find the process pushes them to interview for depth and narrative, rather than race to get factual questions confirmed.

Lastly, reporters should remember that solutions stories are framed thematically, not episodically. SJN has identified and delineated a list of seven "impostors," types of stories often mistaken for solutions journalism that are really advocacy or poor journalism. These include stories that lionize an individual for selfless service, "silver bullets" that claim to solve problems or overstate the effectiveness of a response, PR disguised as journalism that promotes a company's altruism, opinions of think tanks, underexplored solutions tacked on as an afterthought to investigative work, a list of nonprofits addressing a problem and a call out for the reader to donate, and fluffy, one-off features.

Before beginning to report a possible solutions story, ask yourself: *Is the solution actually happening or is it theoretical? Is it about a person doing good deeds or about how a program addresses an issue? Is the response aimed at help-ing one/a few individuals, or does it address a systemic problem? Are my sources only the people who created the response or are handpicked by the organization? Do I plan to include people actually affected and critical voices?* (These last two are questions journalists routinely ask themselves, no matter the type of story.)

INTERVIEWING TO REPORT SOLUTIONS STORIES

As defined by SJN, solutions journalism stories have four essential hall-marks or "qualities": (1) the response and how it works, (2) evidence of a solution's efficacy, (3) insight about how the solution differs from others and might be replicated and (4) limitations. Reporting for each of those qualities requires asking specialized questions.

Response   Breaking news or problem-oriented reporting prioritizes the Five Ws (who, what, where, when and why), often relegating the H (how) to an afterthought. In solutions journalism, the H is the star. In fact, SJN calls the story structure of the most rigorous and thorough solutions jour-nalism the "howdunit." Like a police procedural drama, in a howdunit "You show characters doing the work—trying, failing, trying again—to tell the story of how the project achieved something others could not. You hold the reader's interest by generating curiosity about how the ideas are going to fare."[5] A howdunit structure shows the chronology of characters moving from problem to solution to build narrative tension. Reporters should interview for turning points in sources' lives, asking questions such as, *When did you notice a change in X? When did you start to feel differently about Y?*

In solutions journalism reporting the "how" questions needs to be more "granular" and seeks "infinitesimal detail" reporters usually avoid, said Claudia Rowe, a former *Seattle Times* Education Lab reporter. She explained: "And then how did you do that? Exactly how? Where were you? Did you pick up the phone? Did you knock on the door? Exactly how did you get this kid?"[6]

When you ask those questions, sources "tell you things you didn't even know that you wanted to know," she said.

The reporter ends up with anecdotes that turn into narrative scenes as well as new lines of questioning. Another difference, said former Education Lab reporter and editor Linda Shaw, is that solutions interviewing requires spending more time asking about "process and history" than other types of stories.

Even when writing a less explanatory solutions journalism story with a more traditional news feature structure, reporters still need to ask their sources to be explicit about how the solution functions for the story to provide useful information to readers.

Evidence   All solutions stories must include evidence, but it may be quantitative, qualitative or both, depending on the story. The longer a solution has been around, the more likely quantitative evidence exists. Also, data are more available for solutions involving government agencies or well-funded nonprofits. Yet reporters must still ask questions about the numbers to make sure positive outliers represent a statistically meaningful trend. For earlier-stage solutions or stories about under-resourced groups that may lack data, reporters should ask questions that build their own data, such as, *How many people did your group provide with a free meal last year?*

Stories with little data require the reporter to search for qualitative evidence, but even stories with striking numbers benefit from reporters asking people affected by a response about their experiences. When interviewing for qualitative evidence, reporters should ask questions that showcase how the response changed participants. In this way, the qualities of response and evidence may overlap.

Insight   In my mind, this solutions journalism quality is the most critical. Insight is what elevates solutions journalism above uncritical journalism and distinguishes it from feature writing. For example, a story about a food pantry in your community might make a good feature about residents helping other residents. But absent a related event as a news peg it is not newsworthy in itself, except to reflect the community's humanity.

For a story about a food pantry to become solutions journalism, the food pantry must engage in a systemic attack on food insecurity in an unusual way. Perhaps the food pantry partners with a group that gleans produce from farms, restaurants and supermarkets to subsidize its food offerings and ensures that its clients have access to fresh, vitamin-rich food. In this way, the food pantry is also decreasing food waste, lowering its own costs or fundraising needs for donated canned food and improving the diets of people at risk of not just hunger, but also diseases associated with poor nutrition. The insight here is that nonprofits working together to close the loop on several problems creates better outcomes for those affected and is more sustainable for the responders.

Seasoned reporters will recognize this example as the answer to the proverbial "So what?" asked by editors. Yet finding the insight in a solution is often elusive for student journalists who are less familiar with justifying why a story needs to run now. Asking questions that yield insight is often about getting at the uniqueness news value. Even after reporting is underway, journalists should continue to ask sources what they think is the big picture reason the solution works. I think of insight as the linchpin of a response and suggest asking, *If someone were to try this solution under different circumstances, what is the one thing they should do to make sure the response works?* Another key is interviewing expert sources such as academics who study a problem, even those outside your coverage area. They can provide context about how the solution compares to other efforts and best practices for driving progress on that issue.

Limitations   Including limitations in a solutions story is essential to ensure you end up with quality journalism and not one-source stories or a puff piece. To get at limitations, ask sources who the solution leaves out. If a high school improved its graduation rate, did it improve equally for all student demographics? Don't ask sources to state the solution's limitations, because that can put them on the defensive. Instead, ask questions, such as *What would you do to take the solution further?* or *What do you see as areas for improvement?* As in other types of stories, people may be reluctant to say what isn't working, especially if it involves their job. So, search for critical voices. And be wary of answers about funding. Nearly every organization involved in a solution, whether it is a nonprofit or government agency, is under-resourced. Your story can mention how more funding would help if you explain precisely the difference it would make, alleviating limitations you describe. But don't settle for lack of money as your story's only limitation. Providing concrete examples of sticking points in the response process or people left out of the progress is more useful to audiences than gripes about funding. It also makes your story more nuanced.

By asking themselves and their sources different questions, journalists have the opportunity to create stories that attract wary audiences and provide information typically absent in consumers' news diets. Already, major news organizations, such as the BBC World Service and the *Guardian* have added solutions verticals, partially to address market research findings showing 64 percent of audiences under age 35 seek solutions in their news.[7] Smaller outlets are also finding success with a solutions approach. The *Chattanooga Times Free Press* solutions series The Poverty Puzzle was a finalist for the 2017 Pulitzer Prize in Explanatory Reporting. In many ways, solutions journalism helps journalists continue to do what they do best. Create compelling stories. Hold institutions accountable. Provide useful information. But by asking different questions, journalists (can) hold up a mirror to the world that reflects a much fuller picture.

NOTES

1. Solutions Journalism Network. (2019). Retrieved from: https://www.solutionsjournalism.org/who-we-are/mission.

2. American Press Institute. (2019). Retrieved from https://www.americanpressinstitute.org/journalism-essentials/what-is-journalism/purpose-journalism/.

3. One.org. (2015, April 22). The power of solutions journalism: a conversation with investigative reporter Tina Rosenberg. Retrieved from https://www.one.org/us/blog/the-power-of-solutions-journalism-a-conversation-with-investigative-reporter-tina-rosenberg/.

4. Ibid.

5. Solutions Journalism Network. J-School Curriculum Builder training materials on https://www.solutionsjournalism.org. Page is no longer available.

6. Solutions Journalism Network. (2014, October 7). SJN's Education Lab: On interviewing. Retrieved from: https://www.youtube.com/watch?v= mT13Rxiu1_I&t=30s.

7. BBC World Service. (2015). 5 key research findings about young online audiences from BBC World Service. BBC World Service. Retrieved from https://www.journalism.co.uk/news/five-key-research-findings -about-young-online-audiences-from-bbc-world-service/s2/a588021/.

SEVENTEEN **The Give and Take of Public Relations Interviewing**

Practitioners need to understand the hows and whys of the practice from both sides

DEAN MUNDY

Interviews are conducted for one reason or another by most professionals—from cops to docs. Dean Mundy shows how interviewing is adapted to the specific needs of the public relations practitioner.

I hate the phrase "I'm a people person." I tell my public relations students to never say that they major in public relations because "I'm a people person." It diminishes what public relations does, and it implies that to be successful, practitioners primarily must be adept at working a room, flitting from person to person, while engaging in delightful, witty conversation. Certainly "talking" is an important part of a practitioner's job, but "talking" first requires a heck of a lot of researching, goal- and objective-setting and strategic planning. What we say needs to have purpose.

The same is true for conducting and giving interviews, and interviews have several important purposes in public relations. On one hand, public relations practitioners must learn to conduct interviews at several points throughout the planning process—from environmental scanning to measuring success. On the other hand, public relations has the unique professional mandate to train executives and spokespersons how to *give* quality media interviews. Combined, practitioners must understand both sides of the same coin. This chapter explores both aspects as well as the corresponding challenges practitioners face along the way.

CONDUCTING INTERVIEWS IN PUBLIC RELATIONS

Research is central to everything practitioners do. A public relations program is only as good as the research that drives it, and interviewing is an important piece of that work. Interview subjects fall into categories of "publics," meaning defined groups of people who can affect, or who are affected by, an organization's operations. Publics are both internal and external; they could be employees, clients, business partners, customers, local community members, governments, etc. Each organization-public relationship is unique, and organizations must be in-tune with their various publics' expectations, reactions and needs. Doing so requires, of course, talking to them.

There are three points at which practitioners conduct interviews to learn from their publics: (1) during ongoing informal outreach, called "environmental scanning"; (2) during the first step of developing a public relations program and (3) at the end of a public relations campaign when measuring outcomes.

Environmental scanning is arguably a practitioner's most important (and perhaps most complex) task. It means taking a look at your operational environment—your own organization, the communities where you work and the industry itself—to see what people are saying, where they are saying it and to what effect. On the surface it might seem simple enough; it certainly seems like a smart thing to do. But keeping a pulse on the discourse related to your organization and industry requires a planned, thoughtful, multi-pronged strategy. And while practitioners employ a variety of ways to scan their environment—social media, news media, discussion boards, etc.—one of the best ways is through an informal interview, or more specifically an "intercept interview." In these cases a practitioner "intercepts," or casually asks people for a few minutes to discuss their perceptions of a certain brand or issue.

Intercepting can be tricky, though. You do not want to be too aggressive, and you do not want to take up too much time. We all have had the experience of trying to avoid eye contact with that person 10 feet away, directly in our path, smiling, wearing a name tag and carrying a clipboard. In my experience, though, there are three best practices worth considering:

1. *Tabling*: Let people come to you: rather than standing at a corner with a clipboard, have a tabling event where you create a welcoming, fun space with informational takeaway material, product samples and a space for conversation.

2. *Giveaways*: Everyone likes something free: I once observed a great example of this tactic. In the days following the Chipotle *E. coli* crisis, the company took a variety of measures to begin restoring its image, such as closing all chains for a day nationally for training and communicating "next steps" via the company's social media platforms. Chipotle also employed a kind of intercept technique. Standing in line one day (waiting for my burrito), I observed someone going to various tables, handing out coupons for free menu items. It allowed her to then start a conversation with the people at the table. What do they like about the restaurant? What are their concerns? Do they follow on social media? What was most telling was that the Chipotle representative was not targeting everyone (certainly not me). She was interested in college-age input. After all, students love free food, and they are a key target public for Chipotle.

3. *Community partnering*: Go where your targeted public goes: If you know who your public is, you know the places your public goes. When possible, partner with those organizations to talk to your publics. If one of their trusted organizations trusts you, then you gain instant credibility. I once had a team of

students in my campaigns class who wanted to get a pulse on the local retired community. They partnered with the local library to conduct intercept surveys, which included a question to identify people possibly interested in a follow-up interview. The team hoped for 50 survey responses and a handful of follow-up interviews. Instead, the group received just under 400 survey responses and close to 50 retirees interested in an interview.

Intercepting requires a lot of thought and planning. Just because we have something to discuss does not mean that everyone has the time or interest to engage. As I tell my students, "Always remember that we're way more passionate about our organizations and pet issues than anyone else, so we have to plan our outreach to meet them where they are, not where we're coming from." Yet, we see certain "crash and burns" all too often.

1. *Taking over the intersection*: One of the first rules in public relations is to not assume, or tell, people how they should feel. I deduct five points, for example, from students who use exclamation points in news releases, because it implies to journalists that they should be excited—that this is the best news they will have ever read. So in terms of intercept interviews, one person with a clipboard is fine. Four people, one positioned on each corner of an intersection, can be aggressive. It suggests that what they have to discuss is way too important for us to avoid, and by God you are going to at least consider talking to them.

2. *Shouting repeatedly:* While one person with a clipboard can be a good idea, shouting repeatedly about holding one has risks. First, it can be aggressive and turn people away. Second, it gives the rest of us time to consider the topic, decide we don't want to participate and craft our rejection.

3. *Bad messaging:* It is imperative that you test your messaging before putting it into the field. If you are conducting a tra-

ditional intercept, you have only a moment to get someone's interest. And even if you have followed all of the advice above, a bad message will quickly turn away your targeted public. For example, I once worked on a team developing an awareness campaign for an infant health issue. We realized that our targeted public should be young mothers, and in developing our message hook—how we were going to gain interest from passersby—someone suggested "Do you have a minute to save a baby?" Imagine if that phrase had made it out the door, with everyone running from us thinking we were an aggressive pro-life, anti-abortion organization.

The second instance when public relations practitioners conduct interviews is during the first step of developing a PR program—the research stage, which is followed by the planning, communication and evaluation stages. During this stage, after the primary and secondary targeted publics are identified, in-depth interviews offer practitioners ways to do a deep dive and really identify specific challenges and opportunities

I once worked for a technology company that was trying to recover from executive financial fraud, layoffs and a tumbling stock price. In developing a PR plan, we identified two key publics where we needed to improve relationships: news media (external) and employees (internal). Accordingly, as part of this step, we reached out to journalists and employees to conduct interviews and gauge what both publics sought in order to improve relationships. Journalists expressed the need for more access to executives and transparency. They emphasized that the time was apt because of our new leadership team. Employees told us that while their morale was low, they loved the company; they still had a passion for the brand. Both takeaways provided important data for us to take to our leadership and craft a plan—findings that would not have been evident through quantitative marketing data.

The third main instance when practitioners conduct interviews is during the final (evaluation) stage in the public relations process. At this stage, we measure three things: inputs, outputs and outcomes. Inputs are essentially the resources used (time and money spent) to conduct a campaign. Outputs are what was produced as a result of that investment (number of news releases, social media posts, tabling events, etc.).

The most important measures, though, are the outcomes, which is where the importance of the interview falls. Outcomes tell us what we accomplished as a result of the inputs and outputs, and there are multiple layers of inquiry. The first layer tells us the quantifiable outcomes: the number of likes or shares on social media, the number of resulting news articles, the number of attendees at an event or the number of increased visits to a website.

The second, more valuable, layer of outcomes tells us if we were able to get people to take a certain action or influence their behavior, which is the ultimate goal for a successful PR program. We may have spent a lot of time and money. We may have produced tons of news releases, and social media posts, and events. We may have placed lots of news articles, received a lot of likes and shares and attracted hundreds of guests. But at the end of the day, what did all of that accomplish? Beyond raising money at an event, none of those measures tells you if you were truly successful. What you need to determine, for example, is if your targeted publics saw a news article and did something as a result, or they liked a social media post and then volunteered for your cause.

Interviews, therefore, are quite valuable at this step. They allow you to talk to key targets to gauge their behavior regarding an organization or issue and whether your campaign has influenced that behavior in the way you had hoped. Take the legendary ALS Ice Bucket challenge. The goal was to raise money for and awareness regarding the disease. Determining success for the former certainly is much easier than determining success for the latter. To see if the public is more familiar with ALS after the campaign, though, an interview is ideal, and perhaps the only way to really gauge if the educational element worked.

Certainly interviews by public relations professionals can occur at a variety of other points in public relations work, but the three primary instances are during the environmental scanning process, the first stage of the PR planning process, and perhaps one of the last things during the final, evaluation stage of the PR process.

But for public relations, there's more to the story. Public relations professionals have a dual task of training for interviews with journalists. The next section therefore walks through that mandate and the corresponding rules of "what makes a good interview."

GIVING INTERVIEWS IN PUBLIC RELATIONS

When you work in media relations, as I once did, one of the key practitioner responsibilities is to train your organization's spokespeople—often the executives. And media training can be difficult. It is your responsibility to teach them the core messages to convey, as well as the ways to "stay on message" throughout an interview. In this case, the goal of "staying on message" is not promotional. The goal is pragmatic; it keeps the spokesperson "in bounds."

What do I mean? When you work for a company—particularly a publicly traded company—there are certain things you cannot disclose for legal and competitive reasons. Most often, these discussions relate to finances. If your spokesperson makes a false or presumptive statement, it could suggest that the company is more valuable than it really is, thus inflating the stock price and breaking all sorts of federal laws. Another time this could happen is when an executive breaks confidentiality and discusses a product in development. It would seem like common sense to never disclose something that would hurt a company's competitiveness. Executives get excited, though, and in wanting a good interview can speak too quickly.

Spokespersons must stay on message, therefore, to avoid risking saying too much that might get the organization in hot water or hurt its competitiveness. To that end, there are several rules of thumb that can help spokespersons stay "in bounds" when interviewing with the news media.

It's on the record: The first rule of thumb for public relations practitioners when conducting interviews with journalists is that there is no such thing as "off the record." Yes, there is an unspoken rule regarding journalists keeping "off the record" information confidential, but it is best to keep the interview straightforward and on topic. If the spokesperson wants to say something that should be "off the record," it raises a red flag that the content is not appropriate for the interview itself. Moreover, too much "off the record" information might create suspicion. You do not want the journalist to start thinking, "Hmmm, I wonder what else they're not telling me."

Pardon the interruption: The PR practitioner has what can be an awkward responsibility if the interview is being conducted via a media call. Typically done the day a company releases its quarterly or annual financial earnings reports, a media call involves the appropriate spokesperson(s), the invited media outlets, financial analysts who give the company its financial rating and the PR practitioner. The goal for practitioners is to never say a thing; after introducing the speaker they should fade into the background. That said, it is imperative that the practitioners listen actively, because it is their job to redirect—or even shut down—a comment by the spokesperson that has legal or competitive implications. Again, the importance of staying on message is not to circumvent the interview or spin a response. It protects the company from potential legal and competitive pitfalls.

Become a shadow: During on-site media events, executives often will engage one-on-one with journalists. At these times—similar to a practitioner's role during a media call—practitioners are charged with "shadowing" the executive. Part of this role is to serve as matchmaker, introduce your spokesperson to key journalists and provide any history or context for the conversation. The other part of this role, of course, is to keep your spokesperson in bounds. More than one executive has gotten in trouble by having one glass of wine too many and then talking too freely without the benefit of someone shadowing.

But what are you getting at, really? When I help students prepare for job interviews, I always remember one of media training's key tenets—the fundamental importance of focusing on the premise of the question. It is imperative to consider what they are really asking and why they are asking it. For students, it helps get them get through a tough question they didn't anticipate. For spokespersons, it helps them stay on message and still provide valuable insight. That said, spokespersons also must know that it is OK in many cases not to answer a question; the premise of the question might reinforce that the question is not relevant or even fair. A key part of media training, then, teaches spokespersons that just because a reporter asks, you don't have to answer.

Know when to stop: This final rule of thumb is perhaps one of the most difficult, and it relates to everything we have discussed. A good interview depends on the value of concision. The best corporate spokespersons are experts at answering reporters' questions in the fewest, but most-pinpoint-focused, words. On one hand, it ensures that you are getting directly to the core message. On the other hand, it puts the onus on the journalist to craft really good questions that get to what they need to know. For example, in discussing layoffs with a journalist, I once was asked, "Does this have to do with the company's announced restructuring plans?" I responded with something along the lines of "We're looking at different possibilities at two sites regarding how to maximize efficiencies in lieu of both the restructuring and layoffs." My manager later advised that my response should have simply been, "Yes." She reminded me that the question itself was a yes/no question, and it was up to the journalist to drill further if he wanted.

PREPARING FOR THE UNKNOWN AND UNEXPECTED

Of course, giving and conducting interviews in the daily life of the PR practitioner can sometimes prove challenging. First, practitioners must respond quickly to unforeseen events or queries. Particularly when working with news media, practitioners must be prepared to either give an interview, or arrange an interview, at a moment's notice. Similarly, part of our environmental scanning role requires that we identify potential and emerging issues that require immediate attention. For example, in scanning its operational environment, a soft drink company would be interested to learn that a major city is considering a ban on soft drinks.

In researching the potential issue, the company would want to talk to city officials, perhaps even the mayor. Securing those meetings might prove difficult, but time is of the essence.

These challenges—being ready in an instant to either give or conduct an effective interview—require three things: (1) ongoing media training, (2) constant, consistent messaging, and (3) having a seat at management's table. Ongoing media training provides a sense of confidence that you and your executives are well versed in giving an effective interview. Constant, consistent messaging helps establish an organization's voice— a common thread across otherwise disparate issues or topics. All of this planning might prove a moot point, though, if the public relations function does not have a seat at management's table. It is imperative that practitioners have a relationship with the "C suite" (i.e., CEOs, CFOs, CIOs, CCOs). Certainly it helps with media training. More important, because our environmental scanning responsibility means we have a good sense of an organization's complete operational context, we need to be able to provide valuable counsel to upper management. In the case of the soft drink company mentioned above, not only must we bring the emerging issue to their attention, we also must help them discern the pros and cons of taking a certain position. Doing so not only shapes the public relations program broadly, it also determines how to respond to anticipated media inquiries.

TURNING A PAGE

One of the historical figures who looms large in public relations is Arthur W. Page, the first public relations person to serve as a corporate executive (vice president of AT&T, 1927–1947). He is well known for his seven Page Principles, which he used to guide AT&T's own public relations program. Two of those principles play an important role in guiding effective interviews. The fourth principle, "Conduct public relations as if the whole enterprise depends on it," reminds us that public relations' role is unique in that we must see things holistically, we must understand (and then convey) the bigger picture. His seventh principle, "Remain calm, patient, and good humored," is particularly instructive. The last thing a good spokes-person wants to do is become reactive or even hostile during an interview, because those reactions suddenly become the story (and rightly so), and the opportunity to get your message across has just flown out the window. With good, thoughtful planning, interviews can play a vital role in a pub-lic relations program by helping us learn from, and then engage with, our key publics. Learning how to conduct and give quality interviews takes a lot of practice, and sometimes it can be challenging to convince your spokespersons of ongoing media training's importance. When done well, though, interviews can greatly benefit the public relations function and the organization that function serves.

EIGHTEEN # Interviews with Avatars

*Navigating the nuances of communicating
in virtual worlds*

DONNA Z. DAVIS

What's the difference between interviewing a person
and interviewing a persona? Ongoing research by
Donna Davis delves into that question through the
virtual world with lessons that can be adapted to the
so-called real world.

What exactly *is* an avatar and why would you want to interview one?
Although popularized in 2009 in James Cameron's film *Avatar*, the term
was first used in reference to an on-screen or digital representation of
oneself in 1985 by Chip Morningstar, creator of Lucasfilm's *Habitat*, a
multi-user dungeon (MUD), the forerunner of what are now called mas-
sively multiplayer online role playing games (MMORPG). Avatars may be
photorealistic versions of their human operator or can take on any form,
like the blue, cat-like, human-like creatures that resided in Cameron's
Pandora or perhaps a blood elf, night elf, orc or troll in World of Warcraft.
Regardless of your notions of these spaces as fantasy or reality, they have
become increasingly popular and are now featured in thousands of professional news sources and across social media not only for players or
gamers but for interested consumers and curious observers as well.

Virtual worlds, the lands of avatars, have been growing in significance in recent decades as online games such as SIMS and World of Warcraft and social virtual environments such as Second Life have drawn millions of users worldwide. In 2013 these environments represented $15.4 billion in sales worldwide, according to the Entertainment Software Association, and an estimated 59 percent of Americans play video games. Today many of these environments are used for education, work, entertainment and artistic expression. These "games" are essentially places where many people work, play, socialize and learn via their avatar. They have also drawn the attention of researchers who increasingly explore virtual environments as communities and cultures that have meaning beyond a game.

Preparing for interviews with avatars requires insight into the virtual platform in which you will be interviewing. First, it's important to spend time in the virtual environment to feel somewhat "native" in the space. As is the case in the physical world, to achieve optimal results in the interview context, the interviewee must feel comfortable with the interviewer. Having worked with avatars in the virtual world Second Life for nearly seven years, I have frequently heard individuals complain about people or researchers who come into the virtual world looking for a story with no understanding of the culture or the technology. In these cases, the interviewer is likely to meet resistance from potential candidates. Virtual world enthnographers Tom Boellstorff, Bonnie Nardi, Celia Pearce and T.L. Taylor, who have collectively spent decades across several virtual platforms—Second Life, the game Uru, EverQuest and World of Warcraft—explain that developing trust and rapport "forms the basis for frank, open conversations." As "participant observers" in the virtual cultures they study, they are considered a part of the culture and as such they are able to establish a comfortable connection with their interviewees before they begin. They understand the nuances of the digital environment and are respected as part of the culture. Without that sense of belonging, you would likely be met with resistance.

Next, the interviewer must determine whether the story or research is specific to the virtual world and avatar or if the story will also require a face-to-face interview in the physical world. Consider, for example, what Taylor referred to as "issues of plural existence and anonymity/disclosure."[1] She asks, "At what level is it necessary or desirable to actually prove in some fashion the offline identity/body of a given participant?" Is the story about the avatar, about the human, or both? And do you need to speak to the human as well to complete the story and if so, why? When a story calls for an understanding of activity or behavior exclusive to the virtual world, real life identities may not be relevant.

For example, real life identities are important to the credibility of Blog-TalkRadio. Following the science versus creationism debate in Kentucky in February 2014, BlogTalkRadio's Virtually Speaking Science program featured an interview with Alan Boyle of NBC News, award-winning filmmaker Antony Thomas of HBO's *Questioning Darwin* and Josh Rosenau from the National Center for Science Education. The program was simulcast on Internet radio as well as in a virtual auditorium in Second Life with an audience of avatars. These programs are broadcast monthly to "explore the often-volatile landscape of science, politics and policy, the history and economics of science, science deniers and its relationship to democracy, and the role of women in the sciences."[2] And, while these programs offer "blended realities," the audience is aware of the real life identities of the hosts and guests, yet the guests often make playful choices of how they represent themselves digitally.

Virtually Speaking co-host, science journalist and author of *Me, Myself, and Why* Jennifer Ouellette recently explained that the interviews they host in Second Life allow their guests to choose and style their avatar for the virtual world interview. She explained, "I love interviewing scientists in a virtual world because I love seeing what they pick as their avatar." She continued, "We have our avatars meet in Second Life and—and we talk for an hour." She cited a particular interview with Janna Levin, a professor of physics and astronomy at Barnard College of Columbia University, who "chose a unicorn with bunny ears" for her avatar. This is just one example of the whimsical choices some of the scientists featured on Virtually Speaking Science make as their digital representation in the virtual world.[3]

Similarly, popular blogger Wagner James Au, who writes New World Notes (http://nwn.blogs.com/), frequently reports on trends and activities in a variety of virtual worlds. His blog posts regularly feature interviews done exclusively in the virtual environment that may or may not reveal real-life identities. In many cases, these stories represent the virtual lives and business activities of the individuals who choose not to share their physical world identities. In these situations, if real-life identity will be revealed, individuals often will not participate in interviews. As is often the case in Au's interviews, the story is simply about the avatars and their activity or behavior, not the human operator.

It is also interesting to note that research has shown that people are more willing to open up about themselves when interviewed as an avatar, often because they feel their real-life identities are truly protected and as a result there is the belief that there cannot be any negative consequence.[4] Still, if the story demands an understanding of what happens on the physical world side of the screen, a second interview would be required.

For the interviewer who is new to the virtual world, accepting the identity of the avatar may also be challenging. In a study of effects of avatar appearance on the interviewer conducting virtual employment interviews, researchers found that more attractive avatars had the highest ratings among interviewers, perpetuating the role of stereotype influences, even when computer mediated.[5] If this is so for gender, weight, age and ideals of beauty of men and women, how might a unicorn with bunny ears influence interviewer bias?

In addition to being prepared to accept the appearance of an avatar when conducting interviews in virtual worlds, it is also necessary to understand operational variables specific to the digital environment. These may include an understanding of how time is measured in the world. For instance, in Second Life, days are broken into six-hour increments with the sunrise and sunset cycles each lasting one hour and midday lasting four hours. This accelerated schedule appears to affect the experience of the "residents," as they're called, as well, as they establish relationships more quickly, grow tired of stagnant environments more quickly, etc. The amount of time spent in-world on a regular basis, how long they've been in the game or in the virtual world, how much real money they spend, how many friends they have or groups they belong to, what their primary motivations are for being in the world—such as play, design, business, work or social interaction—will all be important considerations for best understanding the avatars, their experiences and their relationship with the environment.

Other features unique to virtual environments that may influence an interview process are mode of transporting or "teleporting" to locations, what type of location you will meet in, whether you will use text or voice communication, and being cognizant of offline activity that may be occurring during an online interview. For instance, you will not be able to see what the human operator is actually doing while speaking with you in the virtual world. The person may be experiencing interruptions, making dinner, carrying on multiple simultaneous conversations, or any number of possibilities.

When considering the environment for the interview, the interviewer must determine an appropriate location. Several years ago I interviewed avatars to learn about their online relationships. Because these interviews were for research and mandated a secure and private location to ensure protection of the data collected, I created a home environment with a cozy living room with seating in front of a fireplace in a log cabin on a snow-covered mountain. The participants often said they felt "at home" and comfortable in the space, giving them a level of comfort in sharing their information. Still, at their request, two participants were interviewed in their private homes because they felt more safe there.

Likewise, in most virtual worlds, it is possible to secure private space where the interviewer can control who is allowed to be in the area as well as how data are collected. For example, when sharing a text conversation in a public chat box, it is possible for others to read that text if they are in the same vicinity. With proper security settings you can block others from entering the chat range, making local chat secure and private. To further ensure privacy, however, it is recommended to use the "private chat" feature available in the virtual environment. These can be seen, read and accessed only by those in the private chat. The same privacy settings are available when using voice technology in a secure location.

It is important to determine whether an interview will be conducted in voice or text before beginning the interview. One of the most unexpected findings of my study of avatars was their preference for text over voice communication. As I've already discussed, for many individuals, their avatar experience is deeply private and personal and anonymity is paramount. In this case, even voice recognition may be considered a breach of privacy as people can be identified by their voices. In one case, one of my interviewees told me that he never used the voice feature in the virtual world because he had a Southern accent for which he had always been teased. He did not want people to judge him for his voice and chose to communicate only in text. In this regard, he felt he could represent himself as his idealized self, without the judgment he'd always suffered. Similarly, there is a relatively large community of hearing-impaired in the virtual world. For these individuals, text communication is natural, and those with whom they interact may never know that they cannot hear. While seen as "disabled" in the physical world, in this space there is no perceived disability.

Another interesting feature of writing in text is what many of my interviewees suggested was a sense of thoughtfulness about what they "said" when they had to type it out. For example, Avatar LL (name changed to protect identity) explained:

> There is always the possibility of deception through writing. But there is also a veil that is lifted . . . a certain type of inhibition we have when we speak face to face is lifted. Sometimes when we write, we say more what we would not say, because we are at a loss for words in real time.

A separate participant agreed when she wrote, "I think [writing in text] facilitates communication . . . you have to work harder to communicate in typing, you have to emote more, etc. . . . " Yet another interviewee conjectured, "Hmm. I think forcing people to use text—like in my situation—you're more forced to explain your emotion. It makes you more open to yourself, I guess."

This issue of expressing emotion is equally if not more important in virtual interviews than when conducting face-to-face interviews. Critics of virtual interviews argue that when speaking with avatars you do not have the benefit of facial expressions and body language that are generally seen as important to "reading" a person's intent or authenticity. In a virtual environment, as is now common in other digital communication, people have learned to express emotions through text or with the use of "emoticons" or "smilies," textual or printable characters intended to simulate facial expressions and body language.

Additionally, one of the individuals I interviewed revealed that in his physical world he suffered extreme shyness and had never been able to look people in the eye. He was often accused of being aloof or was mistrusted as a result. In this case, his body language was misinterpreted and he felt that he was able to express himself more authentically in a virtual world and via text where he did not experience these visual biases.

The technology itself can also create interesting dynamics when conducting virtual interviews. For example, system crashes or "lag," when connectivity, server speeds or computer issues may cause the environment to close, freeze or slow down significantly, can be misinterpreted as someone logging off (the equivalent of hanging up on someone) or not giving proper attention and appropriate response time to the person you are engaged with. This issue has been well documented for causing interpersonal communication problems in mobile texting and on social media platforms.

Digital slang is also common in virtual worlds (see Table 1). In conducting live text chat interviews, the interviewer must be familiar with text slang and confirm understanding by restating or summarizing responses.

An additional benefit of conducting interviews entirely in text is the assurance of accuracy in interview transcripts. The conversation is collected in real time with no transcription required and as such has no transcription error. Additionally, to best convey the authenticity of the digital culture as it exists virtually, raw text from the transcripts reveals the powerful ways that words and "emotes" (i.e., written descriptions of bodily reactions such as "sighs" and "smiles") can create a rich sense of experience without the use of voice or visual body and facial cues.

Note from the transcription below the following points: (1) Time stamps provide a record of the time of the interview and the potential lag between responses. (2) In this particular interview, the Avatar XX "spoke" in very brief lines and almost in shorthand. The interviewee was a European musician who performed live in the virtual world and had established a number of relationships as a result. (3) I requested that the

Table 1. Common Abbreviations Used in Second Life

Abbreviation	Meaning
☺ or ☹	Emoticon that may also appear as :) or : (to represent a smile or sad face
alt	Alternate account—often people create more than one avatar for use in different settings
AO	Animation override (creates a more natural movement)
Av or Avi	Abbreviation for avatar
brb	Be right back
D/s	Dominant/submissive (to reflect master/slave roles in Gorean or BDSM role play)
FL or fl	First life (an alternative way of saying "real life")
HB or hb	Hurry back
HUD	Head-up display ("worn" on an avatar to provide data)
idk	I don't know
IM	Instant message
kk	Okay
lag	When the system is loading slowly, often causing freezing
LL	Linden Lab—creators of Second Life
LM	Landmark—a digital address or location in Second Life
LOL	Laugh out loud
NC	Notecard—used to save text in a file in inventory
noob or newb	Someone new to the virtual world
OMG	Oh my God! (Oh my gosh!)
ppl or peeps	People
RL or rl	Real life
rofl	Rolling on the floor laughing
SL	Second Life
SLT	Second Life time—Is the same as Pacific time (home of Linden Labs) and is used as the universal time in Second Life for scheduling purposes
SLurl	Second Life URL
ToS	Terms of Service
TP	Teleport
wb	Welcome back

interviewees use "**" to conclude a thought. That way I would not interrupt them if they took a long time between lines. This was very effective in creating flow in the conversation. (4) I made it clear up front that the interviewees should not worry about typographical errors, misspellings or grammar. This put them at ease and created a much more natural flow in the conversation. (5) I am the interviewer, Tredi Felisimo in Second Life.

> [13:24] TREDI FELISIMO: as I was just about to ask . . . what you consider the benefits of the relationships you've experienced in SL
>
> [13:25] AVATAR XX: apart from the emotional bonds
>
> [13:25] AVATAR XX: I think it enriches a lot
>
> [13:25] AVATAR XX: opportunities grow
>
> [13:25] TREDI FELISIMO: what type of opportunities?
>
> [13:25] AVATAR XX: the benefits are really priceless
>
> [13:26] AVATAR XX: well
>
> [13:26] AVATAR XX: I have been to London twice
>
> [13:26] AVATAR XX: to America
>
> [13:26] AVATAR XX: you know
>
> [13:26] TREDI FELISIMO: these are professional opportunities for you
>
> [13:26] AVATAR XX: I can travel all over the world now, and never have to look for a hotel
>
> [13:26] AVATAR XX: now
>
> [13:26] AVATAR XX: that's not from selfishness or how you call it
>
> [13:27] AVATAR XX: but ther's so many ppl who invite me if I will be near them in my travels
>
> [13:27] AVATAR XX: and yes
>
> [13:27] AVATAR XX: professional opportunities are there too
>
> [13:27] AVATAR XX: omg yes!!!!
>
> [13:27] AVATAR XX: **
>
> [13:28] TREDI FELISIMO: Do you think these relationships or experiences have changed you in any way? in RL?
>
> [13:28] AVATAR XX: they have turned my life into the right direction
>
> [13:28] AVATAR XX: if it wasnt for SL I would never have completed my CD
>
> [13:29] AVATAR XX: would never have thought it to be worth to do so

[13:29] AVATAR XX: and this comes from the generous support I have always experienced here in SL too

In another interview, Avatar XX wrote in much longer sentences, even paragraphs, and regularly used ellipses for emphasis or to accentuate her pauses. Also note the conversational tone and textual emote at 6:30.

[6:27] AVATAR XX: oh gosh . . . no, there are challenges . . . but I think that if the relationship is meaningful enough for both parties it isn't really any different to RL . . . in someways maybe it's less challenging as someone may want to cut contact immediately and they can do so (e.g., mute), that really just makes me look at the situation differently . . . the effort we put in to maintain relationships will reflect the strength of the relationship itself . . . and if it wasn't strong then what have you actually lost? you know?

[6:28] TREDI FELISIMO: interesting perspective!

[6:29] AVATAR XX: then . . . my most challenging relationship was with the RL friend . . . I got more insight into who she was . . . and I actually didn't like it . . . that created a lot of problems . . . and a break, I de-friended her for a few months . . . after telling her my thoughts. . . . she saw me RL later and sent me a text apologising and that she missed me . . . I forgave and we have be 're- building' since then **

[6:30] TREDI FELISIMO: we touched briefly already on trust. . . . is that a challenge and if so is it any different than trust in RL (if so why?)

[6:30] TREDI FELISIMO: really interesting about your RL friend . . . that SL was more revealing than RL!

[6:30] AVATAR XX: uh huh *nods*

[6:30] TREDI FELISIMO: glad you're rebuilding

[6:32] AVATAR XX: I'm really thinking hard on this one . . . I'm not sure there is any difference in trust between RL and SL . . . not at this point in time **

Ultimately, the interviewer must decide how to use the text transcript, including misspellings, typographical errors, slang and timing when publishing results.

On a final note, there are also ethical considerations when conducting interviews in the virtual world. Perhaps most significant is when interviewing a vulnerable population, especially those who are emotionally vulnerable. When an interview is taking place exclusively in a virtual environment and no physical identification is provided, the interviewer may encounter tenuous circumstances. For example, one of the individuals included in my interviews sent the following:

> Good morning . . . about 6:00 am, on Saturday, I got a phone call . . . from x's husband,,, threatening to kill me . . . thought i should share,, if I turn up missing . . . his name is, XX, and you are the only person to know this.

What is the responsibility of the interviewer in this case? In another incident when someone expressed concern about a potential stalker, I contacted both mental health professionals and law enforcement. Both dismissed the case as not "being real" since the individuals were avatars. As the lines blur between virtual and physical, these issues are likely to become more salient and concerning. In the meantime, other fields are already addressing the challenges of anonymity and distance in conducting interviews virtually. For example, as a result of the lack of ability to make direct contact with a virtual interviewee, some industries, such as the mental health professions in the United States, have prohibited any professional consulting interviews in the virtual world. Contrarily, corporations such as IBM use the anonymity as an advantage in corporate training environments.

While some may still consider virtual worlds an untamed space of deceit or simply as entertainment playgrounds, new advances in technology such as the development of Oculus Rift may continue to drive more people into the 3-D realm. As the environment reaches mass adoption, understanding how to communicate and interview effectively will become a necessary skill.

NOTES

1. T.L. Taylor. "Life in Virtual Worlds: Plural Existence, Multimodalities, and Other Online Research Challenges." *American Behavioral Scientist,* 43 (1999): 436–449.

2. http://www.blogtalkradio.com/virtually-speaking-science.

3. Author Jennifer Ouellette on SL & LSD interview on *Chaotic Awesome*:

Episode 8 | Character Sheet, http://www.youtube.com/watch?v=SLsY-m5Nfh8 #t=256.

   4. D. Davis. "A Study of Relationships in Online Virtual Environments: Making a Case for Conducting Semi-Structured Interviews with Avatars and What We Can Learn About Their Human Operators." *Advancing Social and Business Research Methods with New Media Technologies.* IGI Global, New York, 2013.

   5. T. Behrend, S. Toaddy, L.F. Thompson, and D. Sharek. "The Effects of Avatar Appearance on Interviewer Ratings in Virtual Employment Interviews." *Computers in Human Behavior,* 28 (2012): 2128–2133.

PART III Sensitivity

NINETEEN **Creating Rapport**

*Effective interviewers focus first
on establishing trust*

ED MADISON

What makes a potential interviewee choose to talk
with a journalist? Ed Madison, who has produced
hundreds of interviews for network and syndicated
television, is convinced that rapport constitutes the
magic ingredient.

Rapport is a seldom-used word that describes an ephemeral state of relatedness. *Ephemeral?* It's another rarely used word that in simplest terms means momentary. Rapport is elusive; gone in the blink of an eye. It is difficult to speak and write about—and yet we intuitively know when it is achieved. There is a sense that we have "connected" with another person. Within the journalistic profession it means our recording devices fade into the background and a rich conversation is free to unfold.

Creating rapport is a process of mutual discovery. It is not about riffling through your list of prepared questions. It's about reaching a level of comfort where the unexpected evolves as a shared experience. But how do you get there? This chapter explores the essence of rapport and offers insights from media masters.

Before retiring in 2014, Barbara Walters was the grand dame of broadcast interviewers. In a career that spanned more than 50 years, she interviewed every American president since Richard Nixon—and many world dignitaries. Oprah Winfrey was inspired by Walters while still a teen, and went on to revolutionize daytime television before launching her OWN network. When Lance Armstrong sought redemption in the aftermath of his doping scandal, he sat with Oprah Winfrey. Their exchange is a textbook lesson in the art of interviewing and achieving rapport that I'll explore further in these pages. I'll also discuss how Walters approached interviewing Winfrey. There is much to learn from watching two masters at work—center stage—under the glare of lights and cameras.

With hot button topics, where the stakes can be high, it is impossible to predict which direction an interview will go. Without rapport, interviews can quickly descend into verbal exchanges that are painful to watch. How painful? Take a look at the links listed at the end of the chapter. Watch Fox News host Chris Wallace lose control of his interview with former President Bill Clinton after asking a line of questions about antiterrorism. Or former President George W. Bush stammer when *Meet the Press* host Tim Russert asked about the necessity of the Iraq war.

At the pop culture end of the spectrum, it can be just as insightful to watch Anderson Cooper match wits with Lady Gaga or rapper Eminem. Links listed below take you to behind-the-scenes segments from *60 Minutes* stories about these superstars that are as informative about rapport building as the actual interviews.

Understanding how and when to pose difficult questions and how to handle unexpected responses is particularly significant. Not all interviews turn adversarial. However, effective journalists accept that they are professionally obligated to probe beneath the surface when necessary—even when it becomes uncomfortable. These are the kinds of examples explored in this chapter.

I'll also share some of my own professional experiences from 25 years of working in the trenches. At age 22, shortly after graduating from Emerson College, I had the privilege of being recruited as a founding producer at CNN. Later, I became West Coast producer at the *CBS Morning Program*, before heading my own media companies, and more recently becoming a professor. Over the years, I've produced interviews with hundreds of celebrities and dignitaries, including Sarah Ferguson (the former Duchess of York), Imelda Marcos, Sir Elton John, Elizabeth Taylor, Tina Turner, Frank Sinatra, Eddie Murphy, Tom Hanks, Halle Berry, Stevie Wonder and other names that will surely date me.

I'm not that old; I just started early. At age 16, while still in high school, I interned at a *Washington Post*–owned CBS television affiliate (then WTOP-TV) at the height of the Watergate scandal. The art of interviewing has fascinated me for as long as I can remember. I've joked that I may have been conceived during a *Tonight Show* monologue.

Journalism, and more specifically having a knack for how to build rapport and best phrase interview questions, is embedded in my DNA. My dad was a pioneer. In 1961, he became the first African-American to join the editorial staff of the *Chicago Tribune*. He covered the first Kennedy–Nixon debate, interviewed then Vice President Nixon, and he knew and often interviewed Dr. Martin Luther King, Jr. Those are stories for another time and place.

The point of this chapter is to prepare you for success in your own journalistic career. You may not be interviewing world leaders and celebrities, but there is much to learn from watching masterful interviewers engaging with them. Most of the examples I'll cite here are from broadcast television, and many of them can be found on YouTube. Even if your mode of publication is not electronic, you'll benefit from studying television interviews. Online sources provide on-demand access to a virtual graduate course in the art of interviewing. Great moments of catharsis, revelation and self-reflection are a mouse-click away.

A good place to begin is with a closer definition of terms. The *Oxford American Dictionary* defines *rapport* as "a close and harmonious relationship in which the people or groups concerned understand each other's feelings or ideas and communicate well" (*Oxford*, 2014). Webster's traces the word's origin to the 17th century and the French word *rapporter*, which means to "bring back" (Webster's, 2014). Translated into English, the word describes a *mutual exchange.*

Both mutual and exchange imply that the participants are on common ground. Thinking of journalistic interviews in such egalitarian terms may seem counterintuitive to those accustomed to use of sports and military metaphors when describing human encounters. Culturally, we often speak in terms of strategies, tactics and maneuvering when talking about interpersonal communication.

There is an old-school sense that effective reporters should be authoritative and heavy-handed in their approach. However, much of this thinking stems from a time before social media when mass media institutions set the agenda for how stories would be framed. Today, audiences are empowered to challenge institutional authority, and often do. Effective journalism no longer functions as a one-way enterprise. The days of publishing a story and being "done with it" are over. Reporters are now expected to be transparent about their practices. Otherwise, they risk the wrath of an increasingly demanding public that may hold them just as accountable for misdeeds as the people they cover (Santana, 2011).

The rules of interview discourse and interpersonal exchange have changed with the times. Contemporary audiences don't want to be "talked to"; they want to be "engaged with." Engagement implies higher levels of participation and less formality. This is the essence of rapport. Consequently, presidential candidates have increasingly sought the informal interview opportunities available through daytime and late night television talk shows where questions are "softer" (Baum, 2005). In these settings, politicians are at liberty to speak about personal matters and hope to be perceived as genuine (Baumgartner & Morris, 2006).

The shows now exemplify this shift in tone, with Jay Leno stepping aside for Jimmy Fallon and David Letterman making way for Stephen Colbert. The move is away from predictable patter and more toward spontaneity (CBSNews.com, 2014). Research confirms that younger audiences reject familiar formats and favor free-form exchange, inclusiveness and fresher approaches, most specifically in entertainment-oriented interview programs (Bibel, 2013; Kissell, 2014). This is not to suggest that tough topics don't call for tougher forums, tougher approaches and even tougher lines of questioning—but you have to get there. Attempting to get a meaningful response from someone in any arena without first building rapport rarely works.

There is a fundamental philosophical shift to make in order to contemporize your approach to interviewing. I argue that it is passé to talk about a dichotomous relationship between interviewers and interviewees, or investigators and "subjects." Framing the interview process in such archaic terms suggests an imbalance of power and significance between the parties involved. Monarchies had "subjects," democracies have participants. Social media and the Internet have altered the rules of engagement.

As we'll explore, the dynamics of an interview can change in an instant. Asking the right question at the right time and in the appropriate venue can make a career. Katie Couric elevated her stature as a journalist when, in their interview, vice presidential candidate Sarah Palin was unable to name a single newspaper or magazine she read to "stay informed and to understand the world" (Mak, 2012). Consequently, asking the wrong question can kill a career. As the *Chicago Tribune* reported, Connie Chung lowered her stature by "tricking Newt Gingrich's mom into calling Hillary Clinton a nasty name" (Royko, 1995). Chung asked 68-year-old Kathleen Gingrich what her son thought of Clinton. When she hesitated, Chung pushed further and asked, "Why don't you just whisper it to me, just between you and me." Mom Gingrich replied in a loud whisper, "She's a bitch." Critics asserted Chung's "just between you and me" comment was intentionally misleading. They argued Gingrich was unaware cameras were still rolling (Royko, 1995).

Students entering the journalism profession often miss subtle and yet significant distinctions about ethics and sensitivity that are fundamental to extraordinary interviewing. Earnest young reporters can be singularly focused on "getting the story" and potentially miss "discovering a story" they might never have imagined. Candor can be achieved, but it should not be by means of coercion. An example is an interview experience I had while interviewing legendary R&B recording artist Smokey Robinson. I was prepared to talk with him about his days at Motown but hadn't expected him to share about his past battles with substance abuse. What got us there was a conversation earlier in the interview about his affinity for the game of golf. Robinson said that golf, for him, was in many ways meditative, a healthier way to escape from the pressures of fame. Healthier? What did he mean by healthier? An unexpected story unfolded. I tossed my prepared questions, intuitively sensing he was willing to explore what had led him down such a dark path and how he recovered. The discussion about golf apparently made him comfortable enough to open up about more serious issues.

When we launched *People Tonight*, the live entertainment news program I executive produced at CNN, we sought to identify our celebrity guests' primary interests and concerns in order to best prepare and establish rapport. Shortly after we debuted, the Screen Actors Guild went on strike, leaving otherwise busy superstars with lots of time and a need to organize their ranks. Our program became a perfect rallying stop for actors who might otherwise not have given our fledgling network the time of day. Guests during that period included Charlton Heston, William Shatner, Ed Asner and Betty White. Our host, Lee Leonard, was very adept at striking the right balance between newsy and light-hearted talk, in effect creating rapport quickly. This ability earned us a good reputation for being trustworthy and fair. We became a place for up and coming actors such as Tom Cruise, Heather Locklear and Lorenzo Lamas to experience being interviewed on television for the first time. A very young Tom Hanks gave us his home number and permission to bypass his publicist should we ever need a last-minute guest to fill time with a game of movie trivia. Triviality can be a great icebreaker.

Barbara Walters often began interviews with unusable (but rapport building) small talk. She also was a stickler for preparation, saying, "The most important thing you can do is your homework" (Pollack, 2013). To prepare for major interviews, Walters would instruct her staff to prepare huge binders of news clippings and transcripts from the person's previous interviews. One objective was to steer clear of commonly over-asked questions. The clips also contained hints about fresh topics ripe for exploration.

She also requested that her guests commit to lengthy amounts of time in front of cameras, and Walters' ability to land "exclusives" was attributed to her relentless pursuit of "hard to get" guests. According to the *Los Angeles Times*, "Walters survived by fashioning a new role for herself: that of the globe-trotting interviewer. She interviewed Fidel Castro in a patrol boat on the Bay of Pigs and scored a joint interview with Israeli Prime Minister Menachem Begin and Egyptian President Anwar Sadat, infuriating competitors like Walter Cronkite" (Gold, 2008).

Walters and Oprah Winfrey share a propensity for obtaining exclusives. Intriguingly, when deciding to share sensitive details with television audiences about their own lives, they've turned to each other. In a 2010 interview, Walters established rapport by asking Winfrey to reflect on her childhood ambition to become a broadcast journalist. Winfrey shared that she had won a local Miss Fire Prevention pageant after stating in the Q&A session that she wanted to become the next Barbara Walters. This light subject banter set the stage for Walters to probe further about Winfrey's more troubling memories of her childhood and about her current relationship with her parents. Notice how Walters followed up after Winfrey's less than candid answer to a question:

WALTERS: How is your father? What is your relationship?

WINFREY: My father is fine. And our relationship is fine.

WALTERS: And your mother; do you see her?

WINFREY: Um, I would not say that I have been the kind of daughter who calls home every week and is checking in with my parents.

WALTERS: You're not terribly close?

WINFREY: I would not say that we're terribly close. (YouTube, 2010)

Winfrey expressed pleasure that success allowed her to provide for her parents' financial needs but offered few details about the present status of their interpersonal relationship. Walters artfully turned the topic to their previous 1988 interview, when Winfrey revealed she had been sexually abused as an adolescent. Notice in the transcript how Walters expresses authentic empathy, as Winfrey reflects on her past.

WALTERS: We know so much about your childhood, and you've talked about it. Knowing that you were abused and survived. I don't know how you did it. But you did. [The video transitioned back to their 1988 interview.] You were actually raped.

WINFREY: I went through the entire fifth grade, every day, thinking, "I'm going to have a baby." At the time I didn't know that you had to be . . .

WALTERS: You make me want to cry.

WINFREY: I weep for the lost innocence, because you're never the same again. (YouTube, 2010)

Walters demonstrated sincerity and compassion at the appropriate moment. Her empathetic approach supported Winfrey in feeling safe. Reflecting on that earlier interview, Winfrey stated:

> As is the case with people who've never told, you've never told because you know that it wasn't safe to tell. And, you know that you are going to be ostracized, put down, and criticized for telling. So that was a really big thing for me. (YouTube, 2010)

Winfrey is also a master at probing into uncomfortable territory with her guests. The tables were turned in 2008 when Walters told Winfrey and viewers about a previous secret affair she had with Sen. Edward Brooke, who is African American. Winfrey also chose that moment to dismiss rumors that she and her best friend, Gayle King, were secretly lesbian lovers (OWN, 2008).

Winfrey elevated the prominence of her fledgling OWN network with another of her many exclusive interviews. When questioning Lance Armstrong about his use of performance-enhancing drugs, she took a distinctive tack by asking how he had told his son and daughters. Armstrong was visibly shaken, yet trusted Winfrey to venture into such sensitive territory. However, she had to pose the question four times and endure several breaks of silence before he candidly revealed the confession he made to his children:

WINFREY: What do you tell Luke? Luke is 13. You have been fighting this thing his entire life. He's 13; he's old enough to know what is going on.

ARMSTRONG: Oh, trust me, they know a lot. They hear it in the hallways; Luke and the girls. Their schools, their classmates have been very supportive. Where you lose control of your kids is when they go out of that space: Instagram, Facebook, Twitter. Then the feedback comes.

WINFREY: But what did you tell him?

ARMSTRONG: Well, first I want to tell you what happened. When this all really started, I saw my son defending me and saying, "That's not true. What you're saying about my dad is not true." And it almost goes to this question of why now? He can't . . .

Armstrong lowered and shook his head pensively, and Winfrey allowed nearly 20 seconds of silence to elapse without interruption.

ARMSTRONG (CONTINUES):   That's when I knew I had to tell him. And he had never asked me. He had never said, "Dad, is this true?" He trusted me. And I heard about it in the hallways.

Armstrong dropped his head again and sighed.

WINFREY: What did you say to him?

ARMSTRONG: Ah, at that time I didn't say anything. That's the time that I knew that I had to say something.

WINFREY: You heard that he was defending you.

ARMSTRONG: Yes, other kids on Instagram replying. It gets ugly. And then at that point I decided that I had to say something. This is out of control. And then I had to have that talk with him, which was just here over the holidays.

WINFREY: (Leaning in) What did you say?

ARMSTRONG: I said, "Listen, there's been a lot of questions about your dad, about my career; whether I doped or did not dope. I've always denied that, and I've always been ruthless and defiant about that. You guys have seen that; it's probably why you trusted me on it," which makes it even sicker. Um, and I said, "I want you know that it is true." And there were the girls, who are twins, and 11—and Luke. And they didn't say much. They didn't say, "But wait, Dad." They just accepted it. And I told Luke. I said . . .

Armstrong dropped his head again, and Winfrey allowed another 20 seconds of uninterrupted silence.

ARMSTRONG: I said, "Don't defend me any more. Don't." (YouTube, 2013)

It was a textbook case in the importance of tenacity. It was essential that Winfrey follow up several times, rather than submit to Armstrong's evasiveness.

Certain topics demand a higher threshold of rapport. Ariane Kunze, a talented multimedia master's program graduate of the UO School of

Journalism and Communication, documents the stories of young survivors of human trafficking in the Pacific Northwest. Building rapport with people who have experienced trauma often requires spending weeks of quality time with no cameras present in order to build trust. Kunze walks a delicate line of bonding with—but not "befriending"—these women. She seeks to represent their stories authentically, not direct their actions. She makes her intentions clear; she is compassionate but the essence of their relationship is journalistic work. They are told to expect fair but tough investigative questions.

Journalists have an implicit pact with their audiences. They are obligated to ask the questions viewers or readers want answered, even when they have to be firm. Making the right calls about when and how to probe comes with experience. There are no hard science equations to rely on to achieve rapport. There are only subjective choices made in the moment.

Intriguingly, the quantitative versus qualitative debate that often arises in social science offers further insights about rapport. Hardline "quantoids" argue there is an objective universe that investigators are to study with little consideration for their personal role—and possible influence. Conventions dictate that they converse and write about their work in the third person, removing any mention of the word "I"—the self who conducts investigations. Traditional journalists also speak of "dispassionate storytelling" and "removing themselves" from the stories they tell (Mindich, 1998). This "just the facts" approach suggests that other observers will (and should) draw similar conclusions. However, is such a state of pure objectivity possible—or even preferable?

A more qualitative approach to interviewing acknowledges subjectivity and nuance. It takes into account that robots do not interview people—human beings do, and they have opinions and personal perspectives. It is appropriate to put your preconceptions aside in most interviews involving politics, religion and similar hot-button issues. Yet other topics, such as human rights and genocide, are not up for debate.

Fairness and transparency are guiding principles that help journalists navigate as they establish trust with audiences and interviewees. It's foolhardy to think you can remove yourself from the equation. Intriguingly, the most revered broadcast journalists have had distinctive personalities.

From Edward R. Murrow to Walter Cronkite to Barbara Walters—the most memorable television journalists have had bold personas that set them apart from their peers, and those characteristics were obvious in their on-camera questions.

When you interview, more than likely your questions won't be shared with an audience, unless you too are a broadcast journalist. Your story will feature only the best quotes or sound bites. Yet your personality will affect the quality of your interview. Are you gregarious or soft-spoken? Would colleagues describe you as being open and accessible or guarded and aloof? What about your mannerisms and social cues? Do you make consistent eye contact, or are you more focused on your note pad? Are you willing to take the time to start with small talk or do you race to get to the point?

Taking notice of the habitual ways we engage with people can be highly enlightening. To take your skills to new levels, make video recordings of yourself doing mock interviews with friends and family. Notice verbal and nonverbal patterns that may prove to be ineffective. Do you ask questions in a manner that is concise and clear, or rambling and ambiguous? Do you catch or miss cues that can lead to richer areas of discussion?

When it comes to interviewing, practice and time are pathways to mastery. Focus first on rapport, and your interviews stand to benefit in new and unforeseen ways. It is the key to developing meaningful stories and crafting memorable journalism.

VIDEO CLIPS

Former President Bill Clinton, Fox News Sunday, 2006: https://www.youtube.com/watch?v=rxWUA764H7E.

Former President George W. Bush, Meet the Press (2:40 into the video), 2004: https://www.youtube.com/watch?v=2_gO34w7oDI.

Lady Gaga and Anderson Cooper, 60 Minutes Overtime: A Tale of 3 Divas, 2011: http://www.cbsnews.com/news/a-tale-of-3-divas/.

Eminem and Anderson Cooper, 60 Minutes Overtime: Behind the Scenes, 2011: http://www.cbsnews.com/news/eminem-and-anderson-cooper-behind-the-scenes/.

BIBLIOGRAPHY

Baum, M.A. (April 01, 2005). "Talking the Vote: Why Presidential Candidates Hit the Talk Show Circuit." *American Journal of Political Science*, 49, 2, 213–234.

Baumgartner, J., & Morris, J. (October 01, 2006). "The Daily Show Effect: Candidate Evaluations, Efficacy, and American Youth." *Peace Research Abstracts Journal*, 43, 5.

Bibel, S. (April 4, 2013). "'The Daily Show' and 'The Colbert Report' Finish First Quarter 2013 as Number 1 and 2 Among Adults 18–49." Zap2it.com. Retrieved from: http://tvbythenumbers.zap2it.com/2013/04/04/the-daily -show-and-the-colbert-report-finish-first-quarter-2013-as-number-1-and -number-2-among-adults-18-49/176487/.

CBS.com. (Jan. 26, 2014). "Jay Leno on Leaving 'The Tonight Show.'" 60 Minutes. Retrieved from: http://www.cbsnews.com/videos/jay-leno-on-leaving -the-tonight-show/.

Gold, M. (May 7, 2008). "Her Turn to Tell." *Los Angeles Times*. Retrieved from: http://articles.latimes.com/2008/may/07/entertainment/et-walters7.

Kissell, R. (March 6, 2014). "Young Viewers Drawn to Jimmy Fallon on NBC's 'Tonight Show.'" *Variety*. Retrieved from: http://variety.com/2014/tv/news/ young-viewers-drawn-to-jimmy-fallon-on-nbcs-tonight-show-1201127115/.

Mak, T. (April 2, 2012). "5 best Couric-Palin 2008 moments." Politico. Retrieved from: http://www.politico.com/news/stories/0412/74735.html.

Mindich, D.T.Z. (1998). Just the Facts: How "Objectivity" Came to Define American Journalism. New York: New York University Press.

OWN (2008). "First Interview: Barbara Walters's New Revelations." OWN Network. Retrieved from: http://www.oprah.com/oprahshow/First-TV-Interview -Barbara-Walterss-New-Revelations.

Oxford Dictionaries. (2014). Retrieved from: http://www.merriam-webster.com/ dictionary/rapport.

Pollack, J. (Aug. 8, 2013). "Barbara Walters on the Art of Interviewing." *Businessweek*. Retrieved from: http://www.businessweek.com/articles/2013-08-08/ barbara-walters-on-the-art-of-the-interview.

Royko, M. (Jan. 5, 1995). "And Just Between Us, Connie Chung Goofed." Retrieved from http://articles.chicagotribune.com/1995-01-05/news/ 95010148_1_men-and-shaper-mom-gingrich-newtie.

Santana, A.D. (June 1, 2011). "Online Readers' Comments Represent New Opinion Pipeline." Newspaper Research Journal, 32, 3.

Tickle-Degnen, L., and Rosenthal, R. (1990). "The Nature of Rapport and Its Nonverbal Correlates." *Psychological Inquiry* 1: 285–293.

YouTube. (2010). "Oprah @ Barbara Walters Interview 2010." Retrieved from: https://www.youtube.com/watch?v=geIWGJi2vQ4.

YouTube. (2013). "Lance Armstrong on Telling His Son the Truth." OWN. Retrieved from: https://www.youtube.com/watch?v=Vq8NgepsFg8.

TWENTY **Cultural Sensitivity**

Some practical considerations
for interviewing across languages

CHRISTOPHER CHÁVEZ

Ask a question in Germany that would elicit a quick
negative response in Oregon and the answer rarely
comes out, "Nein," but instead a thoughtful, "In princip
ja, aber . . ."—in principle yes, but. . . . Chris Chávez points
out the types of errors in interviewing that can easily
occur if journalists fail to consider language and culture
differences.

While in Madrid recently, I had an insightful conversation with two
Spanish colleagues over the topic of language and misunderstanding.
Our conversation centered on the usage of *usted* versus *tu*. You see, in
Spanish there are two separate pronouns for addressing others. Broadly
speaking, *usted* is employed in more formal conditions, while *tu* is designated for informal exchanges. Because my inclination is to address others
formally, I have tended to overuse the *usted*, applying it indiscriminately
to strangers, friends, peers and those in senior positions. If the speech
situation is uncertain, my logic went, why not default to the formal use?

During our conversation, however, my Spanish colleagues informed
me that *usted* could often be off-putting, depending on the context. By
using *usted*, one has the potential to create distance between speakers or
may inadvertently relegate the addressee to the realm of "not one of us."

While I can speak some Spanish, albeit limited, this subtle nuance had escaped me. I simply didn't have the cultural or linguistic codes to understand how this everyday use of language has the potential to offend.

By using this relatively benign example, I mean to demonstrate how the nuances of language are often lost during exchanges between speakers from different cultural and linguistic backgrounds. Sociolinguists have long argued that language is specific to one's particular cultural background. Words reflect our worldviews and are inextricably linked to our personal experiences. But while the meanings of our words are highly intimate, we are beholden to words to communicate our ideas, to report on our experiences and to share our stories. Given the fallibility of language, there is tremendous opportunity for misunderstanding when two speakers from different cultural backgrounds encounter each other. The greater the cultural difference the greater potential for misunderstanding.

Today, we live in a world in which people, information and currency move quickly and easily across borders. That is to say, we live in a much smaller world than ever before, and what happens on one side of the world is more readily felt on another. Furthermore, as media themselves have become globalized, new issues emerge regarding how stories are captured and shared with others. These issues become particularly evident during the practice of interviewing, which is used by journalists, academics and marketing practitioners as they strive to understand the worldviews and lived experiences of others.

At best, the practice of interviewing is fraught with potential misunderstanding. Even under the most ideal circumstances, the interviewer must attend carefully to language in an effort to ascertain the other's point of view or the other's version of the events. During this process, some reassurance may be found in the presumption of shared language and experience. From this perspective, the practice of interviewing may be seen not only as a professional practice but as a rhetorical exchange in which the interviewer poses questions based on the assumption of shared cultural vocabularies and experiences. The interviewee uses that same body of cultural knowledge to interpret the interviewer's question, evaluate its content and formulate a response. Shared cultural knowledge provides the basis for interaction.

During interviews that involve speakers of different cultural and lin-

guistic backgrounds, however, the assumption of shared cultural meaning becomes tentative, presenting greater opportunities for misunderstanding. In addition to the obvious issue of comprehension, political
considerations are inherent in the practice of interviewing. In his discussion of scholarly research, Michael Agar describes the practice as an arrogant exercise in which researchers attempt to ingratiate themselves into a
group of strangers, document their social lives, describe their beliefs and
report on their rituals, all within a relatively short period of time. To complicate this process, researchers bring with them a legacy of colonialism,
which ultimately limits their perspective.

While Agar is discussing the problematic nature of ethnography, the
issues that he raises apply to interviewing in its many forms. For example,
there are times when an interviewer, whether for academic, commercial
or journalistic purposes, drops into a community in an effort to gain firsthand testimony about a given phenomenon. At times, the interviewer is
armed with varying degrees of knowledge of the interviewee's native language and cultural codes. At other times, the interviewer may be working
directly with a translator who also comes to the table with varying biases
and levels of proficiency.

In an American context, there may also be times when the interviewer
is working in his or her home country but may be interviewing someone
new to the country or who has limited proficiency in English. In these
cases, the interviewer may attempt to accommodate the participant's way
of speaking. More often than not, however, non-English speakers are
forced to communicate in a language that is not their own. Or if they are
not capable of expressing their own experiences adequately in English,
their voices may be excluded altogether.

Thus, power is inherent in the practice of interviewing. When writing about the symbolic power of language, Bourdieu argues that despite
a country's actual linguistic plurality, there is a dominant language, the
one spoken by a group that holds the political, cultural and economic
power within a country. Those who can capably speak the dominant language can more readily access the benefits of civil society, while those
who happen to speak a minority language risk marginalization.

It is easy to imagine the scenario in which the journalist working for
a mainstream U.S. newspaper drops into a Mexican migrant commu-

nity with the mission of ascertaining how labor is exploited. However well-intentioned, the journalist wants to capture the experiences of these migrants and convey their stories to an audience primarily composed of English monolinguals. If done well, the interviewer gains professionally from the experience. While it may not seem overt, there are implicit power dynamics inherent in the practice of interviewing. Such exchanges are not necessarily the meeting of two equal participants who happen to speak different languages. Under such conditions, journalists and researchers have natural ways of speaking that enable them to perform with relative ease during the interview process. Whether or not the interview takes place in English, they are in a much better position to control the conversation. Conversely, when Spanish-dominant Latinos are engaged in a conversation with English monolinguals, the imbalance of status and power makes conversation on equal footing impossible. Even the bilingual Latinos often find themselves incapable of holding their own or controlling the conversation in such gatekeeping situations (Zentella, 2003).

In an effort to give interview participants greater opportunity to share their stories on their terms, there are benefits when interviewers and participants share the same cultural and linguistic background. In practice, however, this ideal remains elusive. Despite a changing demographic landscape, news organizations, universities and commercial institutions remain ethnically too homogeneous. Largely as a result of globalizing forces, there has been a greater influx of immigrants from non-European countries. At the same time, the rate of growth for non-Latino whites has decreased. This trend is expected to continue. Demographic projections indicate that by 2023, groups traditionally categorized as minorities will account for a majority of the U.S. population.

Despite these changes, there remain distinctions between those whose stories must be told and those who are in the position to tell those stories. A 2012 Pew journalism study found that newsrooms only vaguely reflect the population. While non-whites make up roughly 39 percent of the total U.S. population, they accounted for only 12 percent of the total newspaper newsroom workforce in 2012. Furthermore, minority groups appear disproportionately affected by the changes to the news industry. In 2011, newsroom employment at daily newspapers dropped 2.4 percent, but for minorities, it dropped 5.7 percent.

Universities and marketing institutions do not fare much better. Despite the country's demographic changes, universities and marketing corporations have resisted any significant diversification despite formidable legal, cultural and economic pressure. In short, there are tremendous disparities between those cultural producers who generate stories and the world in general. The inevitable result is a sort of distorted mirror that vaguely resembles the world as it is and more serves as a reflection of those who are in a position to describe and explain it.

STRIVING FOR A MORE COMPLETE INTERVIEW

In an ideal world, communities of all types would have the power and resources to tell their own stories. But in the imperfect world in which we live, we still rely heavily on mediators to tell our stories. Furthermore, because it is our natural inclination to avoid engaging those who are culturally and linguistically different from us, we risk missing the stories that may be most revealing about any given phenomenon.

Anaïs Nin once wrote that "we do not see the world as it is, we see it as we are." Here, Nin reminds us to remember that ours is not the only perspective and that we must challenge ourselves to see things from multiple points of view. To achieve this ideal, interviewers of all types may learn from social anthropologists who have also had to wrestle with the inherent contradiction involved with capturing and telling the stories of others and have also had to struggle with the challenge of understanding communities that are different from their own. To account for these struggles, social anthropologists practice what they refer to as "reflexivity," which rejects the notion that the interviewer is an impartial and neutral observer. Instead, scholars working in this tradition have argued that researchers are inclined to cling to a "myth of detachment," in which they are presumed to be innocent from their complicity in perpetuating social inequalities. Instead, "reflexivity" is meant to remind interviewers that they carry their own implicit assumptions about the nature of reality. These biases are a result of their personal backgrounds and their professional training, which directs their gaze to certain aspects of human experience that are considered worthy of attention.

Reflexive anthropology assumes that social researchers can rarely, if ever, become detached observers. Rather, their own lived experience both enables and inhibits particular kinds of insight. Thus, the question is not whether interviewers are biased but rather what kinds of biases exist and how might they account for them in their profession. One such strategy is to attempt as much as possible to incorporate various points of view. Different perspectives provide a more complete picture of any given social phenomenon and reveal contradictions. Rather than being locked into any particular perspective, a better understanding of a social phenomenon can be achieved by studying it from a number of positions. These perspectives may include those of interviewer, armed with the perspectives of a discipline, the participants who are being interviewed and, when relevant, the translator who is serving as arbiter between the two.

The benefit of using a translator is that it allows for the inclusion of more voices, particularly those who cannot communicate their stories in English. But it is important to fully appreciate the role of the translator, who acts as an important cultural arbiter. In a 2003 Tribute to Gabriel García Márquez, Edith Grossman provides one of the most revealing insights about the nature of translation. In her speech, Grossman (2003) discusses her longstanding working relationship with the Colombian writer and her process of translating García Márquez's literary works from Spanish to English:

> Fidelity is surely our highest aim, but a translation is not made with tracing paper. It is an act of critical interpretation. Let me insist on the obvious: Languages trail immense, individual histories behind them, and no two languages, with all their accretions of tradition and culture, ever dovetail perfectly. They can be linked by translation, as a photograph can link movement and stasis, but it is disingenuous to assume that either translation or photography, or acting for that matter, are representational in any narrow sense of the term. Fidelity is our noble purpose, but it does not have much, if anything, to do with what is called literal meaning. A translation can be faithful to tone and intention, to meaning. It can rarely be faithful to words or syntax, for these are peculiar to specific languages and are not transferable.

In her speech, Grossman rightfully characterizes translation as an artistic, rather than a technical process. In short, the translator isn't a living, breathing "Google translator" but a collaborator who mediates between two cultures, attempting to link them through language. To achieve this, there is a need for an intimate understanding of the writer's intentions, what Grossman describes as "an ability to see the world through another person's eyes and translate the linguistic perception of that world into another language."

Grossman is also making the point that language is inextricably linked to cultural experience and that there are certain words and phrases so precise to one's experience that they simply do not have a match in another language. For English monolinguals, the idea that a particular concept may not have a direct equivalent in English is not an intuitive notion. In my own research with advertising professionals, participants described being in the awkward position of having to translate ideas written in Spanish to English for approval by English monolingual clients. Under these conditions, Spanish-speaking practitioners expressed frustration that clients couldn't distinguish between the original concept and the translation. Jokes that had relevance in Spanish fell flat in their English translations, leaving clients bemused and reluctant to approve. As one participant I interviewed suggested, clients were merely "talking about the reflection of a thing rather than the thing itself."

Exacerbating the problematic nature of translation is that the practice of translation is frequently done on the cheap. In an effort to save money, the clients have their communications materials translated by anyone claiming to "speak Spanish," resulting in typos, errors and misrepresentations. In some cases, this important task of translation was given to anyone with a Spanish surname. This kind of mischief illustrates misperceptions about language that have the opportunity to obscure rather than reveal meaning. In other words, interviewer or translator and participant may share the same language, but their backgrounds shape the understanding of language. When we typically speak of language (English, Spanish and so forth) we generally speak of it as a single, unified product rather than a living, breathing and evolving set of discursive practices. But sociolinguist Alberto Duranti reminds us that language not only demonstrates diversity in the nature of particular dialects but is also stratified into languages that are common to specific social groups. Consequently, there are forms of language that are specific to professions, social classes, age groups and formal settings.

To account for these many concerns, it is important to be diligent about interrogating the meaning of words. It's vital to use the interview as an opportunity to clarify meanings with the participant and to provide room for participants to elaborate if there is uncertainty. Nothing should be taken for granted. This of course, takes time, which may be a premium in some kinds of interviewing. There is a pressure to meet the deadline, capture the story and move on to the next one. These are the realities of interviewing. But if it's possible, one has the responsibility to attend carefully to the words expressed by another. When describing the hurried conditions in which most cultural production occurs, Bourdieu makes the point that working under pressure negatively impacts the end product. He poses the question, is it possible to think fast? I guess the real question is how can we not?

BIBLIOGRAPHY

Agar, M. (1996). *The Professional Stranger: An Informal Introduction to Ethnography.* San Diego, CA: Academic Press.

Bourdieu, P. (1991). *Language and Symbolic Power.* Cambridge, Mass.: Harvard University Press.

Duranti, Alessandro (1997). Linguistic Diversity. In *Linguistic Anthropology.* Cambridge, England: Cambridge University Press.

Gold, R. (2013). The Atlantic. http://www.theatlantic.com/national/archive/ 2013/07/newsroom-diversity-a-casualty-of-journalisms-financial-crisis/ 277622/.

Grossman, E. (2003). PEN Tribute to Gabriel García Márquez.

Scheiffelin, B.K. Woolard & P. Kroskrity (1998). *Language Ideologies: Practice and Theory.* New York: Oxford University Press.

Zentella, A.C. (2003). "'José Can You See': Latin @ Responses to Racist Discourse" in D. Sommers (Ed), *Bilingual Games: Some Literary Investigations.* New York: Palgrave Macmillan.

TWENTY-ONE **Interviewing for Diversity**

The interview is an important tool not just
for journalists, but for social scientists and
strategists as well

TROY ELIAS

Rounding up the usual interview suspects often
is an easy out for securing interview subjects.
But Troy Elias shows that in order to tell
thorough stories a diverse sample of witnesses
and opinions is crucial.

A recent study based on interviews found that ad agencies use LinkedIn
extensively in hiring but probably don't realize that the social network is
too racially homogeneous to improve diversity.

Another study found—through interviews with journalists—that
engaging in topics that dealt with race and ethnicity led to changes in
news coverage of people of color.

Journalists themselves typically seek out experts to interview for stories
about climate change, but by failing to hear from others, such as minority communities, they fail to grasp that minorities are as concerned about
climate effects as whites. They also miss the fact that minorities, such as
Latinos, are not monolithic in their beliefs.

Interviewing serves a vital function in the process of storytelling and
research. It allows both media professionals and scholars to obtain valu-

able information from a source's personal perspective. In addition, the degree of detail and specificity that emerges generally tends to surpass what respondents are able to provide via surveys or experiments.

Individuals working in disciplines that define success by their ability to unearth human truths and tell compelling stories—journalists, social scientists and strategists—have made tremendous contributions to what we know of the interview process. We have an enhanced understanding of best practices (e.g., be as prepared as you can be, make a great first impression and exert every effort to build trust, be sensitive to possible ethics breaches and, when optimal, adopt a conversational tone, as opposed to cross-examining sources).

While the fine points of the interview process are critical to eliciting a good and credible story or research article, the quality of the final product may be limited if one does not choose the "right" topics and the "right" sources. It is the breadth of diversity within audiences today and their interests that should embolden future journalists, advertisers and media scholars to delve into topics with consequences for an increasingly diverse public.

MEDIA PROFESSIONALS AND CULTURAL INFLUENCE

Through the nature of their work, journalists, social scientists and advertisers tend to establish narratives in the media. When effective, these media narratives resonate culturally at the local or national level. The concomitant result is that these disciplines often tell us what society is like, what it can be, how we fit into the times in which we live, what others think of people like us, and what people like us ought to think of others.[1] Within these vocations, however, homogeneity remains a problem.[2] For instance, roughly 77 percent of newsroom employees, including reporters, editors, photographers and videographers for newspapers and those working in broadcasting and Internet publishing industries, are non-Hispanic whites.[3] For U.S. workers in all other occupations and industries combined, the corresponding figure is 65 percent. Although minorities make up just under 40 percent of the U.S. adult population, they make up only 22 percent of the local television news workforce and only 13 percent of daily newspaper newsrooms.[4] Further compounding the issue, the number of black journalists working at U.S. daily newspapers has declined 40 percent in the past two decades, a loss of about 1,200 employees (the comparable decline for white journalists is 34 percent during the same period).[5] Advertising also has issues with diversity. To wit, as of 2014, the Bureau of Labor Statistics recognizes 582,000 Americans employed in advertising; however, women and minorities remain underrepresented (i.e., less than 50 percent of advertising workers are women, 6.6 percent are black, 5.7 percent are Asian and 10.5 percent are Hispanic).[6] Careers in social sciences reflect similar levels of racial/ethnic underrepresentation. For instance, based on data compiled by the U.S. Census and the Bureau of Labor Statistics, 80.8 percent of social scientists are white, 5.5 percent are black or African American, 5 percent are Asian and 6.5 percent are Hispanic.[7]

These statistics raise questions: What gets lost when storytellers and those responsible for creating media narratives lack racial/ethnic diversity? What pictures of the era in which we live emerge, and are these depictions representative? Moreover, what aspects of contemporary life get overlooked in terms of their implications for minority groups? Unequivocally, the lack of diversity in journalism, social sciences and advertising hinders the ability of media professionals to effectively serve, inform and engage an increasingly diverse public.[8] A dedicated focus on using interviews to examine these issues can be very revealing. The following is an example.

Two years ago, my colleagues and I utilized interviews in a mixed-methodological study to explore the increasing use of social networking sites (SNSs) to discover and evaluate job applicants.[9] Using online survey data from 300 HR professionals, we looked at hiring processes across a broad range of U.S. industries. More relevantly, we conducted interviews with 11 advertising agencies across the U.S. The genesis of our study stemmed from media reports that hiring professionals' reliance on résumés was decreasing and they were becoming increasingly dependent on job applicants' digital footprints, including professional online SNSs such as LinkedIn.[10] Historically, the U.S. Equal Employment Opportunity Commission has urged job applicants not to share their likeness on résumés to limit the likelihood that candidates would be evaluated (and potentially discriminated against) based on their gender, disability, age or race/ethnicity. Yet, in today's digital age not revealing one's physical appearance on professional social networking sites is an aberration. In short, the study explored potential opportunities for bias toward minority job candidates who can no longer easily avoid displaying their physical traits via SNSs. To date, studies that have addressed this topic have typically incorporated field experiments in the form of faux candidate profiles or applications. This study was novel in its use of interviews to question agency decision makers on their processes.

Overall, our study demonstrated that incorporating SNSs into hiring determinations is increasingly commonplace across industries. Moreover, and specifically for advertising hiring professionals, using LinkedIn to cast a wider net was viewed very favorably, especially after first attempting to utilize current employees' SNSs to find candidates—essentially using employees' networks to recruit talent. The reality, however, is that advertising employees were rarely racial/ethnic minorities, and it was questionable whether their networks would provide many potential applicants who were more diverse. Furthermore, LinkedIn also lacked a significant minority presence. Hampton and colleagues[11] found that of those on LinkedIn only 2 percent were black and 4 percent were Latino, while 85 percent were white. Unfortunately, agencies that utilize LinkedIn may not be aware that one of their primary talent pools is so homogeneous. In addition, one interview revealed that women in their 30s were overlooked for account executive positions by that agency because recruiters believed those women were at a point in their lives that required them to spend time away from work based on family commitments. This finding may represent a solitary example of willful discriminatory practices and/or point to a larger trend. Either way, the overall findings might not have been as illuminating without the use of interviews, which provided us with opportunities to ask more pointed and detailed questions and follow-ups. Interviews helped reveal the impact hiring practices have on women and minorities. One other context where interviews may increasingly have implications for America's racial/ethnic minorities is in the area of climate change.

CLIMATE CHANGE—TOWARD THE "RIGHT" QUESTIONS

Climate change represents a problem of substantial magnitude, requiring decisive actions at every level to diminish its environmental impact.[12] People of color are particularly susceptible to its effects, often lacking the resources to recover and to adequately cope with its aftermath. Racial/ethnic minorities, for instance, particularly those of lower income, face undue exposure to air pollution,[13] are most susceptible to labor market displacements[14] and face disproportionate mortality risks due to heat waves[15] than white Americans or those who are more economically advantaged. Media attention and empirical studies have largely failed to adequately examine minorities' response to the risks they face. Journalists and social scientists instead have directed their energies toward almost exclusively interviewing experts, essentially leaving minorities out of meaningful, in-depth climate-change conversations. There are critical questions to be answered, nonetheless, that may be best served by interviewing members of minority groups—especially given their continued expected growth and the depth of insight that's needed to turn the tide on an issue such as climate change.

Early research projected environmentally concerned individuals to be affluent, better educated and white,[16] and recent survey data demonstrate that racial/ethnic minorities are no less concerned about environmental and sustainability issues than white individuals.[17] These findings persist even after factoring in racial/ethnic minorities' economic situation and needs.[18] Yet, even though racial/ethnic minorities care about the environment and share pro-environmental sentiments, their collective orientations (in addition to those of non-Hispanic whites) do not translate into sufficiently impactful environmental behaviors.[19] There may be a number of reasons why.

First, the way in which race/ethnicity has been conceptualized may obscure variations within racial/ethnic subgroups. For instance, research has shown that Latinos are particularly responsive to environmental issues, harboring significantly greater pro-environmental orientations and pro-environmental perceptions of self-efficacy than African Americans and white individuals.[20] However, conceptualizing Latinos' group identity as monolithic or homogeneous fails to acknowledge cultural and socioeconomic differences among subgroups (e.g., Mexicans, Cubans, Puerto Ricans, Dominicans, etc.). Latinos have a wide range of life experiences in the United States and represent individuals of different Latin American heritages and with distinct immigration histories. Given this diversity, Latinos have many options in deciding how to identify and mobilize.[21] Surveys and experiments may only reveal so much.

With interviews, journalists and social scientists can get a much better sense of how Latinos and other racial/ethnic groups' pro-environmental attitudes translate into behaviors. Are there distinctions in the types of pro-environmental behaviors engaged in by Latinos of different ethnic backgrounds? How do those behaviors differ from those of other racial groups (e.g., non-Hispanic whites, African Americans, etc.)? Which racial/ethnic groups are engaging in pro-environmental behaviors experts describe as having the most impact (e.g., eating less meat, avoiding air travel and not wasting food), and what impediments prevent those behaviors from being more frequently adopted? Are there differences in the ecological or carbon footprints of different racial/ethnic groups? Additionally, are certain minority groups more likely to lean conservative, and does their conservatism extend toward their attitudes about climate change? Overall, studies indicate conservatives report fewer concerns about climate change and lower support for ameliorative policies compared to liberals.[22] All of these questions are, arguably, increasingly important to address, and they may best be served by interviews. Preparing students to start thinking about these issues and giving them the tools they need to be able to engage diverse audiences is beneficial for everyone.

For instance, Drew found, using data from interviews with journalists at 28 major U.S. newspapers, that journalists who took on explicit and intentional "racial projects" in their cities ended up "turn[ing] their lens inward, engaging in a critical self-reflection about the complex relationship between racism and their news content, production practices, and newsroom hierarchies."[23] Drew found that by engaging in topics that dealt with issues of race/ethnicity, journalists' awareness about the racialization of news facilitated a reorientation of their relationships to each other and the community, leading to changes inside the newsroom related to hiring, space allocation and news coverage of people of color. Here at Oregon, these are ideals that many of us embrace and that we continue to impart to our students. The value of interviewing in attaining valuable insights and as part of our processes here at the University of Oregon cannot be overstated.

NOTES

1. Turow, J. (1997). *Breaking up America: Advertisers and the new world*. Chicago, IL: University of Chicago Press.

2. White, G.B. (2015). Where are all the minority journalists? The Atlantic. Retrieved from https://www.theatlantic.com/business/archive/2015/07/minorities-in-journalism/399461/.

3. Grieco, E. (2018). Newsroom employees are less diverse than U.S. workers overall. Retrieved from http://www.pewresearch.org/fact-tank/2018/11/02/newsroom-employees-are-less-diverse-than-u-s-workers-overall/.

4. Barthel, M. (2015). In the news industry, diversity is lowest at smaller outlets. Retrieved from http://www.pewresearch.org/fact-tank/2015/08/04/in-the-news-industry-diversity-is-lowest-at-smaller-outlets/.

5. Anderson, M. (2014). As news business takes a hit, the number of black journalists declines. Pew Research Center. Retrieved from http://www.pewresearch.org/fact-tank/2014/08/01/as-news-business-takes-a-hit-the-number-of-black-journalists-declines/.

6. Grillo, G. (2015). The advertising industry needs diverse leadership to thrive. AdAge. Retrieved Feb. 17, 2019, from https://adage.com/article/agency-viewpoint/advertising-industry-diverse-leadership-thrive/297998/.

7. Lam, B. (2015). The least diverse jobs in America. The Atlantic. Retrieved Feb. 17, 2019, from https://www.theatlantic.com/business/archive/2015/06/diversity-jobs-professions-america/396632/.

8. White, G.B. (2015). Where are all the minority journalists? The Atlantic. Retrieved Feb. 17, 2019, from https://www.theatlantic.com/business/archive/2015/07/minorities-in-journalism/399461/.

9. Elias, T., Phillips Honda, L., VanRysdam, M.K., & Chun, J. (2016). A mixed methods examination of 21st century hiring processes, social networking sites, and implicit bias. *Journal of Social Media in Society,* 5(1), 189–228.

10. Gross (2012). Are social media making the resume obsolete? Retrieved Feb. 18, 2019, from http://www.cnn.com/2012/07/11/tech/social-media/facebook-jobs-resume/index.html; Nisen, M. (2013). Moneyball at work: They've discovered what really makes a great employee. Retrieved from http://www.businessinsider.com/big-data-in-the-workplace-2013-5.

11. Hampton, K.N., Goulet, L.S., Rainie, L., & Purcell, K. (2011). Social networking sites and our lives. *Pew Research Center's Internet & American Life Project.* Retrieved from http://www.pewinternet.org/Reports/2011/Technology-and-social-networks/Summary.aspx.

12. Liao, Y., Ho, S.S., & Yang, X. (2016). Motivators of pro-environmental behavior: Examining the underlying processes in the influence of presumed media influence model. *Science Communication* 38(1) 51–73.

13. Grineski, S.E., & Collins, T.W. (2018). Geographic and social disparities in exposure to air neurotoxicants at U.S. public schools. *Environmental Research,* 161, 580–587; Mikati, I., Benson, A.F., Luben, T.J., Sacks, J.D., & Richmond-Bryant, J. (2018). Disparities in distribution of particulate matter emission sources by race and poverty status. *American Journal of Public Health,* 108(4), 480–485.

14. Morello-Frosch, R., Pastor, M., Sadd, J., & Shonkoff, S.B. (2009). The Climate Gap Report. Retrieved Feb. 17, 2019, from https://dornsife.usc.edu/assets/sites/242/docs/The_Climate_Gap_Full_Report_FINAL.pdf.

15. Basu, R., & Ostro, B.D. (2008). A multicounty analysis identifying the populations vulnerable to mortality associated with high ambient temperature in California. *American Journal of Epidemiology,* 168(6), 632–637.

16. Schwepker, C.H. Jr, & Cornwell, T.B. (1991). An examination of ecologically concerned consumers and their intention to purchase ecologically packaged products. *Journal of Public Policy and Marketing,* 10(2), 77–101.

17. Krogstad, J.M. (2015). Latinos more likely than whites to say global warming is caused by humans. Pew Research Center. Retrieved from http://www.pewresearch.org/fact-tank/2015/02/27/Latinos-more-likely-than-whites-to-say-global-warming-is-caused-by-humans/; Leiserowitz, A., & Akerlof, K. (2010). *Race, ethnicity and public responses to climate change.* New Haven, CT: Yale Project on Climate Change.

18. Elias, T., Dahmen, N., Morrison, D., Morrison, D., & Morris, D. (2018). Understanding climate change inactivity across hispanic, African American, and Anglo racial/ethnic groups. *Howard Journal of Communications.*

19. Gifford, R. (2011). The dragons of inaction: Psychological barriers that

limit climate change mitigation and adaptation. *American Psychologist*, 66(4), 290–302.

20.   Elias, T., et al. (2018); Leiserowitz, A., & Akerlof, K. (2010).

21.   Masuoka, N. (2008). Defining the group: Latino identity and political participation. *American Politics Research*, 36(1), 33–61.

22.   Schuldt, J. P., & Pearson, A. R. (2016). The role of race and ethnicity in climate change polarization: Evidence from a U.S. national survey experiment. *Climatic Change*, 136(3–4), 495–505.

23.   Drew, E.M. (2011). Coming to terms with our own racism: Journalists grapple with the racialization of their news. *Critical Studies in Media Communication*, (4), 353–373.

"god bless the ded"

*Why we interview people after tragedy
(even when we don't want to)*

ALEX TIZON

Few jobs are more demanding for journalists
than interviewing the victims of tragedy. Alex
Tizon, a Pulitzer Prize winner, provides some
guidance for facing human loss with respect and
without sacrificing the story.

His daughter's body had been found in the middle of the street. He
didn't know who killed her. He didn't know why she was killed, and why
her body—legs crossed at the ankles, arms outstretched—had been laid
out in the form of a cross. The toll of not knowing showed on his face.
His whole bearing implied a crumbling. When I first met him, Richard
Zapata was 65, a retired media executive, a tall, dignified, silver-haired
man unaccustomed, I would have guessed, to losing his composure. But
as he spoke to me at length about the police investigation, his voice would
crack for a moment. His face would contort. He'd collect himself before
resuming.

Now, many years later, I've forgotten most of what he said, but I still
remember the cracking, and the lines of his face quivering. I remember
trying to keep my own composure. I remember feeling like a jackal for

being there at all, asking questions no considerate person should ask. I had to remind myself that I served a function. I had a job to do.

What exactly is the correct way to conduct yourself in the presence of inconsolable grief? *I don't know.* This is the truest statement you'll read from me. I've done some things wrong, and some right. Every situation differed, and no formula could guarantee a desirable result. In 2 ½ decades of covering news, I've seen mayhem, and I can say that reporting on mayhem is easy compared to what we journalists cover much more often, which is the drawn-out aftermath of mayhem. We walk into the ruins of a fallen skyscraper. We wade through streets-turned-rivers after the storm has passed. We approach a house where a single mother has just learned that her son, 6,700 miles away, was erased by something as impersonal as an "improvised explosive device." We enter these spaces, and come face to face with the people standing there. I don't know any journalist who enjoys that moment. One hot afternoon in Seattle, I walked with a silver-haired man to the exact spot on 24th Avenue South where his daughter's body had been discovered by a streetwalker named Charity. Charity called the police.

"I want to understand," Zapata told me. Every day for months, and as often as he could for many years, he walked the route that he believed his daughter, Mia, had walked on that summer night in 1993. "It's a pilgrimage for me, I guess. I don't know. Maybe I think by doing this, I'll figure out what happened."

FEELING LIKE A JACKAL

As I think of it now, that's exactly why I was there, too. I was trying to figure out what happened: so I could tell the story, so the story could be known by others. So that we could bear the weight of grief together, as a community, and even perhaps help one another arrive at some sort of answer to "why?" The writer Robert Stone said that telling stories involves seeing people suffer and finding some meaning therein. At our best, that's what we do as public storytellers. It doesn't mean there aren't jackals among us, or that compassionate journalists can't be jackals at times. I've certainly had some "learning moments."

During my rookie years at the *Seattle Times*, I covered street gangs as a beat. It involved some covert, mostly low-risk, infiltration. In the late '80s and early '90s, the story of West Coast gangs, with their crack cocaine and propensity to drive by and shoot, was still largely untold. I wanted to tell it. One day I received a tip about a private funeral for a notorious gangbanger killed in a drive-by. I found out the location, a small church, and decided to attend. I didn't identify myself to any of the few dozen people there. Ten minutes into the service a young man in the same pew stood and addressed the gathering. "Hold up, hold up," he said. Then he turned to me, and all eyes turned.

"Who's this motherfukka?"

"I work for a newspaper," I said. Gasps in the crowd. Glares and murmurings of doing me harm. The dead man's mother, in the front pew, looked at me plaintively and said, "You're disrespecting my son. You're disrespecting his family. Do you know that, sir?" She told the others to leave me alone, and she asked me to leave. "Please."

Young and dumb and brazen, that was me. I eventually would have identified myself, probably, but the truth was I hadn't thought it through. At the time, I hadn't yet experienced a death in my family or close circle. Death was still just a concept. I've since sat through the funerals of a beloved grandmother who had lived with me, both of my parents, and several close friends who passed suddenly. I know now the mother was right. I had trespassed on a family's private moment. I added to the affliction. To this day I don't feel sympathy for the dead guy, and if you knew what he had done in his life, you wouldn't either. But his mother, his brothers and sisters, his childhood friends—the ones left to deal with his departure—they deserved sympathy, respect. They had the right to grieve without an uninvited outsider taking notes on them.

I've rung the doorbells of grief-stricken households, and have had a door or two closed in my face. I've approached people at the scene of shootings, accidents, natural disasters, and have been told in various ways, "I'm sorry. Not now." Even when I conducted myself with utmost decorum, I sometimes felt like a heel. I felt it most acutely when I was part of a media swarm. The 1989 San Francisco Earthquake. The crash of Alaska Airlines 261. September 11. Hurricane Katrina. The capture of the

Beltway Sniper. The sentencing of Gary Ridgeway, the Green River Killer, in which the relatives of his 48 victims gathered in a Seattle courtroom. Many in the room spoke of their suffering for the first time. Mothers and sisters wept; fathers cursed. We reporters swarmed. There was no getting around it. From what I saw, the vast majority of us behaved with as much sensitivity as humanly possible given the circumstances.

"I was only 5 when my mother died," said one woman, Sara King, daughter of Carol Ann Christensen, identified in court papers as Victim 22. "The one thing I want you to know is that there was a daughter. I was that daughter, and I was waiting for my mother to come home."

I try to remember this when I'm tempted to feel like a heel, when I get down about my profession. The daughter could have communicated her thoughts in more private ways, but she chose to speak in front of a packed courthouse, with cameras rolling and note-takers scribbling. Why? I think it's for the same reason that a 15-year-old girl in Oklahoma City, Bonnie Martinez, allowed me to ask her questions about her father, Gilbert, who was vaporized when Timothy McVeigh's truck bomb went off in 1995. "I miss everything about him," she told me. It was the same reason why Richard Zapata took me to the spot on 24th where a chalk outline of his daughter's body remained visible for three years. The same reason, I'm guessing, that compelled children in New York City to scrawl notes in crayon and to post them on a bulletin board outside St. Paul's Chapel, one block from the now-gone World Trade Center:

> I feel so sad
> I will always love you Daddy
> god bless the ded

Reporters, at times, swarm, and nobody likes it. Some people will turn us away. Some will be too broken to speak. But many, many others, given the opportunity, want to talk of how it's been for them. They want someone to listen to their story. They want it chronicled, put on the record. Sara King wanted the world to know that she had waited for her mother to come home. The day that my Green River story ran in the *Los Angeles Times* (my then new employer), I got a call from a young woman who had spoken at the sentencing. None of her quotes had been published, and no reporter had interviewed her afterward. She wondered if I might be interested. I told her I couldn't guarantee a story. She spoke to me for 35 minutes. The one thing I remember—I'm not sure why—was that she wished she could thank her sister for the months she spent teaching her how to drive a stick-shift.

This "interview" took no skills on my part. The best thing I did was not interrupt her. I made some occasional sounds to let her know I was listening. In many of my encounters with people in grief, my "technique" was simply showing up and shutting up. That's my five-word crash course on the topic. The showing up part is critical. It's the one aspect that we have control over. We must show up, despite our discomfort, despite the possibility of rejection. Make ourselves available. Be present. If we must, probe as gently as possible. We often need only a few words. Imagine these words as fingers easing out the cork, allowing what's been bottled up to pour forth on its own.

THE DEMON THEORY

It's all that was necessary with Richard Zapata. His affliction was of a particularly cruel kind. There was no answer to the most basic questions: who killed his daughter, and why? We spoke on several occasions over a span of years. When we first met, he said he didn't have much to say, but it turned out he did. The day that I joined him on his pilgrimage, he wasn't much interested in talking about how he felt, and to my credit I never asked. He wanted to talk about the investigation. He spoke of his daughter. Mia was 27, a musician, and "the best of our family," he said. She was an idealist, too trusting for her own good. A couple of times Zapata stopped at an intersection, trying to imagine which route Mia chose.

Police knew that she walked part of the way home after a night out with band members. She stopped at a friend's apartment and left the place at 2 a.m. Her body was found at 3:20 a.m., 1.6 miles from where she was last seen. Eighty minutes, Zapata said. Measurements were what preoccupied him. Coordinates. They were as close as he could get—in my presence, anyway—to talking about the attack, which one detective later described to me as "surpassingly brutal."

The killer had left almost no evidence. Police collected DNA samples but found no matches in criminal databases. All the usual suspects—boy-friends, ex-boyfriends, close relatives and friends—were cleared. Local bands, among them Nirvana and Pearl Jam, raised $70,000 to hire a private investigator. Profilers and psychics were brought in. A forensic psychologist theorized that Mia had been killed by someone who'd done it before, perhaps a serial killer.

Zapata moved from his home in Yakima to a condominium in Seattle, close to where Mia's body was discovered, so that he could conduct his pilgrimages more often. He wound up retracing her footsteps "as many times as I have hair on my head." Police worked the case hard for a couple of years but never got close to identifying a suspect. One of Mia's close friends, explaining the dearth of clues, told me she believed a demon had entered "the earthly realm," took Mia's life, and quickly departed. People in mourning must be given latitude. I told her that anything's possible, I suppose.

Leads dried up. Public attention drifted. The original detectives transferred or retired. Mia's family and friends resigned themselves to the possibility that her murder would never be solved. I had written the initial news briefs in the early days after the murder, and an extensive piece five years later, revisiting what had become a torment to those closest to her. Another five years passed, and I lost touch with Zapata during that time.

One night in January of 2003, I received a phone call from a detective whom I knew only in passing. He wanted to talk off the record. Of course, I said. He was a type of talker who, in reporter's lingo, "buried the lead." Five minutes into a conversation about cold cases and advancements in DNA technology, I still didn't know why he had called. Then he informed me that my stories about Mia's murder, particularly the long piece at the five-year anniversary—the most in-depth article on the case written to date—had become part of Mia's case file. He thanked me for helping to keep the case "on the radar."

"OK," I said.

"I thought you'd be interested to know, although it's not public yet—"

"Right."

"We got him."

I think I took a breath. "What do you mean?"

"We *got* him."

I recall asking him if Mia's father had been notified. He said something along the lines of "we're doing that now."

Nearly a decade after Mia's death, a tall, balding, 48-year-old itinerant fisherman named Jesus C. Mezquia was arrested at his ramshackle home on a remote islet in the middle of the Florida Keys. It turned out that the passing-demon theory was closest to the truth. Mezquia had no known connection to Mia, nor any meaningful tie to Washington state. In the summer of 1993, he had drifted into Seattle, encountered Mia on a dark street, brutalized and killed her, and soon drifted away. He might never have been caught if a Seattle detective had not dug up the case file, re-entered the DNA evidence, and found a match. Mezquia said nothing, and avoided all eye contact, during his trial. He got 36 years.

So one other thing I remind myself when I'm tempted to feel like a jackal is that we reporters can't know the ends to which our stories contribute. We do our jobs with a certain amount of faith. Sometimes a story we tell—one that involves uncomfortable interviews with people in pain, and that draws ire for opening wounds—can help something or someone to not slip into oblivion. And it's our rendering of one party's suffering that often makes the story meaningful or memorable. Being forgotten is easy. Fading is the natural course. Walk into any homicide division or newsroom in any metropolitan area in the country, and you'll find workers laboring to keep up. Yesterday's urgencies must be set aside for today's, and soon yesterday's hardly seem to matter. Zapata did what he could to keep that from happening. I believe the main reason for his pilgrimages to 24th Avenue South, though he couldn't put it into words at the time, was that he didn't want to let go of his grief until it had served its purpose.

"PACK SOME TISSUES JUST IN CASE"

The following thoughts from six storytellers on interviewing people in grief are based on interviews with journalists.

I used to be amazed that people talked in these situations. In fact, they will tell you the most intimate details of their lives. Sometimes, if it was a husband and wife being interviewed, one would be saying something really personal and I'd look at the other and see that he was crying his eyes out. Clearly, he had not heard this before. I'd think, Man, I must be some amazing interviewer. After a few years I realized that it had nothing to do with me: I was just the instrument. People want to tell their stories. They've been waiting their whole lives. All you have to do is get them started. Best way to do that is to ask them something concrete and specific. If a parent has lost a kid who loved to play basketball, ask about his favorite shot, or his best game, something that will get the person to remember details. They want to talk. Let them.

TERRY MCDERMOTT, an award-winning reporter, is the author of *The Hunt for KSM* and *101 Theory Drive*.

I go in knowing it's an emotional situation. And that they might end up crying. And that that might make me cry. It's good to realize you're human and a bit apprehensive in situations like these. (It's also not bad to pack some tissues just in case.) So I often start out saying, "I know this is hard. And I'm really thankful you're taking the time to talk to me." You always want to be respectful when people are allowing you into their lives and their stories, ESPECIALLY in a circumstance like this. It's OK to let them know that you aren't trying to pry (although, let's face it, you are). As gently as possible, I ask about the person they've lost. I get them to recall a scene or a moment or some quintessential action/activity that really shows who the person was. And then I react accordingly, appreciative of what they're telling me. Even if it's unusable. Even if it's not answering your question. But this is how a line of questioning can then turn into a conversation, and that's when the best stories come out.

FLORANGELA DAVILA contributes stories to National Public Radio, Crosscut.com and the *Seattle Times*.

I try to be a bridge between this person who's lost someone dear and all those in the world who will now never have a chance to know him. Because truly, this can be a wonderful thing: a way of helping her distill in her own turbulent heart the one or two things they most remember and love about the person they've lost; the perfect picture they want to leave the rest of the world with, more telling than the prom photo or portrait of him standing by his new car, which she'll also share with me. We sit, and she tells me, a stranger, about how he taught their daughter to ride a bicycle 10 years ago, under the shade of the maple trees. I write it in my story, thinking about my own father and my own bumbling, long-ago self. Someone across the country reads it, and comes to feel the sense of loss in a person he's never met. A bridge has formed in that small moment.

KIM MURPHY, a reporter and editor at the *Los Angeles Times*, won the 2005 Pulitzer Prize in International Reporting.

Journalists are seen in many lights—as crusaders for the truth, as adventurers, as nitpicks, as guarders of the First Amendment. Frequently they are characterized as calloused and badly dressed people who are always looking for the free buffet. One role frequently overlooked is the ministerial role. By choosing this role, you ensure that your interaction, journalist to source, will end up being a two-way transaction where nobody is cheated. The reporter gets the information he is after; the source gets the feeling that he has been heard, and understood. For the time you are with your subject, drop your prejudices and prejudgments. Suspend your disbelief. Listen carefully and sympathetically, whether your source is an angel or a murderer. Try to empathize. Find the common thread of humanity.

MIKE SAGER, author of *The Someone You're Not* and *Wounded Warriors*, is a writer-at-large for Esquire magazine.

When we approach people who have suffered tragedy, our instinct is to presume and protect. We presume that our questions will add to their pain, and we try to protect them from that harm. But who are we to decide for them? Our role is to be fully present and to offer a compassionate ear: to hear about the loved one who is gone, the home that is destroyed, the fear of what's to come, the rage at injustice, the regrets or memories or longings. We give people the chance to tell their stories. If they are offended, I apologize and leave. If they aren't ready, I will come back when they are. The key is to really care about what they have to say, and to believe that theirs are stories that, in some way and at some time, happen to all of us.

JACQUI BANASZYNSKI, winner of the 1988 Pulitzer Prize in Feature Writing, teaches journalism at the University of Missouri.

Your intentions must be simple and good. While your "filming agenda" must be in the back of your mind, your moral sensitivity must be at the fore, and should govern your approach to each person. Have the compassion to allow them to speak as much or as little as they want. Listen as if you were listening to a loved one. Realize that you are privileged to have been allowed into their world at this poignant moment. Your reason for being there is to ensure that their story is heard.

NICK HARDIE is a freelance director and producer who contributes regularly to the Discovery Channel.

TWENTY-THREE

Working Through Trauma

Covering mass shootings is hard on victims'
families and friends—and it's hard on
journalists as well

LORI SHONTZ

Particularly challenging for journalists
assigned to report tragedy is reporting on
random mass shootings. It's a crisis Lori
Shontz researches.

On Oct. 1, 2015, then-president Barack Obama stood at a podium at the
White House, talking about the tragedy that had unfolded that day in
Roseburg, Oregon: A student shot and killed his eight classmates and
his teacher in an English classroom at Umpqua Community College.
Obama had done this before. Fort Hood. Tucson. Wisconsin. Sandy
Hook. Washington Naval Yard. Charleston. This time, he wasn't just sad.
He let his anger show. He pounded on the podium. "Somehow this has
become routine," he said, punctuating each word.

And that's a problem. The routine.

Too often, journalists treat mass shooting coverage—or the coverage
of any breaking news trauma—as though it's just like everything else we
cover. We go into our reporter "routine." We show up, as fast as we can,
so we miss as little as possible as the event unfolds. We gather "color," the

details that we hope will make readers, listeners and viewers care and understand. We look for people to talk to, and we ask questions. Mostly, we find out what happened by asking questions. Lots of questions.

All of this is of vital importance to what we do. As the Society of Professional Journalists' code of ethics puts it, we seek truth. But when you're covering a mass trauma, you've got to keep the second part of SPJ's code in mind: It's equally important to minimize harm.

Maintaining that difficult balance is particularly important when you're interviewing on the scene at a mass shooting or trauma.

I've spent more than three years researching how the UCC shooting was covered and how the community responded to the news media's efforts, and I've reflected frequently on my own days as a general assignment reporter, when I helped cover a mass shooting and the aftermath. Here's what I've learned:

- All journalists need to be aware that even if they don't aspire to be a cops reporter or a war correspondent, there's a good chance that at some point in their career, they're going to have to cover something traumatic.

- All journalists need a basic understanding of trauma—both how it affects the survivors they're interviewing and how it could affect them.

- All journalists need to more frequently deploy one of the most important questions in our repertoire: How do you know this?

- And all journalists need to know it's not a weakness to need help. One of the most important things you can do for your mental health after covering a trauma is to be debriefed—to be not the interviewer, but the interviewee.

BE PREPARED

My colleague Nicole Dahmen and I interviewed 19 of the Oregon-based journalists who covered the UCC shooting for our project Reporting

Roseburg, and the first question we asked was how they got the initial news tip. We found that most of them had been working overnight or early in the morning, reporting stories about the first day Oregonians could legally buy recreational marijuana. With no warning, their assignments changed—or their days continued, for much longer than they had planned.

Only three of the 19 had ever covered a mass trauma. That meant 16 of the reporters arrived on the scene with no experience.

The *Oregonian's* first reporter on the scene, Andrew Greif, was the beat reporter covering University of Oregon football; he was the farthest south of anyone on the staff, so he was interrupted during an interview with the coach and told to get to Roseburg as quickly as possible.

Another of the first reporters on the scene, Joseph Hoyt, was a student at the University of Oregon who had signed up for the *Washington Post's* nationwide reporting network six months previously. His application had never even been acknowledged. The first time he heard from the *Post*, an editor asked him to drive to Roseburg.

Neither of the two young reporters from the *News Review* in Roseburg had been on the job for even a year. SOJC graduate Ian Campbell heard the term "active shooter" on the scanner and wasn't even 100 percent sure what it meant.

All of those journalists—and the other 12 who were also covering such a crime for the first time—told us they wish they had been better prepared. But they knew they had to get to the scene and ask questions.

That's what journalists do: When news breaks, we run out the door. And when we show up at something unfamiliar, we do what we've been doing in any other situation: We identify potential sources, and we ask questions. Troy Brynelson, another SOJC graduate working for the *News Review*, said it was like "a switch comes on where it's just like you're processing everything for a second and then it's . . . I have to work." That's muscle memory, kicking in.

That can cause two problems.

First, memories of trauma can be fragmented—that's how the brain protects itself. U.S. citizens and journalists have learned more about this reality through the #MeToo movement and the testimony of Christine

Blasey Ford, who accused Supreme Court nominee Brett Kavanaugh of sexually assaulting her in high school, and the same phenomenon can happen in a situation like this.

It's important to remember that the information you get during an interview isn't necessarily wrong. The details that a survivor focuses on first, peer-reviewed research on soldiers and sexual assault victims has shown, don't change. But it can mean that some details won't add up, or that you won't get a complete version of what happens.

"That's why the media tends to have roller-coaster stories for the first few weeks," said Kelly Wright, the victim advocate for Douglas County, Oregon, who has worked closely with families affected by the UCC shooting. "Because when you've gone through a traumatic event, recalling those details is beyond impossible in the first few days. Your mind is filling in gaps because it can't live with the fact that you can't remember. You were in shock. You're just in a state of denial."

Second, recounting a trauma over and over can be dangerous for a survivor's mental health. Yet journalists do this all the time. A scrum—a large group of journalists surrounding the person they're interviewing—is a common feature after any breaking news event, from a football game to a Supreme Court hearing. You can't always hear what's been said, or you show up late, so you have to ask again. That's how the scrum works.

That's how it worked after the UCC shooting. Students were bused to the Douglas County Fairgrounds, where their families and friends could meet them. That's where much of the news media went, too. Two reporters, including Rachael McDonald, a reporter for KLCC radio in Eugene, Oregon, noticed a young woman in a Red Cross blanket sitting on a curb.

McDonald said she made eye contact with the young woman, then walked over with another reporter and asked if she were OK. Then, and only then, did she ask if she would be willing to answer some questions. The student, Hannah Miles, agreed.

That's a typical kind of interaction between reporters and witnesses to tragedy, and it's an important part of the job. McDonald and the other journalist asked for her name, for some biographical details and what she could tell them about what had happened.

But this interaction, too, is typical: "More and more reporters were coming up, and they were asking her the same questions," McDonald said. "And I felt sympathy for her because she was having to tell her story over and over again, and it was painful for her to have to relive it. And I think, too, we were kind of like birds of prey descending on a little mouse."

Both of these realities complicate the job of journalists covering a mass shooting or, really, any crime or trauma. "I think for the most part that time down at the fairgrounds was just an exercise in talking to people when they really did not even know what to say," Brynelson said. "I mean, nobody knew what was going on. How did they feel about it?"

Journalists aren't the only people who conduct interviews with crime victims, although journalists' interviews are more public. Other professionals who do this—police, therapists, court officials—are increasingly conducting trauma-informed interviews, in which they explicitly acknowledge what the survivor has been through and give the survivor more control in the interview. These interviews also emphasize the importance of not retraumatizing the interviewee.

Officials still get the information they need. But by using trauma-informed techniques, they do so differently. When they need to, they back off. That's hard to do when you're a journalist and deadline is looming, but it's something you need to consider.

Try this technique: Divide and conquer. There's no formal pool reporting procedure at crime scenes (although I'd argue there should be, especially when hundreds of national reporters show up). So work with colleagues at other news organizations to do something informally. Don't surround the survivors. Share information with one another rather than duplicating someone else's work. Scoops aren't as important at a time like this.

BE A HUMAN FIRST

Hoyt said he'll never forget getting to the fairgrounds to conduct interviews for the *Washington Post*. Some students got mad at him, asking or yelling, "What are you doing here?" or "Get out of here!" or "Can't you see we're grieving?"

"You know," Hoyt said, "the thing is, I completely understand that. I couldn't imagine talking to some person I'd never met before after my son, daughter, brother, sister was involved in a mass shooting."

And it's not only young reporters who feel that way. Eli Saslow, a Pulitzer Prize–winning journalist for the *Washington Post* who is based in Portland, dislikes asking questions at a crime scene so much that he said it took him 10 minutes to get out of the car at the fairgrounds. But he also believes, passionately, that he needs to do it.

"It's my responsibility to journalism to try to do my job well—and if people want to talk, to give them the opportunity to do that," he said. "If they don't, then absolutely, that's totally fine. I understand. That's their right. . . . But I think that the only way we can write things of value is by actually knowing things. The only way for me, anyway, to know things is to go talk to people about them."

This dilemma came up a lot in our interviews for Reporting Roseburg, and it comes up informally, too, when journalists talk to each other. More than half of the journalists said they would not have wanted to answer the questions they were asking of others. Most said they could understand why someone wouldn't want to answer. Yet they asked them anyway—because that, they agreed, is the job.

Hillary Lake, a University of Oregon doctoral graduate who was working for KATU, the ABC television affiliate in Portland, covered the community vigil the night of the UCC shooting. "And part of me didn't want to go up to people to talk to them, to interview them," she said. "Because I put myself in their position. Would I want somebody coming up to me? And I don't know if I could answer that question.

"The only thing that helped me get through that as a reporter was this: What if there was one person who wanted their story told? Who wanted the world to know what they thought about what happened or to remember somebody who had died? To give them that opportunity, that's what we do in these situations."

Here's the thing about trauma—there's no one, consistent response. So Lake is right—some people really do want to tell stories about the loved ones they lost. Elsewhere in this book, the late Alex Tizon writes with empathy and passion about why it's so important to interview victims of trauma. He's right on all counts.

But there's also a case to be made for backing off.

One of the core news values in journalism is timeliness—and like all other news values, it's got pros and cons. The big problem with timeliness is that journalists show up in great numbers immediately after news breaks, and then they fade away. And even when they have the best intentions, reporters cause harm in large numbers. (Another reason why journalists should organize a system for pool reporting at mass trauma events.)

Wright, the victim advocate, told all of the families of those killed at UCC that they didn't need to speak to the news media unless they wanted to. But that didn't stop reporters from asking. One family member turned off his cell phone and turned it back on a couple of hours later—and had 28 messages from news outlets, most of which he'd never heard of. One family got 50 calls—in the middle of the night. Some families had to change their phone numbers.

But a couple of weeks or months later, Wright said, some of those families who hadn't talked were ready. They would have loved to tell their stories. But by then, the news media crowd was gone.

In Roseburg, Saslow was able to stay. He had covered several previous mass shootings and seen the routine Obama lamented—the initial news coverage, the "tick-tock" of what happened at the shooting on about day two, the determination of where the shooter got the gun, etc. "By the fourth day, you know, the stories are about a community healing, things coming back together, the last person gets out of the hospital. And then, it's just the vast silence, at least in the national space. And I knew the story didn't end there, and I wanted to figure out a way to go back and write about the messy reality of how this continues in people's lives."

Two months after the shooting, Saslow wrote "A Survivor's Life," which focused on Cheyeanne Fitzgerald, the youngest survivor at age 16, who was struggling with both physical and mental injuries. "I just wanted to go and spend time and have them be comfortable enough with me that they could start living their lives around me, so that I could see the real thing and not a version of it that was handed to me," Saslow said. "And that takes time, to just sit around."

Try this technique: Focus on resilience. The American Red Cross, which has learned a lot about mass violence in the past 20 years, makes a significant change in its relief operations after 10 to 14 days. At that point, the Family Assistance Center becomes the Family Resilience Center. It's not a surface-level change. It's a reassessing of resources partly because the needs of the families and survivors change, but also because the families will need help for a long, long time to come. Introduce yourself to victim advocates and Red Cross officials early on. Stop by to talk without conducting formal interviews. Let them know that you understand that recovery takes a long time and is a winding road, and say you'd like to be there. Don't look away.

BE CAREFUL OF THE NARRATIVE

Here's what all of this means in practice: When you're on the scene, interviewing people on deadline, you're getting fragments of information from people who have just experienced a trauma and might not—through no fault of their own—be getting everything right. And you've got a self-selected group of people—not everyone is willing or able to speak with the news media right away—who may not be the best people to tell you what actually happened.

So journalists need to be particularly careful in how they use the information they learn from interviewing witnesses and survivors. Even if additional reporting by journalists and investigating by law enforcement determines that the initial reports are incorrect or incomplete, those original news media interviews set the initial narrative, and that's impossible to erase.

In addition, as those details are reported, they can influence the narrative if reporters aren't careful—and don't ask the right questions.

One famous example: Columbine. Dave Cullen, one of the reporters who covered the breaking news, went back a decade later and discovered that most of what the public knew was wrong. In a chapter called Media Crime in his tour de force book, *Columbine*, he writes:

> We remember Columbine as a pair of outcast Goths from the Trench Coat Mafia snapping and tearing through the high school hunting down jocks to settle a running feud. Almost none of that happened. No Goths, no outcasts, nobody snapping. No targets, no feuds, and no Trench Coat Mafia. Most of those elements existed at Columbine—which is what gave them such currency. They just had nothing to do with the murders. The lesser myths are equally unsupported: no connection to Marilyn Manson, Hitler's birthday, minorities, or Christmas.

Cullen detailed how this happened: It turned out that many of the students whom reporters interviewed had been influenced by the news media coverage. Even though television reporters "used attributions and disclaimers like 'believed to be' or 'described as,'" Cullen discovered, the students were learning what may have happened from those reports. (These days, it would be social media.) "Kids 'knew' the [Trench Coat Mafia] was involved because witnesses and news anchors had said so on TV," Cullen wrote.

One of the solutions, he determined, would have been simply to conduct better interviews. If you get in the habit of doing so when you're not under deadline pressure or covering a particularly emotional story, your muscle memory will kick in—to a good end—when you're under deadline pressure covering a difficult story.

Try this technique: Always, ask someone how they know what they are telling you. Don't ask it in accusatory way; you're not trying to catch someone in a lie or a falsehood. You're just trying to get as many details as you can get. Ask it simply: How do you know this?

TAKE CARE OF YOURSELF

In a mass shooting or other such trauma, journalists are first responders. We aren't doing the job that police, firefighters, emergency room personnel and the like are doing, but we are among the first on the scene, and we witness some of the same horror. In addition, through conducting interviews, we hear about more trauma, and we set ourselves up to experience secondary trauma.

This isn't something that newsrooms like to talk about. News happens. So you move on to the next story, and you don't want to show weakness. Or else when the next big story happens, you might not get to be a part of it.

Other first responders get debriefed. They talk to someone about what happened, even if they think they don't need it. And doing so helps them to cope. It strengthens them for future events. But none of the 19 journalists who participated in Reporting Roseburg had talked in-depth about their experiences before we interviewed them for our project. Every one of them thanked us, saying it helped to talk about it.

During the tragedy, many of the veteran journalists on the scene in Roseburg reached out to younger and less experienced reporters, and that kind of mentoring and on-the-job learning is invaluable. But it doesn't substitute for a more formal debriefing. Know that covering a mass shooting or trauma isn't simply about asking questions. It's about answering them, too.

Try this technique: Visit the website for the Dart Center for Journalism and Trauma now, before you might need it. It's got a trove of resources that every journalist should know about, and its section on self-care is particularly good. Covering how communities cope with trauma and crime is important work. Make sure you're in the best possible shape to continue doing it.

BIBLIOGRAPHY

American Red Cross of Nevada. (n.d.). Building resiliency. Retrieved from https://www.redcross.org/local/nevada/about-us/news-and-events/news/Building-Resiliency.html.
Cullen, Dave. (2009). *Columbine.* New York: Hachette.
Dahmen, Nicole Smith, and Shontz, Lori. (2016). Reporting Roseburg. Retrieved from https://reportingroseburg.uoregon.edu/.
Dart Center for Journalism and Trauma. Retrieved from https://dartcenter.org/.

Hopper, Jim. (2018, Oct. 5). Why can't Christine Blasey Ford remember how she got home? *Scientific American*. Retrieved from https://blogs.scientific american.com/observations/why-cant-christine-blasey-ford-remember-how -she-got-home/.

IVOH (2015). Washington Post narrative puts focus on survivor, not offender, of mass shooting. Retrieved from https://ivoh.org/story/washington-post-story -puts-focus-on-survivor-not-offender-of-mass-shooting/.

Office for Victims of Crimes, U.S. Department of Justice. (n.d.). Helping victims of mass violence and terrorism. Retrieved from https://www.ovc.gov/pubs/ mvt-toolkit/.

Saslow, Eli. (2015, Dec. 5). A Survivor's Life. *Washington Post*. Retrieved from https://www.washingtonpost.com/sf/national/2015/12/05/after-a-mass -shooting-a-survivors-life/?utm_term=.b4156f3517a3.

Society of Professional Journalists (n.d.). SPJ Code of Ethics. Retrieved from https://www.spj.org/ethicscode.asp.

TWENTY-FOUR

Interviewing as Connecting

Listening is the key to a meaningful interaction

JULIANNE H. NEWTON

Consider the interview as a medium in which participants seek understanding, suggests communications scholar Julianne Newton. She teaches Oregon students to stay curious and to listen well.

Interview (English)
Entrevista (Spanish)
entèvyou (Haitian Creole)
ראיון (Hebrew)
Agallamh (Irish)
Uiui (Maori)
Ibere ijomitoro (Yoruba)

Interviewing can happen through question and answer.

Or it can happen through the simple but powerful moment of a visual embrace—when eyes meet and two people connect with deep, personal understanding.

Styles vary as widely as interviewers and interviewees: from pure listening to gentle prodding to provocation and from quiet reticence to heartfelt outpouring or emotional outburst and angry denial.

New methods of interviewing—via virtual environment, recording audio and video with sophisticated cameras, research-informed methods for constructing and ordering questions and informing the influence of both interviewer and interviewee on the content elicited, digital tran-

249

scription and analysis software—all complement the tried-and-true practice of face-to-face, in-person interaction between a source of information and a person with a pen and notepad (or a good memory).

As we develop, learn and apply new interview methods, it can be quite evocative to step above the concreteness of everyday practice to theorize a bit. What if we think of the interview itself as a medium?

A medium is simply an environment, a broader concept than the technological assumptions we usually ascribe to the concept of communication media. If we think of an interview as a medium, an environment, we can envision interviewing as a space in which two organisms seek to convey understanding through interaction. Each organism (or person) emerges from his or her own environment and moves into a unique, temporary ecosystem shared with another. The balance—or lack thereof—of power the two organisms negotiate determines the quality of the content they create and share in that ecosystem, with the potential to affect other ecosystems large and small.

Marshall McLuhan's laws of media offer a useful way to ponder the effects of new tools and new ways of interviewing on small and large media ecosystems and to learn the most effective ways to use both new and old forms of professional practice.

McLuhan's tetradic analysis asks:

What is enhanced?

What is obsolesced?

What is retrieved?

What do the new tools and methods reverse into when pushed to extreme?

Thinking in tetrads evokes possibilities rather than prescribes inevitabilities. Tetrads also can reveal both positive and negative potential effects. For example, consider these two tetrads for "recording by smartphone":

Recording by smartphone . . .
    Enhances efficient documentation
    Obsolesces memory and notetaking by hand
    Retrieves accuracy and context
    Reverses into in-depth analysis

Recording by smartphone . . .
  Enhances instant aural and visual connection
  Obsolesces eye-to-eye contact
  Retrieves focused listening and observing
  Reverses into detached interaction

Here are a few more tetrads for you to consider:

Interviewing by Skype . . .
  Enhances immediate connection
  Obsolesces distance
  Retrieves face to face
  Reverses into disembodied intimacy

Interacting via Internet chat room . . .
  Enhances broader connection
  Obsolesces in-person connection
  Retrieves candor
  Reverses into intensified or weakened connection

Interviewing in a virtual world . . .
  Enhances free expression through masked identity
  Obsolesces the directly interpersonal
  Retrieves safety through anonymity
  Reverses into infinite possibility for forms of interaction

Effective Interviewing . . .
  Enhances attention to another person's thoughts and feelings
  Obsolesces isolation in one's own mind and heart
  Retrieves commonality and difference
  Reverses into intensified extension of self

Although working with tetrads can seem confusing at first, imagining them, thinking them through, playing the chords of the effects, which occur simultaneously in what McLuhan called resonating intervals, can awaken awareness of actual and potential ripple effects of new and old tools and methods in our rapidly changing world of infinitely variable environments—or media. They can help us improve interviewing practices, in both practical and theoretical ways.

Regardless of the means of interaction, effective interviewers master the art of listening well. We are learning more about listening through research. Princeton psychologists recently determined, for example, that students who take lecture notes by hand comprehend and remember lecture content better than those who take notes using mobile devices. We also know that something special happens when a researcher listens to a recorded interview, pausing to transcribe, rewinding, pausing again. The process can transport the interviewer back into the intimacy of the original interaction—with the benefit of time—to become consciously aware of the nuances of the conversation.

On the other side of the methodological coin is the opinion that the best listening occurs when the listener neither prods nor empathizes, but, rather, simply listens, connecting with eye contact and later repeating back to the speaker what he/she heard. The idea is that with little feedback from the listener, the speaker has the best opportunity to express his/her thoughts with the least amount of influence from another.

Today's students—the media professionals and scholars of the future—will invent effective ways to practice and deliver journalism in a digital world and to communicate strategically across the globe. Those new strategies employ both old and new methods and tools, occur in different languages, cultures and environments, and work through a full range of platforms. What they have in common—if they communicate effectively—is connection, the seeking of the inner view, the search for insight into and connection with the mind and heart of another. A core tool/process/practice/method in establishing that connection is the interview.

I'm reminded of a story told by photographer Robbie McClaran when he discussed his *Angry White Men* project in my People and Images class a number of years ago. While looking into the eyes of convicted Oklahoma City bomber Timothy McVeigh—via one of McClaran's disarmingly human portraits—a student asked, "How can you photograph someone like that? How can you show him in such a positive way?" McClaran said he finds almost everyone has some ability to connect with another person: "I sensed and connected with his humanity."

The tools of the future will likely include even more direct transfer of information through human-to-human, human-to-machine, machine-to-machine technologies and methods. But the timeless tools of the past—a curious and discerning mind, a wise heart, and the ability to listen—will remain the core of the connection that makes an interview meaningful . . . to find the inner view.

BIBLIOGRAPHY

Association for Psychological Science. "Take Notes by Hand for Better Long-Term Comprehension." ScienceDaily. ScienceDaily, 24 April 2014. www.sciencedaily.com/releases/2014/04/140424102837.htm.
Robbie McClaran. "Angry White Men." http://mcclaran.com/portfolio/angry-white-men/#.
Marshall McLuhan and Eric McLuhan. "Laws of Media: The New Science." Toronto: University of Toronto Press (1988).
Marshall McLuhan and Bruce R. Powers. "The Global Village: Transformations in World Life and Media in the Twenty-First Century." New York: Oxford, 1989.

TWENTY-FIVE

The Equipment Disappearing Act

Cameras and microphones can make an interview better

TORSTEN KJELLSTRAND

Technology can help or hurt an interview relationship, depending on how it's introduced and whom you're interviewing. Torsten Kjellstrand says journalists who rely on sophisticated equipment when they conduct interviews still must act to assuage worries from their subjects about the intrusion of complex recording gear.

Before newspaper photographers started making videos to tell the stories of their communities, those of us who worked as still photographers used cameras that felt as familiar as an old ball cap. Once we began to play in the world of filmmaking, we became people who carried too many bags of equipment we barely knew how to use. For the first time, we also began to record our interviews. Good photographers have always interviewed the people they photograph, because we need the information to understand the stories we tell, and because we need to write accurate, informative captions. But when we began to record our interviews, those interviews became content in a way they never had been.

The assumption we made was that all that equipment gets in the way of an intimate interview, that a camera and microphone will either make a person act for us, or the apparatus will make a person so uncomfortable that it bursts the intimacy of the conversation. I agree that too much equipment and equipment used in a clumsy way can break an interview's potential beyond repair. The break can happen when you point a camera and a microphone at a person.

So the task is to introduce the equipment, notebook or two-camera setup, in a way that makes it less obtrusive, less frightening.

I'll assert that you can introduce equipment in a way that demystifies it. If you use it in a way that lets the person being interviewed in on the process, the equipment can even make the interview better by emphasizing the collaborative nature of many of our interviews. Managing equipment smoothly tells the person being interviewed that you are professional, that you see the interview as important and that you are using your skills to make sure that the result will be accurate and respectful.

I'll talk a bit about how to do this, although there isn't a crisp technical methodology for effectively bringing equipment to an interview in a way that makes the interview better, any more than there is one way to ask people a series of questions that leads them to open up and effectively tell their story in words. People are simply too different for that. Come prepared, so that clumsy handling of gear doesn't call attention to the equipment. And be clear and respectful whether you're hauling gear or not.

On one assignment, I learned that bringing equipment to an interview means we must also bring new sensibilities. I had two cameras and two microphones pointed at a friendly elderly man in his living room. He seemed excited to have so much commotion directed at him. When I put on headphones attached to the digital monitor, however, I could see the friendliness fall from his face, replaced by the kind of look a parent gives a young boy who has just tossed a ball through a window.

"Is there something wrong?" I asked.

"You aren't going to listen to me when I talk today?" he asked.

When I put on those headphones, he thought that I was going to listen to music through my headphones. With that last bit of equipment snapped over my head, I had hidden myself from the conversation. He no longer felt excited, but neglected, until I unhooked the microphone, put it on myself, put my headphones over his ears and talked to him. He heard my voice, smiled broadly. Rather than a barrier, the equipment was now an invitation, a sign that I was taking our conversation seriously.

That story goes a ways toward understanding not only how we should introduce equipment—cameras and microphones, mostly—to an interview, but also why it often makes the interview better.

WHY BOTHER?

But first, let's talk about why you want to bring all that equipment to an interview in the first place. Why would you risk screwing up a perfectly good interview by placing a bunch of recording devices in the middle of it? At the risk of seeming simplistic, the answer is: So you can record the interview for editing and publication. You can do interviews with just a pencil and paper, or you could bring just an audio recorder and microphone. If you believe that all devices put an interview at risk, then the most effective way to have an intimate conversation could just be to sit down and have a look-into-their-eyes conversation without any recording apparatus.

But we're journalists, archivists, anthropologists, linguists, filmmakers and novelists who want very much to record and preserve the conversations we hear, so that we can edit, broadcast, organize and retell those stories in ways that help us bind together ideas and people. We all use tools to help us with this process, and all of those tools can be problematic. Any reporter knows that pulling out a notebook and pen can either shut down a conversation or it can start it up. We've all heard both sides of that: "You aren't going to write this down, are you?"

Or, "Why aren't you writing this down?"

As soon as we bring recording apparatus to a conversation, people know that we are no longer having a friendly chat, but rather they are being asked to share, have an opinion, retell events that we plan to pass along to an audience. This is true no matter what kind of recording device we use, and people clearly react differently to different kinds of devices.

I am agnostic about media. I do not think that one medium is better than another. I do think that each medium offers possibilities for telling certain kinds of stories well, and that we now have new options of using several media together to most effectively present a story to the people at the other end. So, at the risk of kicking an already agitated beehive, here is a brief look at how we can start to think about how to use media. Because most people are not agnostic about media, discussions of how media work often lead to defensive argument. But a conversation about how to introduce media to the interview process can't be had unless we discuss which media we're trying to speak with. This is not an academic inquiry into the fundamental underpinnings of each of these media but rather a reflection of how many of us look at the media as we're deciding how to use them in solving the in-the-field problems of storytelling, often while we are in a hurry.

Writing is the most literal of the media, and it transmits historical and factual information effectively and efficiently. Good writers often "show, don't tell," of course, which makes good writing experiential as well as informational. Telling stories that have already happened and making clear and literal connections between abstract ideas can really happen only in writing, unless you consider re-enactments. Writing can be present tense, past tense or future tense.

Audio also very effectively and efficiently transmits information and can effectively relay stories that have already happened, because it also consists of many words, but audio adds a layer of more abstract "natural sound" that is more experiential than it is informational. Also, audio can give literal voice to the people we interview.

Video/film should really be called moving pictures with audio, but we'll call it video to save me from carpal tunnel syndrome. Video brings visual imagery to the table, with the possibility of showing literal process at one extreme and much more abstract, experiential imagery at the other. Film also adds visual sequencing as an expressive tool, which means we can create new meaning by shoving images close to one another. Video allows the people we interview to express themselves in nonverbal ways, putting great importance on seemingly trivial movements—the wipe of a tear, the subtle shake of a head or the pointing of a finger. Video does present-tense storytelling very well, and it can rely on audio to fill in some past-tense storytelling.

Photography is one step more abstract than video, primarily because it *almost* arrests time, and it appears to show much more than it does. It is a very limited medium from an informational perspective, and it mutes the people we photograph. Photography is very present tense. You cannot photograph the past (although you can show pictures taken in the past), so if you are not in the same space as your story when it happens, you miss it. Much like very formalized poetry, those limits, skillfully used, can unleash emotional power that leads to visceral experiences for the viewer.

Music is the most abstract, and the most misused, medium in the journalistic storyteller's toolbox. Too often, we just spread a thin layer of music underneath a story, and we hope that it adds something we can't articulate to the overall experience. Used well, music enhances the experience of a story, often without the audience being conscious of the injection of emotion, which is why so many journalists are suspicious of music.

All of this is NOT to say, for example, that writing cannot be emotionally experiential. That would be dumbly refuting the power of great literature, among other things. Nor is it to say that photography cannot be used for purely informational purposes—think of photographic evidence in court, for example. It is simply a way of beginning to think about how we select media to use when we're telling a story in multiple media.

All that feels a long way from interview, but it is quite relevant. When you sit someone down for an interview, you have to decide what about that interaction you want to pass along to the audience, and then you choose your tools accordingly.

THE POWER OF MORE THAN ONE MEDIUM

The reason I work hard to remain agnostic about which media stems from the new possibilities we have when we tell stories in more than one medium. This mix of media is not really new, since we've been pairing writing with photographs, sound with moving images, as well as other

combinations, for a long time. What's new is the possibility of mixing so many media at one time to use each to its fullest, which means we avoid using a medium to do something outside of its best use. We can, for example, get the intimacy of visual present-tense storytelling joined to an exploration of a historical story in writing or narrated words.

Let's look at an example from a MediaStorm workshop I participated in a few years ago. We made a short film called *The Amazing Amy* (http://mediastorm.com/training/the-amazing-amy), about a woman continuing to work as a contortionist at an age when most people have moved on to occupations less demanding of a young person's flexibility.

Amy was a great interview, because she loved the attention we gave her. Why? Because she loved the way we gave her that attention. It made her feel important. So, when the crew arrived with equipment, the conversation was all about how Amy's story was worth the effort required. She could see during the interview, and all the other shooting we did, that our attention was hyper-focused, that we listened much more than we talked, that we took her story seriously enough to bother with the hassles of equipment. I really think she felt like we were celebrating her life, which went spectacularly unnoticed most of the time.

In the short film, Amy hooks us with her first seconds on camera. She is on camera in her home (A-Roll):

"It is the best high I've ever had in my life. It's better than sex. It's better than anything. And the energy that's going back and forth is the most glorious, ecstatic, orgasmic experience ever."

The words are strong by themselves, but Amy is waving her arms, shaking her head, making faces, and giving all kinds of visual clues that she strongly feels her assertions. Seeing her gives even her remarkable words a power they don't have on their own.

The next scene cuts visually from the interview (at 00:19 seconds),

but we still hear her words. Amy is dressed up, warming up in the hall of an office building, putting her leg behind her head. A man in business dress walks in, at first oblivious to her presence; then he does an awkward double step as he notices a woman in contortions on the floor in front of him.

The visual tells a present-tense story of their encounter, while Amy tells us that she doesn't function in the "real world. Never have. Never will." We see it, and we hear the story in a double-media punch that neither pictures nor words could deliver by themselves. The words tell us how Amy feels while the pictures show us how the world, at least one part of it, responds to her feelings.

There's another moment in *The Amazing Amy* (starts at 6:10) that shows how one medium can lead to another, using three different media in ways that exploit each medium's strength.

Amy is talking about performing. Her face is tight on the screen.

"It's the only way I know to make people love me is to be a performer."

There's a long pause.

"Cause I never felt like my parents ever really loved me. My father used to say these terrible things like I was a blood-sucking parasite because I didn't have a real job."

The visual cuts from Amy in her home to a rich photograph of her on a stage, by herself, under deep purple light. It's a cue to the audience that we're making a transition from Amy's words to a visual experience, during which the audience can reflect on the words while being handed a mood, a feeling, a sense of Amy's lonely life. But there are two small tidbits from the interview under the visuals.

(6:35) "It made me feel so worthless."

Pause. A cut to a shot of Amy reflected in the window of a bus. The bus starts moving as she looks out the window.

(6:39) "I've had many, many times when I just wanted to go to sleep and not wake up again."

With that, the storytelling shifts completely to visual and almost fully experiential. If the audience doesn't feel her loneliness at this point, the film fails. The interview got us down the field, passed the story to the visual realm, which either fails or succeeds in pushing the story along. Another way to look at it is that the interview provided the context from which the visual story can rise.

One memory,
framed in silver

WHAT DOES THIS LOOK LIKE ON THE GROUND?

So if you agree to entertain my notion that introducing equipment to an interview does not by itself dictate the intimacy or honesty of that interview, how do we work to make it a positive thing? It's one thing to say that equipment makes an interview better, another to actually make it work.

Just like it might be counterintuitive to state that using equipment during an interview can make that interview more, not less, effective, it is also true that adding a second person (sometimes more) to an interview can also make it more intimate and effective. Here's why: when you introduce equipment, you also introduce a bunch of gizmos to manage. If you do an interview by yourself, you will have to split your attention between conducting the relationship of the interview with making sure all that equipment is running as it should. You'll have to focus on the cameras and audio levels. That's more than one person can do well.

Jamie Francis makes some of the most intimate videos you'll see, always with a straight, kind aim at the story, and always with camera and microphone.

> "I've had a personal transformation, from the view that equipment gets in the way to a sense that the equipment can fulfill your obligation to be

respectful of what people are offering you, and respectful of the people who you will tell their story to. I think it is not at all about equipment. It's all about interaction and approach. It's about if you're a good listener and you can make a connection between what people are telling you and what they want to tell you."

He tells the story of an interview with a family that he and a co-worker, Rob Finch, worked with during a campaign for Blue Chalk Media. Both had been with the family for a few days at their ranch in rural Montana, building rapport, getting to know the facts and feel of the story. They saved the interview for last, when they could bring that level of comfort to the conversation. But they made a mistake in asking an audio person to come in at the last minute to help them.

"The guy didn't understand these people, and he had strong opinions about ranching. He shut down the conversation. The equipment was fine; it was the buffoon in the room who caused trouble."

Like many of us, Jamie has covered stories about families who have lost loved ones in war. And like many of us, he tried to approach those stories with the respect and gravity they deserve. He used to think that meant bringing as little equipment as possible to the situation. Then he changed his mind.

"I had always been in that camp that I didn't want to bring a microphone, particularly during interviews with families of soldiers who had been killed. I really regret now that I didn't do sound interviews with those families. The big camera and the big microphone can be a help, because people often want to talk. I think back on the parents of soldiers. The hurdle was getting them to agree to do an interview, and convincing them that you were a person they could trust. And then they were ready to talk, because they were talking about a person they really, really miss. They want them to be remembered. That would have been a perfect time to have the full equipment because it would have matched the importance and gravity of the story we were trying to tell, and it would have given voice to those people, who were often grieving alone and unnoticed."

Years later, working at the *Oregonian*, in Portland, Jamie worked on the story of an aging cowboy named Jack Sweek remembering his one big rodeo day at the Pendleton Roundup. Jamie's story about his interaction with Jack Sweek reinforces the sense that the stories we tell can take on meaning we don't imagine when we start (http://jamiefrancis.com/video/2013/2/21/pendleton-cowboy-jack-sweek-one-memory-framed-in-silver):

"I met Jack at Roundup, when I was working with still cameras. I asked if I could come back and tell his story, this time with video cameras. He thought that was funny. The microphone he thought was particularly hilarious. He said, 'You're just wasting your time!' It was that old 'I'm going to break this camera' thing. He was a very loved man. When he died shortly after we ran the video on our website, I got dozens of emails from people who wanted to tell me that they were very happy that Jack had talked to me and that that story was there. They showed the video at his memorial on the Pendleton Roundup grounds."

Jamie brought equipment to the interview, told the story with that interview and some good present-tense visual storytelling, and his efforts added to Jack's memorial.

"What I found out is that very few people will stand up and say 'I'm really good at interviews and I like talking loudly on camera.' Most people are saying that they aren't good on camera, shy of cameras. But almost always those are the people who are great on camera. They realize, and you realize, that this is for keeps. 'This is my chance to tell my story.' That's what the best interviews are: an opportunity to tell your story and know that people will listen."

While the story of Jack Sweet was a situation where Jamie had to convince a subject to accept the intrusion of equipment into an interview, Jamie also tells the account of meeting a group of ninth-grade Syrian girls living as refugees in a Jordanian refugee camp (http://jamiefran cis.com/video/2013/11/17/syrian-refugees-ninth-grade-girls-escape-death -search-for-life):

"This piece is very dear to me. In the climate of refugees and war, these girls came to find me, wanting to talk to me, with their teacher as a translator. I just set up in the hallway and everyone came through, and the translator wrote down the girls' answers. They wanted to be seen and heard, and I happened to be the person who was there to give them the chance.

"Of course, they noticed the equipment. They wanted to look at all of it and hold it, and they wanted to hear themselves and see themselves after it was recorded, but they also wanted me to get what they were saying. They totally got why I was there, and the equipment helped make sure of that. The equipment organized the story for me and it made it honest, because there was no deception."

DON'T BE THE BUFFOON IN THE ROOM

It's not really about equipment. It's about appearing to be the kind of person people want to talk to, and then actually being that kind of person. The cameras and microphones and notebooks can get in the way, of course, because they highlight the act of recording what's being discussed. That can make people self-conscious. But when you bring equipment, you also have the opportunity to show that you are serious about your work, that the conversation you are about to have is important enough to record and preserve, that you see the interview as a collaboration rather than an act of taking. You have to use the equipment smoothly. To create an honest, useful interview, you have to manage the relationship smoothly, whether you have equipment in the room or not.

PART IV Ethics & Law

TWENTY-SIX **Ethics of Interviewing**

The bottom line is respect for sources

TOM BIVINS

An interview can be combative, intrusive, adversarial or embracing. Longtime ethics researcher Tom Bivins methodically outlines how—no matter an interviewer's style—ethical treatment of a subject and subject matter never need be compromised.

No man who is not in ethical advance
of the average of his community should be in the profession
of journalism.

—Colin V. Dyment, *The Oregon Code of Ethics for Journalism* (1922)

Once upon a time, journalists took notes—with a pen (or pencil) on paper, usually a "reporter's notebook." It was a slim version of a stenographer's pad, designed to fit into a hip pocket or to be neatly tucked into a jacket or some other handy location. It was obviously displayed, and the interviewee could see it, watch the journalist busily scribbling and feel assured that notes were "being taken." No matter that conversation usually progressed faster than notes could be written. There was a psychological comfort in seeing that one's words were being stenographically recorded, with an understanding that what was said would be reasonably accurate. Reporters could always follow up with additional clarifications if needed (and agreed upon in advance). I know this because I have been both a reporter and a public relations practitioner—either seeking information or counseling those who want information released. The interplay of source-reporter has been part of the journalistic interview since its inception. There will always be a constant tension between the needs of the participants, and between what is ethical and what is not.

There are so many variables affecting the ethicality of interviewing that it is nearly impossible to cover them all, so I will attempt only to cover what I consider to be the broader, yet intimately related, issues of mitigation of harm and deception. The more important element is the first. We, as interviewers, are talking about and to human beings. They have rights. They have lives that we may not understand or particularly care about. But, if we are to be ethical journalists, we must learn to go beyond the mere need for a story and begin to appreciate that what we write has an effect on the lives of others. But before we tackle that concern, let's take a shot at defining exactly what we mean by *interview*—a word that journalists often take for granted but one that can mean many things, depending on your point of view.

In order to understand the ethics of interviewing, we must first try to decipher exactly what we expect, as journalists, from our interviews and our sources. Remember, it's not just an interview, it's engagement with a real person. We need also to figure out what we think they want from us by agreeing to the interview in the first place. This motivation will vary widely, from the sought-after interview by the source for public relations purposes to the sought-after interview by the journalist for investigative reasons. The motivation for the interview will decide the approach, and that approach is as much connotative as it is denotative. That is, it's as much what we expect from the interview—and bring to it because of those expectations—as it is a dictionary definition of the format we choose.

Denotatively, *interview* and *interrogation* are closely related terms. According to the dictionary, an interview is a "meeting of people face to face, especially for consultation." We have, in modern times, tended to style this as a "conversation between a journalist or radio or television presenter and a person of public interest, used as the basis of a broadcast or publication." The journalistic sense of this term is at least as old as the late 19th century, and implied a sort of small, mutual admiration society composed of a journalist and a politician. On the other hand, *interrogate* means to "ask questions of (someone, especially a suspect or a prisoner) closely, aggressively, or formally." Both terms derive from Latin. *Interrogate* comes from the Latin verb *interrogare*, which is *to question*—formed from the word meaning *between*, and from the stem *to ask* or *lay claim to*. *Interview* is formed from the same Latin word for *between* and another meaning *to view* or *see*, and, like much of English, passed through French on its way to today's definition. Fittingly, its original meaning was "to see each other, visit each other briefly, have a glimpse of" someone.

Despite their linguistic relationship, these words have grown apart over the years, and we now see them as very different approaches to asking questions. While *to interview* connotes a non-aggressive form of interplay, *to interrogate* summons up more aggressive questioning (i.e., by the CIA, the FBI, the police). It is interesting to note that recently law enforcement entities have begun to describe this approach as *interviewing*—as in "the subject was interviewed." Of course this is all word play, but, as every journalist knows, words make a difference. We may seek an *interview* with supposedly reluctant sources, yet how we treat them may actually be an *interrogation*. This might be determined in advance, as with "hostile witnesses," or on the spot when we realize that they are unwilling sources of information. In either case, we must remember that we still owe any interviewee some basic considerations.

WHAT DO WE OWE THE INTERVIEWEE?

In a recent posting on the website iMediaEthics, managing editor Sydney Smith (2014) talked about informed consent. But what really struck me was the graphic that headed up the story—a fictional consent form. It read,

I understand that being interviewed can:

· Get me fired from my job.
· Get me thrown out of school.
· Damage my relationships.
· Ruin my life.
· Embarrass me.

Because journalists can, and do, affect the lives of those they interview, it is incumbent on them to mitigate that potential for harm. Or, as the Society of Professional Journalists' code points out, "Recognize that gathering and reporting information may cause harm or discomfort. Pursuit of the news is not a license for arrogance." It's interesting to note that the word *arrogance* contains the same Latin stem as *interrogate*: to lay claim to something, as if it were your right. Journalism has always been rife with a sense of self-importance. This is honestly come by, especially given the First Amendment and the early 20th-century charge of the Hutchins Commission—as restated by Bob Kovach and Tom Rosenstiel (2001), "The primary purpose of journalism is to provide citizens with the information they need to be free and self-governing." Thus, the Fourth Estate has a right to feel self-important. Its job description says so. However, self-importance and arrogance are not the same thing.

Arrogance can lead to a feeling of entitlement in the act of newsgathering, especially via the interview. The idea that the journalist's first obligation is to the public and not to the source being interviewed is a common position to take. Obligations to the source may exist, but they are too often outweighed by the "public's right to know." Many journalists, and many journalism codes, attempt to bolster autonomy by preventing interference with the process of newsgathering, by such means as not showing interviewees notes, or not giving them access to raw footage or audio, or not allowing them to correct errors, or, in some cases, even denying them the right of reply. There are good reasons for much of this, the most important being independence. Independence leads to autonomy, which is pretty much guaranteed by the First Amendment, and that autonomy gives journalists freedom from outside pressure, enabling them to make their own decisions. That pressure can come from sources, especially powerful sources, and it can come from the routine of news-gathering itself, with its endless deadlines and constant competition for stories. It's no wonder that journalists not only require autonomy, but they also protect it. However, the specter of arrogance is still too often associated with that autonomy. According to Ted Glasser (2008), "Perhaps more so in the United States than anywhere else, the prevailing view of independent journalism represents the triumph of autonomy over accountability and this, in turn, fuels a curious ethic of defiance."

That's why it's important to remember that journalistic autonomy, as a guaranteed right, brings with it certain obligations. Chief among those is respect for the public served by journalism, and that public includes sources. Canadian journalist and CBC producer Julian Sher (CAJ, 2014) notes that journalists are "also human beings, so we also have to care about the people we are interviewing." He also recognizes that the people journalists interview are more than sources: They are members of the public served by journalists. "You can't have great respect for your public who is reading you and not have respect for the public who agrees to talk to you."

That respect can manifest itself in a number of ways. Contemporary philosophers have laid out some of the obligations we all have, including journalists, to those whom we affect by our actions. As concerns our subject here, several of these are important:

Autonomy   Yes, the same autonomy that journalists expect should also be respected by them. As human beings, we naturally crave the ability to live as free from outside control as possible. Even if we accept that total autonomy is nonexistent, we still deserve at least a modicum of it. Subjects of interviews often are assumed to have voluntarily abdicated that autonomy; however, they probably don't think of it that way. It is our obligation not to force them to surrender more of it than they are willing. As noted in the fictional consent form mentioned earlier, we owe it to our interviewees to be explicit about exactly how much of their ability to control their own lives they are likely relinquishing.

Fidelity   This means being faithful to a promise made, either explicitly (as in a contract) or implicitly (as in a mutual understanding). It plays an important part in trust and honesty. For example, as journalists, we don't always expect honesty from those we interview; however, most of the time we do, especially if they have agreed to an interview. The assumption is that we are engaging in a reciprocal arrangement wherein journalists get their story and the interviewees get something they want in the process. The bottom line here is that if you want honesty from your sources, then be honest with them. In other words, honesty should always be an implied promise.

Justice   This means giving to those who deserve and withholding from those who don't. This is also related to autonomy because it requires a basic level of respect for that of others, not just you. This obligation requires the journalist to ask whether the person being interviewed deserves to be treated with less than the respect owed a normal human being. We must remember that all sources deserve at least some modicum of respect. Although the legal system asserts that even the accused are innocent until proven guilty, the journalistic system too often views this basic right as flexible, especially when the source is either an accused perpetrator or is seeking personal exoneration because of suspected involvement.

Journalists tend to believe that simply inserting the word *alleged* into a story takes care of the legal ramifications; however, it does not absolve them of the obligation to deal with sources as *potentially* innocent. To approach an interview with an assumption of guilt, with the intent to "prove" it, is to deliberately bias the process. Of course, this is obvious to the objective interviewer, but, in practice, we all know that the "gotcha" moment in an interview may override any obligation of fairness. Nonetheless, going into an interview with a basic respect for the interviewee should set the groundwork for, at the very least, a civil conversation.

Beneficence   This means giving to those who need it. This obligation often combines with justice by responding to those who also deserve it. This might be an obligation to respond to the public's right to know, or to the source's right to privacy. In most cases, it also means to improve someone's lot in some way through this obligation. For example, journalists are always citing the public's right to know. The operative justice-oriented question would be, "Does the public really deserve to know this?" as in private information about a source. The operative beneficence-oriented question would be, "Do they (the public) really need to know this?" followed by, "What possible benefit would they gain from knowing this information?" On the source side of the equation, the justice-oriented question must always be, "Does the source really deserve to have his or her privacy violated?" Beneficence is harder to determine on the source side; however, there are times when a discovery made during an interview might lead to a journalist's discarding the information to protect a source or others related to the source. An example of this might involve an interviewee unwittingly disclosing information that could endanger his or her life. It is incumbent on the journalist, under both beneficence and non-injury, to consider this concern before making the information gathered known to others, even if that information would make a good story.

Gratitude   This means reciprocating for something someone has done for you. Interviewees deserve respect from journalists if for no other reason than they are willingly providing information. After all, journalists don't usually force sources into interview situations. Gratitude is reciprocal by nature. That means both sides are getting and receiving something; however, that doesn't negate the obligation associated with the receiving half of the process. For example, even a confrontational interview requires a level of civility (a form of respect perhaps stemming from a sense of gratitude), which might actually net the answers needed instead of an angry retort. As Dan Berkowitz (2009) points out, "The interaction between reporters and their sources is a delicately negotiated relationship," and part of that relationship is built on the journalist's ethical approach to interviewing.

Non-injury   This is pretty self-explanatory but probably the most important of the obligations. It's very possible that as a result of an interview, someone will be harmed—maybe the source, maybe the subject of the story, maybe someone else. That harm could be as simple as injured pride or as serious as economic loss or physical/psychological pain. It is obvious, and frequently pointed out, that journalists must exercise extreme care when interviewing children and those recently bereaved or otherwise traumatized.

Despite this general "guideline," journalists still seek out such interviews, especially during events that garner national attention. Every tragedy has its victims, and tragedy is news. Unfortunately, so are the victims. The long trail of school shootings has illustrated the extremes that some reporters will go to get a story. The 2012 mass killing in Newtown, Connecticut, drew hundreds of journalists from all over the country to a small community reeling from unimaginable horror. A recent study by Charles Deitz (2013) suggests that multiple factors, including excessive competition and lack of context-specific training, resulted in a rush to interview the traumatized residents of this small community. Deitz's own interviews with reporters working the Newtown story showed that they "all had to struggle with their personal moral quandaries during their assignments, from publishing half-truths or hearsay to invading the personal spaces of grieving families and community members."

This sort of example, however, is the most obvious. What about less injurious effects that may still be harmful? Non-injury requires that you think about how you're using the source. When he wasn't carrying on about lying, Immanuel Kant once said, "Act so that you treat humanity, whether in your own person or in the person of any other, always as an end and never as a means only." With this prescription, he set the stage for the championing of individual autonomy and integrity (theirs and yours). Sources deserve some measure of autonomy, as do you as a journalist. The Golden Rule works well here, but the real trick is to balance that against the needs—not *wants*—of the public.

FUNCTIONAL VERSUS MORAL OBLIGATIONS

How should we balance the principle of serving the public with the idea of minimizing the harm we may impose on sources? That is often decided by questioning whether the public really *needs* to know this information or merely *wants* to know it. Remember the tennis star Arthur Ashe? Whatever interviews took place between him and *USA Today* were probably less than cordial, with only one goal in mind—to feed the public's *desire* to know whether Ashe was HIV-positive. Is that enough? If your questions, as an interviewer, are designed to extract information that your audience (and that term is increasingly relevant) is merely curious about, then you are not honoring your moral obligations. You are merely honoring your *functional* obligations to make them happy and you successful.

Functional obligations direct you to decide what's right or wrong depending on the context of whether the act serves your primary stakeholder. For journalists, this could be the news organization—perhaps to scoop the competition, or, at the very least, to prove yourself as a leader in newsgathering. For most journalists, however, that primary stakeholder is usually idealized as the "public." Service in the public interest is, of course, part of the job description; however, public interest may be vastly different from what the public is merely interested in. On the other hand, actually benefiting the public (the obligation of beneficence) can override other obligations to sources and could be viewed as a *moral* obligation—perhaps even construed as an implied contract between the news organization and the public (fidelity). The trick is to balance the functional obligations required to do your job, help your news outlet to succeed and serve the public interest, against your obligations to sources. In an ideal world, they would all mesh, but as we all know, that doesn't always happen. This balancing act is exactly that.

And this final caveat: When we choose to serve the public interest, while likewise serving our own interests, we are not necessarily committing a moral crime. We should recognize that, as human beings, we must not neglect our own interests. That would lead to pure altruism, and, after all, journalism is and has always been a business. The lesson here is to be careful not to pursue *only* your self-interests, however you define them, especially if those interests are masquerading as the public's right to know.

HONESTY AND DECEPTION

How honest should you be? Isn't it a journalist's job to tell the truth? Yes, if you're talking about your stories and your obligation to your public to give them the whole truth in a way that helps them understand the world they live in. But what if that truth can't be told completely because you can't get the information you need to present it? Is it ethical to deceive sources in order to obtain information you deem important?

The short answer is no. Noted philosopher Sissela Bok (1999), in her book focusing on lying, calls it coercive. In other words, a lie causes people to act in a way they might not have acted had they known the truth. "They see that they were manipulated, that the deceit made them unable to make choices for themselves, according to the most adequate information available, unable to act as they would have wanted to act had they known all along." Journalists trade in the truth. It would then seem counterintuitive to assume that lying may be used in order to tell the truth. In other words, if you want to hear the truth, tell the truth. But, as we all know, this doesn't always happen—sometimes for good reasons, sometimes for bad.

Lying requires an intent to deceive. You know you are doing it, and the person you are deceiving doesn't. You can lie outright by stating something that you know is not true, or you can intimate something by nonverbal means. Examples of nonverbal deception might be altering appearance, as in a reporter masquerading as a physician in order to gain access to a shooting victim. Or nodding your head to indicate "yes" when the truth is "no." You can also lie by omission by deliberately leaving out information that can result in altering a person's perception. Some types of omission are more problematic than others. What if the person being interviewed doesn't even know he or she is talking to a journalist? Examples of this include journalists who don't alert potential subjects that they are journalists or who use surreptitious methods to record conversations. But, let's take the source who *knows* that an interview is taking place first.

Subjects who know they are being interviewed expect that what they say will be recorded in some way. Remember that thin reporter's notebook? It had the advantage of being obvious. But what about the not-so-obvious? Glasser suggests that if accuracy is the presiding principle in interviewing, electronic/digital techniques would logically provide for the best result. Given this, it would make sense to assume that if we take out a recorder at an interview, the subject knows what's going on. But should we assume if we are interviewing sources over the phone, for example, that we don't have to tell them they are being taped? It seems logical that if people know they are being interviewed, they would expect that their words are being set down in some way. However, a number of states have laws requiring that all parties in a telephone conversation consent to being taped, even if they know they are being interviewed by a reporter. Oddly, most states and the federal government permit the recording of phone conversations if only one party consents—which means that technically a reporter could record a conversation without the other party knowing. But this applies only to telephone conversations. The law hasn't caught up yet with technologies such as computer-assisted interviewing, complete with face-to-face exchanges, that allow for recording. Regardless of the technology, recording is part of the interviewer's job, and as long as sources know they are being interviewed, there isn't an ethical problem with how it's recorded. But what about people who don't know they are being interviewed, or when the people being interviewed know they are talking to a journalist and are still misled. For example, pretending to be sympathetic to a subject when you may, in fact, be hostile. Or intimating that your interview is not being taped when, in fact, it is. Perhaps the most egregious ethical issue is the latter.

A number of journalism guidelines advise against either misrepresenting oneself or not indicating that you are interviewing someone (both deceptive acts). The most common admonitions include: (1) The information you obtain must be vital to the public interest, not just interesting. (2) There is no other alternative method of obtaining the story. (3) The harm prevented by the information revealed through deception outweighs any harm caused by the act of deception. (4) Full disclosure is provided to the audience about how and why deception was used. This last matches Sissela Bok's "test of publicity" that asks which lies, if any, would survive the appeal for justification to reasonable persons. In other words, deceit must be justifiable and not just rationalizable. Former Poynter ethicist Bob Steele (2002) notes that sometimes the rationale used for deceitful tactics is as unethical as the lies themselves. He says that journalists should never engage in deceit for any of the following reasons: winning a prize, beating the competition, getting the story with less expenditure of time and resources, doing it because "others already did it" or because the subjects of the story are themselves unethical.

The bottom line, then, is when in doubt, err on the side of *moral* obligation, not *functional* obligation. Don't conflate the two. Getting the story is functional. Taking care not to harm someone in the process is moral. And remember, it's a balancing act with the ethical choice already tipping the scale. You'll need some serious counterweight to offset it.

GUIDELINES

For those who crave guidelines, try the following:

· Use fair, responsible and *honest* means to obtain material. Why would you need to be dishonest to obtain an interview? Is the reason that important that you're willing to use unethical tactics?

· Identify yourself and your employer before obtaining any interview for publication.

· Remind the source that an interview for publication is taking place and what that means.

· Treat your interviewees with basic respect. You could view this as simply being professional. If you think they deserve more than that, give it to them. If you think they deserve less, keep it to yourself.

· Be open with them. Ensure they understand all of the potential ramifications of answering your questions, in advance. Answer their concerns, and don't sugarcoat the possible downsides.

· Tell sources if, through some misunderstanding and resultant action on their part or yours, they become more likely to be harmed than they know.

· Don't assume an interviewee is media savvy. Many are not. Never exploit a person's vulnerability or ignorance of media practice. Tell them why you are interviewing them and how you plan to use their information, including whether it may appear across multiple platforms.

- Tell sources whether and how the information is being recorded—especially if you're digitally recording it. If they object to digital recording, ask them why. Remind them that it's the most accurate way of remembering what they say.

- Be honest with them. Don't lie, either by commission or omission. If you leave out information they should know in order to make an informed decision, you are violating their autonomy.

- Don't pretend to be somebody other than a reporter in order to get them to open up. You aren't their friend. You are a journalist. Act like an ethical one.

Finally, revisit the obligations listed earlier and take them seriously. If you don't, you may be thought of as less than ethical—both by your audience and by your peers. And, although what you did might seem to have been the expedient choice at the time, the label "unethical" may well follow you throughout your career. Most of us can easily list those for whom this is already a reality. They probably don't work as journalists anymore.

BIBLIOGRAPHY

Berkowitz, D.A. (2009). "Reporters and Their Sources." In *The Handbook of Journalism Studies*. New York: Routledge.

Bok, S. (1999). *Lying: Moral Choices in Public and Private Life*. New York: Vintage Books.

Canadian Association of Journalists (2014). "On the Record: Is It Really Informed Consent Without Discussion of Consequences?" http://www.caj.ca/on-the-record-is-it-really-informed-consent-without-discussion-of-consequences/.

Deitz, C. (2013). *The Stories Behind the Stories: A Qualitative Inquiry Regarding the Experiences of Journalists Who Covered the Newtown Shooting Spree*. Unpublished thesis, School of Journalism and Communication, University of Oregon.

Glasser, T., and J. Ettema (2008). "Ethics and Eloquence in Journalism: An Approach to Press Accountability." *Journalism Studies*, 9(4), 512–534.

Kovach, B., and T. Rosenstiel (2001). *The Elements of Journalism*. New York: Three Rivers Press.

Smith, S. (2014). "Are Journalists Informing Sources About Possible Interview Fall Out?" http://www.imediaethics.org/News/4420/Are_journalists _informing_sources_about_possible_interview_fall_out__.php.

Steele, B. (2002). "Deception/Hidden Cameras Checklist." http://www.poynter .org/uncategorized/744/deceptionhidden-cameras-checklist/.

TWENTY-SEVEN **Interviewing and the First Amendment**

Good interviewing is based on good information, and courts have provided some help through access laws

TIM GLEASON

Knowing the legal rights of access to information is a powerful tool for journalists. Tim Gleason—a First Amendment scholar—explains how journalists can make use of the potency of the Constitution along with federal and state laws to fuel information gathering and access to news and newsmakers.

The more informed the questions are, the better the interview will be. The more informed the journalist is, the better the story will be. An interviewer who knows something about a topic can ask focused questions that will elicit answers that advance the story. Equally important, the person being interviewed is more likely to engage in a productive conversation with an interviewer who has demonstrated a real interest and some knowledge about the topic.

Let's imagine that a reporter for a student newspaper at a large state university is working on a story about a rumored university proposal to raise tuition by 10 percent for the next academic year. The reporter has an interview scheduled with the university's chief financial officer. She is a very busy person who spends much of her day working on complex questions about the university's budget and finances. The reporter begins the interview by saying, "I hear that the university is raising tuition next year. Can you tell me anything about that?"

This is a lazy question. It indicates that the reporter knows little or nothing about the topic and allows the chief financial officer to take the interview in any direction she may wish to go. Now imagine that the reporter's first question is, "According to the University's tuition proposal for the next academic year, tuition for resident undergraduate students will go up 4 percent and tuition for nonresident undergraduates will go up 7 percent. Average tuition has gone up 15 percent in the last three years. Why is the University proposing another tuition increase?"

How did the reporter know about the university's current tuition proposal and the recent tuition trend line? He may have discovered the information in another news source, but the most authoritative way to know and confirm the information would have been to read the actual university tuition proposal. If the University has formally proposed to raise tuition, it is likely to be a public document and the reporter will have access to it. If there is no formal proposal, the reporter should know this fact before walking into the interview.

In today's news environment there are many times when there isn't time to do in-depth research as a story breaks. It may be that there is only time to do a quick online search, or to read the press release or email that generated the story idea, or to make a quick call to a reliable source. But generating good questions requires some knowledge of the subject. The simple fact is: Uninformed questions result in bad interviews.

What does this have to do with freedom of speech and of the press? Well, in one sense it has everything to do with the First Amendment to the Constitution of the United States and the free speech and press protections in state constitutions, and in another sense it has little to do with these constitutional protections.

The First Amendment protects the right of all of us to speak and write freely:

Congress shall make no law abridging the freedom of speech,
or of the press.

However, the text of the First Amendment is silent on the right to *gather* information. It does not clearly establish any legal right for a journalist or any other citizen to see the city council budget or to see the emails the director of the state's environmental protection agency exchanged with the lobbyist from a major oil company concerning an oil-drilling permit. Several state constitutions—Florida, New Hampshire, North Dakota, Louisiana and Montana—do provide explicit rights of public access to government documents and meetings, but the other 45 state constitutions' free speech and press guarantees do not.

The Supreme Court has not discovered a robust right to gather information from the government in the First Amendment. To the contrary, it has repeatedly declined opportunities to find a broad right of access. Supreme Court Justice Potter Stewart, writing in a law journal, once said, "The press is free to do battle against secrecy and deception in government. But the press cannot expect from the Constitution any guarantee that it will succeed. There is no constitutional right to have access to particular government information, or to require openness from the bureaucracy."[1]

At the same time, the courts have recognized that free speech guarantees would be hollow rights without a public "right to know." For example, Justice Lewis Powell, writing in dissent in a case where the Court found that a television station did *not* have a right of access to a state prison, wrote:

> No less important to the news dissemination process is the gathering of information. News must not be unnecessarily cut off at its source, for without freedom to acquire information the right to publish would be impermissibly compromised. Accordingly, a right to gather news, of some dimensions, must exist.[2]

And in several cases, the Court has stated that journalists have "undoubted right to gather news from any source by means within law."[3]

Access to criminal proceedings and a right to inspect judicial records is the one area where the Supreme Court has established a limited constitutional right of access.

The only exception has been the granting of access to criminal trials.

In *Richmond Newspapers v. Virginia*[4] and then in *Press-Enterprise v. Superior Court*[5] the court did find that there is a First Amendment interest in the public gathering of newsworthy information, but it limited that right to criminal trials.

The degree to which the Court has narrowly drawn any First Amendment right of access to information is highlighted in a California case where the Supreme Court rejected an argument that the First Amendment created a right of access to police records that contained names and addresses of arrested suspects.[6]

The bottom line in this rather depressing history of failed efforts to create a constitutional right of access to information is that, even though the courts have acknowledged the fundamental need for the public to know about the workings of government, journalists can't rely on the Constitution to gain access to that information. However, journalists and the public can look to other sources for limited rights of access to government information.

While the federal Constitution doesn't create a legal right of access to information and only a handful of state constitutions contain language creating a citizen's "right to know," journalists and citizens do have legal rights of access to some government information. These rights are found in federal and state public records and public meetings laws. There are common themes and protections found across these laws, but there are important differences from state to state and from the federal laws to the state laws. It is imperative for a journalist to know the public records and public meetings laws in the jurisdiction where he or she is working.

THE FEDERAL FREEDOM OF INFORMATION ACT (FOIA)

In 1966 Congress passed the Federal Freedom of Information Act (FOIA). It was not the first legislation creating a right of access to government documents, but it was the first effort to create a systematic right of access. It applies to a wide range of records held by the federal government, but by no means is it comprehensive. FOIA applies to federal agencies, but not to Congress, the judiciary or the president's staff. In addition there are nine exemptions under the law that allow documents to be redacted or withheld even if the document is a "public record." The nine exemptions are:

1. National Security   This exemption protects national security information that is properly classified under the procedural and substantive requirements of the current Executive Order on classification. President Obama issued Executive Order 13526 in 2009.

2. Internal Personnel and Practices   Exemption two protects records that are "related solely to the internal personnel rules and practices of an agency."

3. Material Specifically Exempt by Statute   This exemption covers material exempt from disclosure by another federal statute that either unconditionally or conditionally requires that the information not be released.

4. Trade Secrets and Financial Information   This exemption involves commercial or financial information when disclosure by the government would be likely to harm the competitive position of the person who submitted the information; and confidential information that is voluntarily submitted.

5. Inter-Agency and Intra-Agency Memos   This is the "working papers" exemption. It protects inter-agency or intra-agency memorandums or letters that would ordinarily not be released to the public. The purpose is to allow for the free exchange of ideas within an agency. It does not exempt the public disclosure of factual information contained in these documents.

6. Personnel and Medical Files and Similar Files   This is a personal privacy exemption. It protects information in personnel and medical files and similar files when disclosure would constitute a clearly unwarranted invasion of privacy.

7. Investigatory Records Compiled for Law Enforcement Purposes   This exemption is intended to keep information that would interfere with legitimate law enforcement activity out of the public light. There are six categories of information that may be withheld from public disclosure where release of the information is not in the public interest: (1) information that would interfere with enforcement proceedings; (2) disclosure of information that would deprive a person of the right to a fair trial; (3) information that "could reasonably be expected to" invade someone's privacy; (4) information that could reasonably be expected to reveal the identity of a confidential source; (5) information that would reveal techniques and procedures for law enforcement investigations or prosecutions or that would disclose guidelines for law enforcement investigations or prosecutions if disclosure of the information could reasonably be expected to risk circumvention of the law; (6) information that could reasonably be expected to endanger the life or physical safety of any individual.

8. Records of Financial Institutions   The eighth exemption protects information that is contained in or related to examination, operating or condition reports prepared by or for a bank supervisory agency such as the Federal Deposit Insurance Corporation, the Federal Reserve or similar agencies.

9. Geological and Geophysical Information and Data   Protects geological information and data, including maps, concerning wells.

In 1996, Congress recognized the coming of the digital age and addressed in the Electronic Freedom of Information Act some of the changes created by the move from paper to electronic storage of records. Under the EFOIA, records maintained in computer databases are as accessible as paper records and agencies must provide them in the requested format when possible. It also allowed for expedited access to records if there is a demonstrated "compelling need" and said that creating programming to facilitate a database search does not amount to the creation of a record.

FOIA and EFOIA are not helpful on breaking news stories, but they are essential for any serious in-depth journalism covering stories involving the federal government. For an interviewer, the federal public records laws make it possible to learn more about a subject before an interview and to confirm and build on the information provided in an interview. They are powerful tools that journalists should use on a regular basis.

FEDERAL OPEN MEETINGS LAWS

Federal officials hold thousands of meetings every day. As a journalist or as a citizen do you have a right to attend those meetings to observe the government in action? The short answer is "it depends." Two laws, the 1996 Sunshine Act and the 1972 Federal Advisory Committee Act, create a limited right to attend meetings of agencies that are covered by FOIA and advisory committees to the executive branch. Both laws are of limited scope and are full of exemptions and qualifications, but journalists should know about their right to attend meetings.

STATE PUBLIC RECORDS AND MEETINGS LAWS

Every state has public records and public meeting laws that provide access to documents and information held by state agencies and create a right of access to public meetings of government entities. The challenge for journalists is to be aware of the differences among the state laws. For example, in Virginia the state public records law makes records accessible only to state residents, while in most states any person can use the public records law.

The charging of fees for accessing public records is another example of the importance of knowing the law of the state where you are working. In Oregon, a state agency may charge a requester the "actual cost" of the search, review, copying and inspection supervision, while just across the state line in Washington, the agency may charge only a fee for the actual costs of copying the records, and in California only a duplicating fee can be charged, unless the legislature has established a statutory fee that cannot be higher than the direct cost of duplication. In each of these states there is the possibility of receiving a fee waiver, but the process and criteria for getting a waiver are different.

As with the federal FOIA, state public record laws exempt some kinds of information from the public domain. Most state statutes include exemptions similar to the nine federal exemptions. However, many state laws also include many more specific exemptions. For example, at last count the Oregon Public Records law includes more than 40 specific exemptions, as well as an "other statute" exemption. Since the law was first enacted in 1973, hundreds of exemptions have been spread throughout Oregon laws.

Fortunately there are resources available to help journalists and citizens understand and use federal and state public records laws. At the federal level, the *Department of Justice Guide to FOIA*[7] is a valuable resource, as is the Federal Open Meeting Guide put out by the Reporters Committee on Freedom of the Press.[8]

At the state level, the Reporters Committee provides guides for all of the states,[9] and in most states there are both state-provided resources and material created by state-based organizations. For example, in Oregon the Attorney General's *Public Records and Meetings Manual*[10] is an authoritative source for information about the law in Oregon, and Open Oregon, a non-government group, has a website that provides information and guidance about public records and public meetings, including a letter-generating function.[11]

A successful public records request begins with a good letter. The broader the request the longer it will take for the agency to deliver the records and the more expensive the request will be. Of course, frequently the requester doesn't know exactly what information he or she is looking for or where it might be, so the impulse is to make the request as broad as possible. For example, if the request is for "all letters, notes, email or other correspondence containing the words 'student' and/or 'enrollment' between the dates of Jan. 1, 2006, and Dec. 31, 2013, between the University's vice president for enrollment and all university employees," the response will be that the request will generate hundreds, if not thousands of documents and take a long time to complete. In states where the full cost of retrieval may be charged, the cost could run into thousands of dollars.

It will be far more productive to interview people with expertise in the subject of the story and the involved officials, as well as do other background research, before filing a public records request. After those interviews you should have a better idea of the focus of the story and be able to craft a public records request that narrows the timeframe and focuses the request.

The Federal FOIA Ombudsman has a good list of guidelines[12] to consider before you file a public records request:

1. Figure out what you want.

2. Figure out where it is.

3. Ask for what you want and nothing more.

4. Keep an eye on the clock.

5. FOIA professionals are people, too.

STATE PUBLIC MEETINGS LAWS

All of the states have laws governing access to public meetings of state public bodies. If the city council, the state water board, the county council or the city cemetery board of trustees are meeting, it is likely that the meeting is public and subject to the state's public meetings law. While, again, each state law has its own special features, there are common features:

- The public body must provide public notice of the meeting.
- There must be a written agenda that is available to the public.
- There must be minutes taken of the meeting provided to the public in a timely manner.
- No final decisions or votes can take place outside the public meeting.

These requirements make it possible for journalists and the public to see government bodies in action and provide a public record of decisions made.

The freedom of speech and of the press would be a hollow right if the law did not provide a right to gather information from the government. Federal and state constitutions provide limited rights, but federal and state statutes create a public right of access to information. Using these "right to know" laws will greatly improve the quality of the questions asked when interviewing and the power of the stories written.

NOTES

1. Potter Stewart, "Or of the Press," 26 Hastings L.J. 631, 636 (1975).

2. *Saxbe v. Washington Post Co.*, 417 U.S. 843, 846 (Powell, J., dissenting) (1974).

3. For example, *Houchins v. KQED, Inc.*, 438 U.S. 1 (1978).

4. *Richmond Newspapers v. Virginia*, 448 U.S. 555 (1980).

5. *Press-Enterprise Co. v. Superior Court*, 478 U.S. 1 (1986).

6. *Los Angeles Police Department v. United Reporting Publishing Corp.*, 528 U.S. 32 (1999).

7. http://www.justice.gov/oip/foia-guide.html.

8. http://www.rcfp.org/federal-open-government-guide.

9. http://www.rcfp.org/open-government-guide.

10. http://www.doj.state.or.us/public_records/pages/index.aspx.

11. http://www.open-oregon.com/.

12. https://ogis.archives.gov/about-foia/best-practices/requester-best -practices-filing-a-foia-request.htm.

TWENTY-EIGHT **The Interview and Privacy**

Journalists need to be aware of laws involving preparing for, conducting and publishing interviews

KYU HO YOUM

The First Amendment is not a license for journalists to do whatever they want to whomever they wish. Privacy law expert Kyu Ho Youm weighs in on the restrictions interviewers must respect when they practice journalism.

Interviewing is "one of the most basic journalism tools," although its value as a means to obtain reliable and valid information for the public is not entirely uncontroverted (Gordon & Kittross, 1999, p. 291). It is often a deliberate act of information gathering prior to information distribution through publication or broadcasting. News interviews and news dissemination are intertwined, but they are treated differently as a matter of press freedom vs. responsibility.

In the United States, a free press is the rule, not the exception. As Oregon journalism professors Lauren Kessler and Duncan McDonald (1987) observed, however, American journalists "must crisscross [the 'legal minefield']" in finding and reporting news information (pp. 27–28), since their freedom is not absolute. The conduct of newsgathering is fraught with more legal risks than news distribution as expression. This is still the case, although "without some protection for seeking out the news, freedom of the press could be eviscerated" (*Branzburg v. Hayes*, 1972, p. 681).

Privacy and defamation law issues arising from journalistic interviews are not necessarily limited to the interviews themselves. They, more often than not, involve pre- and post-interview processes. Media attorney Eric P. Robinson, co-director of the Press Law and Democracy Program at Louisiana State University (personal communication, April 22, 2014), has identified more than a dozen legal issues, including but not limited to newsgathering interviews.[1] One of the pre-interview issues is whether contacting the interviewee constitutes harassment and stalking or deception. The post-interview issues concern false light invasion of privacy and defamation, which are similar but not identical.[2] These result from publication of the interview stories as distinct from the before- and during-the-interview contexts in which no publication is involved.

This chapter examines several legal issues that deserve close attention from journalists in preparing for, conducting and publishing interviews. Some issues are addressed more in depth than others because their journalistic impact is direct and consequential. Relevant statutes—federal and state—and court cases are discussed. Given the U.S. media's global newsgathering and distribution efforts in the 21st century, international and foreign law should be more relevant than ever. But space limitations constrain the author in regard to touching on non-U.S. law.

I. ACCESS TO PLACES FOR INTERVIEW: INTRUSION?

Speakers' First Amendment rights to distribute information in their possession are "considerably broader" than the First Amendment rights of members of the public to access information that courts hold (Volokh, 2014). This free speech principle in American law applies to journalists, who are no different from ordinary citizens under the First Amendment. When it comes to news interviews, journalists have no special privilege of informational access. In *Branzburg v. Hayes*, the Supreme Court held that "the First Amendment does not guarantee the press a constitutional right of special access to information not available to the public generally" (p. 684).

Public streets, parks and other "traditional public forums" are open to the press because they are also open to the public. Hence, activities, including journalistic interviews, that occur in those places are rarely subject to government regulations, although reasonable time, place and manner restrictions can be imposed. This is also true with the places that are designated as "dedicated public forums."

Newsgathering in public places as a First Amendment right remains confined to judicial proceedings (*Richmond Newspapers, Inc. v. Virginia,* 1980). News reporters can be excluded from the scenes of a crime, disaster or accident on public property to ensure public safety and the efficiency of officials' work on the scenes. A few states, such as California, Ohio and Virginia, recognize a statutory right of media access to disaster scenes in connection with the news media's function of informing citizens about matters of public interest. Under the common law doctrine of professional "custom and usage," journalists in Florida are allowed to accompany officials onto private property when it's a disaster scene (*Florida Publishing Co. v. Fletcher,* 1976). But this custom and usage rule of Florida law is the only one.

Interviews and other newsgathering activities are restricted on government property that is not open to the general public. Journalists do not have special access to prisons, executions, military bases and schools, for they are not public forums. The balancing of the conflicting interests (government vs. news media) is often struck in favor of the government authorities in maintaining their institutional priorities such as prison security and administrative efficiencies.

Entering private property without permission is more likely to be treated as trespass. Unless the state law allows the public free speech activities at private businesses such as shopping malls, there is no First Amendment right to access privately owned businesses. The Constitution of California is a case in point. It guarantees the rights of the public to engage in expressive activities at shopping malls (*Pruneyard Shopping Center v. Robins,* 1980).

Journalists' "ride-alongs" in accompanying law enforcement officers onto private property have raised Fourth Amendment issues over the right to privacy against unreasonable searches. Law enforcement officers were sued for violating the Fourth Amendment (*Hanlon v. Berger,*

1999; *Wilson v. Layne*, 1999), and the Supreme Court held in 1999 that the Fourth Amendment was violated.

Media professionals, whether involved in ride-alongs or not, are prone to be exposed to intrusion litigation when they violate the solitude or seclusion of the subject of their interview without consent. The so-called ambush interview showcases a reporter or film crew visiting the subject's private home or place of business with no prior warning. Whether intrusion as a privacy tort is actionable depends on the subject's reasonable expectation of privacy or on the scope of "consent" to the interview. ·

II. AUDIO AND VIDEO RECORDING: EXPECTATION OF PRIVACY

Journalists often record interviews. One of the oft-cited reasons for journalistic recording is that it helps resolve controversies about who said what when news stories are challenged. But reporters' use of audio and video recorders, especially when they are hidden, raises a host of legal questions. One of the 21 questions posed to media lawyers around the world in *International Libel and Privacy Handbook* (Glasser, 2013) was: "May reporters tape-record their own telephone conversations for note-taking purposes (not rebroadcast) without the consent of the other party?" (p. xxxiv).

In American law, face-to-face recording—that is, recording interviews with audio or video equipment in plain view—is a non-issue because there is nothing private about the recording. When reporters record their interviews over the phone or with a recorder hidden in an in-person setting with no knowledge or consent from those being interviewed, however, federal and state law should be considered.

Under the one-party consent rule, federal law and the laws of 38 states and the District of Columbia allow reporters to record telephone conversations or use hidden recorders for face-to-face interviews. By contrast, 12 states are all-party states whose laws require the consent of all parties for the recording of telephone conversations. In these all-party states, civil or criminal penalties—or both—are imposed for recording of interviews without consent (Reporters Committee for Freedom of the Press, 2012,

p. 2). "Regardless of the state," the Reporters Committee for Freedom of the Press advises, "it is almost always illegal to record a conversation to which you are not a party, do not have consent to tape, *and* could not naturally overhear" (ibid., p. 2, emphasis added).

Which state law will apply when reporters make phone calls to sources in more than one state when the state laws are in conflict, i.e., one-party law vs. all-party law? Does the federal one-party law pre-empt state law? Insofar as the legal issues over interstate phone calls are concerned, the choice of law principles will determine which state law governs the case.

For example, assume that a reporter in Oregon interviews a news source in California and records his or her interview without the consent of the source. The reporter's taping, even without consent, does not violate the law of Oregon as a one-party state, but it might violate California wiretap law, which requires all-party consent, as highlighted by the recorded racist remarks of L.A. Clippers owner Donald Sterling (Snider, 2014). If the Oregon reporter is sued in San Francisco for violation of California law, a California court most likely will apply its state law. As the Supreme Court of California held in a case involving a conversation taped between people in California and Georgia in 2006, the failure to apply California law that prohibits secret recording of phone conversations "would impair California's interest in protecting the degree of privacy afforded to California residents by California law" when the law is in conflict with a one-party state law, in this instance, Georgia (*Kearney v. Salomon Smith Barney*, 2006, p. 100).

The 2006 ruling of the California Supreme Court should not be overgeneralized in predicting which law a court will choose when news interviews involve different state laws. But journalists ought to err on the side of caution when recording interstate phone interviews. The safest journalistic mode of operation here is to assume that the all-party state law will apply.

It is not clear whether the one-party federal law will pre-empt a conflicting state law with regard to interstate communications. To date, there has been no definitive court ruling. But federal law may apply when parties to a journalistic interview are in different states.

The FCC rules are more stringent. For calls that cross state lines, the federal agency requires an individual to alert other parties to an interstate call before recording.

The individual should get consent from all parties before making the call:

- The individual should notify the participants at the beginning of the recording; or

- The individual should use a "beep tone" that is repeated regularly throughout the call (Reporters Committee for Freedom of the Press, 2012, p. 17).

III. CONFIDENTIALITY PROMISES: WHEN TO MAKE THEM AND HOW?

Reporters make promises of confidentiality or more to their sources before and during interviews to obtain information. But they unwittingly create a conundrum for themselves because they cannot always honor those promises. Reporters are sometimes subpoenaed to disclose their confidential sources. In some cases, reporters unmask their sources, albeit inadvertently. Sometimes they decide to break their promises.

The U.S. Constitution does not recognize a privilege for journalists to protect their confidential sources (Fargo, 2010), even while source protection is increasingly accepted in international and foreign law (Youm, 2006). A total of 40 states have shield laws that allow journalists protection against forced disclosure of their sources, but often with qualifications. Various federal shield laws have been proposed over the years, but not much progress has been made. At of mid-2014, the Free Flow of Information Act, a federal shield bill, passed the U.S. Senate Judiciary Committee, and it was awaiting a full Senate vote.

In the "new era of contract journalism" (Sableman, 1997, p. 75), First Amendment lawyer Mark Sableman offers a sobering reality check: "[J]ust about any promise involving any material aspect of an interview or publication can lead to a lawsuit" (ibid., 76).

A number of promise-related challenges for reporters in interviewing have to do with what conditions to accept from sources, including "quote approval" (Sullivan, 2012), not with whether to make promises. This entails setting the rules of interviews in such a way that they'll leave nothing vague. Consequently, there should be no definitional misunderstanding between the reporter and the source on "deep background," "background," "off the record," "not for attribution," and "don't quote me" (Kessler & McDonald, pp. 210–11). Equally relevant is whether sources understand that "off the record" extends only to future remarks and "it can never be used to take one's foot out of one's mouth" (Harris).

Charles J. Glasser Jr., former global media counsel of Bloomberg News, has noted that the biggest problem for reporters in news interviewing is when reporters make promises about tone or content, and their subject feels that a promise was broken (personal communication, April 21, 2014). So, in teaching media law to reporters, one of the "cardinal rules" he emphasized was: "NEVER MAKE PROMISES ABOUT THE STORY" (ibid.).

Glasser's warning reminds journalists of liability for breaking promises, particularly on their own volition. *Cohen v. Cowles* (1991) illustrates a case of "burning the source" in which a news source was revealed by two Minnesota newspapers despite their reporters' confidentiality promises. The Supreme Court in *Cohen* held that "the First Amendment does not confer on the press a constitutional right to disregard promises that would otherwise be enforced under state law" (501 U.S. at 672). The *Cohen* ruling under the promissory estoppel theory does not apply where a journalist breaks the professional promise pursuant to compulsory process during discovery or at trial.

The reporter-source issues do not entirely revolve around source identifiability. The reporter's liability for breaking promises to a news source also can hinge on how the source is portrayed in the interview-based stories. Here more content than newsgathering is in dispute. So misrepresentation, not anonymity, is claimed when the stories place the source in an unflattering light. It is rarely controverted whether the reporter's content-related promises to his source are explicit or implicit. The reporter may be held liable for breach of contract if those provable promises are dishonored, albeit with ethically laudable motives.

IV. INTERVIEW STYLE AND TECHNIQUES: PRECONCEIVED JOURNALISTIC BIAS?

From a defamation and false light tort perspective, journalistic pre-interview conduct may turn out to be more problematic than anticipated when the stories are proved false. Bruce W. Sanford (2014), a leading libel law expert, stated: "Since the degree of care exercised by a libel defendant is assessed with respect to its conduct prior to publication, a reporter's comments during newsgathering are often relevant to the 'fault' question. A reporter's interview style . . . may reveal his attitude toward the truth or falsity of the news report at issue in a defamation action" (p. 8-97).

Just because a reporter is "zealous" in interviewing a source does not automatically lead to a court's conclusion that a subsequent story was published with an absence of due care amounting to "actual malice" in its constitutional sense—knowledge of falsity or reckless disregard for the truth (*Jenoff v. Hearst Corp.*, 1981). Likewise, according to the Minnesota Supreme Court, a reporter's "badgering" of interviewees and asking them "leading" questions did not establish actual malice. Nor were his "abrasive or antagonistic investigatory techniques" tantamount to actual malice (*Diesen v. Hessburg*, 1991). Also, the California Supreme Court rejected a claim by a San Jose city councilman that a reporter's "slick," "devious" and "obnoxious" manner of interviewing people showed actual malice. "The fact that a reporter is aggressive and abrasive in attempting to ferret out information from reluctant individuals is, in itself, hardly surprising," the court held (*Fletcher v. San Jose Mercury News*, 1990, pp. 185–86).

V. QUOTING FROM THE INTERVIEW: MATERIAL CHANGE OF THE ORIGINAL MEANING?

Few would quibble about what the Supreme Court spoke about the substance of news reporting in 1971: "[A] vast amount of what is published in the daily and periodical press purports to be descriptive of what somebody *said* rather than of what anybody *did*" (*Time, Inc. v. Pape*, p. 285).

What "somebody said" is often conveyed through the reporter's interviews. One of the legal questions involved is what latitude reporters have in massaging the quotes from their interviews. The editing of quotes can precipitate lawsuits for defamation or false light invasion of privacy—or both. In a leading misquotation case, the Supreme Court held that even the deliberate misquotation of a public figure cannot be libelous unless the wording materially changes the meaning of what was really said (*Masson v. New Yorker Magazine, Inc.*, 1991). In ruling in favor of journalist Janet Malcolm, the Court said the meaning of the challenged "intellectual gigolo" quotation attributed to the source about himself had not been materially changed.

The misquotation case centered on the application of actual malice due to the plaintiff's status as a controversial psychoanalyst. In other words, the concept of "substantial truth" was applicable to the inaccurate quotation because insubstantial errors were not a substantial basis of the actual malice finding.

Regardless, what are some of the best practices for journalists in quoting from interviews? Attorney Mark Fowler (Jan. 21, 2011) summarizes:

- Do your utmost to get the quotations right. The more inflammatory the quote, the more careful you should be.

- Consider tape recording interviews, especially if they are likely to be contentious. . . .

- If you recall the gist of a statement, but are not confident about the wording, don't put the words inside quotation marks. Report it for what it is: your paraphrase of what was said.

- If you haven't taped an interview, and if you aren't certain that you have precisely captured the interviewee's words in your notes, consider inviting the interviewee to review the quotes before publication. . . .

- Consider preserving your interview tapes and notes for a substantial period after the interview is published. . . .

- Don't take quotations out of context.

VI. INTERVIEW COPYRIGHT: WHO'S THE OWNER?

Interviews are copyrighted in American law because they are "fixed in any tangible medium of expression." But who owns the copyright to the interviews? As a rule, the interviewer can claim the copyright, although the interview copyright issues have not been authoritatively confronted in the United States. "In the absence of some agreement to the contrary, if the interviewee knew he was being interviewed," Fowler wrote, "a court would virtually always conclude that, at the very least, the interviewee had implicitly granted the interviewer a non-exclusive license to publish the resulting interview" (Mark Fowler, Jan. 7, 2011). Canadian law on the copyright ownership of interviews is more clear-cut in that news and other private interviews are copyrighted to "the person who reduces the oral statements to a fixed form that acquires copyright therein," because he or she is the originator of the copyright work (*Hager v. ECW Press Ltd.*, 1998).

In 2000, a federal district court in Illinois rejected an inmate interviewee's copyright claim against an NBC affiliate in connection with its broadcasting of an interview. The court reasoned that ownership of a copyright belongs only to the person who fixes an expression in tangible form, so the plaintiff was not entitled to copyright. The court found that there was no creation on the part of the plaintiff of a copyright work in the videotaped Q&A interview (*Taggart v. WMAQ*, 2000).

On the other hand, a source-centered copyright can be recognized. As implied by a federal district court in 1980, "The author of a factual work may not, without an assignment of copyright, claim copyright in statements made by others and reported in the work since the author may not claim originality as to those statements" (*Suid v. Newsweek Magazine*, 1980, p. 148). Further, even though the content of the interview may not belong to the interviewer, he may claim the ownership of the copyright as the "compiler" of the quotations from the interview (*Quinto v. Legal Times of Washington, Inc.*, 1981).

VII. SUMMARY AND CONCLUSIONS

As in other areas of newsgathering and dissemination, interviewing is not free from legal challenges as an occupational hazard for reporters.

Some of the challenges surrounding privacy and defamation have been old issues. Others such as liability for "burning the source" when news sources have set ground rules and copyright of interview content are more recent ones.

There is no doubt that being a competent news interviewer requires more than professional skill and experience. Critical knowledge of the relevant media law is essential to an able journalist with a passionate commitment to a free and responsible press.

Whether emerging or not, interview-related media law issues should be approached holistically. To a certain extent, interviews are discrete processes: pre-interview preparation, actual interviews, and post-interview publications. But legal issues stemming from interviews are rarely categorizable. Maybe some issues are more related to interview preparation than to the actual interviews—or vice versa. Still, their categorical distinctions might be more apparent than real. As a result, various real or perceived legal issues for reporters in interviewing ought to be placed in context.

Most important, reporters should develop a keen sense of how to identify legal issues and then what to do about them in a timely manner. Media law continues to evolve to keep up with the ever-changing online and offline media landscapes, so reporters need to be extra alert to statutory and judge-made law affecting news interviews.

NOTES

1. Media attorney Eric P. Robinson at Louisiana State University lists the interview-related legal issues that have informed the author's discussion:

- Arranging the interview
  - Identifying/contacting the interviewee
    - Privacy concerns
    - Safety concerns
  - Contacting the interviewee: harassment and stalking/how much is too much?
  - Deception
- Conducting the interview
  - Access to physical locations
    - Private property

- Public buildings
- Prisons
- Use of telephones and other devices
  - Government monitoring
- Audio/video recording
- Publishing/using the interview
  - Confidentiality
  - Copyright
  - Invasion of privacy (publication of personal information)
  - Publication of private facts
  - False light/libel by omission
  - Defamatory misquotations
  - Repeating libel by interviewee

2. While the tort of false light of invasion of privacy and defamation are arguably a distinction without a difference, they are still distinguishable from each other. They both require "falsity" as a fundamental requirement, but false light aims to protect one's interest in "being left alone," while defamation focuses on one's interest in a public reputation. Also, publicity, i.e., broad publication, is a requisite for a false light claim, but it is not essential for a defamation claim. Further, false light requires that the statement challenged be "highly offensive to a reasonable person," but defamation requires that the statement be reputationally injurious. Most important, false light may involve statements that *positively* describe a person, but defamation must involve negative statements (Smolla, 2014, §§ 10:9–10:13).

BIBLIOGRAPHY

Branzburg v. Hayes, 405 U.S. 665 (1972).

Cohen v. Cowles Media, 501 U.S. 663 (1991).

Diesen v. Hessburg, 455 N.W.2d 446 (Minn. 1990), *cert. denied*, 498 U.S. 1119 (1991).

Fargo, Anthony L. (summer 2010). "What They Meant to Say: The Courts Try to Explain *Branzburg v. Hayes*." *Journalism & Communication Monographs*, 12.

Fletcher v. San Jose Mercury News, 216 Cal. App. 3d 172 (1989), *cert. denied*, 498 U.S. 813 (1990).

Florida Publishing Co. v. Fletcher, 340 So. 2d 914 (Fla. 1976).

Fowler, Mark. (2011, Jan. 7). "Who 'Owns' an Interview?" *Rights of Writers*. Retrieved from http://www.rightsofwriters.com/search/label/Confidentiality.

Fowler, Mark. (2011, Jan. 21). "What Are the Risks of Misquoting an Interviewee?" *Rights of Writers*. Retrieved from http://www.rightsofwriters.com/ search/label/Interviews.

Glasser, Charles J., Jr. (2013). *International Libel and Privacy Handbook: A Global Reference for Journalists, Publishers, Webmasters, and Lawyers* (3rd ed.). Hoboken, NJ: Bloomberg Press.

Gordon, A. David., and John Michael Kittross. (1999). *Controversies in Media Ethics* (2nd ed.) New York, NY: Longman.

Hager v. ECW Press Ltd., 1998 CanLII 9115 (FC).

Hanlon v. Berger, 526 U.S. 808 (1999).

Harris, Sam. (2011, May 20). "The Perils of the Print Interview." *The Blog*. Retrieved from http://www.samharris.org/blog/item/the-peril-of-the-print-interview.

Jenoff v. Hearst Corp., 453 F. Supp. 541 (D. Md. 1978), *aff'd*, 644 F.2d 1004 (4th Cir. 1981).

Kearney v. Salomon Smith Barney, 39 Cal. 4th 95 (2006).

Kessler, Lauren, and Duncan McDonald. (1987). *Uncovering the News: A Journalist's Search for Information*. Belmont, Calif.: Wadsworth.

Masson v. New Yorker Magazine, Inc., 501 U.S. 496 (1991).

Pruneyard Shopping Center v. Robins, 447 U.S. 74 (1980).

Quinto v. Legal Times of Washington, Inc., 506 F. Supp. 554 (D.D.C. 1981).

Reporters Committee for Freedom of the Press. (summer 2012). "A State-by-State Guide to Taping Phone Calls and In-Person Conversations." Reporter's Recording Guide. Retrieved from http://www.rcfp.org/reporters-recording-guide.

Richmond Newspapers, Inc. v. Virginia, 488 U.S. 555 (1980).

Sableman, Mark. (1997). *More Speech, Not Less: Communications Law in the Information Age*. Carbondale, Ill.: Southern Illinois University Press.

Sanford, Bruce W. (2014). *Libel and Privacy* (2nd ed.). New York: Wolters Kluwer Law & Business.

Smolla, Rodney A. (2014). *Law of Defamation* (2nd ed.). Eagan, Minn.: Thomson Reuters.

Snider, Bruce. (2014, April 28). "Clippers Controversy: Legal to Record Donald Sterling's Comments?" *FindLaw: Tarnished Twenty*. Retrieved from http:// blogs.findlaw.com/tarnished_twenty/2014/04/clippers-controversy-legal-to -record-donald-sterlings-comments.html?DCMP=NWL-pro_top.

Suid v. Newsweek Magazine, 503 F. Supp. 146 (D.D.C. 1980).

Sullivan, Margaret. (2012, Sept. 12). "In New Policy, The Times Forbids After-the-Fact 'Quote Approval.'" *New York Times*. Retrieved from http://publicedi tor.blogs.nytimes.com/2012/09/20/in-new-policy-the-times-forbids-after-the -fact-quote-approval/.

Taggart v. WMAQ, 57 U.S.P.Q.2d 1083 (S.D. Ill. 2000).

Time, Inc. v. U.S., 401 U.S. 279 (1971).

Volokh, Eugene. (2014, April 25). "Judge Sues Accuser for Libel, Demands
    to See Accuser's Evidence." *The Volokh Conspiracy.* Retrieved from http://
    www.washingtonpost.com/news/volokh-conspiracy/wp/2014/04/25/
    judge-sues-accuser-for-libel-demands-to-see-accusers-evidence/.
Wilson v. Layne, 526 U.S. 603 (1999).
Youm, Kyu Ho. (2006). "International and Comparative Law on the Journalist's
    Privilege: The *Randal* Case as a Lesson for the American Press." *Journal of
    International Media & Entertainment Law, 1,* 1–56.

PART V Et Cetera

TWENTY-NINE

The View from the Assignment Desk

Interviewing in a who, what, when, where and why world

REBECCA FORCE

The journalistic interviewer rarely works alone. Rebecca Force, who teaches broadcast journalism at Oregon, details the collaborative approach to interviewing.

In you want to know something, you ask questions. If you ask questions, you are doing interviews. Reporters do interviews on behalf of people who want to know the answers but would prefer—for a variety of reasons—that the reporter does the asking. Interviews are the building blocks of journalism. They can verify research, provide details, add perspective, lend expertise and unveil the truth. With the help of an interview, the public's understanding of a complex world may be improved and thirst for knowledge temporarily quenched.

Assignment editors facilitate the interviewing process every day. This is a brief look at what goes into the effort.

ASSIGNMENT EDITORS

Assignment editors are the people in the newsroom who are expected to know what is going on in the news. To do that, they talk to reporters and photographers—the eyes and ears of the newsroom. They keep in touch with key sources. They read stacks of newspapers, scan yards of online blogs and check wire reports and social media. They listen to emergency calls on scanners and talk to the people who call in to share what they've seen, what they know or what they would like to know. The AEs then decide—usually in consultation with producers and other editors—what news needs to be covered that day, what form that coverage is going to take and who is going to be assigned to the story.

Assignment editors want it all; they want to have the best story ideas and enough time to cover those stories well. They want to work with the brightest and most talented reporters and photographers, with the most enlightened news managers and with access to an unlimited news budget. They would like all their news sources to be gracious, willing, articulate and honest. But, as the song says, you can't always get what you want.[1]

What assignment editors can do is prepare and evaluate in order to get what they need. If they do that, they have a chance to make the best use of people, equipment, sources and time. That means matching the right reporter with the right source, the right photographer with the best visual opportunities. That means setting up interviews and providing adequate time for news crews to record them—and then write and edit the stories that rely on them—so that deadlines are met and the news-consuming public is informed.

To that end, assignment editors make a slightly different use of journalism's basic questions of who, what, when, where, why and how. The AE has a part to play in deciding why an interview is needed, who should be interviewed, who should conduct the interview, what kind of information it should provide, when the interview should be scheduled, where it should be set and how it should be done.

THE INTERVIEWEE—*Choosing the right person for the story.* If you want to know something about baking bread, you usually don't ask a landscaper; you ask a baker. The baker has standing when it comes to baking bread. The baker has baked a lot of it, and knows the ins and outs of activating yeast, kneading dough and allowing it to rise. Bakers are credible sources when it comes to talking about the effect of a wheat shortage on the price of a loaf of whole grain goodness. And credible sources are what journalists are looking for when they decide whom to ask for an interview. They want to talk to someone who actually knows something about the subject. That means someone who possesses a degree of knowledge that makes it worth our time to ask them to share what they've learned. In the best news environments, journalists are working on behalf of the people who are going to watch or read a report; it follows that journalists should be trying to give those people the best information available. Choosing the right person to interview is a key factor in that equation, and deserves careful thought.

The people we ask for interviews may be experts based on their education, such as an attorney who specializes in immigration law when we report on the laws governing interactions with undocumented workers. Or, it may be that someone's experience makes him or her a good candidate with standing, as in the case of an eyewitness to a disaster or some other newsworthy event. Or, you might try to find an insider when you report on a business or institutional enterprise, as was the case when a reporter recently covered working conditions at an American car company's assembly plant in China. In that case, the factory manager allowed the journalist to interview a handpicked employee but cautioned him that workers were barred from revealing their wages or overtime rates. The reporter finished the "official" interview, and later returned to the factory gates where numerous other employees gave him the information he had requested.

The factory workers would probably *not* have had standing if the reporter had asked them about international business practices or the finer points of running a motor company, but they certainly had standing when it came to talking about their wages, and about the bribes some of them said they had paid to obtain their jobs.[2]

The best interviews derive from asking good questions of people who know what they are talking about. To that end, the desk's address book is filled with the names of people who are in the know and notes on how to contact them. The AE knows which sources are willing to be interviewed, whether they are articulate, who's trustworthy and how to reach them after hours. The longer AEs (and reporters) are in the business, the more contacts they develop, and one good contact can lead to others.

Fat address books are good but frequently useless in breaking news situations. So, AEs need to be nimble. When a disturbed man started shooting people in a Colorado shopping mall, the editors at a Portland, Oregon, television station tapped the social media skills of a University of Oregon intern. She used Twitter feeds to locate people who were trapped in the mall. The station contacted them and subsequently took the lead in the national coverage of the tragedy with eyewitness accounts of what had happened.

THE INTERVIEWER—*Not all reporters are created equal.* The desk may need to decide not only who should be interviewed, but also who should conduct the interview.

For some relatively basic stories, the AE or just about any writer, reporter or photographer can conduct the interview to gather the facts. Easy: Make a couple of phone calls, ask three or four questions, verify the information, write it up. This kind of interview is good for "event coverage," with a focus on the "who, what, when and where," but not so much on the "how" and "why" at this stage of the story. An example would be collecting the details to go with the photos or video shot at the scene of a house fire the previous night.

For the bigger stories we cover, a reporter's intelligence, talent, organization, knowledge, experience and even personality may influence who is going to be chosen to cover an assignment. While these traits aren't mutually exclusive, it is nonetheless true that different reporters have different strengths. In short, a journalist who can't transcend feature reporting is never going to score an assignment to cover the governor's race but may be the best possible reporter to talk to an 8-year-old who has just started her own company.

An AE is going to try to match reporters with their strengths. The smartest might be tapped to cover business or science because they can comprehend the research, speak the language and translate both into something the rest of us can understand. Talented writers who can touch our hearts may be chosen for stories that offer a reporter a chance to do just that. Tracking a complex story might require a journalist with strong organizational abilities. Reporters with a broad understanding of issues or experience covering a beat move to the head of the line because they don't have to be briefed. And if it's a story requiring a pit bull approach, the desk is probably going to turn to the most persistent never-take-no-for-an-answer reporter in the newsroom. Former ABC correspondent Sam Donaldson was one such reporter with a well-earned reputation for dogged determination bordering on irritating rudeness. In his book *Hold On, Mr. President* Donaldson illustrated just why he might be the last person you would ever want to send to cover a feature story.

> If you send me to cover a pie-baking contest on Mother's Day, I'm going to ask dear old Mom whether she used artificial sweetener in violation of the rules, and while she's at it, could I see the receipt for the apples to prove she didn't steal them. I maintain that if Mom has nothing to hide, no harm will have been done. But the questions should be asked. Too often, Mom, and presidents—behind those sweet faces—turn out to have stuffed a few rotten apples into the public barrel.[3]

AEs also care who comes up with a story idea. Most often, the enterprising reporter who brings in a good idea will be the one assigned to cover it.

WHY

When assignment editors or reporters ask for an interview, they already have an idea of the value it might provide. That assessment helps determine where and how an interview might be done and how much time will be budgeted for it. Not all interviews are conducted in person, and not all of them take a long time to complete. Simply put, an interview is underway when you ask someone a question.

Reporters interview people:

FOR FACTS—*Eyewitnesses, insiders and experts can fill in the factual foundation of a news story.* For example, if you are working on a story about one specific homeless person, you can put his or her dilemma in perspective with a paragraph that outlines the scope of the homeless problem with attributable information you might gather from an interview; this might include the estimated number of homeless people in your community on any given night, the makeup of that total (families, individuals, unemployed, veterans, mentally ill, teens, etc.) and perhaps the public and private agencies working on the problem.

FOR FACT CHECKING   Find two sources and check your facts twice; it's a good motto to follow if you want to avoid all kinds of publication errors, including libel. This is just Journalism 101: Get it right.

FOR BACKGROUND AND PERSPECTIVE—*Those in the know can fill in the answers to the question "How did we get here?" wherever "here" is.* As in:
How did the great recession start?
When did you realize that she loved you?
What happened before the Big Bang?

FOR "SPICE" QUOTES—*Many stories benefit from the inclusion of comments from interested or involved observers or participants.* The quotes they provide often give flavor or color to the story rather than facts.
It sounded like a train was coming through the living room.
It's the worst fire I've ever seen.
I couldn't believe she would say that at a public meeting.

FOR PROOF—*The message is, "We didn't make this up."* Sometimes, a reporter needs to get a newsmaker on the record, even if she thinks the source is disgusting, stupid or lying:

"I didn't break any laws, I didn't do anything wrong. This particular prosecutor did everything he could to target me and prosecute me, persecute me, put pressure on my family, try to take our home, take me from my kids, arrest me." *Rod Blagojevich, former Illinois governor, after being convicted on one count of lying to federal officials.*[4] *In his second trial, the jury found him guilty on 17 corruption charges.*

In some circumstances—in the hope of acquiring a useful quote to throw into a story—reporters conduct "drive bys," shouting questions at a news source who is trying to avoid cameras, microphones and reporters. The hope is usually ill-founded, and the value of the effort is questionable. Until the source replies.

FOR BALANCE   This category is about being fair and respecting the reader and viewer. It would be useless to deny that there are a lot of advocacy journalists practicing out there, but all that means is that there are a lot of news consumers at risk of being manipulated by one-sided reports. Don't tell people what to think; instead, interview all sides and give people a chance to make up their own minds.

Note: We often talk about this in terms of "getting both sides of the story." In reality, there are often far more than two.

FOR CREDIBILITY   Most of the time, sources with expertise are more believable than general assignment reporters. Interviewing people who have standing and attributing their responses answers the age-old question, "Says who?"

FOR CONFIRMATION OR LACK THEREOF   The *New York Times* may be reporting that widgets are an environmental hazard and may be quoting an eminent scientist who cites his research in making the claim that widgets cause cancer. You may want to get clarification from the widget specialist at the university or the oncologist at the hospital. You get a local angle on the story at the same time.

FOR INTEREST   Breaking up a report with quotes containing facts, comments and opinions can result in a more interesting experience for the news consumer. We aren't trying to bore them, and while entertainment is not at the top of the agenda either, it isn't a crime to find interesting ways to report the news.

THE STORY   Sometimes, the interview is the story. In 2008 when vice presidential candidate Sarah Palin sat down for an interview with CBS anchor/reporter Katie Couric, that interview was so revelatory that it became a news story covered by reporters everywhere. Or, in 1977 when former President Richard Nixon agreed to be interviewed by David Frost: at the end of four weeks of interviews resulting in 29 hours of recordings, Nixon gave the only apology he would ever offer for the scandal caused by the Watergate crimes. The Frost interview became legendary.

WHEN

Time is the enemy in most news operations; from the moment a shift begins, journalists scramble to research an assigned topic, work with the desk to determine who if anyone should be interviewed, prepare questions, travel to the interview, conduct the interview, travel to the next interview, conduct the next interview (repeat as needed), return to the newsroom, select the quotes, write the story, submit the story for editing, rewrite the story and file it for publication. By the deadline. In the world of multimedia, there are stills and video to be captured and edited for this entire process, as well.

Small wonder that throughout the day, everyone in the newsroom is watching the clock. To defeat the deadline, the object is to send the crews out early to collect information and interviews within the time available.

Usually, there is no option to wait another day to finish a story; "news" by definition is the new stuff . . . not the old. Regardless of whether a reporter works for a television, radio, print or web-based news organization, striving to make deadlines is a reality in the very competitive world of journalism.

In part because of these pressures, assignment editors may initiate an interview before a reporter even knows there is a story to do. In most news operations, AEs are at work before a reporter comes in and might set up appointments for interviews before reporters are briefed. Or the reporter may have generated the idea for the story and set up the interviews herself. In either case, the reporter and editor often share sources and talk about who might be the best person to interview.

They will also negotiate an estimate of how long the interview will take. The desk will plan the day based on such estimates for all the stories that have been assigned and all the reporters who have been assigned to cover them.

WHAT

The form of the story may have a determining effect on the length of interview collected for the story and how it will be used.

The four basic forms of news stories in a broadcast are *reads, VOs, VO-SOTs* and *packages.*

- *Read:* It can take as little as a 10-minute phone call to interview someone for a story that requires no video. An anchor then "reads" the story on air. This type of story can usually be written in 50 to 75 words, and takes :30 or less to read on the air.

- *VO:* If the read is accompanied by video it's called a *voice-over* or *VO.* The viewer hears the anchor reading while watching video. The desk needs to make time for a photographer to shoot and edit that video and the reporter to collect the information and write it up. The estimated length of the story is :30 to :45 on the air.

- *VO-SOT:* This is a read, accompanied by video, accompanied by a portion of an interview with a news source. The *SOT* stands for *sound on tape*—a term quickly becoming archaic in this digital world. This story form usually comes in at less than one minute.

- *Package:* This is a prerecorded story with video, interviews and narration by a reporter. Packages are a favorite form, because they give reporters enough time to get past the "who, what, where and when" of a news story, and into the "why and how." Packages take longer to research, shoot (video and interviews), write, edit and air. It is this form that usually controls the planning of a day for a news organization.

Generally, for a typical package that will last about 1:30 on the air, it will take about 90 minutes to collect two interviews and shoot video to illustrate the story (B-Roll); another 90 minutes to select quotes or "bites," write the script and record the narration; and about 70 minutes to edit the video for the piece. Travel adds time, as does arguing with the desk, eating lunch and—in the smaller markets—picking up a couple of smaller stories. Generally. We're talking averages; there are exceptions to all of the aforementioned parameters. And we haven't even started to discuss the great stories that require weeks of research, days of shooting, writing, rewriting, editing and meeting with editors.

For text, the amount of space dedicated to a story is generally estimated before interviews are conducted or the story is written, based on the formula that strong stories will get more room for more details. The length of stories is measured by word count or—in the case of print stories—by how many inches the story occupies in a column of text. Short stories of 4 to 5 *column inches* (~150 words) are called "news briefs." Briefs are usually *inverted pyramid* (most important information positioned at the top of the story) with few if any quotes. The budget for feature and issue reports is bigger (~500 to 1,500 words) and allows for more extensive use of the information and quotations gathered through interviews.

While online media have more space for publication, they do not use it with abandon. Writing is generally tight, and stories frequently fall in the 250-word-count category. But online can also incorporate all the other story forms and multimedia pieces as well; it is a platform that has the potential to give a story as much room as it needs.

WHERE

For visual impact, we generally like to interview people in their natural habitat. That can be at an office, a ballpark, a farm, the space station or a thousand other places. On his home turf, an interviewee is more likely to be relaxed, and the ambiance provided by talking to him in that space may add to the viewer's understanding of the person talking.

Another choice might be at a site that frames the interviewee's interests: A reporter might meet the opponent of a construction project at the proposed location of that development.

Another option is asking the interviewee to come to the reporter. This is useful for live interview opportunities, or news sources who are passing through an area and don't have a home base.

If video is not needed, an interview can take place anywhere there is a willing source, a phone or a computer connection.

HOW

The outcome of an interview is influenced by the way a reporter prepares for it and conducts it. The desk may assist in the process.

Research is critical, because it can be rather difficult to ask intelligent questions if you know nothing about a subject. The desk can help by giving the reporter the material it has turned up about a story as well as time to do more digging if necessary.

Briefing is useful; the assignment editor has selected the story to be done and should share the reasons for that decision with the reporter. While the interview and final report utilizing it will ultimately be in the hands of the reporter, at the beginning of the day the assignment editor may help explore possible directions the story might take.

Scheduling the interview may fall to the AE as well. That means negotiating an appointment that permits the reporter get to it on time, set up the gear on time and start the interview on time. Promptness is a matter of courtesy and respect for a source; being late is rude and makes everyone cranky.

Choosing the reporter is a strategic decision by the desk, as well. A good story needs a reporter who will do the required homework, be on time, who knows how to put people at ease, and asks questions that serve the interests and needs of a reader or viewer. The AE also wants a reporter who doesn't make assumptions, listens carefully and is open to the occasional unexpected answer that may change the story being done. That means a reporter who isn't afraid to ask challenging follow-up questions, and who strives for accuracy, fairness and balance. Assignment editors keep track of that sort of thing.

AEs also keep track of who comes up with great story ideas. Generally, the enterprising reporter who brings in a good idea is the one who is going to be assigned to do it. It's good for a story to be put together by someone who is interested in it.

Finally . . .

After the reporters are assigned at the beginning of the day, the preparations begin for the night shift and the next day. The AEs have more to read, evaluate and plan. There are calls to be made, interviews to be set. Tomorrow, it all begins again.[5]

NOTES

1. Mick Jagger and Keith Richards, "You Can't Always Get What You Want," *Rolling Stones—Let It Bleed,* LP, Decca Records, 1969.

2. Rob Schmitz, *Marketplace,* "Ford's China Conundrum: Big Profits, Bribery Allegations," www.marketplace.org, Friday, April 4, 2014.

3. Sam Donaldson, *Hold On, Mr. President!* Random House, 1987, p. 20.

4. "By and About Blagojevich in Quotes," *Chicago Tribune,* articles .chicagotribune.com, 6/27/2011.

5. See, e.g., Myth of Sisyphus.

THIRTY Inside Interviewing

What do editors and reporters have in common with interviewers and interviewees?

JOHN RUSSIAL

After an interview is in the bag, John Russial, who teaches editing at Oregon, knows that there should be still another interview before the work is exposed to an audience.

"I'm having a problem with your lead. . . . Is this what you're trying to say?" asks the editor, who then offers an alternative.

"I see the problem, but I'm not sure I agree with what you're proposing," says the writer.

"OK, do you have another idea?" asks the editor.

"Let's try this one," says the writer.

When editors and reporters have this kind of conversation, it usually ends in a story that is better than either the reporter's original or the editor's rewrite. This type of dialogue occurs at news organizations throughout the world. It should occur more often than it does, but when it does, good things happen. Stories get better.

So what do editors and reporters have to do with interviewing—the focus of this book?

More than meets the eye, perhaps. This editor-writer dialogue is really an interview, albeit a specialized one, and though it isn't the same as a reporter talking with a source, some of the ideas might transfer. And stories can get better.

To be sure, an editor-reporter exchange is often a simple Q&A. An editor might ask whether a name is spelled correctly, what support a writer has for a specific assertion or whether the proposed tax increase is 2 percent or is really 2 percentage points.

But it can be more. A dialogue between editor and reporter can lead to an understanding greater than either participant could produce independently. Philosophers might call this a dialectical approach—thesis, antithesis, synthesis. Editors and writers tend to use simpler terms. It's a dialogue. The aim in this type of conversation is to improve a story, a lead, an ending or maybe the overall structure. The approach can help clarify confusing writing or provide a way to explain a complex idea in simple yet still accurate terms. It's a discussion based on respect, and if the planets align properly, on trust. If it's done well, no journalist will be harmed in the process—neither the reporter nor the editor—and both will feel that the final story is better for the effort. And in that sense, it might be a useful strategy for other types of interviewing. It could improve the experience and ultimately lead to better information gathered as well as better information presented.

A science writer, for example, might want to interview an expert in nanotechnology in order to explain a difficult concept to a lay audience in a way that enhances the layman's understanding but does no damage to the science. A business writer might interview a Nobel Prize–winning economist about a concept that goes far beyond simple supply and demand. The interviewee answers a question in technical jargon, and the interviewer attempts to feed it back to the interviewee in a form that readers can understand. The scientist or economist sees the problem (scientists and economists are, after all, pretty smart) and recasts the interviewer's words in a more palatable way—one that preserves important qualification but is more accessible to readers.

The dialectical approach is one technique, but there are others based on good editor-reporter dialogue that might translate to reporter-source interviewing.

Here are a couple of them:

- Keep power out of the discussion
- Use the reader as an ally

POWER FAILURES

Power can be the enemy of dialogue, and it's good to try to keep power out of the process as much as possible. An imbalance of power naturally exists between editor and reporter, and it can lead to testy exchanges. These can breed ill will and intransigence, and they can ultimately yield stories that are not what they could be.

It's a good idea to mitigate the power imbalance so that writer and editor can discuss the story more as equals. The coaching movement in journalism, explained by Roy Peter Clark and Don Fry in *Coaching Writers*, offers some excellent approaches for consultation that remove power from the equation. For example, an editor first asks what the writer likes about the story, instead of starting in on what's wrong with it. And if a rewrite is needed, an editor makes suggestions but lets the writer recast the story.

How might this idea translate into a reporter-source interaction? Much as in the editor-reporter duet, the participants in an interview dance may not be equals. In this case, one has more information than the other, and information can be power. When a journalist interviews an expert, no matter how much background research the journalist does, the expert is, well, the expert. And status differences can lead to arrogance and sometimes even dismissiveness. A former mayor of a large Eastern city was known for this—he had no qualms about publicly belittling interviewers, especially those he felt were unprepared. A power imbalance can create a wall between the one who knows and the one who wants to know.

Disproportionate power can also reside in the interviewer. Some interviewers have much higher status than the people they interview, and they have to be careful to avoid appearing arrogant. Think of a multimillion-dollar network anchor interviewing a trucker or a diner cook. One way to keep power out of the mix is by listening—a point made by others in this book as well as by writing coaches. Listening tells the reporter—or the interviewee—that he or she is important and has something to say. It shifts the balance of power.

Sometimes the issue is more about trust than power. Experts often don't trust journalists because an unprepared interviewer who writes a flawed story can make an expert look foolish, and experts don't like to look foolish. Sometimes trust develops only over time—after experts see that their words or ideas have been reported carefully and accurately. In the short term, one way to improve trust, of course, is to do your homework, as Jon Palfreman and Tim Gleason explain in this book. Another is to show the interviewee that you're serious about getting it right.

William Zinsser says as much in *On Writing Well* when he encourages interviewers to stop the conversation when they need to capture a quote exactly. "I want to make sure I get this right" says a lot to the interviewee. It shows you respect the person you're interviewing and that you care enough to make sure that you report what he or she said accurately. In his chapter in this book, visual journalist Torsten Kjellstrand talked about how it's even possible to communicate this idea of care and professionalism when you set up audio and video equipment—a situation that more typically is construed as intrusive.

DEFUSING CONFLICT

The editing process is fraught with potential for conflict, and so are some interviews. There is a built-in adversarial element in the interaction between someone who writes and someone who critiques that writing. Nobody really likes to be criticized, and criticism can easily produce tension.

There are various strategies for mitigating tension. One approach is to appeal to a third party. The best ally in an editor-reporter discussion isn't even in the room. It's the everyman behind the curtain—the reader—who isn't pulling the strings in a literal sense but who is, after all, the point of the whole exercise. As can happen when editors and reporters talk, appealing to the reader might help interviewer and interviewee find common ground and get beyond personalities if it looks as though they might get in the way. Appealing to an abstraction—"the reader"—may seem a bit artificial, but it also reflects a common understanding. The underlying message is that we're in it together, and we're doing it for someone else—the reader.

These are a few techniques good editors employ in talking with reporters. There are others, such as starting with easier questions and moving to more difficult ones after rapport is established, and again, the coaching movement is a good source of other ideas.

Will such approaches always work? No, and they're not always necessary. If all you need is a simple answer, you ask a simple question. But they can help in situations where things aren't so simple and problems can get in the way.

"Are we on the same page now?" the interviewer asks.

"Yes, I think we are," the interviewee answers.

BIBLIOGRAPHY

Clark, Roy Peter, and Don Fry. (2003). *Coaching Writers*, 2nd ed. Boston: Bedford-St. Martin's.
Zinsser, William. (2006). *On Writing Well*. New York: HarperCollins.

THIRTY-ONE

The Political Interview

Caught inside a tsunami of craziness,
it's easy to miss the bombshell

CHARLES JACO

He said what? Charles Jaco gave the Johnston Lecture at Oregon's "What Is Radio?" Conference. The longtime broadcast journalist notes that interviewers too often fail to listen to the answers to their own questions.

In 1891, Oscar Wilde examined the duality of the critic (read; journalist) and the artist (read: politico) in his essay "The Critic as Artist." The faux Socratic dialogue concludes that people are most prone to illusion when they work toward a defined goal and put their name to it. While that may or may not be a guide for covering politics, and for life in general, the money quote for journalists comes on page 167 of my edition, as Wilde writes, "Man is least himself when he talks in his own person. Give him a mask and he will tell you the truth."

That sums up the difficulty of a political interview, and the time-honored value of having down time and/or adult beverages with the candidate and staff, and getting them to tell you things on deep background that may actually point toward the truth. But in a formal interview, everything is on the record, and canned answers and regurgitated talking points usually obscure the value of any questions that are asked. Thus, this cautionary tale about an interview that changed the course of history by accident.

In August 2012, the Missouri Republican Party held a primary to determine its candidate for the United States Senate. GOP officials were sure that, whoever won, that candidate would become the newest senator from Missouri. The incumbent, Sen. Claire McCaskill, was a middle-of-the-road Democrat who was an early endorser of Sen. Barack Obama for president in January 2008. In the November election, despite an unprecedented turnout of young and minority voters, Obama lost Missouri to Republican Sen. John McCain by around 4,000 votes out of 2.9 million votes cast, a victory margin of around 0.13 percent.

But the closeness of that one race was not really a good indication of political feeling in the Show-Me State. The one-time surge of young people and non-white voters was a political version of Pickett's Charge at Gettysburg, the high water mark of a lost cause. Rural and exurban conservative white voters who showed up election after election gave the state's conservative GOP a super-majority in both houses of the state General Assembly, which, in turn, led to a congressional re-districting map after the 2010 Census that left Missouri with eight congressmen, down from nine, and only two of them Democrats.

President Barack Obama was wildly unpopular in Missouri among likely—read conservative—voters as the state entered the 2012 election cycle. Republican strategists looked forward to November 2012, and, as it turned out, with good reason; the eventual GOP nominee, former Gov. Mitt Romney, ended up thumping the president in Missouri by a whopping 9.4 percent, a relative margin of victory 72 times greater than McCain's 2008 triumph over Obama.

Democrat McCaskill, Republican strategists concluded, might easily be swept out the door because of her close ties to the president. A poll in May indicated the eventual GOP nominee, Republican U.S. Rep. Todd Akin, would beat McCaskill by at least 3 percent. That same poll showed President Obama with just a 44 percent approval rating in the state, with 52 percent of voters disapproving of the president. Sen. McCaskill's only hope was Missouri's habit of having one senator from each party, and of electing Democrats, such as the governor, attorney general, and secretary of state, to statewide office.

All of that was a result of Missouri's political split personality disorder. Its easternmost city, St. Louis, resembles Baltimore or Philadelphia, while its westernmost city, Kansas City, shares an affinity with Denver or Oklahoma City. Residents of its northernmost plains share clipped accents with Omaha and Des Moines, while townsfolk in the southernmost swamps hard against the sinuous Mississippi River speak in the elongated drawls of Arkansas and Tennessee. Any state that gave birth to both Jesse James and T.S. Eliot obviously struggles with an identity crisis.

When the results were tabulated after the three-way August 2012 GOP Senate primary, the winner was Rep. Todd Akin, an engineer by trade who was a five-term congressman representing the conservative white flight suburbs west of St. Louis. Backed by the Republican Tea Party faction, Akin intended to parlay his continual standing as one of the 10 most conservative members of Congress into a Senate seat.

Before he became a congressman, Rep. Akin had been a multi-term member of the Missouri Legislature. During his tenure in public life, I had interviewed Rep. Akin a dozen times or more for both radio and TV. The congressman's position on the House Armed Services Committee (and the deployment of one of his sons to Afghanistan) made him a good candidate for interviews on military affairs, Iraq and Afghanistan.

Our relationship stretched back more than a decade and was perfectly cordial, even though it was clear in conversations that we disagreed on most issues, especially the war in Iraq and his stand on "social" issues. The congressman had always made time to appear with me for interviews, either live on talk radio programs I had hosted, or recorded for a TV assignment, and he always returned my phone calls.

The congressman's opinions on many issues, though, were to the right of most other politicians. While they seemed to serve him well among his Christian conservative base in Missouri's Second Congressional District, they often left many of us scratching our heads. We had an informal term for it: The Akin Effect. As one newspaper editor put it to me, "Interviewing Todd sometimes is like drowning in a tsunami of crazy. He says one thing after another, and it leaves your eyes glazed over."

The political landscape was littered with the fallout from Akin quotes. In June 2011, he said, "At the heart of liberalism is a hatred of God." When confronted by progressive and liberal religious leaders over the statement, Akin replied, "I'm not going to apologize for what I see liberalism doing in trying to take God out."

Three months later, Akin said—all in one speech—that climate change is "highly suspect" and that Medicare is unconstitutional because "I don't find in the Constitution that it's the government's job to provide health care." The next year, Akin supported repeal of the 17th Amendment, which provides for direct, popular election of U.S. senators, saying, "I don't think the federal government should be doing a lot of what it's doing, and a repeal of the 17th Amendment might help to pull that back."

During House budget negotiations in 2010, Rep. Akin called President Obama "a flaming socialist," and two years later continued the theme during a speech where he called federally guaranteed student loans "a stage three cancer of socialism."

In 2006, Akin, in a House floor speech, said, "Anybody who knows something about the history of the human race knows there is no civilization which has condoned homosexual marriage widely and openly that has long survived." In 2012, the congressman supported the anti-gay marriage Defense of Marriage Act, and co-sponsored a bill to stop any same-sex marriages from ever taking place on any U.S. military bases. That same year, he demanded that the United States withdraw from the United Nations.

But no topic caused the congressman to become more passionate than abortion. In a 2008 House floor speech, he called abortion providers "terrorists." That same year, in a C-SPAN interview, Akin said, "You find that along with this culture of death go all sorts of other law-breaking . . . (including) giving abortions to women who are not actually pregnant." Akin firmly believed that abortion should be outlawed completely, including in cases of rape or incest or where the woman's life might be in danger.

So after Rep. Akin won the Republican Senate primary on Aug. 7, 2012, I immediately got on the phone with his press secretary, Steve Traylor, with whom I'd had a good relationship for years. At the time, I reported, wrote, produced and hosted a half-hour weekly newsmagazine on the Fox affiliate in St. Louis. The show, *The Jaco Report*, had been on the air for seven years at the time and had built something of a following in political circles, especially since it was the only local talk program to air during the Sunday morning talk show bloc.

Rep. Akin agreed to appear, which, I later found out, was against the advice of strategists in both the Missouri and national Republican parties. After the primary fight, they had argued, Akin should take time off, maybe head to his family's cottage on Martha's Vineyard, and lay low until after Labor Day. As national party leaders would soon find out, Todd Akin was a man of his own mind and his own convictions, so he ignored their pleas and agreed to come to our studios.

The program ran a half-hour with commercials, which meant we had time for two segments of questions and conversation, each running about 10 minutes. A 20-minute interview is an eternity in TV time, but in real time, it zips by remarkably fast, and given that this was the first sit-down with the Republican nominee for a Senate seat he seemed likely to win, I wanted to make sure I covered as much ground as possible.

Akin arrived at our studios on Wednesday, Aug. 15, to tape a program that was to air Sunday morning, Aug. 19. The first half of the interview covered topics including the Voting Rights Act (the congressman wanted it repealed), federal student loans (he still believed they were de-facto socialism), Obamacare (he said "the government has no role in health care") and Iraq (he still believed the invasion was a good idea, despite the lack of any WMDs).

During the second half, I asked Akin about abortion and how deep his opposition to abortion in any circumstance ran. When he replied that he felt abortion should be illegal under any circumstance, I asked, "Even in the case of rape?"

Assuming that astronomer Dr. Richard Terrile, the director of NASA's Center for Evolutionary Computation and Automated Design, is correct, and that the universe and all of us in it resemble nothing so much as an infinite role-playing computer game, let's pause the action here and consider what has just happened, what is happening and what is about to happen.

What just happened is a fairly standard follow-up to the "sanctity of life" position Akin had tried to articulate in his previous answer. What is happening the moment we hit "pause" is that Akin is just starting his answer, "Well, you know, people always want to make that one of those things, how do you slice this sort of particularly tough ethical question?"

What is about to happen is that in the next nine seconds, Todd Akin will destroy his own campaign, vaporize whatever chances the Republicans had for taking Sen. McCaskill's Senate seat, pulverize GOP hopes for taking control of the U.S. Senate and change the course of American history by keeping the Senate in Democratic hands. And I, along with most people who saw the interview initially, missed it.

Moving the cursor along our Terrileesque timeline, we hear Akin saying, "It seems to me, from what I've heard from doctors . . . ," at the same time the director whispers in my earpiece, "Three minutes. Three," and we see my mind racing, processing the fact that we have 180 seconds left, and I still haven't asked Akin any questions about jobs and the economy in a media market where the recession destroyed at least 40,000 jobs and the average household income plummeted by $7,000 between 2000 and 2010.

Creep the cursor along the existential timeline even more slowly, and you'll hear me thinking, "People are angry and frustrated. Got to ask about jobs and more trickle-down economics," at the same time Akin is saying, ". . . that's really rare. If it's a legitimate rape, the female body has ways to shut that whole thing down. But let's assume that didn't work or something, you know, I think there should be some punishment, so the punishment should be on the rapist and not on attacking the child."

In a nanosecond, I calculated that I had asked Akin about abortion and followed it up, that his position echoed the 2012 Republican Party National Platform—that abortion should be illegal in all cases, including rape and incest—and that I needed to use the final three minutes to grill him about job loss and how the auto bailout he opposed had saved a huge Ford plant in his congressional district, along with his continuing support of the tax cuts implemented by President George W. Bush. At the same time, the Akin Effect was taking hold, as my frontal lobe asked "Wait. What? Did he just say something stupid?" and then responded to itself: "It's Todd. He always says something stupid."

The next words out of my mouth were "Now, on to the economy," which cemented my position among the Twitterati and liberal bloggers over the coming few days as a real-life version of fictional boob anchorman Ron Burgundy, but without his sense of style. One comment, repeated often, really got to me, one to the effect of "This shows what happens when two white males talk. A female journalist would have caught that and followed up."

That bothered me for weeks until I sat down for an interview with Sen. McCaskill, who told me she watched the interview on Sunday morning, Aug. 19, digested it, went outside on her deck with a cup of coffee, and thought, "Well, that was Todd all right." She missed it, too. The crew in the booth missed it. The editors who assembled the piece missed it. In fact, the entire local audience missed it. Not one person—on social media, email or by text or phone—made any reference to the comment at all after the show aired. I personally thought the lead was that Akin wanted to repeal both the Voting Rights Act and the 17th Amendment.

Thus passed Sunday morning, Aug. 19, 2012, in the St. Louis market. In Washington, D.C., however, underpaid and over-caffeinated young researchers for American Bridge to the 21st Century, a liberal Super PAC founded by former self-described "conservative hit man" David Brock, were going through the Sunday political talk shows frame-by-frame, looking for anything with which to trash conservative candidates.

The day was pretty dry. *Fox News Sunday* had on the chief strategists for the Mitt Romney and Barack Obama presidential campaigns. ABC's *This Week* had lower-ranking strategists. CBS's *Face the Nation* had Illinois Democratic Sen. Dick Durbin and anti-tax crusader Grover Norquist. NBC's *Meet the Press* was running with the Democratic governor of Maryland and the Republican governor of Virginia. They had waded through the wonky but innocuous programs and then looked at local programs. Finally, they got to market number 21 and an interview with Congressman Todd Akin, and one of the sharp-eared researchers homed in on Akin's comments roughly 17 minutes into the 20-minute interview.

American Bridge posted the clip on YouTube, where it was picked up by the left-leaning political website Talking Points Memo and posted around 1 p.m. St. Louis time, four hours after the interview aired. By 1:30

p.m. Central time, the first Tweets began to appear referencing the story. At 1:45 p.m., Gawker re-posted the story, and by 2:30 p.m., the *Washington Post* had picked it up, about the same time the *Huffington Post* put up the American Bridge video.

And thus, history. Within hours, my annoyed news director was fielding angry calls from conservatives and Akin's office, I was being praised on Twitter and Facebook for asking the question and excoriated for not following up, and national Republican Party leaders began to call for Akin to withdraw from the race. Within 48 hours, Akin's advantage in the polls became a two-point deficit, then three, then five.

Come election night in November, Mitt Romney beat Barack Obama in Missouri by 250,000 votes. Sen. Claire McCaskill beat Todd Akin by over 400,000 votes. The over 650,000 vote distance between a party's presidential candidate and its U.S. Senate candidate, I was told by a GOP strategist, set a modern record. The Akin clip was used by Democrats in several other races, and Democratic strategists told me it was probably responsible for their Senate victories in Missouri, Montana and Indiana, all of which kept the U.S. Senate under Democratic control.

There are plenty of lessons learned here for journalists covering politics and interviewing candidates and office-holders:

Build a relationship so you can land the interview in the first place   Candidates and the hired help in our governments will almost automatically talk to you if the brand of the company you work for is large enough. But if you work for yourself, or for a lesser-known outlet, it's vital that the interviewee and his or her handlers think you have at least a passing reputation for professionalism.

Know in advance where you want to follow up   My pressing Akin in his abortion views was neither a matter of political gotcha or ideological bias, even though I am, most assuredly, pro-choice personally. It was an attempt to crawl under the hood of a rote political position and see its intellectual underpinnings. I had thought about several questions in advance—abortion, the economy, the entire "government is the problem" mindset—and examined all of them.

Be present!   I was not during the "legitimate rape" portion of the interview. I was thinking about time, and the economy, and was only vaguely aware that Akin had said something discordant. I should have ditched the economic questions and drilled in. I did not. Don't make the same mistake.

Be passionate about your homework   Each question I asked was based on some story I had done previously—pregnant teens struggling with whether to have an abortion; auto and steel workers thrown onto unemployment; people who had struggled to make it to the middle class only to see it jerked away by the financial manipulations of the Great Recession.

Review the interview   The interview was shot on a Wednesday. I had three days to mine the video and find the nugget the Red Bull–fueled researcher for American Bridge found. I went through the interview twice, and the quote never jumped out at me with the force it should have.

Just because you missed it doesn't mean it's not there   As noted, neither I nor Sen. McCaskill nor anyone in the audience who contacted me noticed or mentioned the Akin quote in any way until it went internationally viral, four to five hours after the interview aired. The heart of the interview consisted of 20 seconds out of 1,200 seconds in the interview—roughly 1.6 percent of the entire piece. If an anonymous researcher had not deconstructed the segment frame-by-frame, Akin's comments might not have surfaced for weeks or months, if ever.

Is there a hidden gem buried someplace in that interview you just did? You won't know unless you slog through it word by word.

THIRTY-TWO

Please Don't Ask That Again

The obvious questions are boring; the unexpected ones are energizing

MICHAEL SWAN LAUFER

When mathematics professor Michael Laufer found himself questioned by a long line of all sorts of interviewers, he fast figured out what types of journalists he wanted to talk with and which he wanted to avoid. His calculus can help reporters both when seeking the "get" and during the give-and-take.

There is a gas station off Exit 789 of Interstate 5 in an unincorporated area just south of the Oregon border called Hornbrook. It's prominent in the wilderness there, being the only business you've seen for the last half hour of travel either north or south. The gas station is a Chevron, but the store is independently owned and operated, called "J&D" which makes it all the more appealing to pull over and look to see what it has to offer.

When you walk in, there is a prominently displayed sign next to the cash register with a long list of bullet points:

- Yes, you are in California
- It is 8 miles to the Oregon border
- It's 30 miles to Ashland

- It's 15 miles to Yreka
- Yes, this is the last gas station before the border
- No, there are no restaurants nearby
- The bathroom is around the back, to the left
- No, it does not need a code or a key
- We only take cash
- The ATM is behind you
- Yes, we sell beer
- We also card

The clerk behind the counter pointing at this is not in a bad mood; it's just tiring to answer the same questions again and again

How many times have you had a similar experience? You're in a department store, and you go to ask where the bathroom is and the poor sap you found answers you so quickly you can't make out the answer, and you have to ask again, and you walk away wondering what you did that was so irritating, as you walk under the giant sign that announces "RESTROOMS" on your way to relieve yourself.

Service people endlessly are stuck with this problem: Doing the same thing repeatedly hundreds of times per day gets tiring. Customers are having the experience for the first time, and there is this asymmetry between the two sides of the interaction.

The same dynamic exists between interviewer and subject in the journalism game: someone does something of some note, and all of a sudden goes from having never given an interview to having to field dozens of requests per day. Very quickly the Bill Moyers/Steven Levy ask-stupid-questions-to-get-cool-answers approach tires the subject horribly.

> "So, how did this all start?"
> "What got you interested in this originally?"
> "How has your life changed since this happened?"

Unless you are the very first person who has ever interviewed this person on this subject, there is no reason you should ever ask these things.

First, because if you've done even a shred of homework, you should be able to determine this from previous writings on the person in question. More important, because in all likelihood you aren't going to use it anyway.

I've had the atypical experience of having seen this phenomenon from both sides of the microphone. I have interviewed people and wondered why they seemed impatient with my basic queries. But after having a flash in the pan of the pubic eye, I'd had dozens of reporters coming to ask me the same questions over and over again. Not only was it tiring, but I gave shorter and shorter shrift answers to the generic questions I was tired of hearing.

This happens to everyone. How many times have you been asked, "So, what do you do?" by a stranger at a cocktail party or other social function, and felt that sag of oh-this-again, before you reluctantly try to summarize the entirety of your life's work so that hopefully the conversation can move on? Or at a wedding, having everyone you meet ask how you are connected to the bride or groom?

Even second-line queries are often terribly disappointing.

"Oh, you're a writer? Anything I might have read?"
"Journalism, eh? Woodward and Bernstein have always been heroes of mine."
"So do you, like, travel to interesting war zones and stuff?"

No matter what you do, there is this same asymmetry, where it's the first experience someone has had dealing with the thing with which you deal every hour of every day, and rarely is it that interviewers take a moment to think to a third tier of questions, realizing that their first thoughts might not be terribly profound.

Anyone who has ever had a cast on knows how quickly you get tired of people asking, "So, how'd you break your arm?"

We mustn't judge too harshly those working journalists who are unvalued by their editors, and have to race from one dazzle of public spectacle to the next, and don't have the luxury to ask probing questions, or to write anything but the most cursory pieces on current events. However, if you want to get something meaningful, something beyond the mundane, something really worth reading, you're going to have to go beyond first order. And the great trick of this is to do it *before* you start your interview.

Try this exercise: Sit down as you normally would, and write all the regular first-line questions that you expect to ask in your next interview. Then *don't ask any of those questions.* This is going to force you to find new lines of questioning that will reveal facets of the story that are usually left unexplored.

Of course, it's also an error to trust that the prior reporting is accurate, so you should try to get good source material for the preliminaries. But this can usually be acquired before you have the primary subject in hand. If you still feel the need to double-check preliminary facts with primary subjects, leave those questions to the end, and alleviate their fatigue by feeding them the likely response: "Is it correct that . . ." This will allow them to clear up any errors, while simultaneously not asking for a prepackaged response.

My own story of getting swarmed with reporters is typical. The human rights organization for which I am the spokesperson developed a $30 DIY version of the EpiPen, which we dubbed the EpiPencil. Predictably, despite the many other things our organization does, the requests for interviews poured in, and with them, the predictably generic questions, which immediately became tiring to answer:

"So, how did this project start?"
  "Isn't this unsafe?"
  "What about the FDA?"

The more I got asked these questions, the more prepackaged and dispassionate my answers became. I didn't even want to answer anymore, because it indicated that these interviewers weren't really interested, hadn't done any reading on the work we had been doing and in all likelihood weren't going to include most what I was going to say anyway.

Being interviewed became so routine and generic, I can't differentiate in my memories between most of the different interviews I've given.

But there was one reporter who came to my office whose interview is unlikely to pass from my memory anytime soon.

"What are your parents like?"
  "Who is your favorite philosopher?"
  "Did you have pets growing up?"

Although, I'm sure I was asked the basic contextual questions needed to frame the story, the leading with questions that I hadn't answered dozens of times before turned me off of autopilot and made me think actively about what was being asked, so even when the more predictable kinds of questions came, I was actively engaged, and thinking.

Whether these questions gave her context for the structure of my character or were merely questions to indicate that she was interested in more than getting the basic facts and moving on almost didn't matter. I felt like I was having a conversation with a person and not talking to the top of someone's head watching fiercely scribbled notes of my pat answers going down on paper.

We were having a conversation, like two regular people, and she wasn't mechanically saying "Uh-huh, uh-huh" at random moments in some false attempt to convince me she was listening.

Think for a moment when you race to get the get with a new subject, and think of things that might serve as equalizers. What do you and the interviewee have in common? There is going to be something, guaranteed. Look closely. Look for something you recognize. If you spot a crease on the pants with a little blue chalk on it, maybe you are going to be able to talk shop about shooting pool. Maybe you see short nails and calluses on the left hand and can talk about playing guitar, violin or sitar. Dig for the humanity.

What is there that you recognize? What car is being driven? Why? Every decision is a gesture of consciousness, and the more you can connect, the deeper your understanding of the person will be. Even though you might not use this material either. No need. It will be the scaffold that holds your material together invisibly.

Alan Moore writes fiction. Not just fiction, but fiction in the comic book form. Despite the derisive view that sequential art is not to be given any credence, Alan Moore is considered to be one of the greatest writers of his chosen medium. He was somehow coerced into writing about writing and thence wrote a short volume titled *Writing for Comics*, which I recommend for anyone who has ever considered writing anything in any form about anything at all and wanted it to be good.

He describes his process, which is methodical in the extreme. He first imagines the locale of the setting of his story. If it is a real place, he sends away for the phone book from that place and reads it cover to cover. [Phone books are the pre-Google equivalent of popup ads while searching, for those who have not heard of them.] He would also subscribe to the local paper, and have it mailed to him. If it was a fictional place, he would construct what he imagined the analogues of those things to be for the setting in which his stories were set.

As a journalist, you have the luxury of the fact that everything you ever report on will occur in a tangible locale, and so you will not be burdened by the task of trying to construct a world, civilization or town from scratch. Find the details *first*. When you go to interview someone from El Paso, ask about Chico's Tacos. If someone is from Santa Cruz, ask about the Mystery Spot. If your subject is from New York, for the love of Pete, figure out *which part*, and be prepared to ask about details pertaining to their area.

This sounds like heavy spade work, but it is not. It is no different than asking a Pashtun about interclan politics, what a Russian thinks of Putin or a Singaporean about chewing gum. Get yourself to a point where things feel natural.

Ask yourself: What's the best story you ever heard told? Think carefully. Take a moment.

Most likely it was from a friend at the end of a long night, or at a bar from a stranger who was comfortable enough [for whatever reason] to unload the best material on you. The key is the comfort. If you can get whomever you are speaking with to think of you as a regular sort of person, and your chat as just a regular conversation, then you will get the best story, and it will then be the best story that you get to write.

Ask what is going on later. Is there a vodoun ritual with sacrifices and blood drinking? You better go. Not just that, but you better drink too. Does that seem too scary, and you want to "Just watch"? Decide for yourself how dedicated you are to your craft. Is skydiving the order of the day?

You go too. Decide in advance that you are going to keep up, and that you are going to do whatever strange crazy thing it takes to really get a deep sense of what is going on.

Think of your heroes in journalism; they all did that. Whether it was John Berendt going to the Married Woman's Bridge Club to understand which rumors were flying around regarding Jim Williams in Savannah, Georgia, or Webb Miller walking alongside the Italian army in Ethiopia until his socks were bloody rags. Every great act of journalism, every great interview was steeped in the contextual understanding of whence the event of note came.

And next time you need to pee, look for a sign for a minute or two before asking some poor retail worker for directions.

THIRTY-THREE **Creative Courage and the Interview**

How do we as journalists work and create with courage?

DEBORAH MORRISON

The intersection of creativity and courage is fertile ground for best work and bold process. It's a concept for interviewers to embrace, suggests Deborah Morrison, whether the interviewee is a client, a focus group or a newsmaker.

Our lives as professional storytellers revolve around abilities to observe, question, translate and transform with integrity. As these skills develop over time and with dedicated practice, the process of how information is gathered and shaped takes on even greater importance for individual careers and for the profession. We, as journalists and storytellers and idea professionals, hold that doing this to the best of our ability and for the common good is part of our mission.

This leads to simple questions: How do we develop and sustain professional traits that take us beyond obligation in our work? How do we learn and practice working courageously?

The interview—and its development and successful outcome as a tool for the storyteller—is important to this concept of working beyond obligation. In the best of practices, the interview is imbued with creative courage. This "soft skill" of courageous thinking can be as important as any domain relevant skills (writing and editing and craft, as examples) in paving the path to professional success. The definition of creative courage is a set of relationships: creative courage is the intersection of bravery of thought and generosity of ideas, of visionary purpose and nimble productivity. It is sustained by conviction and tenacity as it is shaped by a person's intrinsic motivation. It is the desire to discover ideas and from that point produce meaningful work beyond the obligation of simply finishing the task. In accordance with the powerful journalistic ethos of truth, creative courage pushes us to create stories above reproach.

We see creative courage manifest in the interview context in a range of ways. Throughout the interview, pivotal points exist where the direction and flow of the discussion can be shaped by the interviewer's perseverance, conviction and bravery. It may be the interviewer asks questions that have not been asked before or uses those questions to form new patterns and concepts. Or, it might be shown in the tenor and tone maintained by the interviewer, how he or she shapes the direction and delivery of the conversation via voice and posture. Whether shown in an isolated moment or developed before and during the interview, creative courage is the fuel of truly transformative work in our profession.

To frame this chapter on creative courage and the interview, I offer perspective by way of my having studied professional creativity and creative process in the idea industry; specifically, the generating, developing and transforming of ideas into value within the advertising and creative media industry. In the case of this text, transformative approaches might be used in regard to the traditional journalistic interview or could reference the audience insight interview used in strategic planning. Though the two have different outcomes (one pursuing information for purposes of building journalistic story, the other for mining discovery around a particular audience or insight), both interview genres grow from a common need for rich and robust information gathered from a conscious "thinking about the thinking" around a topic. This metacognitive approach values informed intuition as much as data as a starting point in the process; it builds on a careful but often rapid cognitive mapping of ideas in order to sort and evaluate their worth to the story. I submit that creative courage is needed for this intuitive process and cognitive mapping, that creative courage supplies momentum that will push the interview to best outcomes.

Three important areas for developing and recognizing creative courage within the interview construct are offered here. First, the power of the question is explored, its inherent relationship to curiosity shown to be a substantive tool in courageous thinking. Second, the importance of finding a voice as an interviewer is studied, using drama and poetry as inspiration for approach. Third, the discovery of new relationships and possibilities is discussed, identifying the importance of this for professions in flux. Though nurturing creative courage as a professional skill set might be regarded as a difficult curricular task at first review, study of the themes presented here offers an important discussion about the need for developing this in our journalistic training.

ASKING BRAVE AND BEAUTIFUL QUESTIONS

Curiosity and courage become the greatest tools an interviewer possesses. It's often been said (by editors, HR directors, creative directors and other supervisors hiring young talent for newsrooms and idea organizations) that curiosity should be among the strongest characteristics of anyone entering the media professions of journalism and advertising. Sharpened by careful research and a dedication to associative and divergent thinking, curiosity leads to the elegant simplicity of "the why." And to find the heart of curiosity, we turn to that basic element, the question.

Warren Berger explores the power of questions to learn and lead in *A More Beautiful Question* (2014). Berger is a journalist who has written articles and books on a range of topics: organizational culture and innovation, the business of change, and the realities of social inquiry in education and business. This book explores the power of inquiry as a general cultural set of values, as well as looks at specific questions pivotal to scientific and entrepreneurial discovery. Quoting Pulitzer Prize–winning historian David Hackett Fischer, Berger notes that questions "are the engines of intellect—cerebral machines that convert curiosity into controlled inquiry" (p. 15). Indeed, brave questions cut across layers of power and politics and education; the courageous question can frame new possibilities, be they confrontational or more in the vein of Appreciative Inquiry as described by Mike Fancher in this text and others.

But how does a question move from simple need for information to a platform of courage and strength? How can the interviewer make space for the courageous question? How can one question beget a more beautiful question in a fertile moment of inquiry within the confines of conversation?

Much has been written in philosophical texts concerning the framing and intent of questions. Those readings have some value in this discussion, yet they often center more on structure and onotological notions of how questions live in the world. For the purposes of understanding the courageous and compelling question and the process for building to it, the better approach is to see the process by which questions happen.

Berger offers a set of simple process points to craft and own strong questions (p. 75). For the interviewer, the process points accentuate a sense of "seeing" an entire topic or direction of inquiry, a type of cognitive mapping of a topic that permits multiple pivot points within a timeline. Further, the last point suggests the most personal approach to a question, one that would require a brave sense of investment in the theme and process. Here's Berger's process of building questions:

- Step back.
- Notice what others miss.
- Challenge assumptions (including our own).
- Gain a deeper understanding of the situation or problem at hand, through contextual inquiry.
- Question the questions we're asking.
- Take ownership of a particular question.

Berger's process for developing "beautiful questions" makes best use of the elements of conviction, bravery and tenacity inherent in creative courage. It emphasizes the power of curiosity in developing questions that will lead to the best information in the interview. If the interviewer is ready to question assumptions and take ownership of specific questions that must be asked, the interview itself becomes a more compelling process.

FINDING VOICE

The interviewer might take on many personas during this process: that of objective interrogator opening doors to find information, of subjective provocateur with agenda offered freely, of storytelling partner collaborating to find new and compelling ways to unravel a story. Each of these requires an interviewer to find a voice, a way of participating in the interview that might be (as example) quiet and observant or aggressive and provocative. In all cases, creative courage—brave and generous thinking, nimble and purposeful—is a catalyst for work of meaning.

John Freeman, author of *How to Read a Novelist* (2013), is by trade a seasoned critic and essayist, shaping his reputation via critical reviews of novels and interviews with the authors of the books he critiques. He notes that he has learned to step into interviews with fewer prepared questions, with more intent on building a dialogue person-to-person, and finding his voice and theme as the interview progresses. As the author talks and as the relationship within the interview continues, Freeman finds the questions become stronger and braver as the conversation grows organically. Though the context of questioner and answerer is the basis of the relationship, Freeman's voice—not the pitch but the perspective and vitality of thought—and his own sense of drama and humor draw out the interesting details from the authors with whom he talks. By his own admission, walking into an interview with fewer prepared questions is at worst foolhardy, at best brave and much more interesting.

What lies behind a voice ready to take the interview to uncharted places? How can we find the brave voice, the appropriate tone and approach to develop meaningful ideas within the interview? What is the value of finding a relevant and dramatic approach to a subject? How might a brave voice work within the framework of "ideas over ego"?

Let's put drama in context. David Whyte, poet and creative consultant to organizations around the globe, writes at length about the need for understanding one's own voice in the professional world. He believes that the dramatic has a place in molding our sense of who we are as professionals. For journalists, this implies a sensibility about where our work belongs, who will read it and why, what we bring to the interviewer's table.

This is not to say that the journalist must be a performer or take liberties with putting himself into the discussion driven by ego. Often, for news interviews specifically, the dramatic voice is not appropriate.

Whyte (1994, p. 19) writes about professional voice and why the dramatic context for a journalistic interview is worthy of consideration:

> Drama is vital, quirky, humorous, tragic, and by its playing out of the stuff of life, lends magnificence to the commonplace.

The notion of finding a dramatic voice from which to conduct the interview does suggest that a storyteller can adapt a way of thinking about the story and find compelling moments in the "commonplace." Indeed, there are moments when the dramatic question or the delicate pause becomes the pivotal point in the interview. From Whyte's perspective as a poet considering the role of professional conversation such as the interview, drama offers an appropriate context for brave thinking and doing for the storyteller/interviewer.

It may be that finding a voice for certain interviews gives power to all concerned. If, by considering her own voice to be an enabler of a truly great story and in doing so shares the interviewee's emotional tone, the interviewer may find more opportunity for the braver and more compelling question. Or, by deciding the voice and tone of this interview is to be humble and quiet, listening as the story unfolds, the courageous moments might come in silence and in a shared moment of understanding. The interviewer's voice determined with purpose and offered bravely can become one of the elements of a successful story.

DISCOVERING NEW PATTERNS AND NEW IDEAS

Developing creative courage is an ongoing professional process. Cultural forces push us to re-imagine how and why we work; for the media and story professions, this means building in a nimble approach to how we gather and create. Staying professionally nimble suggests we understand our process, build in measures for pivoting in the midst of that process, and anticipate those patterns in information that might lead us in new directions. This takes an intuitive sense of what is important and useful to the story. It also suggests a brave standard for the task of discovery. Failure is a tool. New directions lead to revelation. For the interviewer, courage is a constant in this disruptive and optimistic process; courage manifests in preparing for the interview and in maintaining associative momentum from question to answer to question within the interview framework.

In 1975, existentialist psychologist and philosopher Rollo May offered the world *The Courage to Create*, a simple treatise on the place of courage within professional and cultural contexts. In the book, May identifies physical courage and social courage, and then sets up his framework for creative courage:

> Whereas moral courage is the righting of wrongs, creative courage, in contrast, is the discovering of new forms, new symbols, new patterns on which a new society can be built. [. . .] The need for creative courage is in direct proportion to the degree of change the profession is undergoing.

Obviously, journalists and the broad media industry undergo tremendous change on a consistent basis. Patterns in data, design and information evolve constantly. Pattern-seeking and pattern-identifying skills become important when the churn of information and insight are happening at this pace. Critical thinking is based in part on the ability to recognize and recall these patterns of information, and then use that information for predicting new forms and possibilities. Within the interview setting, this pattern recognition drives insight and story to more sophisticated levels. May's treatise was a simple, brave beginning to the conversation around creative courage in the age of ideas.

CONSIDERING THE PLACE OF CREATIVE COURAGE

After such discussion of beautiful questions and determined voice and discovery of new ideas, it should be asked: is creative courage and its place in journalism merely an optimistic possibility for the profession? And from another vantage point: is courage such a part of journalism that to parse it out and look at it diminishes its importance as a reference point?

In a world where "gentle journalism" has been cited as the direct result of profit-based media outlets and the abrupt changes in the profession due to technology and digital culture, it seems that creative courage has a place in this professional discussion. "The death knell of a career is that decision to go with the status quo," a journalist recently told me in a New York symposium. After he said that, he wondered aloud if journalists-in-training should be required to take seminars in confidence and courage. It's a point that sits at the heart of this chapter and this discussion.

Should journalism students be pointed toward creative courage or should courage be a manifestation of personal belief and actions, not trained or mandated, but an extension of self? Certainly, there is opportunity for brashness, uneducated boldness, even maliciousness to hide in the guise of courageous action. And, to be sure, courage is a personal system of beliefs and actions. Our goal in this discussion is to offer creative courage as a concept empowered by intellect and information that shapes meaningful professional work. If, by showing opportunities for brave thinking and delivering tools for acting in this capacity we encourage such actions, I believe we better our profession. Journalism and the broad idea industry are in need of these guideposts.

Creative courage becomes a mindset of transforming ideas purposefully, even fearlessly. As noted in the first section of this chapter, creative courage can be found in the intersection of brave thinking and generous ideas, of visionary purpose and nimble productivity. The power of that intersection gives permission to journalists and storytellers to ask brave questions, find a powerful voice and make sense of a world rife with chaos. In doing so, the work created will be smarter, braver and more valuable to society.

BIBLIOGRAPHY

Berger, Warren. (2014). *A More Beautiful Question: The Power of Inquiry to Spark Breakthrough Ideas*. New York: Bloomsbury.

Freeman, John. (2013). *How to Read a Novelist.* New York: FSG Originals.

Gardner, Howard, Mihaly Csikszentmihalyi, and William Damon. (2001). *Good Work: Where Excellence and Ethics Meet.* New York: Basic Books.

May, Rollo. *The Courage to Create.* New York: W.W. Norton & Co., 1975.

Whyte, David. (1994). *The Heart Aroused: Poetry and the Preservation of the Soul in Corporate America.* New York: Currency Doubleday.

THIRTY-FOUR **Preventing Fires**

Interviewing to identify an
organization's vulnerabilities

KELLI MATTHEWS

Crisis managers use intra-organizational
interviews to identify problems and seek
solutions and to be able to communicate
effectively to the public or to journalists. Kelli
Matthews explores these approaches, which
share some common ground with other types of
interviews, including the journalistic.

Each summer across the West, thousands of men and women head into
forests on fire. Armed with a pickaxe and a shovel, girded in Nomex,
they're trained to do one of the most dangerous jobs on the planet to protect life and property.

When wildland firefighters are on the fireline, the risks they face are
tangible—they see the fire, hear the destruction and violence of the fuels
devoured by flame, smell the burning forest and feel the heat.

Each crew trains, role plays, practices scenarios and draws lessons
learned from fire research and real-world situations. When called, they
hike, fly and parachute into some of the wildest lands in North America.

Sending firefighters into a blaze without training would be negligent.
Yet organizations of all shapes and sizes regularly drop into fighting their
own fires—that is, crises—without planning, training and equipment, or
processes.

For most companies, nonprofits or government agencies, the risks aren't as obvious as a wall of flame, but the figurative fires can burn just as hot and destroy lives, reputations and communities at blistering speed.

Identifying risks and finding ways to correct when possible or build a response plan if needed can shield organizations from crises. Crisis planning starts with crisis prediction and crisis prediction starts with asking a lot of questions.

The interviews designed to predict and prevent crises share some similarities with journalistic interviews. After all, a good interview is a good interview. Getting people to share their stories takes a similar skill set whether you're interviewing to prevent a crisis, write a feature article, put together a news package or even get a job.

HOW IS THIS DIFFERENT FROM A "JOURNALISTIC" INTERVIEW?

In any interview, the interviewer focuses on getting information, and sometimes it's even information that the person being interviewed doesn't want to share—"vulnerabilities," if you will. The primary difference of course, is the outcome.

A crisis manager will interview with the intent to find information that reveals a weakness to be repaired. These interviews give crisis managers the tools they need to build a plan that reflects the real need of the organization. Crisis plans should be a tool to respond, not an academic exercise. The aim is to protect the organization, its employees and other stakeholders from harm. That's not to say that in a journalistic interview, the intent is to harm—it's to report a legitimate story. But what a crisis planner does with the type of information learned in an interview and what a journalist would do are certainly different.

In vulnerability audit interviews, I've learned about drug and alcohol abuse, extreme nepotism or favoritism and crippling communication breakdowns, none of which I'd want to be public in the event of a crisis.

Regardless of the interview's purpose, it's important to develop quick rapport, listen actively to the interviewee and have keen observation skills. Good interviews are based on solid research. Know your subject and your purpose before you walk in the room.

THE VULNERABILITY AUDIT

Leslie Habetler, a now-retired crisis manager who worked for the U.S. Army and U.S. Forest Service, called it "alligator hunting." She explained to organizations that alligators in a swamp are often hard to spot. Just their beady eyes peek above the water. Their prey often doesn't even see the alligator until it's too late.[1] "So let's go find the alligators before someone else does," she'd say.

Jonathan Bernstein, a veteran crisis manager, defines this step of crisis prevention this way:

> Vulnerability audit is a multidisciplinary risk assessment to determine current and potential areas of operational and communications weakness and strength, and to identify potential solutions, because weaknesses may result in emergencies or crises of varying magnitudes if not corrected. An audit is conducted not only to prepare clients for potential crises, but to make them crisis-resistant.[2]

Alligator hunt or vulnerability audit, the point of either is to identify the weaknesses in an organization that, if not recognized, can exacerbate a crisis and create a threat. You simply have to watch a spokesman stammering through a public response to a company misdeed and you can often identify an unrecognized vulnerability.

Watching the evening news, you might find yourself saying—"Why didn't they know that would happen?" or "Wow! They should've seen that coming."

"That" is exactly what vulnerability audits are designed to help find. The results help predict likely crisis scenarios that can either be mitigated with policy, process or people changes or be prepared for in the organization's crisis communications plan. In order to do so, an organization must be open to finding weak spots.

Many organizations are very bad at being objective about their own weaknesses—very bad. Sometimes the CEO is blind to flouted policies, operations managers stop seeing the seemingly no-big-deal misses in machine maintenance or supervisors no longer notice that celebrations at the end of a big project always include consuming alcohol on company property.

The key to a vulnerability audit that serves its purpose is the ability to conduct interviews with the right people and ask them the right questions.

THE RIGHT PEOPLE

Insights about an organization's risk can come from anyone at any level. The interviews must include people from all levels of the organization: executives, managers, legal, marketing, administrative support and line workers. These should be complemented by interviews with a handful of external stakeholders, too. Very few organizations can do this on their own. Bringing in outside advisers to facilitate the interviews brings a much needed third-party perspective and objectivity.

The issues that come up in interviews can also be challenging ones for someone internal to an organization to suss out and, subsequently, address with the leadership. No executive wants to hear all the things that could potentially create or exacerbate a crisis. "It's not that bad . . ." or maybe "That'll never happen to us . . ." The audit interviews give crisis planners the information they need to make hard recommendations and, hopefully, be heard.

With each interviewee, it's the interviewer's job to develop trust very quickly. The interviewees need to be assured that the information is being collected in complete confidence—and that has to be true. Management needs to clearly support this process and confirm with all employees that, if they are interviewed, their answers will remain anonymous and their job is not at stake.

THE INTERVIEW

The importance of building quick rapport regardless of who is sitting in front of you and knowing what questions are going to get you the info you need can't be understated.

According to Robin Dreeke, head of the FBI Behavioral Analysis Program, keep two questions in mind when seeking to draw out information from a source: "What do I want the other person to tell me?" and then "Why should they do it?"[3] Without an outcome in mind of what you need to know, you're unlikely to learn it. And by focusing on the interviewees' motivations, their worldview and why they should want to talk to you, you can direct your questions in such a way that allows for quick rapport and trust. Dreeke provides the following tips for building rapport.

TOP TECHNIQUES FOR BUILDING RAPPORT[4]

- Make sure that both your body language and voice are non-threatening.
- Don't oversell or talk too fast. You will lose credibility quickly and appear too strong and threatening.
- Human beings want to provide assistance and help. It also appeals to their ego that they may know more than you.
- Build the other person up. Remember the focus and let the other person shine in sharing a personal experience.
- Validation allows the interviewee to feel connected and accepted. The reality of an interview of this nature is that you truly believe each person you talk to has a valuable and important perspective. Make that clear.
- Ask "how, when and why" questions. These three little words can create powerful follow-up answers that give you the details you need.
- Offer information about yourself to help a more guarded interviewee make a connection and feel more comfortable.

Other than top executives, those you interview may feel vulnerable themselves. Power structures and hierarchies within an organization can make individuals feel wary about opening up, even if they have something valuable to say. Reassure, validate and provide positive feedback.

Remember the purpose of the interview is to uncover risks, insecurities and vulnerabilities in order for the organization to fix them, if possible, or to understand how to respond to them, if not. With that in mind, the questions will vary widely, but there are several categories of questions to consider and a few examples of questions you might ask.[5]

Business interruption What if your primary place of business was completely unavailable tomorrow and you had no advance warning? Would everyone who works there know where to report for work tomorrow?

Security Are all locks and access codes changed when an employee leaves the organization? Is there any difference in that policy when an employee is fired versus leaving voluntarily?

Compliance If there was a physical crisis related to a part of your business that's regulated, would you be able to accurately say that your level of compliance meets or exceeds requirements? Do you have a positive history with regulators?

Internal communications If I asked 50 people from all levels of the organization to describe the company, would they have an answer that top management would be comfortable with?

Is there a formal rumor control system within the organization that allows employees to fact check or get clarification before rumors take on a life of their own?

Do you have any "loose cannons" on staff whose activities could harm the organization?

Legal Are there any current lawsuits or other legal matters that, if known, could prove embarrassing or potentially damaging to the organization?

Reputation: If we asked 25 customers what they thought about your business, what would they say?

Human resources Are there perceptions by any number of employees that there are issues of discrimination or harassment—regardless of whether they are legally provable?

Are there employees at any level who may be engaged in what some would consider wrongdoing, but the company "turns its head" because these individuals are productive, nice or senior?

Line employees In addition to asking versions of management and staff questions above that line employees can relate to, you should ask specific questions such as these:

- How do you get your information about the organization? Do you feel well informed?

- How does the community feel about this organization? How do you know?

- Describe the training that you receive. Is it effective?

- What is your greatest concern as an employee?

- If you were president of the company, what would you see as the most pressing problems and how would you solve them?

In all cases, probing with "how, when and why" questions can help get at the root of the immediate answer.

Of course there's more to an interview than the questions you ask. Tuning in to body language, voice inflection and all the nonverbal cues an interviewee provides can help you interpret what's being said.

ETHICAL RESPONSIBILITY

Ultimately, as public relations professionals managing crises, we bear a lot of responsibility. There is no tolerance among any of an organization's stakeholders for dishonesty. The end result for an audit is never to figure out how to "cover up" a weakness or "spin" a liability into something positive to protect an image. Lies will always be discovered.

Often the vulnerability audit reveals weaknesses in policies, process or people that need to be fixed, and it's the public relations manager's job to be able to deliver that information and make it clear what the consequences are for a lack of action. If you don't provide honest and direct counsel to your client, your own professional credibility is at stake.

PR professionals must tell the truth so their organizations can, too. And organizations *must* be able to tell the truth. If an organization is reluctant to do so because its behavior is unacceptable in some way to the public, then it must change the way it does business so that it can.

As Ivy Lee, an early 20th-century public relations practitioner said, "Tell the truth, because sooner or later the public will find out anyway. And if the public doesn't like what you are doing, change your policies and bring them into line with what people want."

MY PERSPECTIVE

In addition to studying and teaching crisis communication, my own crisis management experience has been mostly with companies in the wildland firefighting industry. These are the private contractors that supplement the U.S. Forest Service firefighting teams during fire season. It's a dangerous business and not a single fire season goes by without a fatality. Many of the private contractors seek crisis managers to help ensure that when the unthinkable happens, they are able to respond and support their employees and families.

I've seen the devastation on the faces of parents whose sons didn't come home from the fireline and the sadness in the eyes of fellow crew members who had served beside them, and heard the crack of emotion in the voices of CEOs who, despite their own mourning, had to stand and be the leader.

Many of these companies are small, they're family-oriented, and the nature of firefighting is such that employees are very close. When anyone is injured or killed, the company is traumatized. These are good people trying to take care of their families and their communities and do the right thing. Helping them feels like important work.

Every summer I see the news of forest fires and hear the stats about acres burned and property lost and hope to not get the call that means the worst has happened. But if I do, the prevention and planning work I've done with each of these organizations will ensure they can focus on what's important—the employees and families.

NOTES

1. Personal interview.

2. Jonathan Bernstein and Bruce Bonafede, *Manager's Guide to Crisis Management*. New York: McGraw-Hill, 2011. Print. Kindle Edition.

3. Robin Dreeke. "FBI Counterintelligence Division's Behavioral Analysis Program: A Unique Investigative Resource." FBI. N.p. 9 July 2013. Web. 08 June 2014.

4. Robin Dreeke. "Mastering Rapport and Having Productive Conversations." *FBI Law Enforcement Bulletin*, 22 Oct. 2012. Web. 08 June 2014.

5. In part from Jonathan Bernstein and Bruce Bonafede. *Manager's Guide to Crisis Management*. New York: McGraw-Hill, 2011. Print. Kindle Edition.

THIRTY-FIVE **A Picture's Worth . . .**

The right photograph can answer interview questions without words

SUNG PARK

Photojournalist Sung Park teaches multimedia journalism at Oregon.

[Editor's note] When Sung Park captured this image, he was interviewing a nurse at The Center for Scientific Research into Plant Medicine, a clinic in Ghana that treats patients with herbal medicine. She was explaining the close relationship between the clinic and a local hospital where patients are treated with Western medicine. "There is much controversy in the area of herbal medicine, so she was

very clear in describing the relationship between the two institutions and how they work together rather than against each other," Park says about the content of her remarks. Her gesture captures a defining interview moment that punctuates her verbal comments in reference to the hospital. The image helps express the emotional and professional bond between two healing cultures.

THIRTY-SIX

A Few Lessons from the Road

Have a plan, take good notes and be open to possibilities

WES POPE

What a perfect assignment for a news photographer: roam Route 66 and capture images of the locals who live on that legendary road. Wes Pope explains how the verbal interview informs access to subjects and the resulting picture.

Over two decades, I used pinhole cameras made from soda cans to create dreamlike images of life along Route 66 that I turned into a book. If a camera is a passport into other worlds, then a pinhole camera is a magical skeleton key for starting conversations. It engages people on many levels, whether they have ever heard of one or not. I showed one of my pop can cameras to Roy Rogers, and he said, "I ain't never heard that one before." And then he and Dale Evans were hooked.

When you have an assignment for a news organization, it gives you a clear excuse to go places. People can understand who you are and why you are there, even if they don't like the story or stopped trusting the media long ago. Personal work, on the other hand, is often more challenging, particularly at the start. Explaining who you are and why you are there can be a real chore until your project gets going and you are able to simplify your pitch. There is a saying that you need to be human first, but it really takes more than that: you need to be able to tell a good story in order to capture great stories.

What you are working on can seem almost totally arbitrary. Why Route 66? The project could have been about almost anything. My interest was in America and finding home. "Route 66" is something quick, finite; people immediately get it. The pop can pinhole camera aspect takes it a step further: it sounds so implausible that it draws people in. You share something about yourself, and people open up and begin to share about themselves. It is a lesson that continues to inform my work.

STORIES FROM THE ROAD

Perhaps it started with my father's fear of flying. He used to tell a story about being a passenger on a flight that dropped an engine into one of the Great Lakes. He never set foot on a plane again. As a result, my family spent our vacations driving long distances across the West. Without realizing it, it was on these journeys that I became connected to that ancient narrative tradition: the road trip disaster story. It seems to me that the point of any great road trip is to put yourself on the edge of peril, narrowly escape, then come away with a story to tell that can only get better with repeated tellings over many years.

When I was a kid, there was that time we wound up with multiple flat tires on the side of the road in no-man's-land in the Horse Heaven Hills in arid Eastern Washington at the peak of summer. Or that time we hit a deer near Yreka, California, my dad and I pounded the radiator fan flat with a rock outside our motel room. Then my dad traded a case of beer with an old codger who welded up the volleyball-size hole in the radiator so it could hold enough coolant to get us home. In hindsight, I can see the obvious origins of my Route 66 project: head out on the highway and see what kind of stories you can get yourself into. As my grandfather would say, it's all in good fun as long as you keep the shiny side up and the rubber side down. Perhaps as a result of my father's (and grandfather's) tall tales, there is a particular type of story I am attracted to when I talk

to folks on the road: boiled-down stories feel like epic poems of love, loss
and overcoming obstacles. Life lived like a country music song.

A LESSON FROM NEW MEXICO

I started my Route 66 project with a road trip from LA to Chicago in
March 1998. Over the years I lived in five of the eight states along Route
66, and I have family in another (Oklahoma). The stories I included in
the book are a mix of encounters from my road trips and folks I met on
assignment during my career working at newspapers on and near the
Mother Road.

When I worked for the *Santa Fe New Mexican*, the paper published a
monthly series called Our Town, profiling small towns from across the
vast state. The photos ran large in the paper, and the work felt more like
visual anthropology than anything else I encountered in my career. My
favorite Our Town assignment was a story I wrote and photographed
about Pie Town out on the western edge of the state a couple of hours

south of Route 66. My interest in Pie Town started when I came across a set of color photos[1] by Farm Security Administration photographer Russell Lee. Taken in the summer of 1940, the images look vibrant and alive, like they were shot recently. Seeing the photos gave me the inspiration to go looking for traces of Lee's visit.

True to its name, Pie Town had two cafés where you can enjoy an excellent slice of pie but almost nothing else. There is no sign of a gas station, bank or grocery store for miles in either direction. In the Daily Pie Café, I learned about two old-timers who could remember Lee's visit. The first one I tracked down wanted nothing to do with me. Then I found myself standing on Pop McKee's[2] front doorstep. I can close my eyes and picture exactly what it looked like: golden light, the sun low in the sky behind me, a very tall, skinny Santa Claus answers the door. Talking is slow going at first (Pop suffered a stroke years earlier). I open the book to Lee's Pie Town images. As Pop points at the pictures, I am processing his words. That's Pop, right there in the school photo. That's his father, right there, a ringer for Pop, standing on top of a fence post at the town rodeo. And in this moment, after 14 years as a dyed-in-the-wool still photographer, I recognize I have in my hands exactly the wrong tool. My still cameras are failing me; it is moving pictures and sound that I need. Pop's moment of wonderment seeing these images for the first time is a moment I can only play back in my mind. Within weeks I purchase my first video camera,[3] and I haven't looked back.

In journalism and documentary work, you need to think about the right tool for the right job, the right medium for the right moment. In addition to still photography, video, audio and the pen, we have recently gained a new set of Virtual Reality and Augmented Reality tools, each with its own storytelling strengths and weaknesses. There is a saying "Luck is what happens when preparation meets opportunity."[4] I would modify it a bit: have a great plan, take great notes, be prepared, be adaptable and maybe when you stumble into a good situation you won't screw it up.

LEFTOVERS: A FEW LESSONS FROM MY CAREER IN JOURNALISM AND DOCUMENTARY

1. Tell stories from your heart

My dad died of melanoma when I was 16, and I always felt like it gave me a superpower: empathy. I had a connection to subjects who were suffering, and I knew how to be a good listener. And as painful as it is to tell difficult stories, I know how important it is to dig deeper and keep going. What I am trying to say: Don't be afraid to access the part of your heart where you hold your deepest emotions. Then go out into the world and find a way to reflect those emotions back through the words and stories of others. Feel something. Then find go find it and make us feel it too.

2. Plan and remain flexible

There is always a balance between having a mission and remaining open to serendipity. On the Route 66 project, I always had a list of can't-miss stops, but I tried to leave time for detours. Follow your instincts. Remain curious. The sweet spot is finding the balance between sticking to the plan and throwing the plan out the window. Keep doing both for as long as you can.

3. Take great notes

I am a great believer in being in-the-moment and being present while working as a visual journalist. Regardless of recording medium (still camera, video camera, audio recorder, pen), the most critical part of the process is writing in your notebook as soon as you can—notes to yourself—and definitely before you sleep for the night (the brain purges information overnight). If you get a chance, sit in your car and write down at least an outline of key moments before you leave the scene. Then when you get to a café or your hotel, write in detail everything that stood out. What was poignant? What moved you?

4. Process your interviews right away

For interviews you have recorded in video or audio: Online transcription services are cheap these days. However, getting something transcribed is not the same as processing it. You need to go through the material right away and "log" it—keyword it, add ratings, add margin notes.

5. Get organized

Keep track of your notebooks. Develop a filing system and maintain it. In electronic media we say, "There are two types of people in the world: those whose hard drives have crashed and those whose hard drives are going to crash." And while I have learned to carefully archive my negatives and back up my data, I have not always applied the same care to my notebooks. Getting your notes into electronic form and backed up is a good place to start.

LESSONS FROM FRIENDS, MENTORS, HEROES

I didn't go to journalism school, but I have been lucky to have great mentors along the way. These are just a few of the voices I still hear playing in my head. Near the end of his life, my dad said to me, "The most important thing in life are your friends." So I'd like to share what a few of them had to say (paraphrasing).

What Alex[5] said:
Listen to stories, find the parts that are deeply true and share those. The parts that stick their claw hooks in you and rip your guts out. Like one girl he and photographer Alan Berner met in Oklahoma City during their journey across America in the aftermath of the 9/11 attacks. Alex summarized the girl's experiences around the death of her father on the day of the 1995 Oklahoma City bombing. He ends with this: "'I miss everything about him,' she said plainly. She had learned to summarize six years of grieving into a single idea."

What Steve[6] said:
Find people who are making a difference in the world and tell those stories. Cynical old editor types are going to push you away from stories like these, but never stop doing them. Readers will never get tired of seeing them. And because the paper has to get filled every day; might as well put something meaningful into the world.

What Geff[7] said:
The sandcastles you build with your son: those might be the most important creative work in your career. Don't be shy about stealing time and sanity back from your employer. They take so much more from you; you'll

never be able to steal it all back. He always joked about trying to watch a movie, in the theatre, on company time. "That's when you know you are doing it right."

What my grandfather[8] *said:*
He used to say things like: Gettin' old ain't for wimps. Havin' kids is a young man's game. Don't go to bed angry at your spouse. And one thing that is relevant here: Why would you want to be a photographer? Anyone can do that. Meaning: if you are going to do this type of work, you'd better work at it 10 times harder and 10 times smarter than everyone else, because the competition is vast, and there will never be any security in it.

NOTES

1. In the summer of 1940, while on assignment for the Farm Security Administration, Russel Lee and his wife rented out the two-room hotel in Pie Town. They lived in one room, and he converted the other room into a black-and-white darkroom. Meanwhile, he also shot Kodachrome and shipped his color slide film back to Washington, D.C., and wouldn't see the images until much later. I first came across the photos in the book *Bound for Glory: America in Color 1939–43*.

2. The title for my book, *Pop 66*, refers to the pop cans I used to take my photographs. It also references the ties between pop culture and Route 66. And in a smaller way it's a nod to one of my favorite characters included in the book: Pop McKee of Pie Town, New Mexico.

3. A tape-based Sony HDV camera recommended by David Leeson of the *Dallas Morning News*.

4. Attributed to the Roman philosopher Seneca and repeated by football coaches everywhere.

5. Alex Tizon, assistant professor at the School of Journalism and Communication (former *L.A. Times* and *Seattle Times* staff writer). Alex was a friend and colleague who passed away at age 57. This particular anecdote from Alex comes from page 249 in *Telling True Stories*, from the Nieman Foundation at Harvard University. The book is required reading in my classes and a must read for anyone interested any form of documentary work.

6. Steve Ringman, *Seattle Times* photojournalist. I went to school at the University of Washington where all of my journalism training came outside of

any formal journalism program. This lesson came while sitting on the baseline at a Washington Huskies women's basketball game in the early '90s. Ringman had recently moved from San Francisco to join the staff of the *Seattle Times*. I was an undergrad shooting the game for our independent student paper, *The Daily*. I had heard of Steve, but wasn't sure why. "Didn't you win regional photographer of the year?" I asked. "Nope, never did." After more prompts, he sheepishly admitted, "I did win the whole thing, twice." (National Press Photography Association two-time photographer of the year—a prestigious honor.) Next meeting at a basketball game and further badgering on my part: "What accounts for all your success?" Steve: "Lots of drugs." After pulling my leg a little, he shared the answer noted above: Tell stories about people making a difference, and be relentless. Never stop telling those stories. Steve is still one of my greatest heroes, for his early pictures of the AIDS epidemic in San Francisco. And for other life lessons, like taking a step back from his work as a photojournalist in order to focus on being a great dad. Steve is still at the *Seattle Times* doing fantastic photo and video work.

7. Geff Hinds, *Tacoma News Tribune* photojournalist. Geff passed away from cancer a couple of years ago. He was one of the most creative people I have ever crossed paths with. I felt a deep and abiding connection, even though we only had a limited time working together. Geff's comments here are partly in jest and also deeply serious. Find balance.

8. My grandfather, Lynn E. "Bop" Pope, 1919–2017. Bop was born in the Oklahoma panhandle and migrated to Washington state as a small child. The Great Depression was a major influence and having secure employment was a top priority. He spent 65 years as the town barber in Algona, Washington, where he and his beloved wife, Virginia, raised three boys. As a barber he was one of the greatest yarn spinners I ever met.

PART VI **Future**

THIRTY-SEVEN **Re-Thinking the Interview**

*Journalists can learn much from oral
historians and cultural anthropologists,
who know how to listen and watch*

LAUREN KESSLER

Does the journalistic interview—long considered
an American invention—need reinventing?
Lauren Kessler, a practitioner of immersive long-
form storytelling, answers with a hearty yes.

I was midway through recounting a humorous, character-revealing personal story—just the sort of juicy anecdotal material interviewers lust
for—when the guy interviewing me interrupted my story to ask what I
considered a trivial, oddly off-point question. Being a veteran interviewer
myself, I stopped to consider the error of his ways, the *many* ways that
what he had just done was wrong.

For starters, he interrupted me mid-sentence. There really is no worse
behavior for the interviewer, particularly when you've got your subject
warmed up enough to tell a story. But interrupting was only the symptom
of a much larger problem. If there is a cardinal sin in the world of interviewing, it is not listening. He interrupted because he wasn't listening. I
also considered the question he asked, some factoid that had no relevance
to the point I was making with the story. I thought about the nature of his

375

question and how it revealed more than his lack of listening. It revealed how his mind worked. Which was not how mine worked. He asked a question that was important to him, not me. And, not for the first time, I considered how this journalistic practice of asking questions—that is, choosing what questions to ask and in what order, when to follow up, when to let it go—often says more about the interviewer than the interviewee.

And so it seems to me that we've got a problem.

We've got a much-used, much-beloved, downright enshrined method of gathering information and stories that is severely, maybe fatally, flawed. In selecting questions, we journalists direct the conversation. We ask what we think is important—which may or may not be what our interview subject thinks is important. Or has thought about at all. The questions we ask are a product of who we are and how we think. But don't we want to know who the person we are interviewing is and how that person thinks?

I would like to suggest the heretical: Interviewing is a lousy way to get to know someone you want to write about. It is a planned, staged, ritualized encounter that exists outside the real and ongoing life of the interview subject. The "conversation" that is presumably taking place—those who write about interviewing always use the word *conversation*—is not a conversation at all. It is not a back-and-forth exchange of ideas and stories. It is orchestrated, directed and channeled by one of the participants, the journalist, who has an agenda. No, I don't mean an evil hidden agenda (although sometimes that may be true). I mean a plan. The plan is: Collect information and anecdotes, opinions and ideas for the purpose of crafting a particular kind of story of a particular length for a particular audience. Alternately, it may be orchestrated by the interview subject, who has an agenda: Looking smart, creating a platform, furthering a position, promoting a cause, etc.

I'm not suggesting that interviewing never works, that there are no good interviews or smart interviewers. In fact, there have been a handful of astonishingly talented and insightful practitioners of the journalist interview—Bill Moyers and Oriana Fallaci come to mind (and Stephen Colbert can be brilliant, too). But as a journalist who has interviewed hundreds of people and as a writer who has herself been interviewed scores of times, I am not a big believer in the process.

In this staged "conversation," one person—the interview subject—
is expected to spill the beans, whatever those beans might be, while
the other person—the interviewer—remains comfortably opaque and
detached. *Tell me everything while I tell you nothing* is the operative plan.
Trust me (because I say so) *with your story. I'll decide what's important. I'll pick
and choose from what you say in response to my questions. I will then disappear
with the material and craft the story. You can find out what I did with the material you entrusted me with when everyone else in the world finds out, when it's published or broadcast or posted.*

Interviewing is not only a lopsided non-conversation that is a poor way
to get to know someone well enough to write about him or her. It can
also be a dangerous (and lazy) way of gathering facts for a story. It's not
so much that people lie about facts when you ask them—some do; most
don't—it's that they don't know or they misremember. If you want stats,
read the report. Don't ask the person who read the report (among dozens of others) last week. Or even the person who helped write the report,
which may have gone through so many edits and revisions that the person
can no longer remember what made the final cut. If you want facts and
figures, dates, statistics, do the work to ferret out the most credible, best
documented source. This is usually not a person.

Interviewing—if interviewing means asking questions to get responses—
does have a function, albeit limited: If you want a quick opinion about
something you deem important, a quote or a sound bite to fit into a story,
then ask the appropriate person. Otherwise, I would suggest that journalists consider more authentic, more thoughtful ways of delving into the personality and the peccadilloes, the motivations and challenges, the beliefs,
attitudes, quirks (you name it) of a person important to the story they are
crafting.

I would suggest that journalists consider adopting the methods and
mindsets of oral historians and cultural anthropologists. Like oral historians, journalists should pose open-ended prompts that invite the respondent to frame and self-direct the response. They should not ask narrow,
specific questions that come from the journalists' sense of what is important. And, like oral historians, they should listen.

L I S T E N. Listening does not mean keeping your mouth shut while someone else is talking. It means attending to what is being said. It means quieting your own mind and being present in the moment, finding an intensity of focus that allows you to absorb what someone else is saying. Journalists ought to try it more often.

And, like cultural anthropologists who want to learn about people and places, about how others live and the choices they make, journalists should consider the fine art of observation. Yes, watching. Active, vigilant, thoughtful, keen-eyed watching. Ask yourself this: When is a person more likely to reveal something about his or her character—sitting across from a journalist in a staged interview answering journalist-directed questions or when out doing what he or she usually does, when participating in his or her own life, when corralling children or leading a meeting, pumping iron or playing WOW? Someone once said that the very best way to assess a person's character is to see how the person treats his or her dog.

Observation is the challenging act of putting oneself in the right place at what could be the right time. And waiting. It is the active cultivation of curiosity. It is both knowing what to look for and being absolutely open to seeing the unforeseen. It is, as with active listening, about being quietly, intently alert, like an animal in the forest.

Here's something else you might want to consider about interviewing: Although journalists may love interviewing—it gets them out of the office; it is easy and quick (compared to deep research, active listening and focused observation); it can perk up a story with quotes or sound bites—many people actually *hate* being interviewed. I know. I asked them.

TOP TEN REASONS PEOPLE HATE TO BE INTERVIEWED

1. Journalists are ill prepared. They haven't done their homework. It's annoying and insulting.

2. The questions they ask are boring and predictable.

3. The questions they ask are invasive and insensitive.

4. Journalists don't listen. They can't wait for you to stop talking so they can ask the next question.

5. Journalists have their own agenda. They're not actually interested in you. They're interested in some story they've already half-created in their heads.

6. Journalists operate on their own schedule. They want to meet when and where it's convenient for them.

7. Email interviews are the worst. Journalists fire 15 different questions at you. It takes hours to answer all of them.

8. Broadcast interviews are the worst. Journalists don't realize how uncomfortable the camera makes most people.

9. Journalists take my words out of context.

10. Journalists always seem to choose the quotes or the clips that make me look and sound the stupidest.

Bonus #11. Journalists always promise to send links or clips or at least tell you when the story is going to run. They don't.

So there you have it. Although my crowd-sourced survey was decidedly unscientific, I think the results are very much worth considering. They speak to flaws in the interviewing process, most of which are within the journalist's control. (Note that I argue the basic *premise* of interviewing is flawed and that we ought to look at smarter, more thoughtful ways of interacting with people we want to learn about.)

Two things that struck me about the responses I received: First, they were immediate. Fifty-six people responded *within the first hour* of my posting the prompt: "Tell me about your experiences being interviewed by a journalist." Wow. Obviously this is a hot button for some people. Second, many of the respondents were downright angry. They lashed out at journalists using much harsher language than I included in the Top Ten list.

That's something to think about. Hard. When the go-to journalistic method of gathering material from and about people causes this kind of reaction, when it exhibits as many deep flaws as it does, it may be time to re-think our methods.

THIRTY-EIGHT Appreciative Inquiry Interviewing

In this approach, interviews can shift storytelling from what's not working to what might work

MIKE FANCHER

Don't just report the news, former *Seattle Times* executive editor Mike Fancher cautions journalists seeking innovative options. Fancher advocates interviews designed to help solve social ills.

For the nearly 40 years that I was a professional journalist I favored "why" as the most provocative, revealing journalistic question. "Who, what, when, where and how" just didn't seem to compare in bringing meaning to the news.

In recent years I have come to think that journalism needs a sixth "W"—What's possible now?

The driving reason for adding the sixth "W" is the erosion of public trust in professional journalism and the need for journalists to engage with the public to regain that trust.

I believe one cause of this erosion of trust is the sense that the professional journalist's definition of news is rooted too deeply in problems, conflict and negativity. It is a paradigm that limits journalism's capacity to help and inspire people. It can present an incomplete and even distorted sense of reality, an incomplete version of the truth, by failing to explore and report what's working and what might be possible.

Take the story of an urban neighborhood experiencing rapid gentrification. As newcomers move in, longtime residents can be forced out by rising prices for housing and food. High-end boutiques, grocery stores and restaurants replace other businesses that have served the community. Old and new residents are out of touch and often resentful of each other.

The important story of gentrification has been told by news organizations in cities throughout the country, as have stories about crime, failing schools, unemployment, race relations, the environment, etc. In each case, news coverage predominantly focuses on "the problem," what is not working.

"The traditional approach to change is to look for the problem, do a diagnosis, and find a solution. The primary focus is on what is wrong or broken: since we look for problems, we find them. By paying attention to problems, we emphasize and amplify them," writes change management consultant Sue Annis Hammond.

When editors and reporters identify a problem as the basis for a story, "they have already passed judgment on the situation. They have filtered out a lot of information," says Peter Pula, founder and CEO of Axiom News, which uses a concept called Appreciative Inquiry to guide its work. AI shifts the focus from problems to possibilities, which leads to what Pula calls "generative journalism." Generative, according to Pula, because the work gives birth to something new.

What if journalism embraced a new philosophy about interviewing and storytelling that fully explored what's possible? This essay will offer ideas for how Appreciative Inquiry might be useful for interviews that shift storytelling from what's not working to what might work.

To be clear, this is not advocacy journalism. It is not a call for reporting that steers the public toward a predetermined outcome. It attempts to interview and report in ways that help people enrich their own possibilities and achieve their own desired outcomes, while promoting public knowledge and enhancing civic life.

Much of what follows flows from my work with Journalism That Matters, a nonprofit network that supports people who are shaping the emerging news and information ecology. And it flows from conversations with my friend and colleague Peggy Holman, executive director and a co-founder of JTM. Peggy is not a journalist, but she has thought as extensively as anyone I know about how journalism might help people navigate through these uncertain times. She is a leading voice on engagement processes, with two books on the subject.

She posed the question, "What's possible now?" in the closing chapter of her 2010 book, *Engaging Emergence: Turning Upheaval into Opportunity*. She wrote:

> It's a funny thing about cultural stories. We seem to tell more of them that reinforce our belief in collapsing systems than ones that inspire a belief in renewing systems. We find them in newspapers, in magazines, on TV, in movies, and on the Internet. We know that ecosystems flourish, collapse, and arise anew over time. So do social systems. They rise up, become "too big to fail," and weaken, even as something new takes shape. New beginnings are all around us. Yet they become visible only when we ask questions focused on possibility.

Those ideas are at the heart of Appreciative Inquiry, which is a philosophy and methodology for change originated by David L. Cooperrider and colleagues at the Department of Organizational Behavior at Case Western Reserve University. Cooperrider and his frequent co-author Diana Whitney assert, "Human systems grow in the direction of what they persistently ask questions about."

Appreciative Inquiry operates from a premise that in every system something works. Change can be addressed by identifying strengths and doing more of what works, not by simply fixing weaknesses. AI holds that building something new is fundamentally different than fixing something old; creating is often quite different than solving.

In Appreciative Inquiry theory, asking appreciative questions produces immediate changes because the path of the story becomes discovery: what is working and what is possible in the community. Reporting can then explore how and why it is working.

Problem solving and Appreciative Inquiry travel separate paths, according to Cooperrider and Whitney. Problem solving starts with identifying a "felt need," moves to analysis of causes and possible solutions, followed by action planning and treatment. Appreciative Inquiry starts with appreciating and valuing the best of "What is," and moves to envisioning "What might be," followed by dialoguing "What should be."

Cooperrider and Whitney offer this definition:

> Appreciative Inquiry is the cooperative, coevolutionary search for the best in people, their organizations and communities, and the world around them. It involves systematic discovery of what gives "life" to an organization or community when it is most effective, and most capable in economic, ecological, and human terms.
>
> AI assumes that every organization or community has many "untapped and rich accounts of the positive"—what people talk about as past, present, and future capacities—the positive core. AI links the knowledge and energy of this core directly to an organization or community's change agenda, and changes never thought possible are suddenly and demonstrably mobilized.

That definition may not seem to have any relevance to the journalism of the past, but it may be essential to the journalism of the future. Here's why.

Modern professional journalism began as part of the Progressive Era in the first decade of the 20th century and flourished through most of the century. The economic model that supported it fractured as the Digital Age emerged in the last decade of the century. Beyond economics, the old distributive model of journalism does not fit well in a world where people are not satisfied to passively consume news but demand to participate in sharing and creating it as well.

We are living in what authors Charlene Li and Josh Bernoff call the groundswell: "A social trend in which people use technologies to get the things they need from each other, rather than from traditional institutions like corporations." A clear example for journalism is the number of people who say their primary sources of news begins with Twitter, Facebook or other social media.

Li and Bernoff warn, "This movement can't be tamed. And like a flood, it can't be stopped in one place. Often it can't be stopped at all. . . . And while you can't stop it, you can understand it. You can not only live with it, you can thrive in it."

I have promoted the idea that, if journalism did not exist today, it would not be created in the form that it has been practiced for the past century. The values, functions and purposes of journalism are as important as ever, but the distributive model—we create, you consume—is antiquated. If journalism is to survive, and perhaps thrive in the groundswell, it must be re-invented as an interactive endeavor for a networked culture.

This re-imagining of journalism will require journalists to appreciate that public service journalism can be better when members of the public participate as true partners. Or, as the late Cole Campbell, also a co-founder of Journalism That Matters, wrote, when journalists "regard and treat people as experts in their own lives and aspirations."

So what does that mean for journalism, and more particularly, for interviewing and storytelling? What follows is an interpretation of how AI might inform the process of journalism, not a direct application of the methodology.

AI uses what is called the appreciative interview, a one-on-one conversation among people in an organization or community. I believe the appreciative interview technique can be useful to journalists addressing "What's possible now?"

To be clear, Appreciative Inquiry doesn't propose ignoring problems; it presents methods for not being limited by them. Asking about possibilities gets at problems from the other side. Problems end up being expressed as aspirations that can mobilize people to act. The underlying belief, says Pula, is that whatever you pay attention to is going to happen.

In the case of gentrification, an appreciative approach might start with asking residents to describe a high point when the community was at its best and people were most engaged with each other.

- What do you like best about your community?
- What do you want more of in your community?
- What do you most value about yourself as a member of the community?
- What do you most want to preserve about the community even as it changes?
- What are your best hopes for your community?

- What common ground do you see among longtime residents and newcomers?
- What resources does your community have to bring people together?
- What would it look like if people came together in mutual partnership?
- What might you do in your personal life to bring about the change you want to see?

Pula says these questions should be asked at the grassroots, among people who represent the diversity of the entire community. The stories that emerge should be reported in small increments. Mega stories about problems call on readers to quickly pass judgment on the facts, possibly foreclosing on options before they are known. Iterative stories give readers more opportunity to see and weigh possibilities from different perspectives as they unfold, with impact that is immediate and continual.

Pula gives the example of a story in Canada about people with intellectual disabilities being essentially incarcerated in care facilities. They were restrained physically or with psychotropic drugs. Advocates wanted them to be integrated into the community; others were fearful that closing the facilities would leave the people unable to live on their own.

Axiom News used an "asset-based" community development story process, what Appreciative Inquiry calls "the 4 Ds." Peggy Holman of Journalism That Matters describes them this way:

- Discovery—Mobilizing a multiple stakeholder inquiry into the positive core of the system.
- Dream—Creating a result-oriented vision in discovered potential and questions of higher purpose.
- Design—Creating possibility-oriented design propositions of the ideal organization or community. Articulating a design capable of drawing upon and magnifying the positive core to realize the newly expressed dream.

- Destiny—Strengthening the affirmative capability of the whole system. Enabling it to build hope and sustain momentum for ongoing positive change and high performance.

Pula says Axiom News interviewed the people affected, their families and others working in the system to discover what assets existed in the system and community and what outcomes the stakeholders hoped might happen. Axiom followed and narrated the story incrementally as people re-integrated into the community, learning what was being done, how it was working and how it might work better. As results became known, public attitudes and policies changed over time.

Holman says this example illustrates "the activating effect of possibility. People create what they can imagine. When stories stimulate our imagination by helping us envision possibilities that attract us, it mobilizes us to get involved.

"So if journalists want to make a difference, it takes journalism that doesn't just inform, but also engages and inspires. Done well, a natural consequence is that it activates people to get involved. If journalists want to evoke action that addresses problems, then Appreciative Inquiry or solutions journalism is a path towards having an impact. It's a way of activating, not advocating," Holman says.

This activating without advocating by asking questions that expand the range of possibilities is consistent with the first principles of journalism. It resonates with these thoughts from The American Press Institute: "The foremost value of news is as a utility to empower the informed. The purpose of journalism is thus to provide citizens with the information they need to make the best possible decisions about their lives, their communities, their societies, and their governments."

New theories are emerging: journalism as conversation or a relationship with people; journalism as process, not product; journalists as connectors and curators. These new models have varying names: restorative narrative, generative journalism and solutions journalism. All of them introduce possibility as a key element of reporting, whether in covering endemic social issues or disasters.

The Solutions Journalism Network explains its concept this way:

Solutions journalism is critical and clear-eyed reporting that investigates and explains credible responses to social problems.

It looks at examples where people are working toward solutions, focusing not just on what may be working, but *how* and *why* it appears to be working based on the best available evidence, or, alternatively, why it may be stumbling. It delves deep into the how-to's of problem solving, often structuring stories as puzzles or mysteries that investigate questions like: What models are having success reducing the dropout rate and how do they actually work?

When done well, the stories provide valuable insights about how communities may better tackle important problems. As such, solutions journalism can be both highly informing and engaging, providing a reporting foundation for productive, forward looking (and less polarizing) community dialogues about vital social issues.

These new models are not substitutes for traditional methods of journalism. They are complements that should be studied, challenged, improved upon and taught as rigorously as watchdog journalism, accountability journalism or computer-assisted reporting, etc. They should be tested to see whether they generate greater public engagement and trust in journalism.

For journalism educators, students and practitioners intrigued by the notion, here are some appreciative questions that might speed the adoption of the sixth "W" as a journalistic standard:

- "What's possible in journalism now that hasn't been possible before?"

- "What's possible when journalists and the public work together?"

- "How can journalism help people and communities find strengths, assets and best practices?"

- "What are your best hopes for journalism?"

- "What might you do to bring those hopes to life?"

Questions like these are more than an interviewing technique; they are part of an emerging philosophy about the future of journalism.

After all, the questions we ask become the reality we live.

BIBLIOGRAPHY

Hammond, Sue Annis. (1996). *The Thin Book of Appreciative Inquiry*, 2nd edition. Plano, Tex.: Thin Book Publishing Co.

Holman, Peggy. (2010). *Engaging Emergence: Turning Upheaval into Opportunity.* San Francisco: Berrett-Koehler Publishers.

Holman, Peggy, Tom Devane, Steven Cady. (2007). *The Change Handbook: The Definitive Resource on Today's Best Methods for Engaging Whole Systems.* San Francisco: Berrett-Koehler Publishers.

Li, Charlene, Josh Bernoff. (2008). *Groundswell: Winning in a World Transformed by Social Technologies.* Boston: Harvard Business Press.

Wharton, Tony, ed. (2012). *Journalism as a Democratic Art: Selected Essays by Cole C. Campbell.* Kettering Foundation Press.

Whitney, Diana, Amanda Trosten-Bloom, David Cooperrider, Brian S. Kaplin. (2013). *Encyclopedia of Positive Questions: Using Appreciative Inquiry to Bring Out the Best in Your Organization*, 2nd edition. Brunswick, Ohio: Crown Custom Publishing.

AFTERWORD **A Tribute to Ken Metzler**

MIKE THOELE

In the interview class he created at the University of Oregon's School of Journalism and Communication, Ken Metzler always led off his syllabus with a quote from Voltaire: "Judge a man by his questions rather than his answers."

Metzler elevated the asking of journalistic questions to an art form and an academic discipline. Once the editor of the university's alumni magazine, he moved into the teaching ranks at the UO's journalism school in 1971. There he became acutely conscious that students in his reporting and magazine writing classes struggled to reel in the information needed for their stories. Even the good writers, Metzler found, returned from interviews with gaps in their facts, quotes and anecdotes. Too often they didn't know what to ask; sometimes they were afraid to ask it.

Metzler began poking around at the journalistic interview. Soon enough he learned that no journalism school in America had a course-level offering in interviewing. Typically, the subject was a chapter in a reporting text, perhaps good for a lecture or two in a newswriting class. He looked afield and found that dozens of professions—from anthropology to law enforcement to psychology—had done substantially more work on the interview. He probed the literature of those disciplines and, of course, interviewed their practitioners. He learned that, taken together, they had developed a body of knowledge that seemed to contain some universal truths and best practices that would be instructive to journalists.

Metzler was intrigued. Though still new to his academic job, he successfully made a case for the creation of an experimental undergraduate seminar focused on the journalistic interview. Within a couple of years it had become a full-blown course offering in its own right. In 1974, Metzler took a sabbatical to do the research for *Creative Interviewing*. Published in 1977, it was a first-of-its-kind journalistic interview textbook. His laboratory for that original edition of the book was the newsroom of the *Honolulu Advertiser*, where he spent an analytical year interviewing both working journalists *and* their news sources. *Creative Interviewing* would go through three editions and be used by journalism students in universities across America.

Metzler's classes, like his life, were lively and provocative. A writer once described him as "an intellectual Clark Kent." A pilot and a skilled whitewater river runner, the native Oregonian laced his classes with humor, door prizes and elaborate interview setups with role-playing respondents. In time, he became a recognized national expert and a sought-after speaker on media interviewing. He was frequently booked for journalism workshops and conventions, and sometimes for sessions where corporate representatives picked his brain about the business of *being* interviewed. In time, he saw his interviewing insights embraced by some of the professions whose work he had explored in his early research on interviewing, including the business world and the social sciences.

For more than four decades, the interview class has been a staple of the journalism curriculum at Oregon, continuing after Metzler's retirement in 1990 and his death in 2011. In the 40-odd years since Metzler created the class, about 20 faculty members have taught the course, borrowing freely from one another, contributing to the interviewing seedbed at the journalism school and nurturing one of journalism's most fundamental skills. Most of those instructors have retained key elements of Metzler's formula, such as exploring the interview lessons from other professions, emphasizing listening skill, using student-on-student in-class interview exercises, and assigning broader, in-depth interviews in the community. In the class exercises, both interviewer and respondent shoulder a responsibility: the interviewer produces a report or story, while the respondent provides the interviewer a critique memo.

Metzler's real legacy, however, rests with the several thousand journalists who have passed through the field of study he pioneered and taken the resulting interview skills into media work around the United States and the world.

Epilogue

PETER LAUFER

Questions and answers take myriad roles in our lives—from begging to negotiating, from seduction to journalistic inquiry, from political leaders querying advisers to doctors questioning patients. We all interview all the time: at work, in our most intimate lives, casually over the back fence, at the café and saloon and barbershop, and increasingly in virtual anonymity via Instagram and Facebook and Twitter and texting. Discerning the difference between an interview that results in responses of value versus answers that are obfuscation is a sure test of the skilled interviewer.

The actors in the dramas of interviews often switch characters: the interviewee becomes the interviewer in fluid conversations. At times the outcome of an interview is frivolous: the Hollywood puff piece. Other times it is crucial: consider police questioning or words exchanged in the confessional. Interview is such a routine component of our daily lives that it's almost like the air we breathe. We all need good clean air, the gas and lights, bridges and highways, food and drink—and the interview. Yet too often, interviewing is not interrogated itself for its critical effects on personalities and history.

SMILE!

Questions are answered differently in different cultures. Ask, "How are you?" in America, and the automatic answer is "fine" or "okay." But in plenty of other places asking such a question often is taken much more seriously and answered in (sometimes excruciating) detail. Being sensitive to whom you are speaking when asking questions is usually a good idea.

And the how-are-you query leads us to the tale of the smile-past-your-comfort-zone exercise.

Out here in Oregon we sometimes suffer from a little too much of what we tend to call *Oregon nice*. Wherever we go, it's "After you, Alphonse," and "After you, Gaston." A good example is a four-way stop. All four drivers just stop and keep motioning the others to go first. I think I lived here a year before I heard a horn honk. And as we walk down the street and our eyes happen to meet a stranger's, we tend to offer an effusive smile and cordial Western "Howdy!"

When I took the first cohort of Oregon students to study interviewing across cultures and languages for a term in Vienna—and to plant the flag for The Oregon Method overseas—they were all surprised by the austere and secluded public personas they encountered from so many Viennese. Eyes were averted to avoid chance encounters, and when eyes met by accident, the Austrians' eyes almost invariably darted elsewhere. The automatic smile our Oregonians offered in public were at best ignored or met with what the Americans felt was rejection and disdain. Rarely did they receive what they perceived was even a slight positive acknowledgment in return.

It was a great opportunity for an interview assignment all the students railed against in unison. They were sent into the streets of the Imperial City and told to smile at strangers. If they did not receive a smile in return their job was to approach the stranger in question and ask, "Why the frown? Why the stone face? Why the smirk?" or at least, "Why didn't you smile back at me when I smiled at you?"

To ease their stress or timidity or anxiety (or all three) about violating the anti-casual-contact cocoon with which most Viennese seem to surround themselves, students were allowed to work in teams of two. Nonetheless they all returned to class the next day with horror stories about how uncomfortable it made them feel to violate the privacy of the strangers they interviewed. And in almost the same breath they expressed thrilled enthusiasm about how satisfying it was to break through their own self-censoring barriers and intimately question the passersby they chose for interviews.

When we met at the Universitätsbräuhaus for our *auf Wiedersehen* party the entire class agreed that the smile assignment was the one they dreaded and hated the most but that it was the one that made them fearless about asking strangers questions, and so they appreciated it the most.

That's the magic of interviewing—it can reveal and grow the interviewer as well as the subject.

STUDYING THE INTERVIEW IN THE OLD WORLD

Interviews are not just questions seeking answers; they are probing conversations developing relationships that result in sought-after information.

One of the key lessons in my interview course is that we journalists must use the interview as a primary tool as we exercise our distinct place in society. As grandiose as it may sound, we are guardians of democracy. Without us prying into affairs of state and business, culture and sport—the whole spectrum of human activity—society would collapse into an abyss of self-serving corruption, misinformation, disinformation and overall ignorance of current affairs.

Despite this critical role we journalists play, those about whom we report too often denigrate us. Sources are "media trained," corporate headquarters hide on websites with no street addresses, some self-styled citizen journalists pose opinion as fact. Overloaded news reporters too often find themselves reduced to stenographers rewriting press releases.

Hordes of reporters descend on the Big Story, leaving fascinating and critical news left unreported. Critics of journalists, from the White House (as of this writing) to colleagues in the news media (read: some TV and radio talking heads) call us "enemies" peddling "fake news."

It is the old blame-the-messenger story. At the same time, we need access to newsmakers in order to report the news. Were it not human nature to want to talk—especially about ourselves and what we each perceive as our important activities—journalists would find it much more difficult to convince sources to open their mouths.

Still, journalists usually must solicit interview partners. We need to figure out with whom to speak in order to develop the facts and atmosphere needed to tell the stories we're reporting. Too often the result is that reporters act obsequiously in the face of men and women in powerful societal positions. They *ask* for interviews. They allow the interviewee to *grant* them an opportunity to ask questions.

In my classes, students are taught that journalists must demand equal status with interviewees (and the correlation: journalists must not act as superior to those they interview). Together we develop a list of guidelines; here are some examples:

- Don't allow a government or business representative who expects to be referred to by his or her official title to refer to the interviewer with only a first name.

- Control the architecture of the interview venue. Don't accept a seat on a low couch while the interviewee choreographs a dominant role behind a massive desk.

- Interrupt answers—with respect and courtesy, of course—if those answers are not responsive to questions and simply serve to obfuscate.

JOURNALISM IS NOT STENOGRAPHY

But no matter how equitably we may construct the initial interaction with interviewees, no matter how clever we may be eliciting candid answers from our interview subjects, if we allow them to be the final arbiters of our stories, we reduce our role to that of a stenographer. No, that's incorrect and unfair to stenographers. A stenographer accurately records what is said. If we allow interviewees to change quotes because they "misspoke" or decide to "rethink" their position or wish to "restate" their points of view, we become their spokespersons. We lose our integrity as journalists. Ultimately, over time, all we can trade on is our credibility. And if we sacrifice our professionalism in return for access to the newsmakers, we make ourselves impotent vis-à-vis being critical actors helping balance society's powerbrokers.

Too often journalists fold in the face of their interlocutors' inappropriate demands to act as de facto editors. Before publication, too many reporters subserviently offer their stories to the subjects of those stories for what is perversely referred to as "quote approval." It's standard operating procedure in Austria, for example, and a growing worry in America.

When I first taught in Vienna, I was shocked to learn how pervasive quote approval is in Austria. Demands for such prior restraint are based on flimsy arguments such as alleged concern that reporters don't misrepresent quoted statements or leave out a critical component of a quote. As bad as this culture of *Autorisierung* is for Austria, when I returned home to the States I observed a growing trend in my own country of government and business leaders demanding to approve quotes in return for interview access.

New York Times reporter Jeremy Peters wrote an explosive story in 2012 revealing how the Obama campaign demanded approval in return for access. I'm pleased to report that in America journalists are resisting and refusing such demands. The late *Times* media critic David Carr quoted the newspaper's then managing editor Dean Baquet (presumably without seeking his approval first!): "We encourage our reporters to push back. Unfortunately this practice is becoming increasingly common, and maybe we have to push back harder."

We journalists can win this battle, but only if we fight back. The vast majority of newsmakers would much rather get their sides of any story to the public than disappear from view because their demands for quote approval are rejected. We journalists know how to report accurately. News sources can learn how to speak carefully so that they do not need to massage their messages post-interview. Especially in this era of ubiquitous audio recorders (every smartphone is a journalist's Swiss Army knife), *quote approval* is an anachronism that interviewees no longer can hide behind claiming concern about accuracy. We know what they said because their words are recorded.

FURTHER USEFUL TRICKS OF THE TRADE

There are other brazen techniques for breaking through the Colgate Invisible Shield so many of us hide behind in public besides demands like "Why don't you smile?" Acting the fortuneteller can be a clever interviewing tool—as a fortunetelling interviewer, you can take a guess at details of the story, tossing ideas and expectations at the interviewee, and hence (often) eliciting unexpected responses. Even if your hunches are wrong, the resulting answers you get may be just what you need. And the fortuneteller act can be a valuable device for getting past barriers that subjects attempt to establish between themselves and those asking them questions. Tangential queries constitute another such device. Unexpected interview questions completely out of context can develop a productive interviewer-interviewee rapport. For instance, "Do you know where I can get a good sandwich in this neighborhood after we talk?" "This is a great looking desk. Is it cherry?" "I like that painting of those mallards. Are you a hunter?"

And one of the most efficient and useful tools in our kit remains silence. Don't fill that void until you're convinced your interlocutors won't. Odds are they will and what they say may just be your scoop.

ENTRÉE TO THE SOUL

Interviewing done well at least gets questions answered and at best can be an entrée to the soul. And the story we get from an interview benefits from our lifelong curiosity along with rigorous and focused research of the subject.

After studying the interviewing insights in this book that come from my cohort of Oregon colleagues, I only love the interview more. The analysis and guidance offered here are reminders that the interview—crucial for the practice of journalism—can be both great fun and a fine art form.

Through all the challenges encompassing the interviewer—from securing the subject to the final edit—one factor is a constant aid to the questioner: the psychological reality that deep down most everyone wants to talk (especially about themselves).

On that optimistic note, here's to rigorous innovation and civic engagement with *Interviewing: The Oregon Method.*

Contributors

TOM BIVINS is the John L. Hulteng Chair in media ethics and head of the graduate certificate program in communication ethics at the University of Oregon School of Journalism and Communication. He spent six years as a broadcast specialist in Armed Forces Radio and Television and has worked in advertising and corporate public relations and as a graphic designer and editorial cartoonist. He received his BA in English in 1972 and his MFA in Creative Writing in 1974 from the University of Alaska, Anchorage, and a Ph.D. in telecommunication from the University of Oregon in 1982. He is the author of numerous college texts, a book of poetry and several children's books.

MARK BLAINE teaches science and environmental journalism in the School of Journalism and Communication and helped launch the Media

401

Center for Science and Technology, a research center at the University of Oregon. He produces documentaries and has been a reporter, speaker, author and editor for magazines and newspapers.

CHARLES BUTLER is a journalism instructor at the School of Journalism and Communication at the University of Oregon. During his journalism career, Charlie has worked as an editor and writer for such publications as Runner's World, SmartMoney, Sales & Marketing Management, and SportsTravel. His freelance work has appeared in the *New York Times*, Fortune, Men's Health, BusinessWeek and Columbia Journalism Review, among other publications. He is the co-author of two books: *The Golden Rules, 10 Steps to World-Class Excellence in Your Life and Work* (St. Martin's) with Bob Bowman; and *The Long Run, A New York City Firefighter's Triumphant Comeback from Crash Victim to Elite Athlete* (Rodale), with Matt Long.

CHRISTOPHER CHÁVEZ (Ph.D., University of Southern California) is associate professor and doctoral program director in the School of Journalism and Communication at the University of Oregon. His research and teaching interests lie at the intersection of globalization, advertising and culture. Chávez has authored several book chapters, and his work has appeared in peer-reviewed journals, including Consumption, Markets and Culture, Journal of Communication Inquiry and Journal of Spanish Language Media. Prior to his doctoral research, Chávez worked for 10 years as an advertising executive at TBWA Chiat/Day, Goodby, Silverstein & Partners and Publicis & Hal Riney.

DONNA Z. DAVIS is an associate professor and director of the Strategic Communication master's program at the University of Oregon's George S. Turnbull Center in Portland. After a 25-year career in public relations with special interest in advocacy work, she earned her Ph.D. at the University of Florida. Her research focuses on the development of community and relationships in virtual environments and other emerging social media. Her current work focuses on digital social capital formed among people with Parkinson's disease and disability communities in 3-D virtual worlds, where these individuals are able to represent themselves as they choose and function regardless of ability or disability.

TROY ELIAS (Ph.D., The Ohio State University) is an assistant professor in the advertising sequence at the School of Journalism and Communication at the University of Oregon. His research investigates nuances of identity, diversity, media effects and climate change. His research examines the impact of appealing to consumers' identities and its effect on American culture. He has taught courses in Advertising & Culture, Social Influence in New Media Environments, Visual Communication, Advertising Design and Graphics, Media & Society, Understanding Media, and Persuasion. He has published in the Journal of Advertising Research, Journal of Interactive Advertising, Journal of Social Media in Society, Online Information Review, The Howard Journal of Communication and Journal of Homosexuality.

MIKE FANCHER is a retired journalist and journalism educator. He retired from the *Seattle Times* in 2008, after 20 years as executive editor. He was interim director of the University of Oregon's Turnbull Portland Center and the Agora Center for Journalism Innovation and Civic Engagement in 2014–2015, where he also taught digital media ethics. He was a 2008–2009 Donald W. Reynolds fellow in the Missouri School of Journalism and Reynolds Chair in Ethics at the University of Nevada in 2011–2012. Fancher has a degree in journalism from the University of Oregon, a communication master's from Kansas State University and an MBA from the University of Washington. He is an honoree of the UO journalism school's Hall of Achievement.

REBECCA FORCE spent 25 years in commercial broadcasting, most of it in news. She's been a reporter, producer, photographer, anchor, assignment editor, news department director, program director and columnist. She turned to the dark side and began teaching broadcast journalism at the University of Oregon in 1996. On the side, she produced 366 episodes of the weekly television show *UO Today* and created a three-hour documentary on the history of the University of Oregon.

TIM GLEASON is a professor of journalism in the University of Oregon School of Journalism and Communication, where his teaching and research focus on communication law and ethics. In addition, he is the university's Faculty Athletics Representative. He served as dean of the school from 1997 to 2013 and was the recipient of the 2012 AEJMC/ Scripps Howard Foundation Journalism Administrator of the Year Award.

JACK HART is an author, writing coach, professor and former managing editor at the *Oregonian*. He holds a University of Wisconsin doctorate and has taught at five universities. He was a tenured professor at the University of Oregon, where he also served as acting dean of the journalism school and interim director of the school's Portland campus. He has edited all or part of four Pulitzer Prize winners and has also edited winners of almost all of the major national feature-writing competitions. He is the author of *The Information Empire, A Writer's Coach, Storycraft* and *Skookum Summer.*

LISA HEYAMOTO is a narrative journalist and journalism educator whose research, teaching and creative work focuses on community-building through storytelling. She is a senior instructor of journalism at the University of Oregon School of Journalism and Communication. Before joining the SOJC faculty, she was a columnist and reporter at the *Sacramento Bee* and the *Seattle Times*, where she wrote about culture and lifestyle. She is co-founder of The 32 Percent Project, which explores what drives and disrupts public trust in the news media.

CHARLES JACO is a veteran broadcast journalist who has covered politics and war around the world for NBC News, CNN, CBS and Fox. The winner of three Peabody Awards, he is best known for his CNN coverage of Gulf War I and his interview with Rep. Todd Akin that changed the course of the 2012 elections. He has also written books on the Gulf War and the global politics of oil, as well as two novels. He believes the designated hitter is one of the Seven Signs of the Apocalypse.

LAUREN KESSLER (laurenkessler.com) is an immersion reporter and the award-winning author of 10 works of narrative nonfiction. Her journalism has appeared in the New York Times magazine, the Los Angeles Times magazine, O magazine, Salon, Prevention, Ladies Home Journal and elsewhere. She teaches nonfiction storytelling at the University of Washington and leads writing workshops in the United States and abroad. She blogs at laurenchronicles.com.

TORSTEN KJELLSTRAND is a professor of practice at the University of Oregon School of Journalism and Communication, where he continues his work as a documentary photographer and filmmaker. A John S. Knight Fellow at Stanford University in 2003–2004, Kjellstrand began his newspaper work at the *Herald*, in Jasper, Indiana, where he was named Newspaper Photographer of the Year by the POYi contest. He worked at the *Spokesman-Review* in Spokane, Washington, then the *Oregonian* in Portland, Oregon. He studied literature at Carleton College in Minnesota, followed by a Fulbright Scholarship at Uppsala University in Sweden.

MICHAEL SWAN LAUFER worked in mathematics and high energy physics until he decided to use his background in science to tackle problems of world health and other social issues. Perpetually disruptive, he has collaborated in a recent project that makes it possible for people to manufacture their own medications at home. Open-source, and made from off-the-shelf parts, the Apothecary MicroLab medications are within the reach of those who would otherwise not have them. The project that garnered his group the most press was the EpiPencil, an open-source version of the EpiPen that costs only $30 to produce, and $3 to refill.

PETER LAUFER is the author of more than a dozen interview-driven books that deal with social and political issues—from borders and identity to human relationships with other animals. They include *The Dangerous World of Butterflies: The Startling Subculture of Criminals, Collectors, and Conservationists; Slow News: A Manifesto for the Critical News Consumer; Organic: A Journalist's Quest to Discover the Truth behind Food Labeling*, and *Dreaming in Turtle: A Journey Through the Passion, Profit, and Peril of Our Most Coveted Prehistoric Creatures*. Laufer is the James Wallace Chair Professor in Journalism at the University of Oregon School of Journalism and Communication. More about his books, documentary films and broadcasts, which have won the George Polk, Robert F. Kennedy, Edward R. Murrow and other awards, can be found at peterlaufer.com.

ED MADISON's career in media and journalism began as a high school intern at the Washington Post–owned CBS television affiliate in Washington, D.C., during the height of Watergate. At age 22, Madison was recruited to become a founding producer for CNN. His own subsequent companies have provided production services for most of the major networks and studios, including CBS, ABC, A&E, Paramount, Disney and Discovery. Madison holds a Ph.D. in communication from the School of Journalism and Communication at the University of Oregon (2012), where he now teaches.

SCOTT R. MAIER is a professor at the University of Oregon School of Journalism and Communication. A 20-year newspaper veteran, Maier has covered City Hall, the state legislature, Latin America and other news beats. He co-founded CAR Northwest, an industry-academic partnership providing training in computer-assisted reporting. A leading researcher on media numeracy and accuracy, he received the Sigma Delta Chi award for Research about Journalism (a national award by the Society of Professional Journalists). Maier conducts workshops on newsroom math and fact-checking. He also serves as U.S. co-director of the European Journalism Observatory.

KELLI MATTHEWS wears multiple hats as an educator, entrepreneur, professional, volunteer, consultant, trainer and mom. As an instructor in the School of Journalism and Communication, she works to bridge the divide between the academic and professional worlds and train smart, ethical, responsible public relations professionals. She has nearly 20 years of public relations experience, including nearly a decade in crisis planning and management. In that time she has been both interviewer and interviewed.

SIERRA DAWN McCLAIN, a 2019 graduate of the University of Oregon journalism master's program, is a nationally award-winning writer, speaker and visual communicator. She has spoken at international events, covered stories about vulnerable populations and won a university research award for her investigation of the global sex trafficking industry. For three years, McClain was a site director for Campus Life, an international nonprofit serving at-risk youth. She wants to continue giving voice to marginalized people, cultivating empathy and building bridges between communities. In her free time, McClain enjoys mountain climbing, ballroom dancing and oil painting.

TODD MILBOURN is an investigative reporter, journalism instructor and co-director of the SOJC's Journalism Master's Program. Before joining the SOJC, Milbourn worked as a reporter for the *Sacramento Bee* and *Modesto Bee* newspapers, where he produced a string of award-winning investigations. He's also worked as a magazine editor in Prague and as a broadcast journalist for the CBS affiliate in Eugene. As an Agora Faculty Innovation Fellow for 2017–18, Milbourn co-founded The 32 Percent Project, a national community engagement project exploring what drives and disrupts trust in the news media.

DAN MORRISON received his bachelor's degree in photojournalism from the University of Texas in 1984 and his master's degree in public policy from the Lyndon Johnson School of Public Affairs in 1994. Morrison began working as a professional photojournalist as a stringer for the Associated Press in 1982. His work has been published in multiple magazines, newspapers and websites. Morrison has had assignments in over 50 countries, including eight war zones. He was an embedded journalist with a Marine Corps infantry unit in Marjah, Helmand Province, Afghanistan.

DEBORAH MORRISON, the Chambers Distinguished Professor of Advertising at the School of Journalism and Communication, teaches conceptual thinking, creativity and content, and she believes strong university programs should uphold the promise of developing intellect and talent for the idea industry. Her latest book, *Brave Work in the Age of Climate Change* continues the discussion of creative courage in work about climate issues. Morrison is a two-time winner of the SOJC Marshall Award for Innovative Teaching, was named a Grandmaster of The Art Directors Club in New York and served on the board of The One Club for Art + Copy for two terms. She believes brave and generous thinking will save the world.

DEAN MUNDY is an assistant professor of public relations in the University of Oregon School of Journalism and Communication, where he researches how the principles of diversity and inclusion inform best practices in public relations and how local and state advocacy organizations craft their communication strategies. Prior to joining academia, he worked for approximately a decade in the corporate world for Andersen Consulting (now Accenture), the Coca-Cola Company and Nortel Networks. He received his B.A ('96), M.A. ('06) and Ph.D. ('10) from the University of North Carolina at Chapel Hill.

JULIANNE H. NEWTON, professor of visual communication at the University of Oregon School of Journalism and Communication, is an award-winning scholar who has worked as a reporter, editor, photographer and designer for newspapers, magazines and electronic media. Her research applies ethics and cognitive theory to the study of visual behavior. She joined the University of Oregon faculty in 2000 after 15 years at The University of Texas at Austin.

JON PALFREMAN has made over 40 one-hour documentaries, including the Peabody Award-winning series The Machine That Changed the World, the Emmy Award–winning NOVA Siamese Twins and the Alfred I. duPont–Columbia University Silver Baton winner Frontline/NOVA Harvest of Fear. The author of three books, Palfreman is the recipient of the victor Cohn Prize for Excellence in Medical Writing, three-time winner of the American Association for the Advancement of Science science writing prize and a winner of the Writers Guild Award for best script. A 2006 Nieman Fellow in Journalism at Harvard University, Palfreman is currently emeritus professor of journalism at the University of Oregon.

SUNG PARK is an instructor of photojournalism and multimedia at the University of Oregon School of Journalism and Communication. He is also the co-area director of the Journalism Master's Program. In 2013–14 he was a Fulbright Scholar at the University of Ghana where he taught multimedia journalism. Park previously taught at Syracuse University's Newhouse School of Public Communications and at the University of Texas. He worked at the *Austin American-Statesman* as a photojournalist, multimedia producer and picture editor.

WES POPE is co-director of the Multimedia Journalism Master's Program at the University of Oregon in Portland. He has more than 20 years experience working as a visual journalist, including staff positions at the *Chicago Tribune, Rocky Mountain News* and *Santa Fe New Mexican.* He recently published *Pop 66: A Dreamy Pop Can Camera Odyssey Along Route 66* (http://pop66.us). His recent work focuses on 360 video, photogrammetry and drone cinematography. Pope has an MA in Documentary Film and History from Syracuse University.

DAMIAN RADCLIFFE is the Carolyn S. Chambers Professor in Journalism and a professor of practice at the University of Oregon. He is also a fellow of the Tow Center for Digital Journalism at Columbia University; an honorary research fellow at Cardiff University's School of Journalism, Media and Culture Studies; and a fellow of the Royal Society for the Encouragement of Arts, Manufactures and Commerce. An experienced digital analyst, consultant, journalist and researcher, Radcliffe has worked in editorial, research, policy and teaching positions for the past two decades in the UK, Middle East and USA. Find out more: www.damianradcliffe.com.

JOHN RUSSIAL has taught at the University of Oregon since 1992. He worked for 17 years in the newspaper industry, mostly at the *Philadelphia Inquirer* as Sunday copy chief. He is a founding member of the American Copy Editors Society and has written a copyediting text titled *Strategic Copy Editing.* He primarily teaches news editing classes, and his research involves newsroom technology and change.

LORI SHONTZ is a journalism instructor at the School of Journalism and Communication at the University of Oregon. She teaches reporting, writing and sports journalism, and she develops curricula to help student journalists better engage with the communities they will cover. She also is co-founder and co-director of Writing Central, a peer coaching support program for communications writers, and faculty adviser for a student chapter of the Association for Women in Sports Media. Her research interests include journalism education, writing instruction and the links between communities and journalism, with a focus on coverage of mass shootings.

KATHRYN THIER is a nationally recognized instructor of solutions journalism and co-founder and co-director of The Catalyst Journalism Project, a research and teaching collaborative focused on the intersection of solutions journalism and investigative reporting funded by The Solutions Journalism Network and the University of Oregon. In 2017, EducationShift included her on its inaugural EducationShift20 list of innovative journalism educators. She is a former staff writer for the *Charlotte Observer* and *Newsday*.

MIKE THOELE is a journalist who worked three decades as a reporter and editor for Indiana and Oregon newspapers. He subsequently spent nine years as owner/publisher of two Oregon community newspapers. Thoele is the author of three nonfiction books—a collection of profiles, an exploration of the subculture of forest firefighters in the American West and a history of an archetypal Pacific Northwest timber company. As a part-time faculty member at the University of Oregon School of Journalism and Communication, he taught interviewing since 1974.

ALEX TIZON taught journalism at the University of Oregon. His book, *Big Little Man*, was published by Houghton Mifflin Harcourt in 2014. He spent five years as Seattle bureau chief for the *Los Angeles Times*. Before that, he was a longtime staff writer at the *Seattle Times*, where he was co-recipient of a 1997 Pulitzer Prize. He covered some of the most cataclysmic news events in recent times, including the Exxon Valdez oil spill, the eruption of Mount Pinatubo, the 9/11 attacks and Hurricane Katrina. He won the American Society of Magazine Writers' 2018 National Magazine Award for essay and criticism, an Anti Slavery Media Day Award in 2017 from the Human Trafficking Foundation and presented by the British Parliament, and the Asian American Journalists Association 2017 President's Award. He was a Jefferson Fellow and a Knight International Press Fellow based in Manila. He died in 2017 at age 57.

BRENT WALTH is an assistant professor in the University of Oregon School of Journalism and Communication. He worked as Washington, D.C., correspondent and senior investigative reporter for the *Oregonian*, and as staff writer and managing editor of *Willamette Week*. His book, *Fire at Eden's Gate: Tom McCall and the Oregon Story*, is a biography of the state's maverick environmentalist governor. He is a five-time winner of the Bruce Baer award, the state's highest reporting honor, and in 2001 he and three colleagues at the *Oregonian* shared the Pulitzer Prize for Public Service for revealing abuses by the U.S. Immigration and Naturalization Service.

BOB WELCH has been an adjunct professor of journalism at the University of Oregon and is founder of the Beachside Writers Workshop on the Oregon Coast. He is the author of 18 books, including three World War II biographies. As a columnist at the (Eugene, Oregon) *Register-Guard*, Welch was twice honored with the National Society of Newspaper Columnists Best Writing award. He has also won the *Seattle Times'* C.B. Blethen Award for Distinguished Reporting for a series he did on volunteering at a medical clinic in Haiti. He lives in Eugene.

TOM WHEELER taught magazine writing and editing at the University of Oregon for almost three decades. He was a freelancer for Rolling Stone, the former editor-in-chief of Guitar Player magazine and the founding editorial director of Bass Player magazine. He interviewed iconic musicians from Chuck Berry and B.B. King to Keith Richards and Eric Clapton. A consultant to the Smithsonian Institution, Wheeler was interviewed by the *New York Times*, the *Chicago Tribune*, the *Wall Street Journal*, U.S. News & World Report, MTV, NPR, the BBC and CNN. Some of his work is archived at the National Museum of American History. His juris doctor degree was from the Loyola School of Law, and he played guitar with soul singer Deb Cleveland. Wheeler died in 2018.

KYU HO YOUM, professor and Jonathan Marshall First Amendment Chair at the University of Oregon School of Journalism and Communication, has published extensively about media law in the United States and abroad. His articles have been cited by courts in the United States, United Kingdom, Canada and Australia. His research on defamation, privacy, cyberspeech and free press vs. fair trial has been used by journalists, lawyers and others in re-imagining freedom of the press as a human right. Currently, Youm serves on the editorial boards of more than a dozen refereed journals. He holds master of law degrees from Yale Law School and Oxford University and a Ph.D. from Southern Illinois University-Carbondale.

Index